Same-Sex Love in India

Same-Sex Love in India

Readings from Literature and History

Edited by Ruth Vanita and Saleem Kidwai

palgrave

First published in hardcover in 2000 by St. Martin's Press
First PALGRAVE™ edition: September 2001
175 Fifth Avenue, New York, N.Y. 10010 and
Houndmills, Basingstoke, England RG21 6XS
Companies and representatives throughout the world.

PALGRAVE is the new global publishing imprint of St. Martin's Press LLC
Scholarly and Reference Division and Palgrave Publishers Ltd (formerly Macmillan Press Ltd).

ISBN 0-312-22169-X hardcover
ISBN 0-312-29324-0 paperback

Library of Congress Cataloging-in-Publication Data
Same-sex love in India : readings from literature and history / [edited by] Ruth Vanita and Saleem
Kidwai.
        p.   cm.
    Includes bibliographical references and index.
    ISBN 0-312-29324-0
    Indic literature—Translations into English. 2. Indic literature (English)
3. Homosexuality—Literary collections. 4. Love—Literary collections. I. Vanita, Ruth.
II. Kidwai, Saleem, 1951–
PK5461.S26   2000
891'.1—dc21   99-087135

A catalogue record for this book is available from the British Library.

Design by Letra Libre, Inc.

First paperback edition: September 2001
10 9 8 7 6 5 4 3 2 1

Printed in the United States of America

The lamp of history destroys the darkness of ignorance.
         —the Mahabharata

For the two people who introduced
me to the art of story-telling:
my mother,
Lila Marilla Paul,
and my great-uncle,
Charles Sadgun Desai (1888–1974);
and for my partner and swayamvara sakhi,
Mona Bachmann.

—Ruth Vanita

For Siddharth Gautam
(January 25, 1964 to January 13, 1992),
deeply missed friend, in the hope that this book
may answer some of the many questions you used to ask.

—Saleem Kidwai

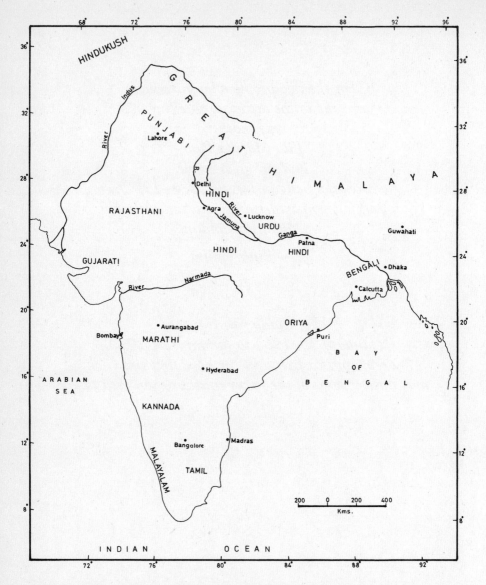

This map indicates the regions in which the languages from which our extracts are translated have a history of being most intensively spoken, read, and written. At different times, many of these languages were also in use in smaller areas in other regions. For instance, Persian and Urdu literature was produced in Telugu- and Punjabi-speaking areas as well. In modern India, people from every region can be found in almost every other region; hence, for example, Hindi and English are in use in most parts of the country, and there are substantial Tamil and Bengali populations in north and west India. Languages not included in this book, such as Kashmiri and Assamese, are not indicated on the map.

Contents

Acknowledgments

A project of this kind is made possible through support, help, and suggestions from many people. We can list only some of them here but we thank also the ones not listed; we apologize if we have inadvertently omitted anyone.

We both are grateful to Anannya DasGupta, Asad R. Kidwai, and Salim Yusufji for research assistance and help with translation; to Sukirat Anand, Shohini Ghosh, Muraleedharan, Sanju Mahale, Bina Fernandez, Sopan Muller, Ashwini Sukthankar, Sandhya Luther, and Sumanyu Satpathy for help with locating texts and authors; to Kirti Singh and Suzanne Goldenberg for lending us their homes in Delhi to work on the book; to Carla Petievich, Kathy Hansen, and Indrani Chatterjee for their warm support and helpful suggestions. We also thank the many people in India and all over the world who responded with helpful suggestions to our inquiries regarding texts in different languages. We are very thankful to Atiya Habib Kidwai for getting the map drawn at short notice.

Ruth Vanita is grateful to the University of Montana for a summer research grant, which was the only funding we received for this project. I would like to thank Kumkum Roy, Anthony Tribe, Aditya Behl, Indrani Chatterjee, and Sumit Guha for reading and commenting helpfully on drafts of my writing at various stages; Harish Trivedi for suggesting the Nirala text; H. S. Shivaprakash, Uday Kumar, Prabha Dixit, Uma Chakravarty, and Alan Sponberg for helpful discussions; Suresh M. S., Kiran Kaushik, Archana Varma, Ashok Row Kavi, Sandip Roy, Christopher and Mrs. Anderson, and Richard Drake for help in locating information. I am deeply grateful to Indrani Chatterjee for spending many days at the Calcutta library tracking down and copying obscure texts. My colleagues at the University of Montana, especially Bruce Bigley, G. G. Weix, Barbara Andrew, Phil Fandozzi, Paul Dietrich, and Casey Charles, have been uniformly supportive. Asha George provided much help, encouragement, and emotional support. Thanks to my family and to my friends, especially Sujata Raghubir, Shohini Ghosh, Mary Katzenstein, Minakshi Sethi, Chris Cuomo, and Darshan and Jetty Kang. Finally, my partner, Mona Bachmann, read and usefully commented on numerous drafts of my writings, located many materials, fruitfully discussed ideas with me, patiently listened to my ravings, and kept me happy and hopeful through difficult times.

Saleem Kidwai would like to thank all those who shared in the pains and pleasures of this project. Particularly, I want to thank Sadiq R. Kidwai for his patience in guiding me through the Urdu materials and Khalid Faruqi for making the Jamia Millia Islamia library accessible to me; Luis Arbeloa for his affection and generosity; C. M. Naim, Muzaffar Alam, Matin Miyan of Firangi Mahal, Khaliq Anjum, and Urvashi Butalia for their help; Parag Pradhan for his effort in locating some authors and helping us get their permission; Ashwini Deshpande and Mehrdad Kia for their help with translations; Yusuf Saeed and Iffat Fatima for source materials; friends like Arun Kapur, Lawrence Cohen, Manjari Dingwaney, Sanju Mahale, Shobha Aggarwal, Shohini Ghosh, Siddhartha Dube, Sujata Raghubir, Sukirat Anand, Suzanne Goldenberg, and Tuhin Chaturvedi, whose support never wavered; Carla Petievich, Kathy Hansen, and Mona Bachmann for their friendship and hospitality; Sushila Sahai and Radha Kumar for providing a warm home for me and the book. And finally my family—my sisters Azra, Hafsa, and Sufia and my nephews Jamal, Saif, and Yasir for their love and support for me, through this project and otherwise. To Asad I owe special gratitude.

Sumanyu Satpathy is grateful to Oriya poet-critic-cultural historian J. P. Das for guiding him in locating, translating and interpreting the Oriya materials.

For granting us nonexclusive world reprint rights, we thank (in order of appearance): for the *Mahabharata,* the Bhandarkar Oriental Research Institute, Pune; for the *Bhagavata Purana, Skanda Purana, Shiva Purana,* and *Padma Purana,* Nag Publishers, Delhi; for Amir Khusro's poems, Mir's autobiography, and Dargah Quli Khan's *Muraqqa-i-Dilli,* Khaliq Anjum of the Anjuman Taraqqi-e-Urdu (Hind); for *Khatirtat-i Mutribi* by Mutribi Samarqandi, the Institute of Central and West Asian Studies, University of Karachi; for the poems of Abru and Mir, the National Council for Promotion of Urdu Language, Ministry of Human Resource Development, Government of India; for the poems of Taban, Insh'a, and Rangin, the Uttar Pradesh Urdu Academy; for the poems of Jur'at, Istituto Universitario Oriental, Napoli; for M. K. Gandhi's letter "Reply to a Query" in *Young India,* Navajivan Trust, Ahmedabad; for Amrita Sher-Gil's letters, Vivan Sundaram; for Suryakant Tripathi Nirala's *Kulli Bhaat* Rajkamal Prakashan, New Delhi; for Josh Malihabadi's and Saaghar's letters, Khaliq Anjum of the Anjuman Taraqqi-e-Urdu (Hind); for Ismat Chughtai's *Tehri Lakeer,* Rajkamal Prakashan, New Delhi; for K. C. Das's story "Sarama's Romance," the author; for Rajendra Yadav's story "*Prateeksha*," the author and Rajkamal Prakashan, New Delhi; for V. T. Nandakumar's *Randu Penkutttikal,* the author and Gokuldas D. of Devi Books, Kodungallore; for Kewal Sood's *Murgikhana,* the author; for Vijay Dan Detha's "Dohri Joon," the author; for Vijay Tendulkar's *Mitrachi Goshtha,* the author; for Nirmala Deshpande's "Mary Had a Little Lamb," the author; for Inez Vere Dullas's poems, P. Lal of Writers' Workshop, Calcutta; for Vikram Seth's poems, the author and Penguin India, New Delhi; for Sunil Gangopadhyay's *Sei Samay,* the author and Ananda Publishers, Calcutta; for H. S. Shivaprakash's *Shakespeare Swapna Nauki,* the author; for Hoshang Merchant's poems, the author and Rupa & Co., New Delhi; for Ambai's "Oruvar Matroruvar," the author C. S. Lakshmi; for Bhupen Khakhar's untitled story, the author.

Preface

Ruth Vanita

"Love"

This book traces the history of ideas in Indian written traditions about love between women and love between men who are not biologically related. Since we are extracting and analyzing written texts, many of them literary ones, what they reveal to us is not so much how women loved women or men loved men but rather how such love was represented or expressed in writing.

A primary and passionate attachment between two persons, even between a man and a woman, may or may not be acted upon sexually. For this reason our title focuses on love, not sex. In most cases where such attachments are documented or represented in history, literature, or myth, we have no way of knowing whether they were technically "sexual" or not. Nor does it seem particularly important to try to establish such facts, especially since ideas of what is sexual and what is not change with place and time. We are more interested in how, at different times and places, primary passionate or romantic attachments between men and between women were viewed—whether they were accepted as an inevitable part of human experience, glorified as admirable and imitable, or vilified as strange and abnormal.

Many societies have viewed romantic attachments between men and between women as perfectly compatible with marriage and procreation, that is, a person may be a responsible spouse and parent, but his or her primary emotional attachment may be to a friend of his or her own gender. It is only relatively recently in human history that the heterosexual monogamous relationship has come to be viewed as necessarily a married person's chief emotional outlet.[1] Although this view is dominant today, in many parts of the world, including many parts of India, the earlier view still coexists with it.

---

1. In Europe, between the twelfth and sixteenth centuries, as a result of new forces that issued in what came to be called the Renaissance and Reformation, the Puritan ideal of

Love need not take an explicitly sexual form, but it is nearly always expressed in language of poetic excess and metaphoric power. Since we deal in this book mainly with written, not visual, texts, such language serves as one marker for characterizing an attachment as "love." In order to establish whether the language justifies such characterization, each text has to be studied in the context of the literary conventions of its time.

When a man is described as swooning at the beauty of another man, or a woman is said to love another woman at first sight, we can be pretty sure that a powerful erotic emotion is being described; in most such cases, however, the text does not describe what the two did in private together, even though we may be told that they spent their lives together under one roof. What matters is not the precise nature of the intimate interaction but the ways that such lifelong attachments are depicted and judged.

We are not concerned in this book with sexual behaviors that are completely devoid of emotional or erotic content. Such behaviors may develop in the context of loveless or exploitative social arrangements or of violence. For instance, in deprived and confined conditions such as prison, and even in other circumstances such as war or gangsterism, men often rape other men or boys to show their power over them. This kind of behavior is a performance of violent rather than erotic impulses. Analysis of these behaviors belongs in a history of rape, not in a history of love or desire between men.[2]

---

companionate marriage as the ideal human state replaced the earlier Christian ideal of celibacy as the ideal state. In the earlier worldview, which drew on elements from ancient Hebrew and Greco-Roman traditions, marriage was a divinely sanctioned social arrangement, the primary purpose of which was procreation. Romantic love, often frowned on by the church, occurred outside of marriage and did not lead to marriage. Romantic friendship, usually between persons of the same sex, was glorified in legend and song as expressive of human nobility. Many stories praised men who were willing to sacrifice wives and children to save a male friend's life. Even after the Renaissance, traces of the earlier worldview persisted. Eighteenth- and nineteenth-century European novels and poetry give an important place to the protagonist's close friend who is often more faithful than relatives or lovers. Lillian Faderman, in *Surpassing the Love of Men; Romantic Friendship and Love between Women* (London: Women's Press, 1981), demonstrates that both married and single women's romantic friendships with one another were socially accepted as a primary source of emotional support for them until Sigmund Freud and others labeled these ambiguous relationships homosexual. In twentieth-century Euro-America the heterosexual couple became more exclusively romanticized in movies and fiction as the individual's primary source of social support, cutting him or her off from kin and friends.

2. The ancient Indian law book, the *Manusmriti*, distinguishes between two women having consensual sex and one woman raping another, punishing the latter far more severely than the former (see p. 25).

"India"

Our use of the term "India" requires some explication. The term in its current form is of relatively recent origin—the composers of the Vedic hymns (in the period beginning ca. 1500 B.C.) did not think of themselves as "Indians." Like many other terms, such as "Hindu" and "Buddhist," it has been applied with hindsight to peoples of the past who did not apply it to themselves. While we are aware that the term, like all terms, is a historical construct, it would be too difficult, for us and for readers, to avoid it or to try to use, in each case, the labels that the writers of these texts may have used for themselves; we have tried, however, to indicate in many cases, what those may have been.

Despite vast differences among regions, linguistic communities, and religious and social groups, there was and is enough commonality in literary and intellectual traditions to justify studying this part of the world as a unit. The cultural continuity between many texts, including those we have chosen, supports this claim. We do not agree with those social scientists who argue that this commonality was an invention of Western Orientalists. In one sense, all commonality is an invention, but this particular invention predates the advent of the British by centuries.

Ancient texts like the *Kamasutra* and the epics do list various regions of what is today called India and catalog the characteristics of peoples of each region; most of the regions of modern India are recognizable in these lists, and some contiguous areas which are not part of India today are included, but more distant regions that were known at the time, such as Greece, are not included.[3] Clearly, a concept of some sort of geographical and social commonality is at work here, although it is not that of the modern nation-state.

The geographical boundaries of any country are arbitrarily marked in different historical eras; the latest boundaries of India were marked in 1947 and have been disputed ever since. Many modern social scientists prefer the term "South Asia," which includes Sri Lanka, Nepal, Pakistan, and Bangladesh. However, like all terms, this term too is not foolproof—is Myanmar part of "South Asia," and if so, given the contiguity and cultural commonalities of Myanmar with Thailand and of parts of Pakistan with Afghanistan, should not the whole unit be reconfigured and renamed? Such problems indicate that, depending on one's point of view, every geographical and social unit shades into its neighbors, and all boundaries are fluid and shifting.

For the purposes of study, scholars have to select units with a certain degree of arbitrariness. Our selection of "India" instead of, say, "South Asia" is as arbitrary as any other and is determined mainly by the limits of our own abilities and expertise. Even so, it is

---

3. See the long list of local sexual customs in Alain Danielou, *The Complete Kama Sutra* (Rochester, VT: Park Street Press, 1994), 141–43. The regions listed include modern Bihar, Uttar Pradesh, Madhya Pradesh, Gujarat, Maharashtra, Andhra, the Konkan, Bengal, and Tamilnadu.

by no means a watertight selection. We have not been able to cover all the regions of contemporary India, and some medieval texts we include were composed in territories that today are part of Pakistan.

"Great" and "Little" Traditions

Social scientists often divide cultural traditions into the "great" and the "little," the former consisting of written texts and rituals established therein, especially those with widespread geographical acceptance, the latter of oral legends, folk songs and stories, local customs, and ceremonies.[4] In the case of India, often these have been identified respectively with the Sanskritic or Brahmanical and the vernacular non-Brahmanical or even anti-Brahmanical.

It is well known that in India, these two clusters of traditions have been in dialog with one another, each drawing on and assimilating elements of the other. Some historians view this as a hegemonic and oppressive phenomenon, with the little traditions getting progressively "Sanskritized" and the great tradition reasserting its dominance by swallowing them up. Other historians, however, view the process as more mutual and interactive. While both cultural strands undoubtedly exist, to accept the former dimension to the exclusion of the latter is to deny the power of the little traditions.

Our materials suggest that the process of assimilation is active on both ends of this cultural spectrum and that it strengthens both. Written texts in India do not speak with one voice. Almost all originate in oral traditions and were built in layers over time. There are more than half a dozen varying accounts of the birth of the god Kartikeya or Skanda in different Sanskrit texts. The fifth to tenth century A.D. merging of the god Murugan, who originates in Tamil oral traditions as a hunter, lover, and warrior god, with the more ascetic Skanda, who originates in Sanskrit texts, revivifies both traditions and allows particular groups of devotees to choose which dimension they wish to focus on.

Written and oral traditions have never been far apart in India. Medieval devotional songs by mystics addressed to individual deities may appear to be remote from Upanishadic traditions but in fact they constantly refer to the Upanishadic idea of the oneness of the individual self with the universal Self. The regional variations of epic and Puranic stories encountered in folk songs, tales, and theater are matched by the variations in Sanskrit texts. This older type of interaction between oral and written texts finds a modern counterpart in cinema, television, and radio, all of which constantly retell old stories from canonical texts in new contexts, freely mixing in

---

4. Although considered outdated by many scholars today, this classification persists among liberal Indians in the form of a general mistrust of the ability of written texts, especially Sanskrit texts, to tell us anything valuable about the Indian people.

with them new elements from such sources as newspaper reports, contemporary fiction, and oral legend.

We do not share the view held by some historians that texts written in languages of the elite, such as Sanskrit, Persian, or English, inherently perpetuate oppressive attitudes to lower castes, tribal peoples, and women; rather, we view all texts as speaking with multiple voices and as open to multiple readings. Texts produced by men in patriarchal and hierarchical societies do not necessarily or uniformly legitimize patriarchal oppression, nor does the stated aim of the author always match what the body of the text expresses and represents. On the other hand, orality is no guarantor of liberatory attitudes nor are lower caste and tribal societies free of gender oppression.

We have chosen to focus largely on written texts, first, because these are relatively more accessible to us than oral sources; second, because we wish to draw attention to the presence of love between men and between women within mainstream literary traditions, a presence that has been almost totally ignored thus far; third, because the antiquity of oral sources is even more difficult to fix than that of written sources, and we aim to demonstrate the antiquity and transformation through time of the ideas whose history we are tracing. For the same reasons, we have, by and large, avoided using previously unpublished materials.

Gender Difference

Many historians have preferred to analyze women's experience separately from men's, on the grounds that in male-dominated societies (and almost all known societies have been male-dominated to different degrees), women's experience is very different from men's. Most feminist historians of love between women have chosen to study these histories separately; they argue that the experiences of men loving men and women loving women have necessarily been very different since men had greater mobility, freedom, resources and power than women, and even those men who did not use these directly to exploit women nevertheless were privileged in ways that women were not. Historians of love between men have tended to relegate love between women to footnotes or epilogs, sometimes claiming that the two experiences were entirely unrelated and sometimes that scarcely any material is available on the subject.

However, some historians and anthologists have treated love between women and between men as closely related subjects, trying to give both equal space in the same volume, on the grounds that in societies that privileged heterosexual marriage and procreation for the majority of people (and most known societies have done this), the choice to organize one's life around love for a person or people of one's own sex was necessarily rendered difficult. The first difficulty may be even to recognize and mentally conceive of such love as primary in one's life. This is generally followed by a series of difficulties in living out this love, given that institutions, such as marriage, rarely exist to formalize it publicly and integrate it into social life. The degree of difficulty has been different for people of different genders, classes, age groups, or communities, and at different times and places in the world—it has ranged from refusing marriage by taking religious vows and joining a same-sex celibate community, to being imprisoned, executed, or put in a mental asylum. Despite the differences in hardships and in options available to men and to women or to people of different classes and communities at different times and in different places, enough commonalities exist both in their situations and in their ways of resolving those situations to make a study of the variations a viable exercise.

Our study suggests that at most times and places in pre–nineteenth-century India, love between women and between men, even when disapproved of, was not actively persecuted. As far as we know, no one has ever been executed for homosexuality in India. This does not mean, however, that there were no difficulties to be overcome. Even when love between men or between women was not trivialized, viewed as inferior to love between men and women, or ignored (and it often was treated in all these ways), even when it was romanticized and to some degree encouraged, society rarely provided institutions that allowed it to be chosen and lived out as primary, in refusal of marriage. People who managed to express same-sex love in this way displayed tremendous creativity in shaping their own lives as well as patterns of community. In the modern world, these communities have often been composed of both men and women, and homoerotically inclined persons have provided each other with support, regardless of gender.[5]

Many of the texts we have extracted support examining representations of female and male homoeroticism together. Texts like the *Kamasutra* catalog sexual interaction between men and between women in the same sections, thus treating them as having much in common. In Puranic and *Katha* literature as well as in folk tales, stories about cross-dressing and the ensuing ambiguity regarding gender and attraction, often play simultaneously with the idea of male-male attraction and female-female attraction. In a whole genre of late-medieval Urdu poetry written by men, we encounter depiction of sexual relationships between women.

Methodology

Selection and Arrangement

The translations included in this book cover a wide range in time and space—Hindu, Muslim, Buddhist, and nonreligious materials, in most of India's major languages including English and in the classical languages. The extracts are arranged in a more or less chronological order and are placed in perspective by a detailed general introduction to each section as well as a brief introduction to each extract.

---

5. We met and developed our friendship in such a community and have drawn on the networks between such mixed-gender communities, both in India and abroad, while working on this book.

The writers of the texts include canonical authors, major and minor literary, political and religious figures, and also obscure people. Some of the older texts are very well known and have been translated many times; however, many of the older texts are little known and have never been made available to an English readership.

In most cases, we know nothing or very little about the lives and loves of the authors. Sometimes, we know the authors to have been involved in same-sex loves; often, we do not know this to have been the case. Some authors purport to be telling their own stories; others seem to disguise possibly autobiographical material as fiction. The texts show a wide range of attitudes toward the love they represent—from celebration to clinical detachment to disapproval to hostility. In many cases, the texts refer to earlier writings and engage in dialog with them. The gender of authors has not determined our selection of texts—we have texts written by women about love between men and by men about love between women.

Most of these writings are of high literary quality, beautifully written, reflective, and nuanced, with a range of emotional tones such as pathos, humor, and compassion. Some of the texts have been included despite their poor literary quality, because of what their content suggests about particular regions and communities at particular points in time.

Translations

The quality of translations is crucial to this anthology. Bowdlerized translations have seriously biased scholars' understanding of several texts, for instance, words referring to beautiful boys in the medieval history *Muraqqa,* have been translated "lads and lasses" (see pp. 175–83). In a recent English translation of the *Krittivasa Ramayana,* where the text describes the two widows of King Dilipa as living together "in extreme love [*sampriti*]," the translator renders this as "living together behaving like husband and wife."[6] In the last line in this section which states that the sage named their child "Bhagiratha" because he was born of two vulvas (*bhaga*), the translation simply omits this etymology and states "The sage then blessed them and gave him the name of Bhagiratha" (see pp. 100–02 for an accurate translation of this text).

We have translated all the Hindi and Urdu and most of the Persian texts ourselves. Translations from other languages have been executed by eminent scholars with whom we have worked closely, going over the translations word by word, trying to keep each translation as close to the letter and spirit of the original as possible and providing glosses, wherever needed, to contextualize particular words. Many flaws, no doubt, must remain, unnoticed by us, and we welcome comments and suggestions from readers.

When we quote texts in our introductory and other essays, we often use standard scholarly translations rather than retranslating the quotes afresh. This is due to our limited resources; this project was for the most part conducted in Delhi, where many

---

6. *Krittivasa Ramayana,* translated Shantilal Nagar and Suriti Nagar (Delhi: Eastern Book Linkers, 1997), section 12, 18–19.

texts are hard to get hold of. The project was largely self-financed, so while we got all the extracts retranslated from Sanskrit, we could not afford to get every quote similarly retranslated. However, wherever the translation seemed doubtful, we did get it checked, and, if necessary, retranslated. We do not always quote the most recent translation. For instance, in the case of the *Rig Veda,* we quote R. W. Griffith's translation, which still remains the standard complete version, used by many Indian scholars. Similarly, we chose Ganguly's version of the *Mahabharata,* recently reissued by an Indian publisher, over J. A. van Buitenen's, first, because the latter was incomplete when our project began, and, second, because the Ganguly version seems to us by and large accurate as well as sensitive, the translator having been educated within the best traditions of both indigenous and modern scholarship. In other cases, though we would have preferred recent translations, we did not have access to them.

Terminology

Michel Foucault, Lillian Faderman, David Halperin, and others have argued that it was only in the late nineteenth century that European and American psychologists and sexologists such as Havelock Ellis, Magnus Hirschfeld, and, later, Sigmund Freud began to think of people as falling into categories based on their sexual-emotional preferences, thus creating the categories of "heterosexual" and "homosexual" people.[7] These scholars claim (a claim widely accepted today but also challenged by many other scholars) that prior to this period, many people performed homosexual acts but were not identified or categorized according to their sexual inclinations.

John Boswell, in his research on Greek, Roman, and medieval Christian societies, and Bernadette Brooten, in her more recent work on love between women in Roman and Christian societies in late antiquity, have shown that such categories did exist much before nineteenth century psychologists reframed them.[8] The terms "homosexual" and "heterosexual" were not used, but other terms were used to refer to those who showed a lifelong preference for erotic attachments to those of their own sex. Plato, in fifth-century B.C. Athens, divided human beings into men who prefer men, men and women who prefer each other, and women who prefer women.[9] Terms like

7. See Michel Foucault, *The History of Sexuality* vol. 1, trans. Robert Hurley (New York: Random House, 1978; French orig. 1976); David M. Halperin, *One Hundred Years of Homosexuality, and Other Essays on Greek Love* (New York: Routledge, 1990), 15–53; Lillian Faderman, *Odd Girls and Twilight Lovers: A History of Life in Twentieth-Century America* (New York: Columbia University Press, 1991).
8. John Boswell, *Christianity, Social Tolerance and Homosexuality* (Chicago: University of Chicago Press, 1980); Bernadette J. Brooten, *Love between Women: Early Christian Responses to Female Homoeroticism* (Chicago: University of Chicago Press, 1996).
9. Plato, *The Symposium,* reprint of translation by Benjamin Jowett (New York: Dover, 1993). In the myth related by the poet Aristophanes, human beings were originally of

"tribade," "Sapphist," "sodomite," and "Ganymede" were used in various parts of ancient and medieval Europe and Asia Minor to refer to women who loved women and men who loved men.

The *Kamasutra* categorizes males attracted to other males as having a "third nature" (see pp. 46–53). Ancient Indian medical texts described categories of people attracted to their own sex, as Michael Sweet and Leonard Zwilling have demonstrated. They have also shown that ancient and medieval Jain texts developed an elaborate taxonomy of such categories, basing some of them not on behavior but on the nature and intensity of same-sex desire.[10]

We have discovered terms that were in use in different languages, at different times and places in India, to refer to same-sex love. In late medieval Urdu poetry, *chapti* (clinging or sticking together) was a word for sex between women as well as for the women who practiced it (see p. 193). This term is still in use today and predates any importation of nineteenth-century European psychologists' terminology. Medieval Urdu male poets, using terms to refer to men who love men, included themselves in these categories (see p. 119). We have also come across creative use of words to indicate same-sex emotions that include and transcend friendship, for instance, *swayamvara sakhi* in the eleventh-century *Kathasaritsagara* (see pp. 46–54).

In our own descriptive analyses of earlier periods, we use phrases like "homoerotically inclined" to describe persons who express same-sex love but in whose case sexual behavior is not established. We use the term "homosexual" to describe same-sex interaction that is clearly sexual. Where the texts describe explicit sexual behaviors, we attempt to stay close to the terms used by the texts themselves.

We have chosen not to use the term "queer," favored by many scholars today because it is deemed wide enough to encompass any unconventional or strange sexual behaviors and self-constructions. For one thing, many of the behaviors and people in the texts we are dealing with are not only not represented as strange or deviant but are upheld by the texts as admirable. Second, the term "queer" is almost too wide for our purposes, as it could include all sorts of behaviors, from fetishism to exhibitionism, which are outside the scope of our inquiry. Some of the texts we extract, especially those that represent sex change, could also be read as texts about transgender, transsexuality, or intersexuality. Our focus, however, is on the texts' homoerotic dimension.

---

three types—male, female, and androgynous. Angered by their pride, the gods cut each one in half. The halves of the originally androgynous whole are men and women who desire to embrace one another; the halves of the originally male whole are men who desire to embrace one another; and the halves of the originally female whole are women who desire to embrace one another. All erotic preferences are thus nonjudgmentally placed on an equal plane, and all love is defined as "the desire and pursuit of the whole."

10. Michael J. Sweet and Leonard Zwilling, "The First Medicalization: The Taxonomy and Etiology of Queers in Classical Indian Medicine," *Journal of the History of Sexuality* 3:4 (1993): 590–607; " 'Like a City Ablaze': The Third Sex and the Creation of Sexuality in Jain Religious Literature," *Journal of the History of Sexuality* 6:3 (1996): 359–84.

Style

As this book is not intended only for South Asianist scholars but also for general readers, we have not used diacritical marks and have spelled Indian language words, as far as possible, phonetically, close to the way they are commonly pronounced—thus Shiva, not Siva. In quotations, the original spelling has been retained. Except for proper nouns, all such words are italicized on first appearance in a particular extract, but not thereafter in that extract. We have tried to explain them on first appearance; where this is not the case or for later appearances, please see the glossary. Recurrent proper nouns are also explained in the glossary.

Periodization

We have divided the book into three sections—ancient, medieval, and modern, with the ancient running from the Vedic period (begins ca. 1500 B.C.) up to approximately the eighth century A.D., the medieval up to the full establishment of British rule in the late eighteenth century, and the modern from then to the present. This division has many flaws, and we considered other kinds of divisions, but opted for this one because it is broad enough to accommodate the highly debatable dating of numerous texts in Sanskrit and vernacular languages in centuries preceding the eighteenth. If the dates of texts could be fixed more definitely, it might be preferable to use a century-based division, although centuries too, of course, are an imposition since they follow the Christian calendar, not the various Hindu ones or the Muslim one.

We use the terms "ancient," "medieval," and "modern" at all times loosely, fully recognizing that these are periods imposed with hindsight, that many texts were composed in stages that overflow from one supposed period to the other, and that each age is shaped by all of its predecessors in visible and invisible ways. Many of the texts position themselves as parts of an unbroken continuum—of devotional, scholarly, or poetic tradition.

Absences

We regret the many absences in this book. Despite our best efforts, we have not been able to find materials in several languages such as Assamese, Kashmiri, and Telugu. We have more materials in northern than in southern Indian languages. This is not due to any preference for northern materials but merely the result of the historical accident of both of us having been raised and educated in the north. Since neither of us knows any south Indian language, we had to depend on others to refer us to relevant materials. We tried our best, through personal contacts and by putting notices in journals and on websites, to find such references. In some cases our efforts bore fruit but in several others we were not successful. In two cases the costs for the publisher's permission to use south Indian materials was more than we could afford.

The materials in languages we know were collected by us over decades of widely eclectic reading, for which there is no substitute in such a search. It is our dearest hope that other scholars will find and translate the wealth of materials that no doubt exist but that we have missed. We would also be very grateful to have such materials brought to our notice, as we are still documenting sources.

Some time periods are better represented in this book than others, and this again is due to our limited abilities and resources. In cases where we had access to more materials than we could include, such as contemporary India, we chose to give more space to materials that are less known, published privately or by small presses, not available in English, or out of print.

Aims

While we disclaim any bias against those literatures that are absent, we do not claim to be completely unbiased and objective on all questions. Bias is unobjectionable so long as it is freely admitted and does not cause conscious misrepresentation of the materials under study. To get the bugbear of "Westernization" out of the way—both of us were raised and educated in urban India and definitely have been influenced by Western thought, as any reader of this book and any educated Indian, including the non-English speaking, necessarily is. It is debatable whether even rural illiterate Indians today are entirely untouched by the "West," and whether to be so untouched is desirable. Neither "Western" nor "Eastern" influence is pure or unmixed and neither has fixed value; more important is what one selects and what one aims to accomplish.

One of our aims is to make accessible many little-known or neglected texts to a general as well as a scholarly readership. Many societies foster the homophobic myth that homosexuality was imported into their society from somewhere else. Thus, Arabs argue that Persians introduced the vice, and Persians blame it on Christian monks.[11] As Boswell shows, Anglo-Saxons blamed it on Normans who in turn blamed it on the French.[12] This kind of myth is very popular in India today. Many believe that the idea and practice of same-sex love were imported into India by "foreigners"—Muslim invaders, European conquerors, or American capitalists. Thus, in 1994, Vimla Farooqi of the National Federation of Indian Women (the Communist Party of India's women's front) asked the prime minister to stop a gay men's conference planned in Bombay, claiming that homosexuality is a result of decadent Western influences.[13] More recently,

---

11. Shibli Nomani, *Shi'r al Ajam*, vol. 4 (1912; Islamabad: National Book Foundation, 1970),155–60. Tariq Rahman, "Boy Love in the Urdu Ghazal," *Annual of Urdu Studies*, 7 (1990): 1.

12. Boswell, *Christianity, Social Tolerance and Homosexuality*, 52.

13. *The Pioneer*, November 1, 1994.

the rightwing Hindu organization Shiv Sena attacked theaters showing *Fire,* and its chief Bal Thackeray stated that "such things are not part of Indian culture."[14]

This myth has not remained confined to an unscholarly readership; its effects are visible in modern South Asian scholarship's tendency, both in India and in the West, either to ignore materials on same-sex love or to interpret them as heterosexual. Indian cinema, theater, television, and fiction are more realistic and sensitive in this regard (see pp. 207–13). As a subcontinent with one of the largest populations and some of the oldest continuous literary traditions in the world, South Asia provides a fertile field for investigations into constructions of gender, sexuality, and eroticism. We hope that this book will help open the way for further research.

The myth that same-sex love is a disease imported into India contributes to an atmosphere of ignorance that proves dangerous for many Indians. In such an atmosphere, homoerotically inclined people often hate themselves, live in shamed secrecy, try to "cure" themselves by resorting to quacks or forcing themselves into marriage, and even attempt suicide, individually or jointly. Their families frequently react with disgust born of ignorance and blame themselves as failures. All of this oppression and suffering has been completely ignored by most political parties and social activists, including supposedly radical ones. The editor of an Indian women's rights journal told us that "such issues" are not important, since Indians face "life-and-death issues." For many homosexually inclined Indians, their sexuality does become a life-and-death issue.

We hope this book will help assure homoerotically inclined Indians that large numbers of their ancestors throughout history and in all parts of the country shared their inclinations and were honored and successful members of society who contributed in major ways to thought, literature, and the general good. These people were not necessarily regarded as inferior in any way nor were they always ashamed of their loves or desires. In many cases they lived happy and fulfilling lives with those they loved. Labels like "abnormal," "unnatural," and "unhealthy" are of relatively very recent origin in India. Even the inventors of these labels, Euro-American psychologists, have already retracted them and come to the conclusion that same-sex love is perfectly natural, normal and healthy for many people.[15]

We hope that people who are not homoerotically inclined will also profit from this book, by learning to acknowledge that some of their ancestors were so inclined, that their writings and writings about them constitute an important part of our common Indian heritage as well as world heritage, and that such acknowledgment is crucial to building a more tolerant, better-informed, less conflict-ridden society that is accepting of all its members and encourages all to explore their full potential for life, love, and creativity.

Finally, we make no claim to be exhaustive, and all our conclusions are tentative and open to revision. The greatest success we can hope for is that our work be rendered outdated by more thorough research.

---

14. *New York Times,* 24 December 1998.

15. The American Psychiatric Association declassified homosexuality as a mental illness in 1974.

Part I

Introduction: Ancient Indian Materials

Ruth Vanita

There is no watertight division between ancient and medieval texts, so most of the patterns traced in this introduction are also relevant to the medieval texts in the Sanskritic tradition, some of which I discuss here. My readings of ancient and medieval texts stress certain patterns, underemphasize others. Other readings, past and present, prioritized other patterns, for example, male-female coupledom or filial, fraternal, and human-divine interactions. The richness of these texts makes available all of these possibilities, and I attempt to render more visible one important and hitherto neglected strand in their weave, without claiming that this is the most important strand.

The cultures that have come to be called Hindu allow for a diversity of belief and practice ranging from monotheism, polytheism and what nineteenth-century German Indologist Max Muller termed "henotheism" (choosing one deity for special worship, while not disbelieving in others) to animism, atheism, and agnosticism. Of these, it is the thriving culture of polytheism/henotheism that has survived over centuries and that is most remarkable for its flexibility, tolerance, and ability to change and grow. In Hindu texts and traditions, both written and oral, there is a god and a story or a variation of a story for practically every activity, inclination, and way of life.

The extracts in this first section are from the the epic, classical, and early Puranic (ca. second century B.C. to eighth century A.D.) periods.[1] My discussion begins with these periods, although I mention some Vedic and Vedanga texts as precedents. Since this first section

---

1. For information on historical events in ancient India, see A. L. Basham, *The Wonder That Was India: A Survey of the History and Culture of the Indian Subcontinent before the Coming of the Muslims* (Calcutta: Rupa & Co., 1981), and Romila Thapar, *A History of India* (Harmondsworth: Penguin, 1966), vol. 1.

contains only a few extracts, I discuss other ancient texts in considerable detail in this introduction.

My discussion of these texts is organized around certain patterns and tropes that emerge in ancient Indian writings as sites for the representation of same-sex attachment and continue to be influential today. These are: friendship as life-defining, often expressed in a same-sex celibate community; sex change and cross-dressing; moving beyond gender; and rebirth as the explanation for all forms of love, including same-sex love.[2] Resistance to marriage often functions to prepare spaces where same-sex attachments can flourish. These patterns acquire different dimensions in Hindu, Buddhist and Jain texts. Miraculous birth of a child to two parents of the same sex is a trope in ancient texts which becomes more prominent in later medieval texts.

Ideals of Friendship

The *Rig Veda Samhita* (ca. 1500 B.C.) presents an ideal of friendship as a very sacred relation. While it represents the man-woman relation as oriented toward procreation, it constructs friendship not as reproductive but as creative. Friendship is identified with the uniquely human power of language, presided over by the great creating spirit, Vak, goddess of speech. Thus, even without a female reproductive figure, human abilities are seen as presided over by female forces.

Naming objects in the universe is the process of befriending them. In this hymn from the *Rig Veda*, friendship is identified as the touchstone of rectitude, indeed of humanity itself—one who has abandoned a friend has no part in Vak, that is, in human interaction. Friendship is the measure of worth—though all have the same biology (eyes and ears), the depth of the spirit varies:

> 1. When men, Brihaspati, giving names to objects, sent out Vak's first and earliest utterances,
> All that was excellent and spotless, treasured within them, was disclosed through their affection.
> 2. Where, like men cleansing corn-flour in a cribble, the wise in spirit have created language,

---

2. Giti Thadani, *Sakhiyani: Lesbian Desire in Ancient and Modern India* (New York: Cassell, 1996), was perhaps the first commentator to examine female homoeroticism in ancient Indian texts. While her readings are often insightful, their persuasiveness is undermined by their focus on a few passages out of context and in a critical vacuum; also, they frequently tend to wishful thinking and exaggeration, for example, her translation of *yuvatyo* (young women) as "evergreen women lovers" is inaccurate (24). One major difference between her approach and ours is that she sets woman-woman bonds in simple opposition to heterosexual bonds, completely ignoring male homoerotic bonds, while we attempt to foreground patterns of same-sex bonding, both female and male, in the overall context of different types of relationships between individuals and groups. Another difference is that she is interested only in explicitly sexual bonding that she terms "lesbian," while we are interested both in this and in other types of romantic same-sex attachment that function as primary without being explicitly sexual.

Friends see and recognize the marks of friendship: their speech retains the blessed sign imprinted.
. . . .

3. No part in Vak hath he who hath abandoned his own dear friend who knows the truth of
    friendship.
Even if he hears her still in vain he listens: naught knows he of the path of righteous action.
4. Unequal in the quickness of their spirit are friends endowed alike with eyes and hearing.
Some look like tanks that reach the mouth or shoulder, others like pools of water fit to bathe in.

(X: LXXI)[3]

This preoccupation with friendship continues in the epics. Krishna and Arjuna are perhaps
the most famous pair of male friends from any ancient Indian text. Modern paintings and calendar art depicting the *Bhagvad Gita* show them alone together in their chariot, engaged in dialog. Arguably, their friendship provides the primary frame for the unwieldy set of texts that
constitutes the *Mahabharata.*

Order is imposed on the epic by the identical invocation with which each of the eighteen
books of the *Mahabharata* opens. This invocation is addressed to the two primal sages (*rishis*)
Nara and Narayana, of whom Arjuna and Krishna are said to be reincarnations: "Om! Having
bowed down unto Narayana, and unto that most exalted of male beings, Nara, and unto the
goddess Saraswati also, must the word Jaya be uttered."[4] The *Adi Parva*, or first book, concludes with Krishna asking Indra, king of the gods, for the boon of eternal friendship with Arjuna. This request sets the tone for the story to follow, wherein every decisive turn of events
in the war is occasioned by Krishna's intervention, which he invariably explains as motivated
by his love for Arjuna.

The story of Nara and Narayana, repeatedly recounted throughout the epic, is important
as it blurs the lines between divine and human—Arjuna too is divine just as Krishna is incarnated as human. Grandsire Bhishma says that these divine sages live in the forest together,
practicing austerities, and their togetherness represents a state of immortal and perfect bliss.
They are born in the human world to fight against unrighteousness. Thus they are placed
both in an eternal past and an eternal present. One of Arjuna's many names is Krishna, the
dark one; he and Krishna are frequently referred to as "the two Krishnas," a twinning reminiscent of the two Asvins in the *Rig Veda.*[5]

---

3. *The Hymns of the Rigveda,* trans. Ralph T. H. Griffith (Varanasi: Chowkhamba Sanskrit
   Series, 1963; originally published 1889), II: 484–85.
4. *The Mahabharata of Krishna Dwaipayana Vyasa,* trans. Kisari Mohan Ganguly
   (1883–1896; New Delhi: Munshiram Manoharlal, 1970, 3rd ed. 1973). Unless otherwise
   indicated, all quotations are from this third edition; parenthetical and footnoted citations
   refer to Ganguly's original volume and page numbers.
5. Further metaphoric mirroring occurs via this name since Vyasa, the poet, who is also Arjuna's grandfather, is named Krishna too, and so is Draupadi, but the term "the two Krishnas" is reserved for Krishna and Arjuna.

The author-narrator, the sage Vyasa, explains to the preceptor Drona that Narayana is the creator of the universe who produced his equal, the great sage Nara, by his austerities.[6] The mystical oneness of Krishna and Arjuna in a previous or eternal form is thus used to explain their inordinate love for one another. Krishna makes more than one declaration of this love, telling Arjuna: "Thou art mine and I am thine, while all that is mine is thine also! He that hateth thee hateth me as well, and he that followeth thee followeth me! O thou irrepressible one, thou art Nara and I am Narayana or Hari! . . . O Partha, thou art from me and I am from thee!" (Vana Parva XII)[7]

It is important to remember that the Krishna of the *Mahabharata* is not the later Krishna of the *Bhagvata Purana* who sports with Radha and the cowherd women. In the epic he is primarily a king and a warrior, not a lover of women. Like most of the other adult men, he is married and a father, but his duties in this role are subordinate to his duties as ruler and as friend of the Pandavas. The husband of Rukmini, Satyabhama, and others, he is not given to extra-marital dalliance. His primary identity is that of Friend.[8]

He and Arjuna are first cousins, and Arjuna marries Krishna's sister, which places them in a particularly intimate relationship.[9] The two men's married state is comfortably integrated into their love for one another, which is repeatedly stated to be primary.

In later versions of the *Mahabharata* and in popular culture today, Krishna's salvation of Draupadi tends to be foregrounded as the most memorable expression of protective love. This emphasis deflects attention from same-sex friendship to cross-sex friendship. In the ancient epic, while Krishna does refer to Draupadi as his friend (*sakhi*), the incident of saving her by lengthening her garment, although moving, is nowhere near as central to the action

---

6. Although Narayana creates Nara, Nara is himself Narayana. This links to other stories of the gods who create offspring singly from their own substance.
7. Ganguly, II: 30.
8. *Sakhya* (friendship or companionship) is the primary form of devotion in the *Mahabharata* and in much ancient literature. It gets replaced by bridal mysticism in some medieval cults which has tended to obscure the continuance of *sakhya* as an important way of conceiving and approaching god in Hinduism.
9. The marriage is arranged by Krishna and Arjuna when Arjuna, during his twelve-year exile in the forest, goes to visit Krishna. The two go on a pleasure trip to the mountains where they "sported as they liked for some time" (*Adi Parva*, CCXX). The word *ramatey* used to describe pleasurable enjoyment in another's company is the same whether two men, two women, or a man and a woman are being described. This suggests that a special ecstasy is not necessarily perceived in heterosexual intercourse. Thus, Arjuna "sports" with Subhadra after marriage (as does Bhima with Hidimva); later, a large group of pleasure-seekers go to the banks of the Yamuna where they spend the day, "everyone sporting according to his pleasure. . . . Some of the women sported as they liked in the woods, some in the waters." Some of these women drink, others dance, sing, and "discourse with one another in private." Krishna and Arjuna go into the woods by themselves and sit alone, conversing happily "like the Aswins in heaven" (*Adi Parva*, CCXXIV).

as are Krishna's repeated interventions to save Arjuna.[10] The story of her rescue is not re-called very often by Draupadi or anyone else, while the tale of her humiliation by the enemy is repeatedly invoked to incite the Pandavas to war.

Krishna clearly states that Arjuna is more important to him than wives, children, or kins-men—there can be many spouses and sons but there is only one Arjuna, without whom he cannot live.[11] It is for Arjuna's sake that Krishna commits several acts in battle that are con-demned by foes as unrighteous and that constitute a debating point even today for readers. For instance, when Krishna by a miracle makes the sun appear as if it has set and then brings it back into the sky, thereby deluding the foes, the only justification he gives for this apparently dishonorable action is his love for Arjuna, which surpasses all other loves: "I, therefore, will do that tomorrow by which Arjuna, the son of Kunti, may slay Jayadratha before the sun sets. My wives, my kinsmen, my relatives, none amongst these is dearer to me than Arjuna. O Daruka, I shall not be able to cast my eyes, even for a single moment, on the earth bereft of Arjuna. . . . Know that Arjuna is half of my body" (*Drona Parva* LXXIX: 153).[12]

Again, when Karna kills Ghatotkacha with the divine weapon he has been preserving to kill Arjuna, Krishna is the only one who rejoices while all the Pandavas mourn. He explains his odd behavior thus: "I do not regard my sire, my mother, yourselves, my brothers, ay, my very life, so worthy of protection as Vibhatsu [Arjuna] in battle. If there be anything more pre-cious than the sovereignty of the three worlds, I do not, O Satwata, desire to enjoy it without Pritha's son, Dhananjaya [Arjuna], to share it with me" (*Drona Parva* CLXXXII: 424).[13]

This love symbolizes the love of the human self and the divine Self. Krishna is much more aware of these eternal dimensions than Arjuna is, and he often tells Arjuna about these di-mensions, most clearly in the *Gita*. But the human side of Krishna also surfaces through this love, notably in the anxiety he feels whenever Arjuna is threatened.[14]

---

10. Draupadi, wife of the five Pandava brothers, is publicly humiliated by her husbands' cousin who tries to strip her naked. She appeals to Krishna, who, although not present, intervenes miraculously, causing her garment to lengthen infinitely, thus preventing her from being disrobed.

11. When Aswatthaman asks Krishna for his discus, Krishna reproaches him for the inap-propriateness of this request, saying that even "Phalguna [Arjuna] than whom I have no dearer friend on earth, that friend to whom there is nothing that I cannot give including my wives and children" has never made such a request (*Sauptika Parva*, XII).

12. Ganguly translates the last phrase as "half of myself" (VI: 154). However, the Sanskrit ex-plicitly refers to the body: *sharirardha*.

13. Ganguly, VI: 153.

14. Krishna stresses his human limitations when he explains to the sage Utanka why he could not prevent the war. He says that he is limited by the nature of his incarnation. Incar-nated as a human being, he could only use human means of pacification, as when he tried to mediate between the foes. It would not be right for him to intervene with divine force to prevent war.

This love humanizes Krishna; through it he emerges as an emotional being, vulnerable to grief and joy. He tells Satyaki that as long as Karna was in possession of the fatal weapon, he (Krishna) could not sleep or be happy because of his anxiety regarding Arjuna. Arjuna too is similarly protective of Krishna—when Karna pierces Krishna with five arrows Arjuna blazes with anger and shoots such a shower of arrows that all the foes flee, leaving Karna alone. The human dimension of their love is evident too, when, after the war is won, Krishna and Arjuna take a pleasure trip together, similar to the one they took before the war:

> Vasudeva and Dhananjaya [Krishna and Arjuna] were highly pleased when the Pandavas had suc-ceeded in regaining and pacifying their dominions, and they deported themselves with great sat-isfaction, like unto Indra and his consort in the celestial regions, and amidst picturesque woodland sceneries, and tablelands of mountains, and sacred places of pilgrimage, and lakes and rivers, they travelled with great pleasure like the two Aswins in the Nandana garden of Indra. (*Aswamedha Parva* XV)

When Krishna must return to his city, Dwarka, on his last night at Hastinapur:

" . . . all of them entered their respective apartments. Krishna of great energy proceeded to the apartments of Dhananjaya. Worshipped duly and furnished with every object of comfort and enjoyment, Krishna of great intelligence passed the night in happy sleep with Dhananjaya as his companion" (*Aswamedha Parva* LII).

When parting, all the heroes embrace Krishna and fall back: "Phalguna [Arjuna] repeat-edly embraced the Vrishni hero [Krishna], and as long as he was within the range of vision, he repeatedly turned his eyes towards him. With great difficulty, the son of Pritha [Arjuna] withdrew his gaze that had fallen on Govinda [Krishna]. The unvanquished Krishna also [did the same]" (*Aswamedha Parva* LIII).[15]

As in the Vedic song quoted earlier, speech is crucial to relationship in the *Mahabharata*. It is when dialog breaks down that violence erupts and escalates. Violent action is remembered repeatedly as that which breeds more violent action—the dragging of Draupadi by the hair leads to all the violent killings in war. But the bulk of the poem consists of speech as action. These dialogs take place between all kinds of people—ancestors and descendants, divine or semidivine beings and humans, animals and humans, teachers and students, servants and mas-ters, fellow seekers of wisdom, husbands and wives, male and female friends (Krishna and Draupadi), brothers, and female friends (Draupadi and Satyabhama).

But the most important ongoing conversation is that between Krishna and Arjuna. It is ap-propriate then, that the apotheosis of their relationship is expressed in the *Bhagvad Gita*, where Krishna's thought unfolds in response to Arjuna's questions, doubts, and requests. It is im-portant that this central philosophical moment is cast as a loving conversation between two men. As in the *Vedas* and *Upanishads*, the conversation between divine and human (or even

---

15. Ganguly, XI: 14.

nonhuman) creatures fosters the possibility of the human becoming divine or, rather, realizing its own divine nature and the divine nature of all things. The *Gita* only reiterates what Krishna says in his many declarations to and about Arjuna—that he and Arjuna are not two but one.

The metaphor of chariot rider and driver as inseparably paired (also found in somewhat different form in ancient Greek philosophy) is made literal in the image of Krishna driving Arjuna's chariot. Krishna's refusal to act (he does not take up arms in the war) links him and Arjuna with the famous Rig Vedic image of the two birds who sit on one branch, one eating while the other looks on. Ultimate and temporal reality are figured in this same-gender pair. While Krishna is god, he is also definitely man, which is evident in Arjuna's moving cry when Krishna reveals his universal form as Vasudeva.[16] Arjuna asks Krishna to return to the human form he knows and loves, that of the beautiful Krishna, and also asks him, as god, to forgive any transgression Arjuna may have committed in the course of their intimacy: "It behoveth thee, O God, to bear my faults as a father his son's, a friend his friend's, a lover his beloved's [*priyah, priyaya,* both nouns masculine]" (*Bhishma Parva* XXXVI: 82).

Friendship and Marriage

If the sanctity of companionate love in marriage is indicated in the symbolism of the seven steps taken together in the wedding ceremony, the companionship and love of friends is, in many ancient texts, given an equal status in the recurrent, apparently almost proverbial, phrase *saptapadam hi mitram* which can mean "seven steps taken together constitute friendship" or "seven words spoken together constitute friendship."[17]

It would appear that sometimes certain ceremonies were performed to express commitment in friendship. Thus, in the *Ramayana,* when Rama and Sugriva swear friendship to one another, this friendship, which is also a political alliance, is ratified by Hanuman lighting and worshipping a fire, which Rama and Sugriva then walk around. Further research is needed to determine whether the "seven steps" of friendship have anything to do with this kind of ceremony, that is, whether seven steps were taken around the fire. But the play on words in *saptapadam* defines speech as the essence of this kind of friendship: "He is a friend who shows affection for another, who gladdens another, who makes himself agreeable to another, who protects another, who honours another, and who rejoices in the joys of another" (*Mahabharata, Karna Parva* VII: 42).[18]

---

16. Krishna reveals this form to only one other man, the sage Utanka.
17. In the wedding ceremony too, the seventh step is said to be taken for *sakhya* or "friendship." Thus, no sharp line is drawn between the friendship of conjugality and that of same-sex bonding.
18. Ganguly, VII: 105. This canonical definition is repeated often in very similar words in other texts, for example in the *Panchatantra* (see p. 42).

Although both the main story and many supporting stories celebrate filial, parental, and marital love and fidelity, a persistent strain in the *Mahabharata* represents conjugality and parenthood as obstacles to the love of friends which, for men, may symbolize the path to perfection. The text itself is conflicted here—some stories represent liberation as unobtainable without marriage and procreation. Yet asceticism often is represented as the highest and most powerful state through which humans attain deification. The state of companionable asceticism is the state of true happiness, as opposed to illusory happiness. Thus, Rishabha tells Sumitra: " . . . while travelling among sacred places, I arrived, O lord, at the beautiful asylum of Nara and Narayana. . . . Within that retreat the Rishis, Nara and Narayana, always pass their time in true pleasure" (*Santi Parva* I, *Apadharmanusasana Parva* CXXVII).[19]

In contrast to the selfless love of friends, the love of parents for children often is posited as self-seeking. Thus, when Ghatotkacha is to be sacrificed in battle, Krishna tells him: "O Ghatotkacha, sires desire sons for achieving their own objects. Children, those sources of good, are expected to rescue their sires both here and hereafter" (*Drona Parva* CLXXII).[20]

The pathos of the children burdened by this expectation is exemplified in the life of Bhishma as also in the deaths of Ghatotkacha, Abhimanyu, and all the children of the Pandavas and Kauravas.[21] Finally, when Arjuna's one remaining grandchild, Parikshit, is stillborn, Krishna revives the infant by invoking his own acts of truth and righteousness, foremost amongst which is the perfect love between him and Arjuna: "Never hath a misunderstanding arisen between me and my friend Vijaya [Arjuna]. Let this dead child revive by that truth!" (*Mahabharata, Asvamedha Parva* LXVIII).[22] Thus, procreation, which legitimates conjugality, is symbolically mediated by same-sex friendship. The dead child is given new life by the power of male friendship constructed as the perfect relationship.

On the other hand, parental love may conflict with the love of companions, as in the story of the sages Bharadvaja and Raivya, "two friends" who live together in the forest from their boyhood, "ever taking the greatest pleasure in each other's company" (*Vana Parva* CXXXV).[23] The "unequalled love" between them is disrupted when their sons fall out. Impelled by grief for his erring son who was killed by Raivya, Bharadvaja curses his friend but then laments: "Blessed are those to whom children have never been born, for they lead a happy life, not having to experience grief. Who in this world can be more wicked than those who from affliction,

---

19. Ganguly, VIII: 276. Recounted by Bhishma.
20. Ganguly, VI: 400.
21. Another example is that of their ancestor Puru, who, as a dutiful son, gave up his youth to his father Yayati and in reward was blessed to be the progenitor of the line. Painful self-sacrifice often is integrated into the father-son relation.
22. Ganguly, XII: 134.
23. Ganguly, III: 281.

and deprived of their sense by sorrow consequent upon the death of a child, curse even their dearest friend!" (*Mahabharata, Vana Parva*, CXXXVII).[24]

Arjuna is called a *brahmachari* (celibate) because he approaches his wives only for purposes of procreation, and this is one reason for his prowess in battle. Bhishma describes a man who goes to women "for the sake only of offspring" as one who overcomes all difficulties (*Mahabharata, Santi Parva* I, *Rajadharmanusasana Parva* CX).[25] In one of Bhishma's accounts of creation, he tells Yudhishthira that sex and marriage came into being only when the human race degenerated. In the earliest times people lived as long as they chose and

> Sexual congress, O chief of the Bharatas, was then not necessary for perpetuating the species. In those days offspring were begotten by fiat of the will. In the age that followed, Treta, children were begotten by touch alone. The people of that age, even, O monarch, were above the necessity of sexual congress. It was in the next age, Dwapara, that the practice of sexual congress originated, O king, to prevail among men. In the Kali age, O monarch, men have come to marry and live in pairs (*Santi Parva* II: CCVII). [26]

Bhishma goes on to advise against attachment to children:

> As one casts off from one's body such vermin as take their birth there but as are not on that account any part of oneself, even so should one cast off those vermin of one's body that are called children, who, though regarded as one's own, are not one's own in reality. From the vital seed as from sweat (and other filth) creatures spring from the body, influenced by the acts of previous lives or in the course of nature. Therefore, one possessed of wisdom should feel no regard for them (*Santi Parva* II: CVII).[27]

Such denigrations of sex and procreation are often read today, especially by some feminists, as evidence of misogyny and body-hating asceticism.[28] Although this dimension does exist in many contexts, another important aspect should not be overlooked. Most societies, today as in ancient India, glorify procreation to an extent unnecessary for propagation of the species, thus fostering near-universal marriage and parenthood, with disastrous consequences for the natural environment (for the views of a modern Hindu priest at Shri Rangam on this, see pp. 216–17). Modern commentators' post-Freudian biases often lead them to valorize heterosexual sex and monogamous heterosexual marriage as the highest form of human bonding, as well as the form most conducive to a high status for women. This assumes that women's status in

---

24. Ganguly, III: 285.
25. Ganguly, VIII: 240.
26. Ganguly, IX: 83. It is generally agreed that the *Santi Parva* consists mainly of later additions.
27. Ganguly, IX: 84.
28. If read in this way, they could be discredited as proceeding from the celibate and childless Bhishma. However, Bhishma is one of the most spiritually evolved characters in the epic.

society is wholly determined by marriage. However, other scholars argue that societies which exalt celibacy above marriage provide more avenues for women (and men) to acquire learning, power, and mobility in the context of same-sex community.[29]

Comments such as Bhishma's can be read as a critique of the institutions of compulsory marriage and parenthood, which cause immense suffering to many—both to those who do not have children and to those who do. The *Mahabharata* abounds with stories of people, often royal people, who are miserable because they are childless. However, the poem also repeatedly reminds its audience that the entire tragedy of the war that destroys so many lives is caused by the inordinate love of Dhritarashtra for his wicked son, Duryodhana. In the framing dialogue between Sanjaya and Dhritarashtra, Sanjaya, while narrating the story of the war to the old king, constantly reproaches him for not restraining his son. Similar reproaches are voiced by almost everyone involved, including the wise Gandhari who is Dhritarashtra's wife and Duryodhana's mother. Dhritarashtra acknowledges his fault repeatedly and curses himself for his mindless attachment to his son.

Read in this context, Bhishma's comments posit choice against lack of choice. The nature of biological offspring is determined by their own *karma*, or actions and desires in past births. (We would say inherited genetic patterns.) Parents cannot choose their children as people can choose the friends they love. The relation between parent and child originates in speechlessness. It is figured as an area of darkness and potential destruction. The imagined earlier ages when children were created by acts of will and by touch connect with stories of miraculous birth that I shall examine later. Here we see the imagination straining beyond compulsory procreative sex, grounded in the inequalities of marriage and parenthood, toward past and future utopias.

In a somewhat different but related strain, the sun god Surya tells the unmarried girl Kunti that virginity is a state of autonomy, and desire is naturally free. Although his argument functions in part as a seduction speech, it carries a certain extracontextual power because Surya is the god of light and life, and he emphasizes that as the sustainer of life in the universe he cannot act unrighteously. Kunti says that her giving in to him would break the law of obedience to elders and would besmirch family honor. He replies:

> O thou of sweet smiles, neither thy father, nor thy mother, nor any other superior of thine, is competent to give thee away! . . . It is because a virgin desireth the company of everyone, that she hath received the appellation of *Kanya*, from the root *kama* meaning to desire. Therefore . . . a virgin is, by nature, free in this world. . . . And how can I, who am desirous of the welfare of all creatures, commit an unrighteous act? That all men and women should be bound by no restraints, is the law of nature. The opposite condition is the perversion of the natural state. (*Vana Parva* CCCV)[30]

---

29. See, for example, Janice Raymond, *A Passion for Friends: Toward a Philosophy of Female Affection* (Boston: Beacon Press, 1986).
30. Ganguly III: 594–95. In one recension, Surya says that "this is what the Smritis say."

Here Surya would appear to be putting forward an ideal, wherein virginity is not physically defined (Kunti remains a virgin even after having a son by him) but is an autonomously creative state defined by free choice. Several ancient Greek goddesses, such as Artemis and Athena, were termed ever-virgin (*Aie Parthenos*), in the sense of being unmarried and autonomous, even though they engaged in sexual activity. Surya also states that the natural state is for desire not to be bound by laws.

Perhaps the most interesting story of the conflict between procreative sex sponsored by the family and individual evolution in same-sex company is that of Narada's influence on Daksha's sons. Narada, the divine sage, tends to be represented as an undomesticated bachelor, free-floating and very mobile, acting as messenger and often as troublemaker. However, he is also very wise and in the *Srimad Bhagvatam* (attributed to Vyasa, the purported author of the *Mahabharata*), the trouble he makes for Daksha is inspired by this wisdom. Daksha advises his sons to perform austerities in order to have children. Narada explains to them that this is a futile, illusory aim, and it is much more important to know the divine by means of living an ascetic life. Daksha is extremely annoyed when all his sons are persuaded by Narada's argument. He produces a second set of sons and sends them on the same mission of begetting children. Narada advises these young men too to follow the path taken by their brothers.

When he succeeds, Daksha is infuriated and rebukes him, calling him "shameless" and "most cruel" for "disturbing the hearts of youths." He accuses him of "having destroyed our religion which is obtained by begetting offspring." The narrator Sukadeva remarks that Narada patiently listened without retorting, because forbearance is a virtue of the pious, and god himself is forbearance.[31] This conflict between the father who advocates procreation and the older male teacher who advocates celibacy is reenacted repeatedly, much later in history, in such cases as those of the medieval Sufis (see pp. 148, 185) and that of Shri Ramakrishna (see p. 231).

Although it is important that ideals such as those expressed by Surya and Narada are adumbrated, even if at a utopian level, they do not determine the narrative of the epic, which is embroiled in patriarchal imperatives. The autonomous mother-child unit (Ganga-Bhishma; Kunti and her divinely fathered sons) is pushed into the background. The unmarried Kunti is ashamed to acknowledge Karna, her son by the sun god. At every point, when the naturally autonomous mother-child unit is replaced by patriarchal compulsions to marry and produce legitimate male heirs, tragedy ensues. Kunti's abandonment of Karna creates his deep sense of injury and leads inexorably to his death at the hands of his brother. Earlier, the fidelity of goddess Ganga's son Bhishma to patriliny leads to tragedy when he, who would have been a just ruler, gives up the throne to his weak half brother.

31. *The Srimad-Bhagvatam* of Krishna-Dwaipayana Vyasa, trans. J. M. Sanyal (New Delhi: Munshiram Manoharlal, 1970; 3rd ed. 1984), vol. 1, 550–54.

It has often been remarked that the *Ramayana* is structured by grief and separation, the primary states generated by the action. Rama's perfection consists of his strict adherence to the patrilineal, filial, conjugal, and fraternal ideals that, the logic of the narrative indicates, can lead only to separation. Paradoxically, the *Mahabharata*, built around the eruption of conflict within the family (for this reason, the book is traditionally not kept in Hindu homes), communicates to the reader a greater sense of togetherness. Rama will not fight his father for his rights, so he must leave his father, who dies of grief. The Pandavas, bonded to each other and to their mother in a mother-children unit, fight those who are in the position of father to them—paternal uncle, grandfather, teacher—but the conflict ensures proximity and even bonding between apparent foes. Bhishma dies surrounded by all his grandsons and Dhritarashtra lives on after his sons' deaths, surrounded by his nephews who dutifully act as sons.[32]

Impelled by *dharma*, which dictates that a wife who has lived in another man's house on her own, cannot be accepted by her husband, Rama abandons his wife. Impelled by another reading of dharma which teaches that a friend or companion cannot be abandoned, Yudhishthira refuses to enter heaven without his faithful dog. Rama's action leads to separation and grief for all concerned; Yudhishthira's action leads to joyful reunion with all, both friends and foes. There is, of course, a larger sense in which union may occur in the *Ramayana* too, but the storylines of the two epics tend to suggest that familial ideals lead to separation while companionate ideals foster union.

Miraculous Birth

In most mythologies, divine, heroic, and semidivine beings are of miraculous origin. Their birth from virgins, from human-divine intercourse, or from a single parent, male or female, signals their difference from ordinary mortals. The forms taken by these miraculous births are significant for understanding a culture's changing readings of gender and sexuality. For instance, birth from a human woman and a god or a human man and a nymph may reinforce the primacy of normative heterosexuality, whereas birth from a single parent may suggest a desire for freedom from compulsory heterosexual coupling, and birth from same-sex parents, whether human or divine, an aspiration toward dual mothering or fathering outside of heterosexual marriage. All of these kinds of birth appear in ancient and medieval Indian texts, showing an openness to different possibilities.

One of the most common forms of miraculous birth in these texts is that blessed by a sage or a deity who gives some special food to a man and his wife or wives. This is the way Rama and his brothers are conceived. Sometimes this process goes awry when a man consumes the

---

32. The tendency of modern versions to focus on the war should not obscure the fact that about one-fourth of Vyasa's poem concerns life after the war. The Pandavas reign for thirty-six years after the war, before they renounce the world and proceed to the forest.

food meant for the woman or when two women consume the food meant for one. These variations may result in male pregnancy and childbirth (as in the case of King Saudyumni who drinks the consecrated water meant for his wife and gives birth from his thigh (*Mahabharata, Vana Parva* CXXVI) or in both women giving birth to half a child each (as in the case of Jarasandha, who has a third mother in the demon woman Jara who joins the two parts of his body together) (*Mahabharata, Sabha Parva* XVII, XVIII).

Another kind of miraculous birth is direct emergence from one of the elements—Sita's from the earth, Draupadi's from the fire. This is similar to parthenogenetic birth from a divine being; the great goddess in the *Devi Mahatmya* gives rise at will to a large number of goddesses, her emanations or attributes, as does Parvati in the *Shiva Purana*. A human variant of this is when sages' sperm produces children outside a female womb. Drona and Kripa are both born in this way. The heterosexual connection is retained here, however, as the sperm is ejected only when the sage sees a beautiful woman.[33]

Another kind of miraculous birth is that which results from the interaction of two persons of the same sex. This is the case in some stories of the births of Kartikeya and Ganesha (see pp. 77–84). Sometimes one of the two male parents assumes a female form. This could suggest many things—a disguise, a sex change, or an illusion. One example is that of Harihara, son of Shiva and Vishnu (see pp. 69, 94–95). Another is that of Aruna, god of dawn and charioteer of the sun, who takes on a female form in order to sneak into an all-female gathering where women dance naked for each other's entertainment. As a woman, Aruna sleeps with both Indra and Surya and has a son by each.

As important as miraculous procreation by a same-sex couple is nurturing by dual mothers and fathers. In the context of polygamy and polyandry, dual mothering and fathering may lead to conflicted relationships, exemplified by the wicked stepmother, in the Indian context most famously in Kaikeyi's banishment of Rama, son of her cowife Kaushalya. Equally important, however, are the all-pervasive references to, and descriptions of, the father's other wives as comothers and to uncles and aunts as additional parents. Rama's equal love and respect for his father's cowives is stressed as normative, but even his less perfect brothers like the hot-tempered Lakshmana are shown sharing such a fond relationship with at least some of these women. The most explicit case of cowives as partners and joint mothers is perhaps that of the medieval text where King Dilipa's cowidows produce a child by mutual sexual interaction (see pp. 100–02).

---

33. It is interesting that single-parent birth tends to be autonomously willed when the parent is a female but inspired by the sight of a female when the parent is male. The goddess's emanations are all reflections of herself and would seem to look forward imaginatively to modern cloning, as the fructifying of sperm in a vessel other than the womb seems to anticipate test-tube babies. Neither possibility seems to have much troubled the ancient Indian imagination.

The children of the Pandava brothers by their common wife Draupadi and by their separate wives merge into a group of "children" in relation to the "parent" generation. Their deaths are mourned by all the parents in common. These representations may mirror common social reality in many traditional Indian households, where children are nurtured by many adults, and the most nurturing adult is not necessarily a biological parent.

Any culture's ideas of procreation and parenting are crucially related to its ideas of original creation and parenting of the universe. Ancient Indian texts offer many different creation stories, not one, and these stories continue to proliferate in medieval texts as new divinities come into being and become the focus of worship for different groups. Thus, goddess worshipers see a female primal force as original creator, while followers of Vishnu and of Shiva identify their chosen deities with the first creative force. The imaginative space available for multiplicity works in tandem with the social reality of many parenting figures to allow for nonbiological parenthood as an acceptable reality. In the *Rig Veda*, the earliest Indian text, which, in later times, is constructed as normative, we find such patterns emerging.

Dual Motherhood and
Same-Sex Pairing in the *Rig Veda*

Various creation myths are adumbrated in the *Rig Veda* and the other *Veda Samhitas* and *Upanishads*. The songs present a recurrent vision of the universe as pervaded by natural forces functioning as parent figures, whose protection is sought by humans. These parent figures often are addressed as father and mother; very often, too, they are conceived as pairs of mothers or groups of mothers. Thus, Heaven and Earth (Dyaus and Prithvi) are ambiguously gendered and are sometimes addressed in the same hymn as Father and Mother, as twin mothers, and as Friends:

> 2. The Twain uphold, though motionless and footless, a wide-spread offspring having feet and
>   moving.
> Like your own son upon his parents' bosom, protect us, Heaven and Earth, from fearful danger.
> . . . .
> 5. Faring together, young, with meeting limits, Twin sisters lying in their Parents' bosom,
> Kissing the centre of the world together. Protect us, Heaven and Earth, from fearful danger.
> . . . .
> 9. May both these Friends of man, who bless, preserve me, may they attend me with their help
>   and favour.
> . . . .
> 10. . . . .. Father and Mother, with your help preserve us. . . ..
>
> (I: CLXXXV)[34]

---

34. Griffith, I: 248–49.

Agni, one of the most important deities in the *Rig Veda* (after Indra, the largest number of hymns address him), is repeatedly described as "child of two births" (*dvijanman*), "child of two mothers" (*dvimatri*), and occasionally, "child of three mothers" (the three worlds). Agni, the god of fire, is identified as the principle of light, heat, purification, and life. His two mothers are sometimes Heaven and Earth (the sun, moon, and stars are the fires of heaven) and some-times the two sticks from which fire was generated for the sacrifice.[35] These two parents some-times are identified as father and mother but, far more often, as two mothers.[36] The gender of the firesticks (*arani*), in Sanskrit, is feminine. The lower arani is laid flat, and the upper arani (referred to as "the Matron" in the following hymn) is rapidly rubbed against it. The firesticks developed into a small swastika-shaped wooden machine. In either case, it is friction, not pen-etration, that generates fire.[37] Numerous hymns celebrate this process of creating life from two female figures:

1. Here is the gear for friction, here tinder made ready for the spark.
Bring thou the Matron: we will rub Agni in ancient fashion forth.
13. Mortals have brought to life the God immortal. . . .
The sisters ten, unwedded and united, together grasp the Babe, the new-born Infant.

(III: XXIX)[38]

Agni is not only born of two mothers but also is nourished by groups of mothers. He is suckled by Day and Night, and produced from the firesticks by the ten fingers who are per-sonified as ten maidens, the daughters of the divine artisan, Tvastri:

1. To fair goals travel Two unlike in semblance: each in succession nourishes an infant.
One bears a Godlike Babe of golden colour: bright and fair-shining is he with the other.

---

35. See Alfred M. Hillebrandt, *Vedic Mythology,* trans. S. Rajeswara Sarma (Delhi: Motilal Banarsidass, 1990).

36. The *Bhagvata Purana* (IX. 14.49) provides a heterosexual interpretation of the *aranis.* In the *Mahabharata,* however, only the mother is identified with the fire-stick. A passage ex-tolling the importance of the mother as the dearest of all beings notes "Of this union of the five elements in me due to my birth as a human being, the mother is the cause as the fire-stick of fire" (*Santi Parva,* Part II, CCLXIII). A more intellectualized reading occurs in the discourse of a Brahman to his wife, recounted by Krishna to Arjuna: "intelligence devoted to Brahman is the lower Arani; the preceptor is the upper Arani. . . . From this is produced the fire of knowledge" (*Aswamedha Parva,* XXXIV). Theosophist Madame Blavatsky commented that the secret mystical meaning of the female arani had been "per-verted into phallic significance" by a materialist later age (H. P. Blavatsky, *Theosophical Glossary,* New York: Theosophical Publishing Society, 1892).

37. For an interpretation of this friction as an all-female erotic and creative force, see Lawrence Durdin-Robertson, *The Goddesses of India, Tibet, China and Japan* (Clonegal, Eire: Cesara Publications,1976) s.v. arani.

38. Griffith, III: 343.

2. Twashtar's ten daughters, vigilant and youthful, produced this Infant borne to sundry
quarters.

(I: XCV)[39]

A recurrent metaphor for the pairs of mothers is that of two sister cows.[40] These cows are spontaneously generative, like the later Surabhi—they become fruitful without being impregnated. The cow-calf/mother-child unit emerges as an autonomous one, with no father or an entirely shadowy and insignificant father in the background. The pairs of mothers are envisioned as loving not only their children, but each other:

4. . . .. One Mother rests; another feeds the Infant. Great is the Gods' supreme and sole dominion.
. . . .
11. Ye, variant Pair, have made yourselves twin beauties: one of the Twain is dark, bright shines
the other;
And yet these two, the dark, the red, are Sisters. Great is the Gods' supreme and sole dominion.

(III: LV)

The vision of multiple motherhood here provides the worshiper with the reassuring sense of a nurturing universe.[41] Whether embodying natural or social forces or both, the gods as sons of mothers are comforting figures.

Agni embodies, among other things, the principle of nurturing friendship.[42] Although he is also addressed as conqueror and protector, the emphasis is on warm and loving friendship: "Safe be my bliss, O Agni, in thy friendship" (III: XXXIV: 21), in contrast to Indra, warrior and slayer of foes. Other natural forces, such as rivers, also are personified as coupled mothers who seek each other and live and move together, without male companions:

1. Forth from the bosom of the mountains, eager as two swift mares with loosened rein contending,
Like two bright mother cows who lick their youngling, Vipas and Sutudri speed down their waters.

(III: XXXIII)[43]

The *Rig Veda* tends to celebrate individual deities but when it does celebrate pairs, they are predominantly same-sex pairs—twins, sisters, comothers, friends—rather than conjugal cou-

---

39. Griffith, I: 124.
40. In *Sakhiyani,* Giti Thadani comments on the implications of this for same-sex love.
41. If to have one mother is to be blessed, then to have two or more mothers is to be doubly blessed. In many religious mythologies, gods and heroes are specially blessed in this way. They are raised by a loving pair of two women—mother and grandmother, biological and foster mother, or mother and aunt.
42. See M. Winternitz, *A History of Indian Literature* trans. S.Ketkar (Calcutta: University of Calcutta, 1959), vol. 1, part 1, 76.
43. Griffith, I: 353. The river Vipas is the modern Beas, the other river, Sutudri, is the modern Sutlej.

ples.[44] The pattern of praising male-female couples is scarcely visible here. It becomes prominent later in Puranic literature.

In the *Kaushitaki Upanishad*, a number of sacrificial rituals are outlined that people can perform to obtain certain objects, such as prosperity and progeny. One of these rituals (II: 4) is for one who "desires to become dear [as life] to any man or woman, or to any men or women." The person is advised to offer oblations, saying "Your speech I sacrifice in me, so and so [name of the desired person]," "Your Breath I sacrifice in me," and so on, proceeding through the person's eye, ear, mind, and intelligence. Thus, all the person's faculties are sought to be attracted and his or her dislike sacrificed. When the sacrificer rubs the butter over his limbs and tries to approach or touch the desired people or even converses with them from windward, "He becomes beloved indeed. They long for him indeed." Noteworthy here is the neutrality of the ritual as far as gender is concerned. It would seem to allow for a person of either gender to perform it in order to be beloved by a person of either gender.

Sex Change, the Forest, and the Undoing of Gender

Perhaps the best known sex change in ancient Indian literature is that of Amba into Sikhandin (see p. 31). The pattern of the cross-dressed girl-child, the wedding of two women, and the pressure for one of them to change into a man after marriage is a persistent one in Indian texts, right down to the Rajasthani folk tale "A Double Life" (see p. 318). Interestingly, real-life weddings between women in modern India repeat some aspects of this narrative pattern (see p. 209).

It is significant that the sex change in the *Mahabharata* story, as in the modern folktale, takes place in the forest with the aid of a forest-dwelling spirit or nonhuman being with semi-divine powers. The forest in these ancient texts appears to be a space where transformations happen—between species, orders of being, and genders. This in part relates to its being outside the sphere of normative order and in part to its being the place where ascetics live and acquire miraculous powers. It is in the forest that Amba performs austerities and receives a boon; when she is reborn as Sikhandini, it is in the forest that the Guhyaka exchanges sexes with her. The gods, of course, being already possessed of powers of metamorphosis, do not always need to retreat into the forest to undergo a sex change, as is clear from the Puranic story of Vishnu's volitional change into Mohini (see p.69).

When a woman changes into a man, she generally wishes to remain a man. Of course, Bhishma refuses to accept that Sikhandin is a man, but it is clear that Sikhandin has all the

---

44. The term most frequently used for such a paired relationship is *jamitva*. It is used with reference to the Asvins and also, frequently, for brother and sister or for twins, as in the famous Yama-Yami dialog (*Rig Veda*, X: X). *Jami* is also used as a synonym for "sister." For a reading of the male-female significations of the term, see Kumkum Roy, *The Emergence of Monarchy in North India, Eighth to Fourth Centuries B.C., as Reflected in the Brahmanical Tradition* (Delhi: Oxford University Press, 1994), 246–49.

attributes of a man—he produces children with his wife, is an acclaimed warrior, and so on. It is significant that in Hindu texts, women are rarely reborn as men. They are reborn as more and more virtuous women, even as women ascetics. All other lines—those of caste, class, and even species—seem to be easier than the gender line to cross via rebirth. Amba, despite the boon she receives, is reborn as a girl, Sikhandini, and has to be changed into a man.

When a man changes into a woman, the change is much more ambiguous. Thus Vishnu as Mohini is still called "Hari"—Hari and Hara (Shiva) are the parents of Ayyappa (see p. 95). When the sex change takes place in order to enable the man to bear a child, it is temporary, as in the case of Aruna. In one account of the birth of Sugriva and Bali, their parent is a male monkey who plunges into a pool in search of his own reflection, which he takes to be another monkey. He emerges as a beautiful woman, has two sons by Indra and Surya, and changes back to a male monkey next morning. So he is called both father and mother to his sons.[45]

When Arjuna is cursed to live as a woman for a year, he retains his brawn and manly ways—he seems to be not so much a woman as a hermaphrodite or a cross-dressed man of the kind found in the *Kamasutra* and the Tamil epics. In the *Matsya Purana*, King Ila, while wandering in the forest, enters a grove where Shiva and Parvati are sporting. To please Parvati, Shiva has willed that any male who enters this grove will be turned into a female. In the *Ramayana* version of this story, Shiva himself has turned into a woman in the course of love play with Parvati, so everything in the forest turns female too. So Ila is transformed into a beautiful woman and his horse into a mare. The woman Ila gets married to Budha, son of the moon. The brothers of King Ila intervene and get Shiva to transform him into a *kimpurusha* (literally, "what?man"), a type of being who is a man one month and a woman the next month. In this alternating state, Ila, now known as Sudyumna, produces children both as man and as woman. Ila is an important figure, being the founding ancestor of the lunar (*Chandravanshi*) Kshatriyas. In the *Ramayana*, Ila, when of one sex, does not remember that s/he ever belonged to the other sex. Here, the sex change occurs in a homoerotic ambience—in a forest where Parvati sports with Shiva in the form of a woman and in an all-female environment.

For a man to become a woman and remain a woman seems to be a disaster in many texts. In the *Bhagvata Purana*, Narada tells King Pracinabarhis a cautionary tale—that of Puranjana, whose excessive love for women led to his rebirth as a woman. The moral of the story, according to Narada, is: "Renounce the householder's stage of life [lit. women's house] with its talk about extremely lustful and lascivious gatherings" (IV.29.55). However, a new pattern emerges in the later *Puranas*, influenced by ascendant Vaishnava devotion, wherein men aspire to become women (as opposed to this happening to them involuntarily). This pattern be-

45. *Adhyatma Ramayana,* trans. Rai Bahadur Lala Baij Nath (New Delhi: Oriental Books, 1913, 2nd ed. 1979), 196–97, *Uttara Kanda,* III: 6–15. This medieval text is part of the *Brahmanda Purana.*

comes dominant in the medieval period, when erotic love displaces friendship as the main form of devotion, and men wish to be reborn as women and to live as women, in relation to god (see p. 65). The story of Sumedha and Somavan shows a man becoming a woman and happily living as one (see p.72).

Buddhist and Tamil Texts: Refusing Marriage

In Buddhist texts sex change acquires a different meaning—it is related to liberation. Women are frequently reborn as men. Either rebirth or a sex change within one's lifetime is often a necessary step toward becoming a *bodhisatta*. While the liberation desired is from the cycle of births, it also carries, as is clear from "The Songs of the Elders" and "The Songs of the Female Elders," the resonance of liberation from the burdens of marriage and domesticity. This has been noted by feminist commentators with regard to female elders, but what has not been noticed is that for some elders, both male and female, choice of the same-sex community of the monastery is directly related to same-sex attachment or to the refusal of cross-sex marriage.

Thus, two women, both named Sama, left the world out of grief at the death of their dear friend Samavati, a lay disciple.[46] The princess Sumedha refused to marry and cut off her hair to resist the marriage her parents had arranged.[47] Posiya attained awakening when disgusted by his wife's sexual advances.[48] Atuma left home and was ordained when his mother wanted to find him a bride.[49] Sudanta left the world to follow his friend. The two of them lived in the hills and devoted themselves to religious exercises.[50] Sariputta and Moggallana, two of the Buddha's chief disciples, were together as friends in two previous births.[51]

Particularly poignant and suggestive is the story of Sangha Rakkhita, a monk who lived in the forest with a companion monk. One day he saw a doe whose love for her fawn kept her from going far from it; lacking grass and water close by, she was famished. Seeing her, he realized that one who is bound by attachment suffers. Observing that his companion was "cherishing many wrong thoughts," he admonished him by telling him the story of the doe. Both of them attained awakening.[52]

---

46. *Psalms of the Early Buddhists,* trans. Rhys Davids (London: Luzac, 1964), "Psalms of the Sisters (*Therigatha*)" XXVIII, XXIX, 32–34.
47. *Psalms of the Early Buddhists* LXXIII, 164. Compare the stories of ancient and medieval Christian virgin saints who resisted marriage by disfiguring themselves and also the stories of Indian medieval women mystics like Avvaiyyar who miraculously grew old to dissuade persistent suitors (see p. 63).
48. *Psalms of the Early Buddhists,* "Psalms of the Brothers (*Theragatha*)" XXXIV, 39.
49. "Psalms of the Brothers (*Theragatha*)" LXXII, 72–73.
50. "Psalms of the Brothers (*Theragatha*)" XXXVI, XXXVII, 41–42.
51. "Psalms of the Brothers (Theragatha)" CCLIX, 340–42.
52. "Psalms of the Brothers (Theragatha)" CIX, 98–99

John Garrett Jones, in his extended and sensitive analysis of the *Jataka* stories, has noted a similar pattern of foregrounding the love of male friends in these stories: "There is no constantly recurring wife for the bodhisatta. . . . Where friendship is concerned, the situation is quite different. There *is* a constantly recurring friend for the bodhisatta and the friend, unlike the wife, always has a predictable fidelity. . . . In nine cases out of ten the friend will be identified as Ananda."[53] Jones shows that in many of the stories, "the boys . . . grow up together, . . . are extraordinarily good looking and are the closest of friends" (105). *Jataka* story 498 narrates "three former births of the bodhisatta and Ananda, first as two Candala outcasts, then as two deer, when 'they always went about together . . . ruminating and cuddling together, very happy, head to head, nozzle to nozzle, horn to horn' then as two osprey—behaving in much the same way" (107). Jones also points out that when both the bodhisatta and Ananda are animals, the friendship seems more idyllic "without the sad possibility of human faithlessness to mar the picture . . . though even at the animal level it should be noted that the friends concerned are always male" (111).

In *Jataka* story 27 the Buddha explains the intimacy of two monks by narrating their former life and inseparable friendship as an elephant and a dog. In *Jataka* story 346, an old teacher, Kessava, is so attached to his pupil, Kappa, that he falls ill when they are separated by the king. The king's personal attention and his physicians fail to restore Kessava so he has to be sent back to the Himalayas where he is rapidly cured "by the mere sight of Kappa." This is explained to the king:

"The food may coarse or dainty prove,
May scanty be or much abound,
Yet if the meal is blest with love,
Love the best sauce by far is found."

Jones comments: "Sex and marriage; love and friendship; there can be no doubt that this is the way in which the Jatakas, on the whole, see it. Sex and marriage on the whole are bad; love and friendship on the whole are good. . . . This differs from the canonical position [wherein] sex and marriage are bad, but so are love and friendship." (115).

Somewhat similar patterns of choice between conjugality and same-sex community are visible in the second- to third-century Tamil epics *Shilappadikaram* and *Manimekhalai*. The first tells the story of the faithful wife, Kannaki, whose righteous anger burns up the city of Madurai when its ruler unjustly kills her husband, Kovalan. The other woman in this epic is Kovalan's mistress, the courtesan Madhavi, who becomes a Buddhist nun and is very sympathetically portrayed. In the sequel *Manimekhalai*, the eponymous protagonist, the beau-

53. John Garrett Jones, *Tales and Teachings of the Buddha: The Jataka Stories in Relation to the Pali Canon* (London: George Allen & Unwin, 1979), 105. This excellent study is one of the few on ancient India that takes homoeroticism into consideration in its analysis of texts.

tiful daughter of Madhavi by Kovalan, refuses all her suitors and dedicates herself to the pursuit of charity and knowledge. She is aided in this endeavor by many different women, and the relationships among these women frame the story.

Manimekhalai is pursued by the prince Udayakumara, but even after she learns that she was his wife in a former life, she refuses to act the faithful spouse. She is protected and aided by human women, ranging from her mother to her close companions, Vasantamala and Sutamati, and others she meets during her travels, such as the matron Atirai. A number of goddesses also intervene to rescue her at crucial moments. The poem opens with a dialog between the goddess Champu and the river Kaveri embodied as a nymph. The goddess takes the nymph on her lap and henceforth the city Puhar gets two names, in honor of the two women—it is called Champapati and Kaveripumpattinam.

Manimekhalai grows up in a women's world—the only family she knows is the matrilineal kinship of the courtesan. (Her grandmother and mother are named but she has never seen her father or any of his kin.) The transition from this world to the same-sex world of the nun takes place through a series of female interventions. The goddess Manimekhala (note the near identity of the two names) spirits away the sleeping Manimekhalai to a beautiful island where she awakens "like a newborn child who with astonishment discovers a world unknown where nothing remains of the familiar places and persons of its former life."[54] This second paradisal birth endows her with multiple mothers; as she explores the island, calling out to her friend Sutamati and recalling her father's death, she recollects her former lives and meets both Manimekhala and the goddess of the island, Tivatilakai. Since Udayakumara, although warned by several women and by the goddess herself, refuses to desist from his pursuit, he meets his just deserts. To escape him, Manimekhalai disguises herself as one of her acquaintances, a married woman, and this woman's husband kills Udayakumara in a fit of jealous rage.

When she wishes to study the various schools of thought, Manimekhalai assumes a more drastic disguise. She turns into a man because most teachers will not accept a female student. The Buddhist teacher Aravana Adigal (possibly the third-century philosopher Nagarjuna) is an exception, and as she is persuaded by his teaching, she returns to her female form and becomes a nun.

The text carefully contrasts this happy ending with that of the *Shilappadikaram*. Kannaki appears to Manimekhalai and tells her that although she and Kovalan went to heaven when they died, they will have to be reborn when their accumulated merit is exhausted. Manimekhalai's choice of the nondomestic path, her steadfast refusal of heterosexual alliance, enables her to seek enlightenment in this lifetime. Also, her life, although not without its sorrows, is filled with adventure, friendship, and learning, and is on the whole much happier than either Kannaki's or

---

54. *Manimekhalai by Merchant-Prince Shattan*, trans. Alain Danielou (New Delhi: Penguin, 1993), 35.

Madhavi's. Kannaki, married very young, suffered betrayal soon after her wedding and was widowed thereafter.

Philosophy and the Undoing of Gender

In Buddhist and Hindu (and somewhat differently in Jain) traditions, gender itself is questioned. The philosophical basis of this questioning closely resembles the deconstruction of
gender in our own times by such thinkers as Monique Wittig and Judith Butler. What these
philosophers would call the social construction of gender that only appears to be "natural,"
ancient Indian philosophers call "illusion" that only appears to be "real."

In Buddhism, a *kalyanamitra*, or compassionate friend, is one who instructs and supports
in the dharma. Many women, such as Asha, Prabhuta, and Vasumitra, play this role. The next
step is to become a bodhisatta. There are many examples of women becoming bodhisattas,
then becoming men, and, finally, becoming Buddhas, but scholars like Diana Paul argue that
there is no female Buddha within non-Tantric Mahayana Buddhism.[55] Two women bodhisattas, Candrottara in the third- to fourth-century *Candrottaracaritrakaranasutram* and Sumati in
the third-century *Sumatidarikapariprccha*, dispute the need to change their sex. They argue
that since no object or person has innate characteristics, and Emptiness is the only reality, so
a woman too has no innate characteristics and there is nothing to be transformed.[56] In so arguing, they point to a discrepancy between Buddhist philosophy and practice, insofar as there
is a sharp discrimination between the rules governing monks and nuns.

Goddesses in Mahayana Buddhism perhaps originate in the feminine gender of abstract
nouns in Sanskrit that then become personified as autonomous deities. In the *Vimalakirtinird-
esa* a goddess, when asked by the monk Sariputra why she does not change her sex although
she has the power to do so, replies that she has found no innate characteristics of females despite her twelve-year search for them and therefore she cannot change. To demonstrate this to
Sariputra, she turns the tables on him by transforming him first into a likeness of herself and
then back into his own form. She asks him what the innate female characteristics are and he
is forced to reply that such characteristics "neither exist nor do not exist." The goddess explains: "Just as you are not really a woman but appear to be female in form, all women also appear to be female in form but are not really women. Therefore, the Buddha said all are not
really men or women. . . . All things neither exist nor do not exist. The Buddha said there is
neither existence nor nonexistence."[57]

55. Diana Y. Paul, *Women in Buddhism: Images of the Feminine in Mahayana Tradition* (Berke-
    ley: Asian Humanities Press, 1979).
56. See *Vinaya Pitaka*, trans. Frances Wilson, in Diana Y. Paul, *Women in Buddhism*.
57. Paul, *Women in Buddhism*, 230–31.

One of the most extended debates on the question of the reality of gender is that re-counted in the *Santi Parva* of the *Mahabharata*, a late section composed under the influence of Buddhism. The debate takes place between King Janaka, epitome of the enlightened Hindu sage, and Sulabha, a Yogini mendicant who doubts that he is really enlightened. Sulabha appears in Janaka's court uninvited and takes possession of him by her Yogic powers. Janaka explains to her that he has attained a state of freedom from duality even though he is living in the world. He goes on to reproach her, saying that though she has renounced the world, she is really not free from desire. As a woman, she had no right to enter into Yogic union with him. He notices her youth and beauty, asks who her husband is, and accuses her of being impelled by sexual desire.

Sulabha replies with a long, scholarly speech, quoting Hindu philosophers of various schools. She demonstrates that no creature, not even a king, has an independent or separate existence from other creatures. Referring to the Vedic trope of fire generated by the friction of sticks, she shows that all creatures are a mixture of the same elements. She shows that her Yogic or intellectual connection with him is not a physical connection; she touches him only with her understanding, not with any part of her body. Indirectly reproaching him for his vanity, she asks: "Indeed, as thou thyself seest thy own body in thy body and as thou thyself seest thy soul in thy own soul, why is it that thou dost not see thy own body and thy own soul in the bodies and souls of others? If it is true that thou seest an identity with thyself and others, why then didst thou ask me who I am and whose?" (*Santi Parva* II: CCCXXI).[58]

Janaka is silenced, and Sulabha wins the debate hands down.

There is a direct connection between the nonreality of gender and the nonabsoluteness of heterosexuality. If the two categories, "man" and "woman," are not ultimate categories but are merely created by society to foster certain social roles, and to uphold institutions such as marriage, parenthood, and patrilineal inheritance, then the heterosexual relation ceases to be the most important one. If human beings are turned by society into "men" and "women" through such mechanisms as dress, social roles, division of labor, and learned mannerisms, there is no natural or innate reason why an individual should be attracted or attached only to a member of the other gender category. A particular man and woman may be complementary to one another, but two men or two women may also be complementary to one another. Complementarity may then be a product not of the category but of individual difference and likeness. It may vary infinitely as do individual human beings.

Socially engendered categories change over time as society changes, and new categories come into being. As we shall see, ancient Indian texts constructed more than two gender categories. While the terms "homosexual" and "heterosexual" come into being in the nineteenth century, attraction, attachment, and sexual interaction between men, between women,

---

58. Ganguly, X: 67 (57–72).

and between men and women are as old as all known societies. The terms, tropes, and language for understanding these phenomena, cross-sex as much as same-sex, vary widely.

If we cease to see "men" and "women" as all-important categories, individual relationships can be seen on their own terms instead of being categorized and labeled. Ancient Indian philosophy provides us with tools to undo the categories of gender and of sexuality. However, some ancient Indian texts also attempt to construct categories of intermediate or alternative gender and sexuality.

Constructing Categories:
Legal, Medical and Erotic Treatises

The *Shastras* and *Sutras* are manuals or treatises, containing varying degrees of prescriptive and descriptive content. They belong to the epic period, that is, approximately the last centuries B.C. up to the fourth century A.D. Their aim is to outline how human beings can achieve the four goals of life: *dharma* (fulfilling the law of one's being), *artha* (material, including monetary, success), *kama* (pleasure and desire, including sexual fulfillment), and *moksha* (liberation from the cycle of rebirths). These texts are compendiums—they refer to many earlier texts and scholarly traditions. The most important are *Manavadharmashastra*, also known as *Manusmriti*, a compendium of laws and penances composed ca. the first century A.D.; Kautilya's *Arthashastra*, a treatise on economics and statecraft; Vatsyayana's manual on erotic arts, the *Kamasutra*, which will be examined separately (pp. 46–54); and the medical texts, *Charaka Samhita* and *Sushruta Samhita*.

If late nineteenth-century European sexologists invented such terms as "invert," "the third sex," and "homosexual," the Kamasutra's term "the third nature" refers to a man who desires other men. Whether the man concerned is feminine looking or masculine looking, the Kamasutra emphasizes that this external appearance makes no difference to his desire for men.

Michael Sweet and Leonard Zwilling, in their studies of the medical texts, grammatical texts such as Patanjali's second-century B.C. grammar, and Jain texts, have demonstrated that the concept of a third sex, with various ambiguous subcategories such as *kliba*, *pandaka*, and *napunsaka* (all varieties of the neutered), "has been a part of the Indian worldview for nearly three thousand years."[59] They argue that this concept evolved during the late Vedic period and was incorporated into grammar as a third gender in the sixth century B.C. Ancient and medieval Jain thinkers, debating whether women could attain liberation or not, argued that there were three types of desire (*veda*): male, female, and third-sex desire, of which the last was the

59. Michael J. Sweet and Leonard Zwilling, " 'Like a City Ablaze': The Third Sex and the Creation of Sexuality in Jain Religious Literature," *Journal of the History of Sexuality* 6:3 (1996): 359–84.

most intense, and all of which could be experienced by anyone, regardless of biological sex.[60] While categorizing men who desire men as "women" on the basis of their desire but simultaneously as "men" in gender, they also noted that desire may be fluid and transient. Thus, in the *Strinirvanaprakarana* (ca. 814–867) the Jain philosopher Sakatayana pointed out that a person may be capable of being sexually aroused by the same sex, the opposite sex or even a nonhuman animal. This is close to the worldly wise stance of the *Kamasutra*.

In the *Arthashastra*, there is a wide category of *ayoni*, or non-vaginal sex (also mentioned in other texts, such as the *Mahabharata*), which, whether with a man or a woman, is punishable with the first fine (IV.XIII.236). The first fine is the lowest fine, payable in grades for robberies of three types of not very high value. The medium fine is for robbery of large animals, gold, slaves and immovable property. Interestingly, women who have sex with each other have to pay a lower fine than do men who have sex with each other. But a woman who sleeps with an unwilling woman has to pay her a large amount of money. Clearly, this text treats heterosexual vaginal sex as the norm but makes no particular distinction between oral/anal sex occurring between men or between men and women. While homosexual sex is unsanctioned, it is treated as a minor offense. Many types of heterosexual vaginal sex are punishable much more severely; for example, the seduction or rape of a minor girl of equal caste is punishable with cutting off the man's hand or a heavy fine; if she dies, the man is to be killed (IV.XII.231).[61]

The *Manusmriti* appears even less judgmental in its famous prescription that a man who has sex with a man, or with a woman in a cart pulled by a cow, in water, or by day, should bathe with his clothes on (XI: 175).[62] XI: 174 prescribes that a man who sheds his semen in nonhuman females, in a man, in a menstruating woman, in something other than a vagina, or in water has to perform a minor penance consisting of eating the five products of the cow and keeping a one-night fast. This is the same penance prescribed for stealing articles of little value. XI: 68 states that "sexual union with a man is traditionally said to cause loss of caste." The phrasing suggests that this traditional idea is replaced by the penances prescribed here.[63]

Sex between nonvirgin women incurs a very small fine, while a man or a woman who manually deflowers a virgin has two fingers cut off (VIII.367; 369). The underlying idea is that loss of virginity will adversely affect a girl's chances of marriage. A virgin who "does it" to a virgin

---

60. See Padmanabh S. Jaini, *Gender and Salvation: Jaina Debates on the Spiritual Liberation of Women* (Berkeley: University of California Press, 1991), especially 79–89.
61. See the similar interpretation by Pratap Chandra Chunder, *Kautilya on Love and Morals* (Delhi: Gian Publishing House, 1987), 128–29.
62. *The Laws of Manu*, trans. Wendy Doniger with Brian K. Smith (Delhi: Penguin, 1991).
63. Religious penances do not foreclose the possibility of judicial penalty. Many of these penances apply only to Brahmans; in some cases, Brahmans might have been more subject to purity taboos and therefore other castes may have avoided strictures, while in other cases the latter might have been more severely penalized.

has to pay double the girl's dowry and is given ten whiplashes. The verb used for manual defloration is *kri*, to "do" or "make," and its meaning is clear from the context. Mutual manual stimulation or oral sex that does not involve deflowering, although mentioned in treatises on erotics like the *Kamasutra*, is not mentioned here as punishable. Again, various heterosexual offenses such as cross-caste adultery, rape, and abduction incur much heavier punishments than any homosexual act.

In contrast to these legal texts, the medieval text, the *Narada Purana*, trying to suit the punishment to the crime, provides a more comical and less enforceable penalty for those who have nonvaginal sex: "The great sinner who discharges semen in non-vaginas as in masturbation, in those who are destitute of vulva (*viyoni*) and uterus of animals, shall fall into the hell Retobhojana (where one has to subsist on semen)" (I.XV.936). The *Skanda Purana* issues a general warning designed to scare off everyone, declaring that those who have homosexual sex or different varieties of sex (*prakirna maithunah*) become impotent.

In the medical text *Sushruta Samhita*, a man who can have an erection only by sucking the genitals and drinking the sperm of another man is called an *A'sekya*.[64] This condition is ascribed by *Sushruta* to such a man having been born of scanty paternal sperm. *Sushruta* also states that a child without bones is the product of a sexual act between two women. If the sexual secretions of two women unite in the womb of one of them, conception may take place and a boneless child is then born.[65] The medieval *Krittivasa Ramayana* makes imaginative use of this space provided by the ancient medical treatise (see pp. 100–102).

Attempts at categorization in ancient texts vary in sophistication, and often contradict one another, which suggests that no one form of categorization was dominant. This confusion is perhaps endemic to all attempts at categorizing what is fluid and uncategorizable. Twentieth-century categories such as "heterosexual," "homosexual," and "bisexual" are equally flawed and reductionist, as is clear from the many questions they leave unanswered. (For example, does duration, intensity or frequency of experience determine preference? What about fantasy? What is the role played by the force of circumstance/proximity/opportunity?).

Overall, it may be said that those ancient texts that do attempt categorization certainly subordinate nonpenetrative as well as nonheterosexual sex to penetrative heterosexual sex. They also tend to take a somewhat derogatory view of those who are homoerotically inclined. The range of terms used for such persons suggests a groping for words rather than complete social integration and widely understood categories. Many of these terms spring from heterosexual assumptions, ascribing effeminacy, impotence, or some sort of inadequacy to nonheterosexual persons.

On the other hand, there is also an overall tolerance and relatively nonjudgmental attitude, and an absence of violent persecution. As in many traditional cultures, including medieval

---

64. *The Sushruta Samhita,* ed. and trans. K. L. Bhishagratna (Varanasi: Chowkhamba Sanskrit Series Vol. XXX, 1991), II: 36–40.
65. *Sushruta Samhita,* II: 46–49.

Christianity and later Hinduism, the main divide in ancient Hindu and Buddhist texts seems to be that between sex and celibacy rather than between different types of sexual behavior.

Explicit References to Sexual Relations

In the epics, as in the erotic and medical treatises discussed above, one comes across explicitly sexual interactions between men and between women that are not categorized. One example is the well-known description in the *Valmiki Ramayana* of the women Hanuman sees in Ravana's palace and in the other houses in Sri Lanka. They are described as lying semiclad in each others' arms as if with male lovers. Their being Rakshasa women may allow the author a certain freedom in his depiction of their sexual behavior, but not all Rakshasas are represented by Valmiki as evil, and Hanuman also feels guilty about having violated the privacy of these women. He concludes that since his voyeurism happened inadvertently, it is pardonable. The *Mahabharata* contains references to oral sex, to sports and diversions in which women dress as men and men as women, and to forbidden sex that is to be punished with going about in wet clothes and sleeping on ashes.[66]

Given the widespread popular assumption in modern India that boy prostitution, eunuchs and even anal sex appeared only following the advent of Islam, it is important to note that in pre-Islamic texts, men and boy prostitutes and dancers who service men are represented in descriptive, nonjudgmental terms, as normally present in court and in daily life, evidence of the affluence and splendor of urban culture. Male servants performing oral sex on their masters are mentioned in the *Kamasutra*. In the *Rajatarangini*, chronicles of the kings of Kashmir, the licentious king Kshemagupta is described as addicted to anal as well as vaginal sex, has male favorites whom he caresses in public, and fills his court with "harlots, knaves, imbeciles and corrupters of boys."[67]

In the *Shilappadikaram*, a king called Nurruvar Kannar whose kingdom is in the Gangetic plain sends as tribute to the Chera king Shenguttuvan a large number of gifts including animals, jugglers, musicians, dancing girls and "one thousand brilliantly dressed *kanjuka*, boy prostitutes with long carefully burnished hair" (166).[68] These boys are described as "fine-spoken" (167). Later, Shenguttuvan, in order to humiliate the army chiefs

---

66. Markandeya's account of the end of the Kali Yuga refers to women using their mouths as vaginas (*mukhebhagaha striyo*) and becoming hostile to their husbands (*Vana Parva*, CLXXXVIII; Ganguly, III: 378). Shree's account of the decline of the Danavas, which focuses on their disregard of caste, age, gender, slave, and other hierarchies and their neglect of purity, ritual, and charity, describes their enjoyment of cross-dressing (*Santi Parva*, II: CCXXVIII, Ganguly, IX: 149).

67. *Rajatarangini: The Saga of the Kings of Kasmir,* trans. Ranjit Sitaram Pandit (New Delhi: Sahitya Akademi, 1968 [1935]).

68. Prince Ilango Adigal, *The Shilappadikaram,* trans. Alain Danielou (Delhi: Penguin, 1965).

he has defeated, parades them chained to male prostitutes. These prostitutes are termed "Aryan *pedis*" and described as having "drawn-in cheeks, black tufts, sunken dark eyes reddened at the corners, large earrings, red lips, white teeth, thin bamboo-like arms loaded with gold bracelets, fake breasts, thin waists, and circlets on their shapeless ankles, that made people laugh" (176). These prostitutes are not boys but adult men and are dressed as women; they may be close to Vatsyayana's men of the "third nature." In any case, they are clearly not eunuchs because the latter are mentioned as a separate category who dress as women and serve the women in the women's quarters of the palace (181).

Also interesting in this text is the Brahman boy dancer who performs at court the dance of the hermaphrodite, or of Shiva and Parvati united in one body. The description of the dance shows that male and female are perceived as active and passive, since the dancer swiftly moves the traditionally "male" right side of his body while keeping his traditionally "female" left side silent and motionless (182). In the *Manimekhalai*, boy dancers in the street perform a dance called *pedi* in which they dress as hermaphrodites. These boys wear artificial beards, long hair, breasts and protuberant sex organs.

Rebirth: The Justification of "Impossible" Loves

Rebirth seems to me the single most significant factor in the Indian understanding of same-sex love. It is important in ancient texts and continues to be important in folktales and in daily life and conversation today (see p. 216).

The concept of previous births serves to legitimize actions perceived as improper in the present life. Between simple social acceptance and outright social rejection is the gray area made possible by the concept of rebirth. This is clear in cases when two people of different castes fall in love. Instead of simply condemning the people concerned, it is possible for others to explain their attraction as involuntary because caused by attachment in a former birth. This enables the family and society to absolve the lovers of blame and to gradually accommodate the relationship.

Thus, when Prince Avantivardhana in the *Kathasaritsagara* falls in love with Suratamanjari, a Chandala girl, and wants to marry her, his father says, "Since the heart of our son is thus inclined, it is clear that she is really a girl of another caste who for some reason or other has fallen among the Matangas."[69] He then relates a story of a Chandala man who fell in love with a princess. The god Agni appeared and revealed that the man was actually Agni's son by a Brahman woman. (Here is a clear-cut case of miraculous birth being used to legitimize a son born of a nonmarital relationship.) The princess's father had a dream informing him of this, and the marriage took place. Avantivardhana's father argues that Suratamanjari must have

---

69. *The Katha Sarit Sagara,* trans. C. H. Tawney (Calcutta: Asiatic Society, 1880; New Delhi: Munshiram Manoharlal, 1968), 490. All page numbers refer to this 1968 edition.

been his son's beloved in a previous birth "and this is proved by his falling in love with her at first sight" (491). This arguing backward from the fact (falling in love proves that they were linked in a former birth) works to sanction the relationship. Another case involved is that of a fisherman who fell in love with a princess "for destiny never considers whether a union is possible or impossible" (491). This formulation, again, is interesting for its willingness to accept that a relationship considered socially impossible may be predestined. Her father hears a heavenly voice telling him that the fisherman was a Brahman in a former birth and the princess his wife.

Avantivardhana's troubled father is consoled by this explanation of otherwise unacceptable unions: "In this way a connexion in a former birth usually produces affection in embodied beings. . . . creatures are completely dependent upon connexions in previous births, and this being the case, who can avoid a destiny that is fated to him . . . ?" (493–95). The concept of destiny and fate clearly functions here in an enabling rather than disempowering way. To confer respectability upon the marriage, the king calls 18,000 Brahmans and asks them to eat in the Chandala girl's father's house. They prefer to perform self-torture at Shiva's shrine. But Shiva tells them in a dream that the girl's father is really a Vidyadhara reborn as a Chandala, so they consent to eat food cooked outside the Chandala quarter but served by the girl's father. Hearing about all these dreams, the girl's father now tells the king an elaborate story of how he himself was a Vidyadhara cursed to become a Chandala, and the marriage then takes place.

I have quoted this story at length to demonstrate that even the normally most impossible marriage, that between an upper-caste person and an outcaste, can be made acceptable by drawing on the possibilities of rebirth. In the many stories quoted in the preceding sections as well as in the extracts, rebirth of one kind or another is constantly called on to explain same-sex attachments from that of Krishna and Arjuna, to that of female friends in the *Kathasaritsagara* (p. 86), to that of the bodhisatta and his friends in the *Jataka* tales. An attachment that appears inexplicable for its intensity, its suddenness or its unconventional object can be understood both by the participants and by those around them if placed in the frame of former births. Even unhappy endings to such attachments can be seen as nonfinal; for example, joint suicide or dying together can be read as entry together into another birth under, it is hoped, more favorable circumstances.

Secondly, rebirth makes fluid categories and boundaries, even those that appear most biologically fixed, such as species and gender categories. Further, the basic Hindu idea, variously expressed, that the universal spirit pervades all things means that in the ultimate analysis nothing is abnormal or unnatural. Even gods and demons are akin rather than absolutely distinct. Stories of warfare with demons and other evil beings, including the normative war between Rama and Ravana, often end by explaining that the demon engaged in war in order to attain death at the hands of a god or a good man, thus merging with god or returning to an original high status from which he or she had fallen due to wrongdoing.

In this context, people inclined to alternative sexual behaviors are also expressions of divine play or *leela* (see pp. 61–62). Invocations to a particular god or goddess, when he or she is henotheistically being identified with ultimate reality, often take the form of saying that she or he is everything, including all apparent opposites. Oppositions get resolved and are revealed as illusory in the universality and allness of god. Thus Shiva is addressed (in a long catalog that identifies him with a series of opposites): "Thou art male, thou art female, thou art neuter" (*Mahabharata, Santi Parva I, Apadharmanusasana Parva* CCLXXXV).[70] Ancient texts too aspire to this compendious condition, and through that aspiration, to inclusiveness, to embracing every possibility, leaving nothing out. As the *Mahabharata*, in its concluding section, famously puts it: "That which occurs here occurs elsewhere. That which does not occur here occurs nowhere" (*Swargarohanika Parva V*).[71]

Finally, rebirth, by bringing mortality into the debate, automatically makes socially constructed categories such as caste, class and gender seem less important. In the face of the common creaturely fate—death—how important is it to condemn attachments that violate the bounds of humanly constructed categories? Rebirth focuses on the disembodied spirit, thus diminishing the obsession with the biological difference between men and women; conversely, the idea of the spirit retaining its attachments into the next birth foregrounds the importance and value of attachment itself, regardless of the form taken by the object of that attachment.

---

70. Ganguly, IX: 326.
71. Ganguly, XII: 291.

Vyasa's Mahabharata:
"Sikhandin's Sex Change" (Sanskrit)[1]

Introduced by Ruth Vanita

The story of Sikhandin is perhaps the best known case of sex change in any ancient Indian text. *Sikhandin* later became a term to refer to eunuchs and men of doubtful sexuality. The story is remarkable for the cluster of motifs associated with the sex change—rebirth, the cross-dressed girl-child married to another girl, her desire to be a man, and the uncertainty regarding the permanence of the change. Some of these motifs occur in stories of sex change in other mythologies.

The events preceding the following extract relate to the princess Amba (lit. mother) who, along with her two sisters, was abducted from their *swayamvaram* (ceremony where a woman chooses her husband) by Bhishma (lit. terrible, so called on account of his terribly difficult vow to remain celibate) who wanted them as wives for his brother. Amba told Bhishma that since she was already in love with another king, she should be allowed to marry him. Bhishma agreed and Amba went to the man she had chosen, but he refused to marry her because he considered her defiled by the abduction. Amba returned to Bhishma but his brother could not marry her now, since she had declared herself affianced to another. Bhishma himself could not marry her as he had taken a vow to remain celibate. Furious, Amba sought the assistance of many heroes, including the mighty Parshurama, to take revenge on Bhishma, but none could help her as Bhishma was invincible on account of his vow. Amba then retreated to the forest and practiced severe austerities, worshiping Shiva. When he appeared to her, she told him that she had no womanly desires left, but she wanted revenge on Bhishma because he had prevented her from fulfilling the duties of a woman. She asked for the boon of manhood so that she could kill him. Shiva told her she would obtain manhood in her next birth and would remember the incidents

1. Edition used for this translation: *The Mahabharatam: Text as Constituted in Its Critical Edition* (Pune: The Bhandarkar Oriental Research Institute, 1971, 1976).

of this life. Amba entered the fire, after which she was reborn as a girl, Sikhandini, who later was changed into a man.

Sikhandin literally means "the crested one." Peacocks are often called *sikhandin* and peahens *sikhandini*. Although Sikhandini is born to kill Bhishma, it is interesting that her desire for a sex change is triggered not by the wish for revenge but solely by the complications consequent on her marriage to another girl; that is, gender becomes a problem in the context of youthful sexuality. In an ancient Greek story recounted by the poet Ovid (43 B.C.–17 A.D.), Iphis was a girl brought up as a boy, who fell in love with another girl, Ianthe, and lamented that this love was "impossible" to fulfill. By a divine boon, she was changed into a man and they got married.[2]

In the following extract, Bhishma, before the war, is telling Duryodhana the story, so that the king is forewarned and can try to ensure that Bhishma does not encounter Sikhandin in single combat.

◆   ◆   ◆

Translated from the Sanskrit by Kumkum Roy

Udyoga Parva

5.189.2 onward.

Bhishma said: "O great king, the chief and beloved wife of King Drupada had no son. So the king worshiped Shankara [Shiva] in order to get a son. He performed severe austerities to ensure my destruction, saying: 'May I get a son from Mahadeva, not a daughter. O lord, I want a son so that I can take revenge on Bhishma.' The god of gods replied: 'You will have a female-male (*stripumans*). O king, stop performing austerities, as it will not be otherwise.'

"Returning to his capital, he told his wife: 'O lady, I have performed great austerities to get a son. According to Shambhu [Shiva], we will have a daughter who will become a son. Despite my repeated requests, he said, 'This is what is fated; it cannot be otherwise. What is destined will happen.'

"Then, O king, when her season came, the intelligent wife of Drupada approached her husband. I was informed by Narada that in due course the wife of Parsata (Drupada) conceived, as was destined. The lotus-eyed lady bore the embryo in her womb. O delight of the Kurus, the mighty king Drupada looked after the well-being of his beloved wife out of affection for his son."[3]

---

2. See Ovid, *Metamorphoses* (Philadelphia: Paul Dry Books, 1999), 9: 666–797.

3. One verse is missing here from the critical edition.

"O king, a beautiful daughter was born to the sonless monarch Drupada. But his illustrious wife announced: 'A son is born to me.' King Drupada got all the rituals performed for the concealed one as if she were really a son. . . . Believing the words of that god of immense energy, he concealed the fact that the child was a girl and said: 'He is a boy.'

"The king performed all the rituals of birth for the child as if she were a male, and named her Sikhandin. I was the only one who knew the truth, on account of my spies, through Narada, and through my knowledge of the words of the god and the austerities of Amba."

5.190. Bhishma said: "Drupada took great care of that daughter of his, and taught her writing as well as the various arts. O king, the child learnt archery from Drona. O king, the child's golden-hued mother urged the king to find a wife for their daughter who was like a son. Then Parsata, seeing that his daughter was in the full bloom of youth, consulted his wife.

"Drupada said: 'On the word of the trident-bearing god, I have concealed this daughter of mine; she has become a young woman who increases my sorrows. What the lord of the three worlds has declared will never be false. Why indeed would he tell a lie?'[4]

"The wife said: 'O king, son of Parsata, listen to what I have to say, and then decide on your course of action. O king, his wedding should be performed according to custom. I am sure that the word of the god will come true.'"

Bhishma said: "Having made up their minds, the couple chose the daughter of the king of Dasarna. That lion amongst kings, Drupada, having examined the families of all the kings, chose the daughter of the king of Dasarnaka as Sikhandin's wife. The king of the Dasarnakas was known as Hiranyavarman, and he gave his daughter to Sikhandin. The king of the Dasarnas, Hiranyavarman, was extremely powerful and virtually invincible, with a large army.

"O best of kings, some time after the marriage, the daughter of the king attained puberty, as did the daughter Sikhandini. After the marriage, Sikhandin returned to Kampilya and the wife soon came to know that she was a woman. The daughter of Hiranyavarman, knowing her to be Sikhandini, shyly informed her nurses and female friends about the daughter of the king of Panchala [Drupada]. Then, O tiger amongst kings, those nurses of the Dasarnakas were very sad and sent messengers to the king. They went and told him how he had been deceived. Hearing this, the king was furious.

"O bull of the Bharatas, hearing that news after a few days, the king was overcome with rage. Then the furious king sent a messenger to Drupada. Reaching the palace, the messenger of Hiranyavarman called Drupada aside and spoke to him in secret: 'The king of the Dasarnas is enraged at your deception and says, "You have ill-advisedly insulted me by

---

4. The last two sentences are attributed to the king in some manuscripts and in the critical edition and to his wife in others.

seeking my daughter's hand for your daughter. Just wait, O wicked one, you will reap the fruits of this deception today, as I will kill you, along with your relatives and advisers.'"

5.192.9 Bhishma said: "The king wondered how he could avoid war with his kinsman, and prayed to the gods. . . ."[5]

5.192.17 "Hearing her parents' conversation, and seeing them overcome with grief, the intelligent Sikhandini was filled with shame. She thought, 'They are grief-stricken on my account.' Consequently, she decided to end her life. Having made up her mind, and overwhelmed with sorrow, she left the palace and entered a dense, desolate forest. This, O king, was the abode of a Yaksha named Sthunakarna. Men avoided entering the forest as they were afraid of him. In the forest was Sthuna's palace, plastered with mud, filled with smoke of fried paddy, with high walls and a gateway. Sikhandin, the daughter of Drupada, entered, and emaciated her body by fasting for a number of days.

"Then the Yaksha Sthuna, who was compassionate, appeared before her and asked: 'Tell me at once why you are making such an effort. I will do it [what you want] for you.' She replied again and again: 'You will not be able to do it.' 'I will,' replied the Guhyaka [the Yaksha]. 'O princess, I am the follower of the lord of wealth [Kubera]. I can grant boons, I can even give that which cannot be given. Tell me, what is it you are seeking?'

"Then, O Bharata, Sikhandin narrated everything to Sthunakarna, the chief of the Yakshas: 'O Yaksha, my father will meet his doom very soon, as the enraged lord of the Dasarnas marches against him. The king is mighty, courageous, and wears golden armor. Therefore, O Yaksha, protect me, my father and mother from him. You have already promised to assuage my distress. With your blessings, may I become a perfect man, O Yaksha. O great Yaksha, bless me until the time that king leaves my city; be gracious, O Guhyaka.'"

5.193.1–11. Bhishma said: "O bull of the Bharatas, the Yaksha reflected on hearing these words of Sikhandin and said: 'This was destined for my sorrow, O Kaurava, O auspicious one. I will fulfill your desire but listen to my terms. I will give you my malehood for some time. Promise me you will return on time. I am the master of immense powers; I can fly and change my form at will. Through my grace save your city and your relatives. O princess, I will bear your femaleness for some time. Promise me, and I will do what you desire.'

"Sikhandin said: 'O lord, I will return your maleness to you. O wanderer of the night, bear my womanhood for some time. When the king of the Dasarnas, Hiranyavarman, returns, I will become a girl and you will be a man.'"

---

5. The term used for "kinsman" is *sambandhin,* which refers to kin created by marriage, especially to one's child's in-laws.

Bhishma said: "Having spoken thus, O king, the two of them made a contract and entered one another's bodies. O Bharata, the Yaksha Sthuna bore the femaleness while Sikhandin obtained the beautiful form of the Yaksha.

"Then, O king, Sikhandin of the Panchalas, having attained manhood, entered the city joyfully and went to his father. He told Drupada everything that had happened. Drupada, too, was overjoyed, and, with his wife, remembered the words of the great god. Then he sent a messenger to the king of the Dasarnas, saying: 'My child is a man. May you believe my word.'

5.193.25–52. "Hearing the words of Drupada, the king, filled with sorrow, sent a number of beautiful young women to find out whether Sikhandin was a female or a male. O lord of the Kauravas, those who were sent, having ascertained the truth, joyfully announced to the powerful lord of the Dasarnas that Sikhandin was a man. The king was pleased with the news and spent some time happily with his kinsman. The king was also pleased with Sikhandin and gave him wealth—many hundreds of elephants, horses, cattle and slave women. Treated respectfully, the king left, after scolding his daughter.

[In some versions, but not in the critical edition, there is a line here: "After the departure of the king Hiranyavarman, who was satisfied, Sikhandini was very happy."]

"Some time later, Kuvera, who is carried around by men, made a journey through the worlds and came to Sthuna's abode. Floating above the house, the lord of wealth observed that the house of the Yaksha Sthuna was decorated with beautiful garlands. It was fragrant with the smell of paddy and flowers, it was washed and swept, decorated with flags and banners and full of food and drink of various kinds. Seeing that well-adorned place, the lord of the Yakshas addressed his followers: 'This house of the brave Sthuna is well adorned. However, why does he stupidly refrain from greeting me? Seeing that he does not come forward to greet me, I have decided to inflict a severe punishment on him.'

"The Yakshas said: 'O king, a daughter named Sikhandini was born to King Drupada. The Yaksha has given his male attributes to her for some reason. He has accepted her womanly attributes, and, having become a woman, stays at home. That is why, from shame at being possessed of the form of a woman, he does not come to greet you. . . .'"

Bhishma said: "The lord of the Yakshas commanded again and again: 'Bring Sthuna, I will punish him.' O king, he, ordered by the king of the Yakshas, came and stood before him as a woman, ashamed. Then, O joy of the Kurus, the angry giver of wealth cursed him: 'O Guhyakas, let the womanhood of this sinful one remain as it is.' Then the great lord of the Yakshas said: 'Seeing that you have humiliated all the Yakshas by giving Sikhandin your attributes and taking the attributes of womanhood from her, and seeing that you, of wicked intellect, have done something which was never done before, you henceforth will be a woman and he a man.'

"The other Yakshas begged again and again, trying to soften Vaishravana [Kuvera] in favor of Sthuna, and requested him to set a limit to the curse. To all his followers, who hoped that the curse would be limited, the great lord of the Yakshas replied: 'When Sikhandin is killed, the Yaksha will regain his own form. . . . '

"Receiving the curse, Sthuna remained there, and Sikhandin came to him the moment the time was up. Approaching him, he said: 'I have come, O lord.' Sthuna responded again and again: 'I am pleased with you.' Seeing that the prince Sikhandin was honest, he told him all that had happened. The Yaksha said: 'O prince, I have been cursed by Vaishravana on your account. Go where you will and live happily in the world as it may please you. I think that both your coming here and the arrival of Paulastya [Kuvera] were foreordained and could not have been prevented.'

5.193.59–63. "This is how, O best of the Kurus, Sikhandin, the excellent charioteer, the son of Drupada, was born as a woman-man. O bull of the Bharatas, the eldest daughter of the king of Kashi, who was well known as Amba, was born in Drupada's family as Sikhandin. If he approaches me, armed with the bow, to fight, I will not even look at him for a moment, nor hit him. This vow of mine is known throughout the world. O joy of the Kurus, I will not use my arrows against a woman, one who was once a woman, one whose name is like a woman's, or one who resembles a woman. For this reason, I will not kill Sikhandin."

Manikantha Jataka (Pali)[1]

Translated by Kumkum Roy

This story was told by the Master while he was at the shrine of Aggalava near Alavi, about the rules for building cells.

Some monks who lived in Alavi were going around begging everyone for materials for constructing their cells. They went on and on: "Give us a man, give us somebody who can do a servant's work." People were annoyed at this constant begging and pleading, so much so that they were startled and ran away whenever they saw the monks.

It so happened that around that time Mahakassapa (a senior monk) entered Alavi in search of alms. As before, people ran away as soon as they saw the elder (*thera*). After mealtime, he returned, summoned the monks and asked: "Earlier, it was easy to get alms in Alavi; why has it become so difficult now?" They told him why.

Then he went to the Blessed One who was at the Aggalava shrine and told him all.

The Master summoned an assembly of the monks of Alavi and asked: "Is it true that you are troubling everybody for help to build your cells?" "It is true, O lord," they replied. Having scolded the monks, he said: "O monks, even the Serpents who live in the realm full of all kinds of jewels detest begging; how much more would men from whom it is as difficult to get a coin as it is to skin a stone?" With that, he told a story of the past.

"Once upon a time, when Brahmadatta was the king of Varanasi, the Bodhisatta was born in the family of a prosperous Brahman. When he was old enough to run about, another blessed soul was born to his mother. When they grew up, both the brothers were so distressed at the death of their parents that they renounced the world and lived in leaf huts which they made on the banks of the Ganga. The hut of the elder brother was on the upper Ganga while that of the younger one was on the lower Ganga.

One day, the Serpent King named Manikantha (lit. Jewel Throat) left his palace and, taking the shape of a man, wandered along the banks of the Ganga. He came to

---

1. This translation from V. Fausboll, *The Jatakas with Its Commentary* (London: Truber and Co., 6 vols. 1877–1896).

the hermitage of the younger brother and, greeting him, sat on one side. They talked pleasantly to one another and grew so fond of one another that they could not live apart.

Manikantha would often come to visit the young ascetic. He would sit and talk with him, and when it was time to leave, because of his deep love for the ascetic, he would cast off his body, embrace the ascetic in his folds, hold his great hood over his head, and lie for a little while. Then, when his love was satisfied, he would let go of the ascetic's body, bid him farewell, and return to his palace.

Due to fear, the ascetic grew thin, disheveled, pale, more and more yellow, and his veins bulged out of his skin.

One day, he paid a visit to his brother who asked: "Why are you so thin and disheveled? Why have you lost your color and become more and more yellow? Why do your veins bulge out?"

The other told him all.

The first asked: "Do you wish the Serpent to come or not?"

"I don't."

"What ornament does the Serpent King wear when he comes to visit you?"

"A precious jewel," he replied.

"Well, when the Serpent King next comes to visit you, as soon as he is near you but before he can sit down, you should beg, 'Give me that jewel.' The Serpent will leave without embracing you in his snaky folds. The next day, stand at the door and beg for it as soon as he comes, and on the third day just as he surfaces from the waters of the Ganga. Then he will never come near you again."

The young ascetic promised to do as he was told, and returned to his hut. The next day, as soon as the Serpent King came and stood there, he said: "Give me your beautiful jewel." The Serpent hurried away without sitting down. The next day, standing at the door, the ascetic said: "Yesterday you didn't give me your jewel. Today, you must." The Serpent slipped away without entering the hut. On the third day, as he was emerging from the water, the ascetic said: "This is the third day I am asking you for a gift. Give the jewel to me." The Serpent King, remaining in the water, refused, and replied with two verses:

> I have plenty to eat and drink because of this jewel which you desire.
> I will not give it to you, who ask too much
> Nor will I visit you again as long as I live.

> You frighten me like a young man brandishing a sword.
> I will not give it to you, who ask too much
> Nor will I visit you again as long as I live.

With these words, the Serpent King plunged into the water, and went to his palace, never to return again.

Then the ascetic, not seeing the handsome Serpent King, became even more thin, more disheveled, more pale, more yellow, and his veins protruded even more than before.

The elder ascetic thought: "Let me see how the young one fares." Going to him, he found that he was more yellow than ever.

He asked: "How is it that you are even more sickly than before?"

He replied: "It is because I do not see that beautiful Serpent."

The elder ascetic said: "This ascetic cannot live without the Serpent King."

So saying, he recited the third verse:

> Do not beg of those who are dear to you.
> Excessive begging makes you hateful.
> The Brahman begged the Serpent for the jewel.
> He disappeared, never to return again.

Then he said: "Do not grieve any more," and having consoled him, the elder brother returned to his own hermitage, and then the two brothers cultivated their faculties and virtues and became worthy of attaining the world of Brahma."

The Master said: "Thus, O monks, begging is disliked even amongst the Serpents who live in a palace full of seven kinds of jewels; how much more so amongst men?" Having taught them the lesson, he identified the birth: "Ananda was the younger brother, while I myself was the elder."

Vishnu Sharma's Panchatantra *(Sanskrit)*

Ruth Vanita

As with most other ancient and medieval Sanskrit texts, the dates of the *Panchatantra* are impossible to fix with certainty. Like the other *Katha* cycles, it is a compendium of stories, arranged like Chinese boxes, story within story. Of all ancient Indian texts, it has probably had the greatest influence on world literature. Between the sixth and the eighth centuries it traveled via Pehlevi, Syriac and Arabic, to Europe, and between the eleventh and the eighteenth centuries, versions appeared in Greek, Latin, German, Spanish, French, English, Armenian, Hebrew and Slavonic languages. Although the earliest Sanskrit versions are lost, a large number of medieval Sanskrit versions exist as well as many versions in other Indian languages. While some of the stories are of ancient provenance, dating back to the epic period, others were added much later.

The *Panchatantra* (lit. five *tantras* or narratives/strategies/theories) purports to have been composed by an eighty-year-old Brahman scholar Vishnu Sharma, at the request of a king whose five sons were averse to learning. The frame narrative tells us that through these stories, the scholar succeeded in educating the young men in all the arts requisite to being good rulers.

Friendship is the primary theme and the structuring relationship of the *Panchatantra*. Although the text is framed as an instruction manual for princes, and friendship as political alliance is represented as an important aspect of a king's ruling strategy, the dimension of friendship as life-sustaining at a personal level also emerges as highly significant, and not just for kings. As Chandra Rajan remarks, "it is friendship that is given a special place and set above all other relationships."[1] Of the five books, three revolve around same-sex friendship,

---

1. Visnu Sarma, *The Pancatantra,* trans. Chandra Rajan (New Delhi: Penguin, 1993), Introduction, xlv. All further quotations in English are from this edition. Sanskrit quotations are from the critical edition, Sudhakar Malviya, ed., *Panchatantram* (Varanasi: Krishnadas Academy, 1993).

with only Book Three focusing on inherited enmity. The first two books are entitled "Estrangement of Friends" and "The Winning of Friends."

Although all the protagonists in the major framing stories are animals, they function in many ways as stand-ins for humans. It is noteworthy that all of them are male and none of them is represented as married although they are not ascetics either. They are depicted as living happily together and enjoying each other's company. These friendships are not mere social acquaintances; they are life-defining, primary relationships. The friends provide each other with all kinds of support and are even ready to sacrifice their lives for one another. Most of these friends do not have any other relationships of greater importance; in the one instance where a male is married, the wife perceives her husband's male friend as her rival and tries to destroy the friendship.

The friendships between these creatures are odd, however, insofar as they occur between members of different species—lion and bull; crow, deer, tortoise, and mole; and ape and crocodile. This oddness could, of course, have many implications, some of which I shall explore below. At least one of these implications could relate to gender and sexuality. If the categories "man" and "woman" are socially constructed as both opposite and complementary to one another, playing out the action between beasts rather than humans could have the effect of defamiliarizing and undoing the categories.

The oddness of life-defining friendship between creatures of different species could stand in for the oddness of life-defining friendship between persons of the same sex. Both appear unconventional, even "unnatural" in that they appear to defy biology, social custom, and inherited traits.

This "unnaturalness" is explicitly debated in the text, in relation to the question of whether friendship is possible between grass-eaters and flesh-eaters, for example, between lion and bull. When the lion and bull become intimate friends, it does not occur to them that this is strange. The apparent difference between the powerful lion and the comparatively powerless bull is bridged by a common "nobility," and the difference between the wild warrior lion and the domesticated, learned bull is bridged by conversation. We are told that the lion becomes civilized through conversation with the bull. The two friends spend all their time in private talk, unattended by others. This dismays one of the jackals who begins to sow discord between the friends, on the basis of what he perceives as the unchangeably different "natures" of lion and bull.

Here lion and bull could stand for the powerful warrior king, the Kshatriya, and the learned but weak Brahman who acquires influence through his eloquence or, in later times, for Muslim and Hindu. The jackal stresses the difference between flesh-eater and grass-eater, and also speaks disparagingly of the bull's dung and urine, arguing that worms will breed in this excreta and infest the wounds on the lion's body. Given the sacred status of cow dung in Hindu ritual, which Muslims tended to view as unhygienic and even disgusting, the metaphor seems carefully chosen and feeds into the jackal's larger argument that the apparently weak can undermine the strong in unexpected ways.

The jackal succeeds in fomenting mistrust between the friends and provoking a battle in which the lion kills the bull. However, the jackal's view of this odd friendship as undesirable is undermined by another jackal who lectures the lion on his folly in having listened to an evil advisor and destroyed a faithful friend. The lion repents too late. (Some Arabic versions mete out poetic justice by having the evil counselor executed.) Thus, the text could be in part a meditation on the inevitability and simultaneous fragility of friendships between ruler and ruled. This sort of debate continues in the colonial period in texts about friendships between the British and Indians.

In Book Two, the only book with a "happy ending," same-sex friendship is exemplified in its most exalted form. The four friends here—the mole, crow, deer, and tortoise—are all relatively powerless creatures, although some are vegetarian and others are not. To begin with, the mole refuses the crow's proffered friendship, because, like the jackal in Book One, he thinks there can be no lasting friendship between "natural" enemies—he points out that he is the food of the crow. The crow, who is deeply impressed by the mole's skill and intelligence, persists in his persuasions.

After they have had a long debate, the mole hiding in his burrow and the crow aboveground, the crow produces his clinching argument. He points out to the mole that since they have conversed for so long, they have become friends whether the mole likes it or not:

"Wise men have declared this:
comradeship is when seven words are spoken
(or seven steps together taken).
Friendship has been thrust upon you,
O friend; so listen to my words." (II: 36)

Quoting the ancient texts, the crow says that friendship with good people occurs at first sight, *maitri syaddarshanatsatam*, and also after seven words are spoken together (see p. 7). The friendship is then ratified by an embrace and by sharing each other's food. Each brings his own kind of food—the crow a piece of buffalo meat and the mole rice and millet grains, of which both partake.[2] On the other hand, eating each other's food is not an essential prerequisite of friendship, for the deer is not shown eating meat yet he is an intimate friend of the crow. One sees here a sensitive and nuanced approach to the question of interdining as it relates to intimacy.

---

2. As a variation of beef, buffalo meat would not be eaten by at least some groups of Hindus by late antiquity. However, in the debate on vegetarianism waged in Buddhist texts and also in the *Mahabharata,* eating the flesh of a creature that one has not killed for the purpose of eating, would be acceptable to some. The crow does not of course, kill the buffalo, but finds its carcass, freshly slaughtered by a tiger.

In this section, there is an emphasis both on passionate emotions and on the physical delight experienced by a friend's touch as well as in intimate or intellectual conversation. When the crow embraces his friend the tortoise, the narrator comments:

> "Can sandal-paste blended with chill camphor
> or snowflakes delightfully cool, compare
> with the refreshing touch of a friend's body?
> They are not a sixteenth part of this delight." (II: 45)[3]

The metaphor of sandalwood is often used in the context of erotic contact, for example, the princess Sasiprabha in the *Vetalpanchvimsati* story cycle narrates how she felt when Manahsvamin carried her in his arms: "Then contact with his body made me feel as if I were anointed with sandalwood ointment, and bedewed with ambrosia. . . ."[4] After embracing, the crow and mole sit together, "their bodies still thrilling with happiness" (*pulkita shariro*).[5] The narrator remarks here that the embrace of a friend after many days is invaluable—no price can be set on it.

The destitute and exiled mole relates the sad story of his life and comments that the heart that lacks a true friend is empty, just as a home without a child is empty. The mole is restored to mental well-being by the reassurances of his friends who tell him that he should treat their homes as his own. The crow thanks the tortoise for his hospitality and places the joys of friendship on par with those of lover and beloved:

> "Those who enjoy happy times,
> friends with dear friends,
> lovers with their beloved,
> joyful with the joyous,
> only they fully taste Pleasure's quintessence—
> and live life to the fullest;
> they are the salt of the earth." (II: 162)[6]

Later, when the friends meet every day to converse, the narrator comments that men of intellect experience physical pleasure even without women, because "their skin tingles, their limbs thrill," relishing witty conversation (II: 171).[7]

---

3. Rajan, 209.
4. *The Katha Sarit Sagara or Ocean of the Streams of Story,* trans. C. H. Tawney (Calcutta: Asiatic Society, 1880; Delhi: Munshiram Manoharlal, 1968) II: 301–07, Vetala 15. All further references to the *Katha Sarit Sagara* are to this 1968 edition, and volume and page numbers also refer to it.
5. Rajan, 209.
6. Rajan, 248–49.
7. Rajan, 254.

The four ideal friends in this section are all male, all unmarried and without children or other domestic ties. Each has his own daily routine, but they all draw emotional support from each other. Their love is tested when one of them is caught by a hunter and the others risk their lives to save him. The tortoise exclaims that it is better to give up one's life than to be separated from one's friends because life is regained when we are reborn but friends, once lost, cannot be found again.

This poignant remark stresses an important point about imagining rebirth. While former births can function as a psychologically satisfying explanation and legitimization of present intimacy (see 28–30), it is not so easy to be confident that present intimacy will renew itself in the next birth. The word used here for "separation" is *viyoga*, a word normally used in erotic and romantic contexts. The tortoise addresses his friend here as *vara* which is normally used to mean "lover," "husband" or "bridegroom," and literally means "chosen one." This Book concludes with all the four friends living "happily in mutual friendship and affection."

In Book Four, the story of the ape and crocodile's friendship begins and continues in the same way as the story of the four friends in Book Two, but it is disrupted because one of the friends, the crocodile, is married, and his wife intrudes. The male crocodile meets the male ape every day and spends the whole day conversing with him and sharing sweet, juicy fruits with him. The erotic symbolism of the fruit is interesting; it seems to satisfy the crocodile who, like the lion vis-à-vis the bull in Book One, never has any desire to eat the ape. As long as same-sex friendship and cross-sex conjugality subsist in different spaces, they coexist peacefully. The female crocodile never appears on shore but stays at home. When, later, she desires to eat the ape, she orders her husband to bring him to her; she does not go herself to hunt. This very un-crocodile-like behavior is clearly a reflection of the wife secluded in the women's quarters at home who resents her husband's intimacies in the world outside.

The crocodile inadvertently provokes his wife's jealousy by carrying her some of the fruits every day, thus bringing domestic and public spaces into contact and conflict. When she inquires where he gets the fruit, he tells her that his intimate friend provides it. The wife then demands that he bring her the ape's heart (liver, in some versions) to eat because one who lives on such sweet fruits must have a very sweet heart. Once again the symbolism here is significant since the heart (or liver) is the seat of emotion and passion.

Refusing to kill his friend at his wife's behest, the crocodile defines the love of friends in a way that recalls the Vedic formulation of friends as born of Vak (see p.2): "One brother [*bandhu*—the word also used for close companion] is born of the mother and the other is born of Vak [the goddess of speech]. Wise men say that that the brother born of Vak is superior to the one born of the same womb" (IV: 6). He also remarks that the ape is "the source of this sweet fruit" therefore, he cannot kill him.

In a section in some versions that is always omitted in popular retellings today, the wife's speeches suggest that her murderous desire to eat the ape's heart is inspired not so much by greed as by suspicion and jealousy. She insists that the ape must be a female, not a male, and that the crocodile's daily and lengthy intercourse with the ape is sexual in nature. She accuses her husband of sighing for another when he lies with his wife at night and adds that his kisses are cold and passionless. She finally concludes: "if she is really not your beloved then why won't you kill her when I am asking you to do so? Again, if the creature is truly a male ape, as you say, what kind of affection is this that you feel for it?"[8] She then threatens to fast to death, and her husband gives in. Noteworthy here is the possibility of unconventional heterosexuality (cross-species sex between male crocodile and female ape) and also of some strange "kind of affection" between two males.

In the later part of the story, not commonly included in popular retellings today, the crocodile, after he has been outwitted by the ape, tries his best to win back the ape's friendship. The ape, although angrily refusing to renew the friendship, in effect prolongs it by continuing to tell stories to illustrate his arguments regarding the crocodile's folly and perfidy. So, the relationship does continue through storytelling, which structures all relationships throughout this text.

While the crocodile is engrossed in these stories and has forgotten all about his wife's vow to fast to death if she does not get the ape's heart to eat, he gets a message that she has kept her vow and has died. Distressed, he thinks of entering the fire with her corpse but is dissuaded by the ape. The storytelling continues; the crocodile, counseled by the ape, defeats an enemy and lives happily alone in his house for many years.

Here the clash between conjugality and comradeship develops to a murderous and suicidal point where the wife loses out, so that happy male singleness can prevail. Although irrevocably damaged by the clash with normative heterosexuality as exemplified in the institution of marriage, the same-sex friendship is not altogether destroyed.

---

8. Rajan, 355

Vatsyayana's Kamasutra[1]

Ruth Vanita

The Kamasutra is perhaps the world's most famous work on erotics. However, it is much more than that. As its opening definition of *Kama* indicates, it is about all types of desire. It defines *Kama* as the mental inclination toward the pleasures of the senses—touch, sight, taste, and smell. Contrary to texts that identify procreation as the aim of sexual activity, the *Kamasutra*, while giving procreation due importance, states that Kama "finds its finality in itself."[2]

Although probably a composite text, the *Kamasutra* is attributed to Vatsyayana, who appears to have been a Brahman scholar residing in the city of Pataliputra (modern Patna) around the fourth century A.D., during the reign of the Gupta kings.[3] This was a period of great material and cultural prosperity for the region. Vatsysyana states that his *Kamasutra* is a compilation of several earlier texts on erotic science. At the outset, he outlines a genealogy of authors on erotics. He traces the science ultimately to the lord of all creatures, Prajapati, to the primal sages Manu and Brihaspati, and to Shiva's companion, the bull Nandi. Among the human scholars he names are the Babhravyas, or disciples of Babhru, Charayana, Suvarnanabha, Gonardiya, Ghotakamukha. The section on courtesans in the *Kamasutra* purports to be a reproduction of a work by Dattaka, which he composed with the aid of a famous courtesan.

In the course of the text, Vatsyayana constantly cites the differing opinions of several scholars on particular issues, before giving his own opinion. Thus, at every point, he emphasizes that different points of view are possible and that no one opinion can claim absolute validity.

---

1. I am particularly grateful to Kumkum Roy for her helpful comments and corrections of my mistakes in this essay.
2. KS I. 2:12. Alain Danielou, *The Complete Kama Sutra* (Rochester, Vermont: Park Street Press, 1994), 29. Unless otherwise indicated, this is the translation quoted throughout, both of the *Kamasutra* and of Yashodhara's *Jayamangala* commentary. I do not always agree with Danielou's translation but have quoted it when it appears to be satisfactory.
3. For convenience, I follow the convention of referring to Vatsyayana as the author.

He also repeatedly refers to the varying customs of different regions, times, communities, and the preferences of individuals, stressing that all these must be taken into account before choosing or judging a course of action.

The text commences by placing Kama in perspective as one of the three aims of life, pursued by all living beings.[4] Vatsyayana advocates the study of this text by both men and women. He emphasizes that not just courtesans but other women too must study the *Kamasutra*, and that young girls should be instructed by older, more experienced women, in its theory and practice. He lists sixty-four arts as necessary to be studied by all people in order to be attractive. These include vocal and instrumental music, dancing, needlework, cooking, gardening, woodwork, flower arrangement, word games, and decorating the home and oneself. He states that a man who knows these arts is attractive to women and that a woman who knows these arts can always earn a living as well as be successful in love.

Thus, although specific portions of the *Kamasutra*, such as the sections on how to win other men's wives, are largely addressed to the cultivated adult male city dweller, the text does attempt to outline a more general theory on the arts of life and love.[5] It also specifically addresses and incorporates the points of view of particular agents, such as young and inexperienced boys and girls, younger and older courtesans, younger and older cowives, males of the "third nature" attempting to seduce other men, and so on.

The text is constituted of *sutras*, which are brief, almost cryptic statements, accompanied by verses from literature that are illustrative of the types of activity described.[6] In a recent essay, Kumkum Roy draws a distinction between the prose and verse sections of the text, reading the former as more normative and the latter as more descriptive. The difference is between recommending and permitting. It is important to note that variations which are not recommended may be permitted and that, as Roy points out, this text, unlike the *Manusmriti* and *Arthashastra*, is not punitive even when it attempts to delineate ideals. No sanctions are pronounced for deviations.[7]

The *Kamasutra* attempts to catalog types of sexual behavior and also to categorize those who are given to these types of behavior. To begin with, a normative adult male city dweller's

---

4. The fourth aim of life, *Moksha* or liberation, is not included here, presumably because desire pertains to the material world and liberation entails freedom from desire.

5. Kumkum Roy, "Unraveling the *Kamasutra*," *Indian Journal of Gender Studies*, 3:2 (1996): 155–170, characterizes the text as focused on upper-class male desire. This formulation does not account for the courtesan as protagonist or for the seduction technique suggested to men of the third nature who desire other men.

6. *Sutra* literally means "thread." These cryptic statements, characteristic of ancient Indian texts, lend themselves to exegetical commentary that, as it were, weave the fabric from the threads.

7. I read the text as more oriented to mutuality than does Roy. She assumes that feminists would necessarily be opposed to violence in sex. That consensual violence in sex is not specific to heterosexual sex is clear from much evidence in many cultures, and several feminist thinkers, both lesbian and heterosexual, argue for it as a legitimate form of sexual expression.

lifestyle is described, stressing its elegance and sophistication. Women are categorized in various ways. One set of categories is based on temperament and inclinations, for instance, the energetic, the melancholic, the whimsical. Another set of categories is based on relations with men—the virgin, the widow, the one who belongs to another, the courtesan. A third set of categories is related to degrees of autonomy—the one who acts as her own intermediary (*Swayamdutika*), the woman linked to a close female friend (*Samasyabandhu*), the self-willed or autonomous woman (*Svairini*). Yet another set of categories is that based on physical features, especially the size of the sexual organs, and for this there are corresponding male categories, based on similar criteria.

Friendship is given an important place in this text too. Women categorized as avoidable by a man include not only a priest's wife, a royal woman, his male friend's wife but also his own female friend. A *snehamitra* (loving friend) is described as one with whom one played as a child or who is similar to oneself.

The *tritiya prakriti*, literally, "third nature," is mentioned in the initial classificatory chapter (I.5:27). Danielou translates this as "third sex" but "third nature" is more accurate and suggests too the wider connotations of the term. The medieval commentator Yashodhara (ca. twelfth century A.D.) explains that "the third nature" is *napunsaka*, neither man nor woman. This constitutes a medieval reading of the text. He adds that these people get pleasure from oral sex.

Anal Sex

Given the popular misconception that penetrative anal sex was introduced into India after Muslim rule, it is important to note that it is mentioned in the *Kamasutra* as one of the many types of copulation: "Copulation below, in the anus, is practiced by the peoples of the South" (our trans.) (II. 6: 49). There is no pejorative tone or implication here.

The next sutra (II. 6: 50) states: "Penetration of men (*purushopasripta*) will be described in the chapter on women behaving like men (*purushayita*)" (our trans.). The term *purushopasripta* is repeatedly used in the eighth chapter entitled "*Purushayita*."[8] This behavior is said to arise when a man is tired after intercourse. The text says that a woman should behave in this way if the man is tired, if he likes it or if she likes it. The word used to describe her actions is *Purushopasripta*. The term *Upasripta* or *Upasarpan* when used to describe a man doing it to a woman indicates both mounting and penetration. So what does it mean when a woman is the agent and the man (*purusha*) is the focus of the activity indicated?

---

8. Burton translates the chapter title as "On Women Acting the Part of a Man," Danielou as "Virile Behavior in Women."

Modern translators Madhavacharya and Richard Burton understand it as vaginal penetration with the woman on top of the man.[9] Danielou translates it as anal penetration of the man by the woman, with a dildo. Another word used to describe the woman's action here is *yuktayantrene* (joining of the instruments)—*yantra* is used in the *Kamasutra* both for the genitals and for a dildo. The text here distinguishes between external (*abhyantara*) and internal *purushayita*. Danielou translates this as the woman penetrating the man between the thighs and anally.

A further complication is introduced from II. 8: 7 onwards. The text says that these are the actions a man does to a woman, but they are being described in a chapter that deals with woman's agency, because a woman too can perform all these actions. Both Burton and Madhavacharya translate the section with the man as agent, noting that a woman too can do all this to a man. This is followed by a description of opening the lower garment, rubbing the hand between the thighs, caressing, kissing gently and roughly, and penetrating. Neither translator explains how the woman is to do the last or what is being penetrated in this case. Danielou translates the entire description with the woman as the agent, which fits the chapter title. However, even if we follow Burton and Madhavacharya's gendering of the agent here, they and the text make it clear that the agency is reversible.

The next crux occurs at sutra 11. In Madhavacharya's translation, since this is a description of a man acting on a woman (although the purpose of the description here is to indicate how a woman can imitate all these actions), sutra 11, which refers to a virgin as the object, indicates a man having sex with a virgin. How this is relevant to a chapter on a woman acting a man's role remains unexplained. Since in Danielou's translation the woman acting like a man is the agent in the entire description, when a virgin appears as the object, the sentence translates as a description of the experienced or manlike *purushayita* woman having sex with a virgin.

In Danielou's translation, the modern Hindi commentator Devadatta Shastri explains this as a virgin learning the art of love from an older woman or a prostitute. This is plausible because the text elsewhere does refer to a girl learning the arts of love in secret from an older experienced woman. In sutra 13, the word *svairini* (self-willed woman) occurs with the description of rough lovemaking. Madhavacharya translates this as an intimation to the man that he can act roughly with an experienced and self-willed woman. Danielou translates the *svairini* as the agent here, who acts roughly with the virgin.

If Madhavacharya's translation is accurate, this description would appear to be quite irrelevant to the chapter on "Purushayita" or "Woman Acting Like a Man" in which it occurs. Rough lovemaking by a man, as well as between a man and a woman, has already been described in detail earlier, in the sections on biting, scratching, beating, sighing, and crying out.

---

9. Sanskrit text with Hindi translation by Pandit Madhavacharya, *Kamasutram* (Bombay: Venkateswara Steam Press, 1911, reprint 1995). *The Kama Sutra of Vatsyayana,* trans. Sir Richard F. Burton ([1883] Delhi: Penguin, 1993).

The purpose of the present description is that the woman acting like a man imitates all the actions of the man. If we translate this description as a man with a virgin, is the implication for the imitating woman that she should act in this manner with a virgin boy? While Danielou's translation of the term *svairini* as "lesbian" is misconceived, his overall translation of the sense of the passage is at least plausible. Also, the practices described are not unique to this section—elsewhere, in the section on the women in the royal women's quarters (V.6:2), the text describes women penetrating one another with vegetables.

Sutra 19 is important. It refers to the hands being used like an elephant, that is, the first and fourth finger being turned down into the palm and joined together, and the middle finger then being used for penetration like an elephant's trunk. Yashodhara explains that the "elephant's trunk" could also refer to an artificial instrument. Madhavacharya translates this as the man using the hand or a dildo on the woman, especially when he has had his orgasm and she is still unsatisfied. Again, he does not explain how the woman acting like a man, who is the subject of this chapter, is to copy this. This verse is the best indicator that at least by implication some sort of penetration by the woman, with hand or dildo, is referred to, whether the object is a man or another woman.

Danielou uses the word "boy" throughout this chapter for the male being penetrated but the text consistently uses *purusha* ("man"). It would appear that Danielou's association of "sodomy" (the term by which he anachronistically translates *purushopasripta*) with youths leads him to use the word "boy." If a male is being penetrated here, it is a man, not a boy.

Madhavacharya is uneasy with the references to internal *purushopasripta*. He asks what it is, and answers that it is vaginal penetration. But then why does it have a different name? *Upasripta* (penetration) is the term used in the text for vaginal penetration by a man; joining the term with "man" to form the term *purushopasripta* must refer to a special form.

Oral Sex and the Third Nature

This chapter is immediately followed by chapter 9, on *Auparashtika*, or oral sex. It opens with the statement that the "third nature" is of two types—those who take the form (*rupa*) or appearance of a woman and those who take the form or appearance of a man. This statement is nonpejorative. Yashodhara in his commentary identifies the third nature with the *napunsaka* (neuter) and adds that the ones who take the form of women have breasts and long hair while the ones who take the form of men have mustaches and beards. Vatsyayana goes on to say that the ones who take the form of women behave like women in their dress, adornments, manner, tone of voice, sweetness, timidity, and shyness. Vatsyayana does not mention artificial breasts or long hair, such as transvestites mentioned in medieval texts have, and such as Yashodhara, writing in the twelfth century, mentions. Madhavacharya, writing in the twentieth century, goes still further to describe a hermaphroditic body that is like a woman's except for the vulva. He appears to be describing modern *hijras*.

Sutra 6 is very interesting because it clearly dissociates feminine appearance from men who like to perform oral sex on men. It states that those who take the form of men hide the fact that they desire men and earn their living as hairdressers or masseurs. Yashodhara remarks that there is no real difference between the desires of these two types—those who take the form of men want the same pleasure but other men will not approach them directly because their desires are not evident. This is followed by an extended and graphic description of the way the masseur with a masculine appearance goes about seducing his customer, the sexual advances made by both, the teasing words exchanged, the manual stimulation of the penis and the eight types of oral stimulation that build up to orgasm for both parties.

Vatsyayana expresses no outrage at these desires of the "third nature." He then adds that various types of women also perform oral sex on men. As in the case of heterosexual lovemaking in water, which he describes as pleasurable but declares is opposed to the texts, because it pollutes the water, he remarks at the close of the extended description of fellatio that it is inadvisable because it is opposed to the texts. Yashodhara adds regarding cunnilingus that it is a polluting act to kiss the place in which one ejaculates.

In this case, unlike in the case of sex in the water, Vatsyayana adds his own opinion that oral sex is not wrong for one who frequents courtesans, and even the other objections can be similarly overcome. Yashodhara glosses this to mean that if it is a "custom of the country" or region, it is allowable. There follows a list of peoples in different regions who practice or avoid oral sex. Vatsyayana states in verse 34 that the texts differ on matters of purity, so one should act according to local custom as well as one's own inclinations and beliefs. In VII.2:3, he remarks that oral sex can arouse a man who, due to age or excess, has trouble getting an erection.

Sex between Men and between Women

II.9: 35 and 36 are of crucial importance because they describe sex occurring between two people categorized as men rather than between a male categorized as a "man" and a male categorized as belonging to the "third nature." These verses indicate occasional and even regular sexual behavior between men, which may or may not be exclusive.

Sutra 35 states that young men servants, wearing earrings and flowers (these are worn by the elegant male city dweller too), perform oral sex on men. The word used by both Vatsyayana and Yashodhara is *yuva* or young man, translated by Madhavacharya as *launda*, a modern Hindi word for "boys" that connects directly with *laundebaaz*, the Urdu word for pederast or boy-lover. Danielou too inaccurately uses the word "boy" to translate Yashodhara's *purusha* ("man") here.

Yashodhara uses the term *sadharana* (ordinary) to describe acts mutually performed such as oral sex by a man and a woman on each other, and *asadharana* for acts that are not mutual but one way, such as oral sex by the masseur of the third nature or by a young male servant or actor, performed on a man. Sutra 36 describes as *sadharana* a mutual act of oral sex peror actor, performed on a man. Sutra 36 describes as *sadharana* a mutual act of oral sex performed by two male friends on one another. These friends are both explicitly termed *nagarika* by Vatsyayana, that is, both have the full status of the city dweller who is the agent in much of the text.

This sutra (II. 9: 36) says that two such men who are well-wishers of one another and have deep trust in one another mutually practice the act with each other. Danielou translates the term *parigraha* here as "marriage" between the two men. Yashodhara elaborates on the relationship between the two men, using the term *maitri*, or friendship, to describe the trust and affection between them. They take turns to perform oral sex on one another. Since this is mutual activity, Yashodhara says it indicates that women too can mutually engage in it. He quotes a verse that describes women in the women's quarters of the house, who, in complete mutual trust, lick one another's vulvas.

Finally, Vatsyayana remarks that everything that is described does not have to be performed, just as medical texts mention eating dog's flesh for certain illnesses but this does not mean this is a recommended edible. But every type of sex has to be described because there are some people, some occasions and some places where these acts may be performed. So one should perform or not perform them, bearing the place, time, texts, context, and one's own inclinations in mind. In the brilliant concluding verse to this chapter, Vatsyayana remarks that these are acts performed in secret and the human mind is ever-changing and unstable, so who knows when, how, and why a person may do any of these acts.

This verse well expresses the sophisticated and worldly wise tone of the *Kamasutra*. As a compendium, it attempts to exhaust all possibilities and to mention every possible type of sexual behavior. Sex with animals, manual sex between women (III. 3: 9), the making and use of dildoes and penis sheaths (VII. 2: 4–14), piercing of sex organs (VII. 2: 15–24), different types of group sex, imitating animal sex, and what are today called sadomasochistic practices such as biting, scratching, and beating, even to the point of killing the partner (this last is definitively condemned), all are described.

Many of these are merely mentioned in passing; some are described in detail. Sex between men and between women is described in some detail, and is often mentioned in passing too. Distinctions are made between those who have a special inclination for it and those who practice it occasionally. A distinction is also made between mutual interaction of male friends or female friends and hierarchical one-way interaction of masseur and customer, servant and employer, or young girl and older woman training her.

Another noteworthy feature is Vatsyayana's treatment of oral sex as the primary form of same-sex sexual interaction. He is clearly aware of anal sex performed on men and also penetration with a dildo. However, here, as in other ancient Indian texts, oral sex, not penetrative sex, is represented as the model of sex between men. This leads one to wonder why penetrative sex later came to displace oral sex in the popular imagination as the primary form of sex between men.

The primacy of oral sex in ancient texts could be related to the general symbolic primacy of eating practices and of food in these texts. In the *Vedas*, *Brahmanas*, and *Upanishads*, the universe is often described as a constant circulation of food and all relationships as ever shifting between food and feeder. Food has occupied a major place in Hindu worship from the earliest times. It is the main substance exchanged between gods and mortals, between humans, and between human and nonhuman animals. Other types of substances are very often visualized as food. Births in the epics and *Puranas* are frequently brought about by the consumption of miraculous foods. So it is not surprising that sex of all types should be visualized as the consumption of bodily fluids and secretions.

The history of the *Kamasutra* demonstrates the continuity between periods that we term the ancient and the medieval. Sanskrit commentaries such as the twelfth-century *Jayamangala* by Yashodhara continue the scholarly practice of accretive composition, and many erotic treatises, such as the *Kokashastra* and the *Anangaranga*, were composed throughout the medieval period both in Sanskrit and in other languages. Many of these drew on the *Kamasutra*, as it had drawn on earlier texts.

Part II

Introduction: Medieval Materials in the Sanskritic Tradition

Ruth Vanita

During the period from approximately the eighth to the eighteenth centuries A.D., Islamic culture took root in the Indian subcontinent. Various regional and religious cultures including the Muslim, Buddhist, Jain, and Hindu (Vaishnava, Shaiva, and Shakta) interacted during this period, producing a range of cultural practices that have been highly influential for subsequent periods. Although altered by modern developments during and after the colonial period, many of these practices still exist in recognizable form today.

Among the texts generated in this period are those in Sanskrit; those in Sanskrit-based languages, many of which took on their modern forms at this time; those in the southern Indian languages; and those in the Perso-Arabic and Urdu tradition. In the first three groups, the texts we look at belong to the following major genres: the *Puranas*, which are collections of religious stories, compiled between the fourth and fourteenth centuries; vernacular retellings of the epic and Puranic stories; *Katha* literature or story cycles; historical chronicles produced in courts; and devotional poetry.[1]

I will here discuss developments of the patterns discussed earlier in the introduction to ancient materials and new developments consequent on the spread of new types of devotion known as *Bhakti*. Bhakti was a series of movements centered on mystical loving devotion to a

---

1. For an overview of the literature, see Sukumari Bhattacharji's two books, *The Indian Theogony: A Comparative Study of Indian Mythology from the Vedas to the Puranas* (Cambridge: Cambridge University Press, 1970), and *History of Classical Sanskrit Literature* (Hyderabad: Orient Longman, 1993).

chosen god that began around the seventh century A.D. in south India and spread throughout the subcontinent.

One major tendency in medieval texts is that of commentary on and exegesis of ancient canonical texts. Often this commentary takes the form of intellectual play with concepts, retelling well-known stories to draw out their imaginative potential and elaborating on what were under-stated suggestions in earlier texts. This kind of commentary is often found in the texts generated by Bhakti. Contrary to the popular stereotype, Bhakti poetry is not always a spontaneous emo-tional outpouring; it is frequently informed by a thoroughgoing engagement with philosophical concepts drawn from earlier texts and carries on a sophisticated dialog with those texts.

During the British period, Christian scholars constructed a theory of medieval Bhakti that was later developed by Marxist scholars and remains prevalent in India today. In this view Bhakti was a movement of the oppressed, especially the lower castes, the poor, and women, who criticized and even rejected the so-called Brahmanical tradition, including its philosophi-cal texts such as the *Vedas* and the *Upanishads* and also its ritual practices, substituting instead the direct and loving relationship of the devotee with a personal god. Furthermore, *Bhaktas* ("devotees") advocated communal harmony between Hindus and Muslims.

However, this account of Bhakti is too simplistic.[2] The idea that there are several paths to lib-eration from the cycle of births and deaths is found in major Brahmanical texts, including the *Upanishads* and the *Bhagvad Gita*; one is the path of knowledge (*Jnana*), another the path of love (*Prema*), both paths being variants of Bhakti. While many medieval mystics emphasize emotional devotion, others, especially the Sants, also emphasize intellectual devotion. Medieval Bhakti tra-ditions represent a significant growth, in scale and in form, of ancient devotional traditions. They also incorporate major new interpretations of ancient texts. While lower-caste people, women, and Muslims were often prominent devotees, so were upper-caste people such as Brahmans, kings, and chieftains.[3] Bhaktas do not discard ancient texts but rather cite them to prove that any-one can attain salvation through devotion and that to exclude untouchables or Muslims is wrong. For instance, Shri Chaitanya pointed out that Krishna ate in the house of Vidura, an outcaste.[4]

---

2. A seminal study that takes issue with received wisdom in this regard is Krishna Sharma, *Bhakti and the Bhakti Movement: A New Perspective* (New Delhi: Munshiram Manohar-lal, 1987). See also Ashis Nandy, *The Intimate Enemy* (Delhi: Oxford University Press, 1983), 61.

3. For an example of how caste mingling is susceptible of differing interpretations, see Ed-ward C. Dimock, *The Place of the Hidden Moon: Erotic Mysticism in the Vaisnava-Sahajiya Cult of Bengal,* new foreword by Wendy Doniger (Chicago: University of Chicago Press, 1989), 216–21. Dimock interprets the Sahajiya men's use of low-caste and "untouchable" married women as ritual sexual partners as "perhaps . . . contempt for the Vedic and Brah-manical tradition." I would interpret it as exploitation. The epics are full of examples of upper-caste men's sexual relations with low-caste women.

4. Dimock, 79.

When orthodox Brahmans castigated Bhaktas for breaking caste rules, the Bhakti texts usually show not an all-out conflict but a rapprochement occasioned by divine intervention. A miracle causes the orthodox to regret their rigidity; simultaneously, the devotees, and sometimes even god himself, agree to undergo ritual penance for breaking the rules. A more one-way capitulation is generally represented when the conflict is between the devotees and Muslims in authority try-ing to convert them.[5]

As Peter van der Veer has argued, Nirguna ascetics' disregard of caste distinction was a "far cry from an active religious protest against caste discrimination."[6] This disregard, feasible in the peripatetic life of the ascetic, became problematic in a sedentary existence. Historically, as Bhakti spread and took root, ascetic tendencies were domesticated, a process still ongoing in some traditions (see pp. 98–99).[7]

5. These points can be illustrated from a major hagiographical text produced by late me-dieval Bhakti, Mahipati's (1715–1790) 40,000-line Marathi verse collection of the lives of devotees, entitled *Bhaktavijaya,* translated by Justin E. Abbott and N. R. Godbole, *Sto-ries of Indian Saints* (1933; Delhi: Motilal Banarsidass, 1996). Although composed com-paratively late, the text draws heavily on earlier texts such as those composed by Jnaneshwar and Namdev. Mahipati begins in orthodox style by invoking Saraswati, the great sages, and the Vedas. Although his devotion is addressed to the *saguna* (with attrib-utes) deity, he is careful to acknowledge that this is the same *nirguna* (without attributes) deity whom even the *Vedas* could not fully describe. For examples of upper-caste devo-tees, see the stories of the Brahmans Jagamitra Naga, vol. I, 311–319, Ramdas of Dakur, vol. II, 1–6; Kalyan and Niradha, vol. II, 14, Bhanudas, vol. II, 109–21. Better-known Brahman Bhaktas are Tulsidas, author of the *Ramcharitmanas,* Surdas, Chaitanya, and Ramdas. For the story of how Namdev, on Krishna's instructions, feasts the Brahmans as prescribed, how Krishna undergoes ritual penance for having broken caste rules and how the orthodox Brahmans express regret and are embraced by Krishna, see vol. I, 207–58. A similar story is narrated about Eknath. In contrast, when a king tries forcibly to con-vert Bodhla to Islam, a miracle turns cooked flesh into flowers, and Bodhla leaves in dis-gust without accepting the proffered wealth (vol. II, 328–29). The erring king is embarrassed but not embraced. Muslim devotees of Vishnu such as Latibsha similarly de-feat Muslim kings (vol. II, 345–47). In the case of direct conflict between a Hindu upper-caste authority figure and Muslim authorities, the latter are represented as discomfited and defeated. See the story of Shivaji's visit to Tukaram and the defeat of the Muslim army sent to capture him (vol. II, 208–15); also the story of how Muslims in Bedar attack devo-tees holding a musical procession to celebrate Rama's birth, whereupon Hanuman ap-pears and destroys a mosque, killing many inside it. The Muslim king then donates money to the devotees for their celebration (vol. II, 362–66).
6. Peter van der Veer, *Gods on Earth: The Management of Religious Experience and Identity in a North Indian Pilgrimage Centre* (London: Athlone Press, 1988), 93. See also 175–76.
7. Mark Hölmstrom, "Religious Change in an Industrial City in South India," *Journal of the Royal Asiatic Society of Great Britain and Ireland,* No. 1 (1971): 28–40, argues that Bhakti represents a religious universalism in which devotees are religiously equal but socially bound by caste values.

In this context, I will briefly outline some of the spaces hospitable to same-sex love that emerge in medieval texts, in relation to the patterns I traced in ancient texts.

Multidimensional Divinities

Medieval devotion was directed not to the Vedic deities but to the pantheon of Puranic gods and goddesses. The marvelously flexible and multiple lives and doings of these new deities are recounted in the *Puranas* (literally, "old stories"). The eighteen major *Puranas* were composed in what are today classified as the later ancient and early medieval periods. Like most early texts, they are extremely difficult to date with exactitude. The earliest Puranas were probably compiled around the second and first centuries B.C. One redaction took place around the fourth century A.D. Most *Puranas* were completed by the seventh century A.D. but the latest were probably completed by the thirteenth century.[8]

In the *Puranas* the new pantheon of gods, which replaced the Vedic gods and is still in place today, emerges and is fully fleshed out. The Vishnu family and the Shiva family came to be worshiped in different shapes on a large scale. In separate but related developments, mother goddesses returned to prominence and proliferated in the context of Shaktism and Tantrism.[9]

The single most remarkable feature of medieval stories of the deities is their multiplicity and variability. Almost any variation that can be imagined exists somewhere. Capable of taking on any form, the divine is made available in multiple ways. Puranic catalogs of eulogies make a point of celebrating the chosen deity, whether Shiva, Vishnu or anyone else, as infinitely flexible and available—as male, female, neuter; as animal, bird, tree, jewel, river; as present in all elements and all forms of life. Again, these are not new concepts in Hindu tradition but important medieval restatements.

Paradoxically, the numerous ritual taboos of everyday practice coexist in the texts with stories and accounts of the divine in which nothing is taboo. The Puranic gods are not just celebrated as omnipresent in a philosophical sense; the stories of their doings represent them as taking on all forms, incarnating as different types of creatures (for instance, Vishnu is incarnated as a boar and a fish) including humans of different ages, castes and genders. The absence of any clear-cut philosophical boundary between gods and humans, or indeed gods and other

---

8. For the dating controversies, see *Classical Hindu Mythology: A Reader in the Sanskrit Puranas,* ed. and trans. Cornelia Dimmitt and J. A. B. van Buitenen (Philadelphia: Temple University Press, 1978), Introduction; and Wendy Doniger O'Flaherty, *Hindu Myths* (Harmondsworth: Penguin, 1975), Introduction.
9. Mother goddesses are prominent in the pre-Vedic Indus Valley civilization but were subordinate and relatively unimportant in the *Vedas.* For not fully explained reasons, they reemerged in a big way in late antiquity.

living beings, allows for the deifying of all actions and every way of life. This has important im-plications for our study.[10]

Bridal mysticism flourished in the poetry of Shaiva as well as Vaishnava mystics, male and female. Although Shaivites and Vaishnavites engaged in debate and, at times, in conflict, there are numerous instances, both in written texts and in legend, of highly creative rapprochement between the two devotional traditions. Interestingly, play with ideas of undoing gender, sex change, same-sex love, and miraculous birth frequently occurs in the context of such rap-prochement. If Shiva, as is well known, often represents the union of male and female princi-ples (the Ardhanarishwara image where the deity has a half-male, half-female body, or Shiva and Parvati in fusion), he also represents the union of two male principles (the image of Har-ihara, which is all male but half Shiva and half Vishnu). The legend of the birth of Ayyappa from Shiva and Vishnu is a variant of this theme (see p. 94).[11]

The latter story generally has been read by modern scholars as an example of patriarchal male bonding of the kind that Gayle Rubin and Eve Sedgwick have termed homosociality.[12] Stories in the epics and *Puranas* of autonomous male reproduction have often been read as ex-pressive of male womb envy. Another strategy for avoiding the obvious eroticism of such sto-ries as that of Agni swallowing Shiva's semen has been to claim that both males are really identical—thus Wendy O'Flaherty argues that Agni, as erotic fire, is synonymous with Shiva. She similarly argues that in the Mohini story (see p. 69), Vishnu and Shiva, rival deities, are reconciled and metaphorically united through the concept of Harihara.[13] Conversely, because

10. Richard J. Hoffman, "Vices, Gods, and Virtues: Cosmology as a Mediating Factor in At-titudes toward Male Homosexuality," *Journal of Homosexuality* vol. 9, nos. 2 and 3 (Win-ter 1983, Spring 1984): 27–44, argues persuasively that polytheistic religions take a more flexible view of gender roles and a more holistic view of sexuality in the cosmos than do monotheistic religions and that this is why Hindu texts and societies have not denounced or persecuted homosexual activity in the same way as many Judaic, Christian, and Islamic texts and societies have.

11. Arjuna, one of whose titles is Savyasachin, or "ambidextrous," is associated with Shiva in Draupadi cults; this suggests that, like Shiva, Arjuna knows how to unite the left, the female side, with the right, the male side, of the body. See Alf Hiltebeitel, *The Cult of Draupadi Mythologies: From Gingee to Kuruksetra* (Chicago: University of Chicago Press, 1988), 207.

12. See, for example, Robert P. Goldman, "Transsexualism, Gender and Anxiety in Traditional India," *Journal of the American Oriental Society,* vol. 113, no. 3 (1993): 374–401. Sedgwick, in *Between Men* (New York: Columbia University Press, 1985), derives the theory of ho-mosexuality from anthropologist Gayle Rubin and applies it to literary texts. According to this theory, many male-dominated societies are based on strong bonds between men that are reinforced through the exchange of women. The taboo on sexual interaction between men functions to empower male bonding by making women sex objects to be exchanged as gifts or fought over as prizes. Women's bodies become the site for men to relate to one an-other as rivals or allies, these being the most powerful bonds in the social dynamic.

13. Wendy O'Flaherty, *Women, Androgynes and Other Mythical Beasts* (Chicago: University of Chicago Press, 1980), 320–23, especially the argument that the Vishnu-Shiva union

in this story Vishnu assumes the form of a woman, Mohini, the text also can be assimilated to a framework that privileges heterosexuality. Thus O'Flaherty includes the story in her discussion of Shiva's adultery, unproblematically treating Mohini, in this context, as a woman.[14]

Modern readings of this kind function to avoid the implications regarding love between men in the specific text under analysis. It is interesting that south Indian medieval elaborations of the story of Shiva and Vishnu's union do not try to avoid these implications, but rather emphasize them by stressing that Ayyappa is the son of two males (see p. 97). His refusal to marry a woman assumes special significance in the context of his nearly all-male following and his close companionship with Vavar. Another legend recounts that he returns from heaven to dwell in the forest because he cannot work out the nature of his relationship with Parvati, who is the wife of one of his fathers yet is not his mother. He remains in the forest, puzzling over the question put to him with regard to this relationship. This remarkably unafraid and speculative set of legends raises questions without providing definitive answers. It constitutes an indigenous tradition of exegesis of canonical texts, which stands in remarkable contrast to heterosexist interpretation of the same texts by twentieth-century South Asianists.

Another story about Mohini is unique to Tamil texts.[15] In Tamil versions of the *Mahabharata*, by Peruntevanar and later by Villiputtur and Nallappillai, Arjuna's son Aravan offers himself as a sacrifice to Kali to ensure victory for the Pandavas.[16] He asks for three boons before he dies, of which one is that he should be married before his death. Since no parent would give a daughter to one who is about to be killed, Krishna appears as Mohini and marries Aravan for a night.[17] This festival is celebrated annually by modern *hijras* in Tamilnadu, who identify with the transgendered Krishna.

"proves a theological rather than a sexual point," 323. I would argue that the theological point does not erase the erotic one, just as Shiva and Parvati's ultimate oneness does not erase their conjugality. See O'Flaherty, *Siva: The Erotic Ascetic* (Oxford: Oxford University Press, 1973), 273–87, for a heterosexualizing discussion of the Agni-Shiva episode. She has modified her position with regard to some of these texts such as the Mohini stories in her most recent book *Splitting the Difference: Gender and Myth in Ancient Greece and India* (University of Chicago Press, 1999), which appeared while our book was in press.

14. *Siva: The Erotic Ascetic,* 228–229, in chapter VII, section F, "The Adultery of Siva."

15. This episode is not found in the Sanskrit *Mahabharata*. A prewar sacrifice occurs in other languages; for instance in Telugu traditions Ghatotkacha is the victim. "But Aravan's sacrifice is found only in the Tamil tradition," Hiltebeitel, *Cult,* 318.

16. Aravan's name in Sanskrit is Iravan, which some scholars have derived from *ida-vant,* one who possesses the Sanskrit *ida* or that part of the oblation which makes the sacrifice fruitful. Interestingly, this is close to the name of Ila, the king who undergoes a sex change in the Valmiki *Ramayana,* and becomes a *kimpurusha,* male half the year and female half the year (see p. 18). Modern followers of the cult, however, derive the name Aravan from the Tamil *aravu,* or snake.

17. See Hiltebeitel, *Cult,* chapter 15, "Aravan's Sacrifice."

Similarly, the *Krittivasa Ramayana* account of the birth of Bhagiratha from the union of two women constitutes a medieval fleshing out of an ancient medical text's statement that a child born of two women's sexual interaction will have no bones (see p. 100). The *Krittivasa Ramayana* rewrites this frightening prediction when the boneless child is miraculously cured by an ascetic.

Fluid Intimacies

Corresponding to the multidimensional divinities, medieval devotion developed many ideas of intimacy between devotees and deity as well as between devotees that crucially shape Indian ways of relating even today. Some of these forms of intimacy can be found in ancient texts as well, for instance, the relationship between male teacher (*guru*) and male students. They become fictive kin, with students being incorporated into the guru's family and related fraternally to one another; the relationship also can become primary for both teacher and student in an ascetic context.

New forms of intimacy also develop in the medieval period. One of the most important is the worship of god as a child, which grew to enormous proportions in the context of medieval devotion and continues to flourish today. Medieval versions of the ancient epics construct the childhoods of Rama and Krishna, and medieval mystics dwell at length and with great delight on the doings of these divine children who, at another level, are seen in every child.

Unlike the trope of bride and groom, which is common to Hindu, Christian, and Muslim mysticism, the trope of god as small child and devotee as parent is relatively specific to Hindu mysticism.[18] In bridal mysticism god is the husband or male lover to whom the devotee as wife or female lover is often subordinate, but when god is worshiped as a child the devotee assumes *vatsalya bhava*, or the tender, protective love of a parent for a child. This love is unconditional and all-accepting. Paradoxically, the trope also represents the deity as mischievous and whimsical and the devotee as mature and amused by the deity's doings.[19] As Sudhir Kakar has argued, this attitude is in tune with Indian parental attitudes toward children, especially male children, which tend toward protective indulgence rather than punitive repression.[20]

The *Puranas* and the later devotional songs that celebrate the pranks of the baby Krishna and the actions of baby Rama emphasize the beauty and freedom of divine play (*leela*) in the universe. This play rewrites acts that conventionally would be considered wrong, even scandalous, and

---

18. See Evelyn Underhill, *Mysticism* (London: Methuen, 1912), for a seminal account of cross-cultural patterns in bridal mysticism.
19. The Christian trope of god as parent emphasizes love but also fear and chastisement. The Hindu devotee identifying with the deity's parents is never seriously punitive. Any attempt to chastise the divine child (Yashoda scolding Krishna for his pranks) quickly dissolves into embraces and caresses. This non-punitive attitude is also evident when god is conceived as parent.
20. Sudhir Kakar, *The Inner World: A Psycho-analytic Study of Childhood and Society in India* (Delhi: Oxford University Press, 1981).

legitimizes them as joyful and innocent. Many of these behaviors are erotic in nature, for example, the adolescent Krishna's teasing the milkmaids, stealing their clothes and forcing them to emerge naked from the water to beg for their clothes. A nonjudgmental attitude to eroticism is evident in these texts, the word used for such activities being *krida*, "play" or "sport." The identification of god with child lends itself to a worldview in which all activity is essentially innocent. If the universe is a manifestation of god's playfulness, then actions that appear unlawful may ultimately be part of the workings of a larger law. A remark like that of Christopher Isherwood's guru Prabhavananda, asking him to see Krishna in his male lover, is related to such a view of human activity (see p. 216).

Medieval mystics figure god simultaneously as spouse, friend, and child. Poets such as Surdas, Tulsi, and Meera see no contradiction in taking the attitude of a lover, a friend, and a parent in songs to their chosen deity. At one level, this represents a sophisticated understanding of intimacy, foreshadowing modern psychologists' perceptions that the beloved is never just one thing but always more than one, and brings out the child, the parent, the companion and the spouse in the lover. At another level, it also moves the idea of intimacy beyond the confines of the patriarchal family where roles are much more rigidly circumscribed by gender and age.

The contrast between life in the patriarchal family and life in the family of devotees emerges sharply in the songs of those mystics who provide us with some autobiographical details along with the description of their relation to god. Thus, Bahinabai (1628–1700), the Maharashtrian mystic, describes her marriage to an authoritarian and violent man, which contrasts with her loving relationship to god, to her guru and to the cow and calf she adopts. The latter four figures enter into a parent-child relationship with her, where she is both parent and child. Her accounts of her former births participate in this fluidity, as the calf, for example, is sometimes born as her child and sometimes as her teacher.[21]

In real life, people playing familial roles are often tightly bound by them and behave harshly to others as a consequence. Even in a household of devotees, the harshness does not disappear. Thus, Janabai, the Maharashtrian mystic who was a maidservant in the household of the major mystic Namdev (1279–1350), writes how other members of the household, themselves devotees and poets, such as Namdev's mother, mistreated her. In contrast, god appears to her as a loving female friend and companion. Janabai is unique among women mystics in envisioning god as a female and the relationship between god and devotee as subsisting between women.[22]

21. Bahina's songs are popular even today. She was the only medieval woman mystic to compose a verse autobiography. See Justin E. Abbott and Narhar R. Godbole, *Bahina Bai: A Translation of her Autobiography* (1929; Delhi: Motilal Banarsidass, 1982).

22. See Ruth Vanita, " 'At All Times Near': Love between Women in Two Medieval Indian Devotional Texts," forthcoming in Francesca Canade Sautman and Pamela Sheingorn, eds., *Same-Sex Love and Desire Among Women in the Middle Ages* (New York: St Martin's Press, forthcoming).

Marriage Versus Same-Sex Spaces

With the near disappearance of Buddhism from India around the eleventh century A.D., organized monasticism on any significant scale also disappeared. However, religious celibacy as an option did not die out; it merely took different forms. One general pattern found in the lives of most major medieval Bhaktas and Sants is that of resistance to marriage. Sometimes this resistance took the form of active refusal to marry or leaving the spouse. Stories abound about how miracles occurred to help women mystics avoid marriage or avoid living with their husbands. To cite a few, the Tamil Shaiva devotee Karaikalammaiyar (ca. 600 A.D.) was suddenly transformed into an emaciated woman after her husband, frightened by the miracles she performed, left her; the ninth-century Tamil Vaishnava mystic Andal refused marriage and, at the age of sixteen, was absorbed into Vishnu's stone image; the Kashmiri Shaiva Sufi Lal Ded (born ca. 1320) left her husband and wandered about naked, singing and dancing in ecstasy; and the sixteenth-century Rathori princess Meerabai is said to have survived drinking poison given by her irate husband. The twelfth-century Kannada Shaiva mystic Mahadeviakka is said, in varying legends, either to have refused marriage or to have left her husband. Her poems sharply criticize heterosexual relations and also claim that there is no essential difference between men and women. Even those women devotees who did stay married significantly altered the conjugal roles, often converting their spouses into fellow devotees.[23] These women do not reject the marriage institution but rather transform it dramatically, by claiming to be married to god.

In another variant, *devdasis*, women dedicated at temples, were ritually married to a deity, either male or female, and thereafter lived outside the space of conventional marriage. While in some cases this degenerated into temple prostitution, it also allowed the development of matrilineal communities of women whose lives may in some ways have been less circumscribed than those of married women.

The pattern of women mystics' resistance to dutiful wifehood has been noticed often by feminist scholars. Equally important but less noticed, however, is the resistance to husbandhood expressed in the lives and writings of many male mystics who left their wives or refused to act as dutiful husbands and fathers. Often they see conjugality and parenthood as selfish preoccupations that obstruct devotion to god and to all god's creatures. There is a long tradition of male mystics who do not perform the primary duty of a patriarch—to earn and support the family. Rather, when wealth is given to them by god or by devotees, they distribute it to others even though their own families are in dire poverty. One example is the Maharashtrian Varkari mystic Namdev.[24] Both his mother and his wife reproached him for neglecting

---

23. For their lives and writings, see Susie Tharu and Lalitha K., eds., *Women Writing in India 600 B.C. to the Present,* vol. 1 (Delhi: Oxford University Press, 1993).

24. Founded in the late thirteenth and early fourteenth centuries, the Varkari tradition still has a large mass following today. The Varkari deity Shri Vitthal or Vithoba is identified

his family. They also reproached god for distracting Namdev from his duties. When god provided wealth to Namdev, he was distressed and immediately distributed it.[25]

The same sort of story is told about several other saints in the Varkari tradition, including the seventeenth-century poet-mystic Tukaram (died ca. 1649), who was Bahinabai's guru. Tukaram continued to live with his family but did not perform the duties of a householder. His poems record, rather amusingly, his constant discord with his wife on this account. She objected to his spending all his time and energy singing the praises of god in the company of other devotees who, she felt, were eating them out of hearth and home. She insisted that he should earn and support his family. Tukaram refused and berated her as an obstruction to his devotions. Some feminist commentators read this resistance to the normative life of the householder as misogyny and immoral irresponsibility.[26] But, in the context of Bhakti, where numerous women mystics resisted domestic roles, male mystics' similar resistance also can be read as part of a larger attempt to create alternative life patterns.

While women, because of their subordination, bear heavier burdens in marriage and parenthood, men are also weighed down by these burdens. Married off early, often against their will, Indian men, in traditional families even today, are expected to provide not only for wife and children but also for their parents, younger siblings and dependent relatives, including widowed, orphaned, and disabled aunts, uncles, cousins, nephews, and nieces. This kind of household is the one described in many medieval texts. The ideal man is supposed to uncomplainingly sacrifice his own interests to the upkeep of this entire extended family.

God as parent of the community of devotees sets up a family that often conflicts with the reproductive family of everyday life. The devotee's primary family and ancestry become the chosen one, not the biological or marital one. Several male devotees chose celibacy over marriage. Ramdas, author of the *Dasbodh*, is said to have run away to become an ascetic while his wedding ceremony was in progress. The sixteenth-century Hindi poet-mystic Tulsidas, author of the *Ramcharitmanas*, the most influential medieval version of the Rama story, is said to have seen the light when, as a doting husband, he followed his wife to her parents' house and she reproached him, saying that if he loved god as he loved her, he would have attained enlightenment long before. Tulsi then left her and became devoted to Rama.

Many male mystics, such as Surdas and even Kabir (the latter by and large operated in the Sant tradition of Nirguna Bhakti, following the path of knowledge), use the trope of bridal

---

with Krishna but has a Shiva emblem on his head, and would seem to represent a merging of Shaiva and Vaishnava devotional traditions.

25. Namdev lived in Pandharpur but traveled widely. His verses and those of his wife, mother, sons, daughters, and maidservant appear in the huge collection entitled *Namdev Gatha*. Some of Namdev's verses also appear in the Sikh scriptures, the *Guru Granth Saheb*.

26. See, for example, Parita Mukta, *Upholding the Common Life: the Community of Mirabai* (Delhi: Oxford University Press, 1994), especially 116–17.

mysticism. In such poems, a male mystic typically uses feminine verbs for himself, even though his name, used in the poem's signature line, is male. He addresses a male god as lover or husband and identifies himself with the bride waiting for the bridegroom or the female lover Radha waiting for the male lover Krishna. He uses the tropes of the veiled face and the vermilion, just as female mystics like Meera do. In Vaishnava devotion, all devotees tend to identify with the female who desires union with the male deity. The sixteenth-century Gauriya Vaishnavas, followers of Shri Chaitanya (see p. 103), developed an elaborate theology of bridal mysticism. Intensely emotional relationships often develop between male devotees participating in such mysticism.

The Ramanandis, an all-male community in eastern India, said to have originated in the fifteenth century, are devotees of Hanuman, the monkey god, incarnation of Shiva, and servant of Rama. The ascetic branch of the order is militaristic while the celibate devotees in the temple identify with Hanuman and other males who are said to have taken on the form of Sita's female servants in order to serve her. Through their devoted service to Sita, these "women" friends vicariously participate in her union with Rama. In Ayodhya today, these male devotees take female names, dress as women, and are even said to experience menstruation. They organize their daily routine around the service of Sita and Rama, carrying their images through the day's activities of bathing, eating, love play, and so on.[27]

The seventeenth- and eighteenth-century Vaishnava Sahajiyas, who were influenced by Tantra, interpreted male identification with the woman lover somewhat differently. They saw *kama*, or desire, as male, and *prema*, or selfless love, as female, therefore male devotees identified with Radha's and the other milkmaids' love for Krishna. Through highly ritualized sexual intercourse with a woman who was married to another man (as Radha and the milkmaids were married to other men), the male devotee attempted to "become a woman" and thus purify his love for Krishna.[28]

It is in these contexts that Puranic stories about the sex change of devotees such as Narada and Arjuna (see p. 90) and the rebirth of males as females, in order to enjoy love play with Krishna, assume significance. It is important to notice that gender, like the body itself, is seen as a garment, a disguise, which is assumed at birth and shed at death; therefore, it conceivably can also be assumed or shed in life by one who is suitably prepared for such changes. Gender is not rigid and unchangeable, nor does it fully determine the self. The self ultimately exceeds gender as well as other categories such as age, caste and class. An enlightened person can realize this in a way that most people cannot.

Parallels and even overlap regarding both celibacy and gender fluidity are found among Indian Sufi male mystics (see pp. 117–18, 130).

---

27. See van der Veer, *Gods on Earth*.
28. See Dimock, *Place of the Hidden Moon*, 158–64.

God as Friend

Another kind of household within which the intimacy of same-sex friendship partially displaced that of conjugality was the community of friends with god as the chief friend. This kind of household, drawing on the ancient model of the guru's *ashram*, plays a very important imaginative role in constructing relationships.

Modern scholarship has tended to focus on bridal mysticism more than on friendship mysticism. In fact, many devotees, individually and collectively, related to god as *Bandhava* or *Sakha*, companion or friend. This is a relationship foregrounded by many poets, especially those in the Sant tradition, such as Kabir, Nanak, Jnaneshwar, Namdev, Tukaram.[29] *Sakha bhava*, or the mode of devotion expressed as friendship, is a dominant mode in the practice of the Varkari devotional community of western India.

As distinct from *shringara bhava* or the mode of erotic love where the devotee approaches god as lover, *sakha bhava* enables the devotee to approach god as friend, usually a same-sex friend. This mode allows for greater equality and reciprocity in the relationship since the hierarchies involved in heterosexually constructed gender do not come into play. A devotee's relation to the deity is one of tender and intimate love, often expressed in the image of two mirrors facing one another. As this image implies, perfect devotional love involves the loss of separate identity—it is impossible to tell which mirror reflects which being. Significant here is the emphasis on sameness rather than difference as crucial to relationship.

Miraculous Birth

On the whole, medieval retellings of ancient stories have a tendency to introduce a happy ending. A famous example is Tulsi's medieval Hindi retelling of the Rama story in his *Ramcharitmanas*. Tulsi leaves out the episode narrated by Valmiki in the Sanskrit *Ramayana*, of Sita's final rejection by Rama and her subsequent sinking into the earth. It is perhaps in part from this tendency to aspire to what may seem an unrealistic happy ending that a uniquely Indian legitimization of same-sex love emerges in some medieval texts where children are miraculously born to two males or two females.

Indian culture is heavily child-centered, and the birth of a child makes all well. Even today, marriages disapproved of by parents, such as intercaste and intercommunity marriages, are often accepted after the birth of a child. The ancient texts repeatedly state that the primary purpose of marriage is to produce a child, especially a son. In this context, it makes sense that same-sex coupledom should be sanctioned if it can result in offspring. Legends imagine this happening in two ways—either through one partner's sex change (see p. 72), or, more radi-

---

29. See *The Sants: Studies in a Devotional Tradition of India,* ed. Karine Schomer and W. H. McLeod (Delhi: Motilal Banarsidas, 1987).

cally, as in the births of Ayyappa or Bhagiratha, through the miraculous divinely blessed birth of a child to the same-sex couple. A third possibility was imagined parthenogenesis, especially in the case of goddesses, triggered by some sort of interaction between friends (see p. 82).

Intimacies within the Household

Many of the themes I have adumbrated unfold in the ancient and early medieval compendiums of stories—folktales, animal fables, and popular retellings of Puranic stories.

While the option of friendship in singleness may be available to men, love between women in the *Katha* literature is framed in the context of marriage, especially polygynous marriage in royal or wealthy merchant households. The patterns that emerge here anticipate medieval and modern representations of love between women within the family. In the *Kathasaritsagara*, a story cycle compiled in the eleventh century, female friends frequently play the stock role of confidante and go-between. This is a purely functional role, and the friend disappears from the narrative once she has furthered the heterosexual romance.

However, in some other stories, friends acquire different degrees of importance. Thus, when the princess Mahallika's marriage is arranged, she persuades her father to marry her twelve friends (who are her subordinates, girls taken captive from other kingdoms) to her husband. When her husband mildly protests, she scolds him, arguing that since he has married so many other women, he should have no objection to marrying her friends for her sake. She tells her friends that she would like to have them with her to avoid feeling isolated among her husband's other wives who are strangers to her (I: 428–31).[30]

In the more elaborate frame story, the minister of King Udayana of Vatsa wants him to marry the princess of Magadha, Padmavati. To facilitate this political alliance, he persuades Udayana's queen, Vasavadatta, to go away in disguise and he burns her palace, so that her husband thinks her dead. Vasavadatta goes to Magadha in disguise and meets the princess: "And Padmavati, when she saw the queen Vasavadatta in the dress of a Brahman woman, fell in love with her at first sight" (I: 110). Padmavati keeps Vasavadatta with her in the palace. The description of her attraction to Vasavadatta is sensuous in detail: "And Padmavati perceived that Vasavadatta was a person of very high rank, by her shape, her delicate softness, the graceful manner in which she sat down, and ate, and also by the smell of her body, which was fragrant as the blue lotus" (110). This mutual love makes the status of cowife more acceptable to both women, who, however, strenuously protest against the king's taking any more wives.

The desire to be cowives and thus to prevent separation has to be understood in the context of virilocal marriage where a married upper-class woman's mobility and freedom of alliance

---

30. *The Katha Sarit Sagara* trans. C. H. Tawney (1880; New Delhi: Munshiram Manoharlal, 1968). All page numbers refer to this edition.

were severely constrained. This becomes very clear in the story of Somaprabha and Kalin-gasena; the two women are attracted to each other at first sight and plight their troth with joined hands and embraces, feeling that they were linked in former births (see p. 85). Somaprabha tells Kalingasena that they can meet frequently as long as Kalingasena is unmar-ried, but as soon as she marries, they cannot visit each other because it is not proper for a mar-ried woman to enter another man's house alone. Once Kalingasena becomes embroiled in various relationships with men, Somaprabha manages to visit her only on occasions such as her daughter's wedding.

Even the rare stories of single women befriending one another in the forest tend to finally get enclosed in the frame of marriage. Thus, the princess Hemaprabha goes to live in the for-est after her father insults her by slapping her. There she meets a female mendicant who took to this life when her father kicked her. They live together until they remember their former births as wives of a king and his minister, and reunite with their former husbands (121–24). This pattern brings to mind Amba's comment in the *Mahabharata* that a woman cannot ful-fill her *dharma* unless she marries. However, it is noteworthy that this narrative pattern keeps the two women together by marrying them to closely linked men, thus maintaining their re-lationship even while subsuming it in the institution of heterosexual marriage.

In one of the Vetala's stories, a series of sex changes, caused by a magic pill, enables an artful young man, Manahsvamin, to sleep with an unmarried girl on the pretext of being her friend and also to sleep with a married woman whose cowife he has become. While he is in female form, another man falls so deeply in love with Manahsvamin that he neglects his new-lywed bride Mrigankavati and "bitten by the great snake of fierce passion, he suddenly be-came distracted" (304). After Manahsvamin is married to this man, he sends his new husband off on a pilgrimage in order to avoid sleeping with him. To seduce his cowife Mrig-ankavati, he tells her the story of Ila's transformation into a woman and his/her relationship with Budha. This telling of an ancient story of involuntary sex change to legitimize a volun-tary sex change is an early example of a medieval reading of an ancient canonical text in a dif-ferent context, aimed at foregrounding a particular tradition of ambiguous sexual behavior. Manahsvamin then changes back to a man each night to sleep with Mrigankavati and changes into a woman by day. This is a kind of speeded-up variation on Ila's monthly sex change as a *kimpurusha* (see p. 18).

Bhagvata Purana: *The Embrace of Shiva and Vishnu (Sanskrit)*[1]

Introduced by Ruth Vanita

In one of the primal myths, the ocean was churned by gods and demons in order to get from it nectar, the essence of immortality. The ocean yielded a number of treasures, including the wish-fulfilling cow, and finally, a jar containing the nectar. The gods and demons quarreled over it, and the demons got hold of it. The gods appealed to Vishnu for help, and he assured them that he would take the form of a beautiful woman, Mohini (the enchanting one) in order to delude the demons into giving up the jar.

The story of Shiva's attraction to Vishnu is related in at least three *Puranas* which date approximately from 850 to 950 A.D. In the *Brahmanda Purana*, Parvati stands with her head lowered in shame when Shiva chases Mohini. In the *Shiva Purana*, the seven sages collect Shiva's semen and infuse it into Gautama's daughter through her ear. She then gives birth to Hanuman, the monkey-god.

The traditional interpretation of the story is that Vishnu's *leela* (play) is to make Shiva forget that he is a man and become attracted to his Mohini form. However, it is noteworthy that in this version, as well as in Telugu versions,[2] it is Shiva who asks Vishnu to assume his Mohini form, because Shiva missed seeing it earlier and heard about its beauty. So Shiva is aware of the ambiguous nature of this male-female form. In the context of religious drama where men and boys traditionally played, and still often play, female roles, audience awareness of and response to the man disguised as a woman would be comparable to Shiva's. In other stories, Shiva himself takes the female form during love play with Parvati (see p. 18). The stories suggest the

---

1. Ca. 950. Text used for this translation is *Bhagvata Mahapuranam* (Delhi: Nag Publishers, 1987), originally published by the Shri Venkatesvara Steam Press, Mumbai, no date.
2. Cintalapadi Yeallanaryudu, *Vishnu-maya-vilasamu* (Madras: Vavilla Ramasvami Sastrulu, 1970). I am grateful to Professor V. Narayana Rao for this reference.

fluidity of gender in sexual interaction. For the story of the son born to Shiva from his interaction with Vishnu/Mohini, see pp. 94–99.

Translated by Kumkum Roy

8.8.41–46 Shuka said, "Meanwhile, the supreme lord Vishnu, the knower of all kinds of strategies, took the virtually indescribable form of an exceedingly wonderful woman. This form was a pleasure to behold. Its color was that of the blue lotus; all the limbs were beautiful; the ears and earrings were symmetrical; the face had beautiful cheeks and a shapely nose. The waist was slender, borne down by the weight of breasts heavy with the onset of youth. The eyes seemed to be perturbed by the hum of bees which were attracted by the fragrance of the mouth. A garland of full-blown jasmine adorned the mass of hair. The beautiful neck was adorned with a necklace and the lovely arms with armlets.

"Covered with a shining cloth, the island-like part between the hips appeared beautiful. The sound of tinkling anklets accompanied the movement of the feet. The hearts of the leaders of the demons were inflamed with passion in a moment on account of the shy smiles, the arching of the eyebrows, and the playful glances."

[The enchanting Mohini distracts the demons into giving the jar of nectar to the gods. The god Shiva, who is not present on this occasion, hears an account of the incident and is curious to see this unusual form of Vishnu so, accompanied by his wife Parvati, he goes to pay him a visit.]

Shiva said, "I have seen the incarnations you assumed while playing with the three energies [Purity, Heat and Lassitude, of which the universe is composed]. I long to see the womanly body you adopted. We have come because we are very curious to see that form which deluded the demons and enabled the gods to drink the nectar."

Shuka said: "At this request of the trident-bearing god, the lord Vishnu laughed and replied to the lord of mountains with words full of deep meaning."

The lord said: "When the jar of nectar had gone into the hands of the demons I dressed as a woman in order to arouse the curiosity of the demons and accomplish the task of the gods. O best of the gods, as you are so eager, I will show you that form which arouses desire, and which is highly valued by passionate men."

Shuka said: "Speaking thus, the lord immediately disappeared. Shiva waited there with Uma [Parvati], looking for him in all directions. Then, in a garden with many-colored flowers and trees with red leaves, he saw a beautiful woman. She was playing with a ball. She wore a girdle, and a beautiful cloth covered her lower parts.

"It seemed as if her waist would collapse with the weight of her heavy breasts which trembled as she rose and bent with the ball, as well as with the weight of her necklaces and hips, as her tender leaflike feet went from place to place. The pupils of her large eyes anxiously followed the movements of the ball in various directions. Her face, framed with her dark flowing hair, looked beautiful, while her cheeks shone with the radiance of her earrings. She was tying her fine cloth, which had come loose, and tidying her disheveled hair with her beautiful left hand while hitting the ball with her other hand. She enchanted the entire world with her powers of illusion.

"On seeing her playing with the ball, smiling shyly, glancing at him, the god, gazing at the woman and being looked at in return by her, forgot himself as well as Uma [Parvati, his wife] and his attendants. The ball slipped from her hand and rolled away. She followed it while a gust of wind blew off her cloth and girdle. The lord Shiva stood staring.

"Seeing that beautiful charming woman who tried to attract him with her eyes, Shiva fixed his heart on her. Being deprived of his wisdom by her, completely oblivious of discernment, overwhelmed with passion, and quite shameless, he approached her even as Bhavani [Parvati] looked on.

"Undressed as she was, she seemed to be very shy as he came to her. Laughing, she went behind a tree but did not stay still. The lord, his senses out of control, overpowered by desire, followed her as a lordly elephant would a she-elephant. Chasing her, he caught the unwilling woman, pulled her by the hair, and held her in his arms. The lord held her in a close embrace, just as an elephant holds a she-elephant. She struggled in his grasp, and her hair was disheveled.

"Freeing herself from the arms of the bull-like god, she, the illusion created by the god, ran swiftly, her heavy hips swaying. Completely vanquished by the enemy, passion, the famed Shiva followed the footsteps of the woman who had been created by Vishnu of miraculous exploits.

"While pursuing her, his semen, of unfailing power, fell, just as that of a prize bull chasing a fertile cow, or a lordly elephant a fertile she-elephant. O king, wherever the semen of the great one fell to the earth, there were fields of silver and gold. Hara [Shiva] pursued her over rivers, lakes, mountains, forests, gardens, and the abodes of sages.

"When his semen was completely drained, O best of kings, he realized that he was exhausted by the illusion of the god, and he recovered. It is said that, realizing the greatness of his own soul and of the universal soul, he was not surprised at what had been done by the lord of unknowable power.

"Vishnu was very pleased to see that he was neither remorseful nor embarrassed. He resumed his own masculine body."

Shuka said: "O king, having been honored by an embrace from the lord who bears the mark of Shri Vatsa, Shiva paid his respects, circumambulated him, and returned home with his attendants."

Skanda Purana:
Sumedha and Somavan (Sanskrit)[1]

Introduced by Ruth Vanita

This story, from the *Skanda Purana* (compiled ca. 700–1150), is a variation on the familiar theme of the miraculous sex change. Set in the context of medieval devotion, it highlights the idea of the devotee being in a sense more powerful than the deity. The devotee's powers of perception are able to transform a man into a woman, and not even a deity can undo the transformation.

What is interesting here is that the transformation is almost volitionally brought about by the low-caste woman devotee, Simantini. She sees through the disguise and knows that Somavan is a man dressed as a woman, but instead of denouncing him, she chooses to see and worship the goddess in him. This suggests that she perceives the "womanhood" in him and, by worshiping it, makes it manifest.

While the narrator is careful to stress that it is only after the sex change that Somavan/Samavati expresses attraction for Sumedha, the story does suggest that this attraction may have been latent in their relationship. This suggestion is highlighted at the end when Parvati says that Saraswat's new son will be "pure-hearted." By implication, Somavan (whose name derives from *soma*, the intoxicating drink of the gods) was not pure-hearted. She adds that by marrying Sumedha, Samavati will enjoy the pleasures of fulfilled desire. According to the doctrine of *samskaras*, one becomes what one desires to become and may be reborn as whatever one mentally dwells upon in one's dying hours. Fulfillment of all desires may be seen as a necessary step toward ridding oneself of those desires and attaining liberation.

A similar suggestion is built into the framing of the story by same-sex bonding—the boys' fathers are friends and the story stresses that the boys grow up together, dress alike and are

1. Translated from *Sriskandamahapuranam* (Delhi: Nag Publishers, 1986), originally published by Shri Venkatesvara Steam Press, Mumbai, no date.

educated together. The narrative presents them as a perfectly matched couple in every respect except that the possibility of marriage seems excluded by the sameness of gender. When the fathers think the boys should marry, no prospective brides are named—that the enterprise ends in the two marrying each other fulfills a desire that seems to be latent in the opening phrases. When the boys dress as a couple, they may not be just obeying the king but bringing out denied possibilities in themselves.

In devotional texts, the deity often is represented as containing all possibilities. Shiva and Parvati represent sexuality, among other things, as is clear from the symbolism in their temples of the *linga* and the *yoni*, the male and female genitalia respectively. Shiva and Parvati are even said to be present in every child in the form of the genitals. In Hindu devotional ritual, it is common to worship god in human persons; thus, on their wedding day, bride and groom are worshiped as gods. Simantini follows well-established practice when she worships the couples as Shiva and Parvati. Where she modifies this practice, or brings out its latent possibilities, is in choosing to worship a male couple as a sexual and conjugal unit.

Although the story heterosexualizes the couple, they are not punished but ultimately rewarded with marital bliss. Such stories suggest how traditional notions of the fluidity of gender can work to the benefit of same-sex couples.

Translated from the Sanskrit by Kumkum Roy

3.3.9.2. The charioteer said: "There was an excellent Brahman named Vedamitra in Vidarbha. He was wise, and well versed in the *Vedas* and *Shastras*. He had a friend (*sakha*), a Brahman named Sarasvat. Both of them lived in the same place and had great love for one another. Vedamitra had a diligent son named Sumedha, while Sarasvat's son was known as Somavan. Both boys were of the same age, they dressed alike, they were of equal status and learning, and they were initiated into Vedic learning together. They studied the Vedas along with the subsidiary texts, logic, grammar, legends and myths, as well as the complete *Dharmashastras*. They were skilled in all kinds of arts, and were sage-like even in their childhood. The joy of their fathers was boundless, as they possessed every possible virtue. Then, when they were sixteen years old, and handsome, those happy fathers, the best of the Brahmans, called them and said: "O sons, you have completed your studies and are brilliant. This is the right time to marry. Now you should please the king, the lord of Vidarbha, with your skills, and, obtaining plenty of wealth from him, you should get married."

Having been advised thus, those two sons of the Brahmans went to the king of Vidarbha and pleased him with their talents. When he was satisfied with their learning, the two Brahman boys told him that they were poor, and had demonstrated their skills in order to obtain wealth and get married.

Hearing what they wanted, and in order to find out the truth about popular beliefs, the king of Vidarbha laughingly spoke as follows: "Simantini is the virtuous queen of Nishada. She worships Mahadeva [Shiva] along with Ambika [Parvati] on Mondays. On that day she worships the foremost of Brahmans, versed in the Vedas, along with their wives, and offers vast quantities of wealth, out of great devotion. One of you will go disguised as a young woman, while the other will go as her husband. Thus you will be a Brahman couple. You will go to Simantini's house as a bride and groom. Having entered there and after obtaining plenty of wealth, you will return to me" (17).

[The boys say it is improper to deceive a devotee, but the king insists.]

3.3.9.28 The king made Somavan, the son of Sarasvat, take the form of a woman, with clothes, ornaments, collyrium and other things. He seemed to be a wife, through wonderful artifice. With his earrings, ornaments and the use of fragrant substances, with his eyes glistening with collyrium, with his attractive form, he seemed like a glowing young woman. Having become a couple at the orders of the king, the two sons of the Brahmans went to the land of Nishada, thinking: "What will be will be."

On a Monday they went to the palace with the best of Brahmans and their wives. They were greeted as guests, and their feet were washed. The Brahmans were seated on excellent seats. The queen then offered worship to each one of the distinguished Brahmans with his wife.

Seeing the sons of the Brahmans who had come to her, she realized that they were a couple in disguise, but, smiling to herself, she regarded them as Gauri and Maheshvara [Parvati and Shiva]. She invoked Sadashiva [the eternal Shiva] in those excellent Brahmans, and the goddess, the mother of the universe, in their wives. She worshiped them with unalloyed devotion, with fragrance, garlands, incense, and waved lamps before them (35).

3.3.9. 42 Of those two sons of the Brahmans, she worshiped one after identifying him with Haimavati [Parvati] while she worshiped the other after contemplating him as Mahadev [Shiva]. After being worshiped, they took leave of her and went away.

She [Somavan] forgot her masculinity and, overwhelmed with passion by the god of love, was attracted to the best of Brahmans and said: "O my large-eyed lord, you are so completely handsome. Please wait. Do you not see me, your beloved? Here, before us, is this lovely forest with big trees in bloom. I want to enjoy myself with you to my heart's content."

Hearing this, the Brahman who was walking ahead thought it was a joke and continued to walk on.

Once again, the young woman said: "Wait! Where are you going? I am under the unbearable spell of the god of love. Come and enjoy me. Embrace me, your beloved—let me drink from your lips. Afflicted by the arrows of the god of love, I can go no further."

On hearing these words, never heard before, he became suspicious. Turning around to see who was following him, he was awestruck.

"Who is this with eyes like lotus petals, with full and raised breasts, with slender waist, with large hips, as tender as a blossom? Has my male friend become a beautiful woman? Let me ask him everything."

Thinking thus, he said: "O friend, your appearance and behavior are unprecedented. So are your words, like those of a woman overpowered by desire. You know the *Vedas* and the *Puranas,* you are celibate and in control of your senses. You are the self-controlled son of Sarasvat. Why do you speak like this?"

Addressed thus, she replied: "O lord, I am not a man. I am a woman, named Samavati. I am here to give you sexual pleasure. If you doubt this, O beloved, examine my limbs."

On hearing this, he examined her secretly at once. Seeing her, with her naturally luxuriant tresses, with her beautiful hips and breasts, and her lovely form, his passion was somewhat aroused. The wise man controlled his wandering mind with an effort and, although he was astonished for a moment, he said nothing more in reply.

Samavati said: "Now that your doubts are dispelled, come and enjoy me. O my beloved, see this forest which is suited for sexual pleasures with a lovely woman."

Sumedha said: "Do not speak thus. Do not violate the norms as if you were intoxicated. Both of us have understood the meaning of the *Shastras.* Why do you speak thus? You have studied the *Shastras,* you have the ability to discriminate, and you are of a good family. How can you behave like a lover? You are not a woman but a man, learned and wise. Realize yourself through introspection. Or is this a disaster which has befallen us because of what we tried to do? We deceived our parents on the advice of the wily king. We have done that which ought not to have been done, and now we enjoy the fruit of our actions.

"All improper acts lead to the destruction of the well-being of men. So you, the learned son of a Brahman, have attained the despicable state of womanhood. A man who strays into the forest leaving the well-trodden path gets pricked by thorns. Similarly, he who abandons his own people is attacked by fierce wild beasts. Clinging to your conscience, follow me quietly to your home. Your womanhood may disappear through the grace of the gods and Brahmans. Or, if you are destined to remain a woman, then, O beautiful woman, once you are given to me by your father, you can take pleasure with me. Alas, this is amazing, alas, this is a great sorrow, the great power of sin. Alas, this is the effect of the power which the queen has acquired by worshiping Shiva."

Although he repeatedly scolded her, the woman, overwhelmed with passion, embraced him forcibly and kissed his tender, budlike lips. Although the patient Sumedha was molested by the new woman, he brought her home and narrated everything.

On hearing this, the two Brahmans were angry and overcome with grief. Taking the two boys with them, they came to the king of Vidarbha. Then Sarasvat addressed the king who had engineered the deception: "O king, look at my son who has followed your instructions. . . . My son, who has attained the hateful state of womanhood, now suffers the fruit (72).

3.3.9.76 On your account my lineage has been destroyed, as has the path of Vedic learning. O king, tell me, how can I, the father of only one son, obtain salvation?"

Hearing the words of Sarasvat, the king was filled with great wonder at the powers of Simantini. Then the king called all the great sages of boundless luster, and, having worshiped them, prayed for his [Somavan's] manhood. They replied: "Who can reverse the will of Parvati and Shiva, and the greatness of their devotees?"

Then the king took the best of the sages, Bharadvaja, and went with him to the two foremost of Brahmans and their sons. Going to the temple of Ambika [Parvati] on the advice of Bharadvaj, they worshiped the goddess with difficult vows (81).

3.3.9.84 Then Gauri [Parvati] asked the king: "What is your wish?" He replied: "By your grace may he get his masculinity." The great goddess replied: "What has been done by my devotees cannot be undone even in a myriad years."

The goddess said: "By my grace, he [Sarasvat] will have another excellent son endowed with learning, modesty and long life. He will be pure-hearted. Let Samavati, this daughter of the Brahman, be Sumedha's wife. United with him, let her enjoy the pleasures of desire."

Having spoken, the goddess disappeared. The king led the way as they went to their respective homes, bound by the order. Shortly thereafter, by the grace of the goddess, Sarasvat, the Brahman, obtained a son who was even better than the previous one. He gave his daughter Samavati to Sumedha and that couple enjoyed great bliss for a long time.

Shiva Purana:
The Birth of Kartikeya (Sanskrit)[1]

Introduced by Ruth Vanita

Kartikeya, the son of Shiva, is the god of war, leader of the army of the gods, and, in some traditions, patron of wisdom and learning. Represented as a handsome youth riding on a peacock, he is usually considered a bachelor and is widely worshiped in south India as Subrahmanya and Murugan. He is also called Kumara (which means both "unmarried" and "slayer of the demon Mara") and Guha (from "cave," suggesting also "hidden," "secret"). In several ancient texts, we are told that women were not permitted to enter his shrines. Even today, women cannot enter his ancient temple at Sandur near Mysore. In one aspect, he is worshiped by women to obtain a son, as he is the protector of children and youth. This protective role is a benevolent inversion of his hostility to procreation and childbirth, an aspect evident in his leading troops of underworld beings, including eight planets who cause children's diseases.[2] As the Tamil Murugan, he is the god of love and revelry, often erotically associated with a tribal woman Valli.[3] Although sometimes represented courting and marrying, he is most frequently represented flanked by both wives but touching neither, holding on to his lance instead.[4] It would appear that the Murugan cult developed from the merging of an early hunter and fertility god with the Sanskritic Kartikeya.

---

1. This translation from *Shiva Mahapuranam,* ed. Pushpendra Kumar (Delhi: Naga Publishers, 1981).
2. For an account of these male and female demons, see *Mahabharata, Vana Parva* II: CCXXVIII, CCXXIX.
3. Fred W. Clothey, *The Many Faces of Murukan: The History and Meaning of a South Indian God* (The Hague: Mouton Publishers, 1978), points out that despite Tamil purists' desire to claim Murugan as a purely Tamil god in origins, fifth-century Tamil Sangam literature, the earliest to mention him, already shows the influence of the Sanskrit epics.
4. Clothey, 79, 85.

However, in most other parts of the country as well as at the Palani temple in Madras, he is represented as celibate.[5]

One of his names, Skanda, is suggestive of his birth from Shiva's semen, for it appears to be derived from the verb *skandri* (to attack, leap, rise, be spilled) and literally means "that which is spilled or oozed, namely, seed."[6] This name also may provide a link with the shrine to "Sekunder," on top of a hill associated with the Murugan temple at Tiruppankunram, which Muslims visit and equate in some obscure way with Murugan. This name appears to be a dis-tortion of Iskandar or Sikandar, still used in India for Alexander. Some scholars argue that this association is because the Skanda cult is influenced by that of the Greek god Dionysos (who was born from the thigh of Zeus).[7]

The several accounts of Kartikeya's birth differ in detail but agree in ascribing his origin to the male principle alone. In the *Mahabharata*, he is the son of Agni, god of fire. Indra needs to find a commander who can lead the divine army against the demon Taraka. The army is em-bodied as a lady, Devasena (lit. army of the gods), who is in search of a husband to protect her. Attracted by the Krittikas (Pleiades), the wives of the sages, Agni discharges his semen into the hands of one of them, named Swaha.[8] She throws the semen into a lake, from whence springs Kartikeya, also known as Skanda (lit. cast off, since he is born from cast away semen). Suckled by the Krittikas, he comes to be called Kartikeya.

He is a highly energetic child, whose sports terrify the universe. At his birth, "the nature of males and females, heat and cold, and other pairs of contraries, was reversed" (CCXXV). Afraid that the child will dethrone him, Indra throws his thunderbolt, but instead of killing Kartikeya, it merely produces from his body another fierce-looking youth called Vishakha. Indra then worships Kartikeya and installs him as the commander of the army. This installa-tion is represented through the metaphor of marriage to Devasena, who is merely an embod-iment of the army. Kartikeya is also called Senapati (lit. lord/husband of the army). He is described as having "mysterious charm" and beauty; he is also called Kanta (the handsome), Lalita (the beautiful) and Brahmacharin (vowed to celibacy). The *Mahabharata* remarks that the mountain on which Agni discharged his semen was itself created from Shiva's semen, and

---

5. The paradox of being married and celibate is not perceived as a contradiction by wor-shipers—this is a paradox also embodied by gods like Shiva and heroes like Arjuna. A very popular legend gives one explanation for Kartikeya remaining unmarried. Kartikeya and his brother Ganesha engage in a contest to decide who will marry first. The one who can go around the world first will win the contest. Kartikeya sets out on his peacock but Ganesha, on his rat, circumambulates his parents, since he considers them his world. Ganesha wins the contest and Kartikeya refuses to marry at all.

6. Clothey, *Many Faces,* 49.

7. Clothey, 3, 41, 125, 196–97.

8. As the name indicates, this lady is merely a personification of the sacrificial ritual. Each time an offering is made to the fire, it is accompanied by the word *swaha.*

as Kartikeya was formed from Shiva's energy entering into Agni, he is the son of Shiva as well as Agni.[9] So, Kartikeya, the leader of an all-male army, is the son of two males and also produces other males parthenogenetically from his body without the mediation of a female.[10]

In the *Shiva Purana* (ca. 750–1350), a later text, appears the better known account wherein Kartikeya is born from Agni swallowing Shiva's semen. The text is clearly aware of the implications of this act, as Parvati repeatedly denounces it as "wicked" or "impure," and Shiva also tells Agni his action was "improper." However, as in the *Smritis* and *Sutras*, oral sex between males, although not considered wholly proper, is far from being an unforgivable or even uncreative act. Agni suffers from a "burning sensation," which is relieved when, on Shiva's instructions, he transmits the semen into the wombs of the sages' wives who in turn drop it into the Ganga. Falling from the Ganga into a forest of grass, the semen produces the beautiful Kartikeya who is adopted and nursed by Parvati. Thus, the son of two males is purified by the mediation of various natural forces and is ultimately accepted by his father's wife.

In the *Skanda Purana*, a text devoted to the celebration of Kartikeya, Agni, disguised not as a dove but as a male ascetic, interrupts the intercourse of Shiva and Parvati, and then receives the semen in his hands and swallows it (I.1.27). The rest of the story is basically the same. In the eleventh-century *Kathasaritsagara*, it is Shiva who summons an unwilling Agni and deposits his semen in him; Agni tries hard to avoid this but fails.

◈ ◈ ◈

Translated by Kumkum Roy

4. 2: 9–12 [Shiva and Parvati are locked in what appears to be an eternal embrace. The gods are worried, as this does not seem to be leading to the birth of the promised son who will lead the divine army against the demons. They decide to interrupt Shiva politely, by singing his praises. Shiva leaves Parvati without discharging his semen and appears to them.]

Shiva said: "O immortals, listen to what is of concern. What has happened has happened. Now let him who will accept the semen I discharge." So saying, he let it fall on the ground. Urged by the ageless ones, Agni became a dove. He swallowed the semen of Shiva with his beak.

O sage, in the meantime, the daughter of the mountains [Parvati] also arrived there. Since Shiva was taking a long time to return, she came and saw the brave gods. Having

---

9. Markandeya's explanation, *Vana Parva* II: CCXXVIII, Ganguly, III: 461–62.
10. Apart from Vishakha, he produces Skandapasmara in this way (*Vana Parva,* CCXXIX).

heard all that had happened, Shivaa [Parvati] was filled with rage. [She curses them with childlessness since she herself has become barren due to their interruption.]

19–21.Brahma said: "The all-pervading goddess cursed Vishnu and all the other gods. She then turned to the purifying one [Agni], the eater of Shiva's semen. Parvati said: "O pure one, may you become an indiscriminate eater of all things.[11] You fool who have accomplished the task of the gods, you do not know Shiva's principles. You rogue, most wicked one, follower of the wicked advice given by wicked ones, you have eaten Shiva's semen which is neither proper nor beneficial for you."

[Shiva's semen gets transferred to the gods along with offerings made to them in the sacrificial fire, and it literally burns them. They find a way out by placating Shiva with praises. Agni, himself fire, is also burned by the semen and has to approach Shiva.]

42–48.Then, O sage, the troubled god of fire praised Shiva with folded hands. Agni said: "O lord of gods, I am your foolish and deluded servant. Forgive my offense and extinguish the burning sensation I feel. O Shiva, lord of all, you are compassionate towards the distressed."

Brahma said: "Hearing the words of Shuchi [Agni, the pure one], Shiva, the lord of all, with compassion for the distressed, was pleased and said to Pavaka [Agni, the purifier]: 'By eating my semen you did that which was improper. Therefore, by my order and because of your excessive sinfulness, your burning sensation has not subsided. Now that you have sought refuge in me, O pure one, you will be happy. Because, now that I am pleased, all your sorrows will be destroyed. Carefully deposit my semen in the womb of a good woman. You will be happy and completely freed from the burning sensation.'"[12]

[The wives of the sages, having bathed, dry themselves in front of the fire. Agni transmits the semen to their pores through his flames. Suspecting their wives of inchastity, the sages discard them. Distressed, the women discharge the semen on Himavat (the Himalaya Mountains, personified as father of Parvati). Burned by it, Himavat throws it into the river Ganga who in turn throws it into a forest of grass where it becomes a handsome boy. His appearance makes Parvati and Shiva very happy. Kartikeya transforms Vishwamitra, the sage born in the warrior caste, into a Brahman priest to enable him to perform purificatory rites for his birth.]

---

11. Parvati is being sarcastic here in addressing Agni as "pure," but the questions of purity and pollution are seriously in consideration throughout this narrative. Consuming semen may seem like a polluting act; on the other hand, fire, in Hindu thought, is the ultimate purifier. Fire is also the element of sexual and other energy in the human constitution. Metaphorically, fire swallowing semen renders the impure pure. Semen too is ambivalent—it represents energy and is usually very valuable, especially here, where it is discharged by Shiva, the pure one.

12. Shiva's reproaches are double-edged, as it was he who initially discharged the semen and asked whoever would to receive it.

Shiva Purana:
The Birth of Ganesha (Sanskrit)[1]

Introduced by Ruth Vanita

Ganesha, the elephant-headed god, is the son of Shiva and Parvati. The many differing accounts of his birth agree in describing it as occurring outside the womb.[2] In some versions he is created by Shiva alone, and in others, from the bodily fluids of Shiva and Parvati mingling outside the body; but in most versions, such as that extracted here, he is created by Parvati alone. A folk etymology of one of his names, Vinayaka (without a *nayaka* or leader, that is, peerless), relates it to his origin, that is, he is created without a male agent (*nayaka*). Parvati creates rather than produces him. She fashions him as the Jewish Yahweh creates man out of clay. Her creative role is distinct from the common view of woman as merely a receptacle for the creative male seed.[3] She rubs Ganesha out of her body—this recalls the

---

1. This translation from *Shiva Mahapuranam*, ed. Pushpendra Kumar (Delhi: Naga Publishers, 1981).

2. For an exhaustive account and sensitive interpretation of these stories, see Paul B. Courtright, *Ganesha: Lord of Obstacles, Lord of Beginnings* (New Delhi: Oxford University Press, 1985).

3. Wendy O'Flaherty, *Women, Androgynes and Other Mythical Beasts* (Chicago: University of Chicago Press, 1980), reads the outcome of unilateral female creation as "less auspicious" (50) than such creation by males, because Ganesha is created out of dirt (37–38) and a demoness participates in his creation. I disagree with this reading because there could hardly be a more auspicious outcome than Ganesha himself and, further, residues from a divine body are purifying in Hindu tradition, as in cow's dung and urine, food offered to gods and consumed as sacred leavings, or the water used to wash icons, which is later drunk by devotees. Kunal Chakrabarti, who views Puranic religion as the outcome of Brahmans' attempt to reassert their control over lower castes, tribals and women, reads Ganesha's "unnatural" (his term) birth and celibacy as expressive of oedipal and incestuous compulsions but makes no mention of homoerotic ones ("Divine Family and World Maintenance: Ganesa in the Bengal Puranas" in *From Myths to Markets: Essays on Gender*, ed. Kumkum Sangari and Uma Chakravarti [New Delhi: Manohar, 1999], 56–84).

churning action that is so creative in Hindu myth—from the Puranic churning of the ocean to the Vedic friction of the two female firesticks which produces the fire god.

In the *Shiva Purana* (ca. 750–1350), Parvati clearly chooses to create Ganesha to protect her autonomous space from constant invasion by her husband. Her female friends (whose names, Jaya and Vijaya, mean Victory) suggest this act of creation to Parvati; it is while they are bathing with her that Shiva is prevented by Ganesha from entering the bath, and they urge Ganesha on to war against Shiva and the other male gods. Parvati goes on to create female beings parthenogenetically, to aid Ganesha in his defense of her. Although Shiva triumphs by brute force, his triumph is temporary. He and the other gods are terrified by Parvati's irresistible power, and Ganesha has to be revived and honored.

In another version, Ganesha's all-female origin is more explicit. Here Parvati's bodily residues are washed with her bathwater into the Ganga, where they are swallowed by Malini, an elephant-headed female who goes on to give birth to Ganesha (Jayadratha's *Haracaritacintamani*).

In most traditions, Ganesha is celibate. In those traditions where he is wedded to two wives, Riddhi and Siddhi, they are personifications of his own qualities of prosperity and success, rather than goddesses with any individual character. That he is metaphorically wedded to the army of male Ganas is suggested in his name Ganapati (lord/husband of the Ganas), which parallels his brother Kartikeya's name Senapati (see p. 78). He is childless and is generally represented as a perpetual child, chubby and adorable.[4] As the auspicious remover of obstacles, he is worshiped all over India at the commencement of every important endeavor, including literary composition, religious ritual, and educational or business enterprise. As guardian of the door, a role he plays for Parvati, his image is placed at the entrance of homes and shops. He is the god of wisdom and learning, often represented reading or writing. He is the scribe of the *Mahabharata*, which he wrote at Vyasa's dictation. He also represents the fusing of animal, human and divine powers, through the fusion of elephant head with human body and divine four arms.

---

4. See Courtright, *Ganesha,* 110–25, for an interesting discussion of the motifs suggesting castration (beheading), eunuchism (guarding the women's quarters), homosexual oral sex, comic oedipalism, and celibate marriage (one tusk detached and held by the wife), associated with Ganesha. Courtright also points out that the twentieth-century, largely female cult of the new north Indian goddess Santoshi Ma attempts to domesticate Ganesha by claiming him as her father (124). See also Rohit and Ashwini, "Delving into Tradition," *Pravartak* (April-June 1994), 5.

Translated from the Sanskrit by Kumkum Roy

4.13.9–39 Brahma said: "Ganapati [Ganesha] was born a long time after Shiva's marriage and his return to Kailasha. Once upon a time Jaya and Vijaya, the two female friends of Parvati met her and had an animated discussion: 'Although all the Ganas (the followers of Shiva), headed by Nandin and Bhringin, are supposed to be ours, in reality they all obey Shiva's commands. . . . O sinless lady, you should create one who belongs exclusively to us.'"

Brahma said: "The goddess Parvati found that the beautiful suggestion made by her two friends was good, and she decided to act on it. Once, when Parvati was immersed in her bath, Shiva scolded Nandin and entered the inner apartment. The beautiful mother of the universe was embarrassed by Shankara's [Shiva's] untimely intrusion and rose from her bath. At that very moment, the goddess decided that the playful suggestion made by her friends was indeed wise, and would bring her happiness.

"When the incident occurred, Parvati, the great goddess, the auspicious one, thought to herself: 'I need a servant of my own, for whom my orders will be the last word, who will not be swayed at all. That indeed is most desirable.' Accordingly, the goddess created a man, endowed with all the attributes, out of the dirt of her body.

"He was flawless, beautiful, large, brilliant, strong and valorous. She gave him all kinds of clothes and ornaments and blessed him profusely: 'You are my son, my very own, I have none apart from you.' Thus addressed, the man bowed to the auspicious one and said: 'Tell me what is to be done and I shall do it.' Hearing this, Shivaa [Parvati] replied: 'O child, listen to me. From today you will be my gatekeeper. You are my son, you belong to me, I have none other than you. O my son, nobody, by any means, should enter my inner apartments without my permission. This is my command.'"

Brahma said: "O sage, having said this, she gave him a very strong stick. She was filled with delight on seeing his beautiful form. She kissed and embraced her son out of love and mercy, and then installed the lord of the Ganas [Ganesha] at her door, with the stick in his hand. The brave son of the goddess, standing, armed with the stick, at the door, wanted to do what was good for Parvati.

"Having installed her son Ganesha at the door, the auspicious goddess began to bathe with her friends.

"At that moment, O excellent sage, the playful Shiva, skilled in various arts, arrived at the door. Not knowing him to be Shiva, his mother's consort, the lord of the Ganas said: 'O lord, you cannot enter now without the permission of my mother. Where are you going? My mother is taking her bath now.' With that, he barred his path with the stick.

"Shiva, on seeing him, said: 'O stupid one, do you know whom you are holding up? Don't you know, O wicked one, that I am none other than Shiva?' Ganesha then beat him with the stick. The great god, the master of various sports, addressed his son angrily.

"Shiva said: 'O fool, you do not know that I am Shiva, the husband of the daughter of the mountain [Parvati]. O child, how can you prevent me from entering my own house?'"

Brahma said: "Then, O Brahmana, just as Mahesha tried to enter once more, the leader of the Ganas grew furious and beat him again and again with his stick.

"Then Shiva grew angry as well and summoned his Ganas, saying: 'Find out who this is and what he is supposed to be doing.' After saying this, Shiva waited angrily outside his house. The lord, engaged in worldly activities, is capable of many wonderful sports."

[While the Ganas and Ganesha argue, Parvati's friends advise her not to give in, as Shiva should not enter her apartment without her permission. They say that Shiva is too proud and squeezes her like a crab. Parvati agrees and the women tell Ganesha to stand firm. This angers Shiva, who says that if he were to give in, all would say he was subservient to his wife. In the ensuing battle, Ganesha, although a mere boy, single-handedly defeats the Ganas and all the gods, including Kartikeya, Shiva's son and the god of war. Parvati then creates two Shaktis, or female embodiments of her powers, to help Ganesha. After displaying great heroism, Ganesha is defeated by Shiva who cuts off his head.

Parvati then creates thousands of Shaktis and orders them to deluge and dissolve the universe. At this, all the gods and Shiva are terrified. The gods pray to her as the eternal cause of creation, its only sustaining power and the only cause of its dissolution. When they ask her forgiveness on Shiva's behalf, Parvati says the universe can be spared if Ganesha is restored to life and given an honorable status among the gods. Shiva agrees, Ganesha's head is replaced with an elephant's head, and everyone is delighted.]

Somadeva Bhatta's Kathasaritsagara: Kalingasena and Somaprabha (Sanskrit)[1]

Introduction by Ruth Vanita

This eleventh-century compilation of story cycles, attributed to Somadeva Bhatta, recounts the adventures, amorous and otherwise, of both male and female members of royal and aristocratic families. This story of the premarital love of a princess for a married woman anticipates in interesting ways the premarital collegiate woman-woman romances common in twentieth-century Indian fiction.

Translated by Kumkum Roy

[Queen Taradatta, the wife of the king of Takshashila, gave birth to a beautiful daughter.]

6.2.5. On seeing the newborn child, the father Kalingadatta was disappointed at not obtaining an equally lovely son instead. [A Buddhist monk consoled the king by telling him a number of stories.]

6.2.45–48. Having spent the day in the monastery listening to such stories, the king returned to his palace. When he once more began to grieve at his daughter's birth, a Brahman who had grown old in the house asked: "O king, why are you so sad at the birth of a jewel-like daughter? Daughters are better than sons, and are auspicious in both this world and the next. How can kings trust sons who are greedy for the kingdom and eat up their fathers like spiders?"

---

1. This translation from *The Kathasaritsagara of Somadeva Bhatta,* ed. Pandit Durgaprasad and Kasinath Pandurang Parab (Bombay: Nirnaya Sagara Press, 1903, 2nd ed.)

6.2.98. The princess Kalingasena grew up in her father's house amongst her female companions. She played in the palaces and the forests, like a wave on the playful ocean of childhood.

One day, the Asura [demon] Maya's daughter, Somaprabha, was traveling through the sky and saw her on the roof of the palace, absorbed in play. While still in the sky, Somaprabha saw her beauty, capable of bewitching even an ascetic's mind, and with feelings of love aroused, wondered: "Who is she? If she is an incarnation of the moon, then how does she shine during the day? If she is Rati, where is Kama?[2] I think she must be an unmarried girl, a celestial being born in the palace on account of a curse. I am sure she and I were female friends in a previous birth. My mind which is overwhelmed with affection for her, tells me so. Therefore, it is only appropriate that I should choose her as my friend once again."[3]

Thinking thus, and not wanting to frighten the young girl, Somaprabha became invisible and descended to the earth. Taking the form of a human girl in order to reassure Kalingasena, she approached her slowly.

Kalingasena thought: "Here is a princess who is very beautiful. She has come on her own to me. She deserves to be my friend." She rose from her seat and embraced Somaprabha. She offered Somaprabha a seat and asked her about her family and her name. Somaprabha replied: "Wait a while. I will tell you all." Talking to each other, they took one another's hands, and swore to be friends. (6.2.110)

6.2.189. As the sun set, Somaprabha took leave of her friend who was eager that she come again. She flew up into the sky in a moment, filling those who saw her with wonder, and soon reached home. Seeing that amazing sight, Kalingasena entered her house, perplexed: "I do not know if my friend is a Siddha, an Apsara, or a Vidyadhari [various types of celestial beings]. That she is divine is obvious from her flight through the air. It is also known that divine women come to mortal women, drawn by extreme affection. Was not Arundhati the friend of the daughter of King Prithu? Did not Prithu succeed in bringing Surabhi [the celestial cow] from heaven to earth because of this love [between Arundhati and Prthu's daughter]? Did he not, by drinking its milk, return to heaven in spite of his fall? And were not perfect cows born on earth after that? So I am fortunate to have this celestial friend. When she returns in the morning, I will skillfully ask her about her family and name." Thinking thus, Kalingasena spent the night there. Somaprabha too, spent the night in her own house, eager to see her again. (6.2.198)

---

2. *Rati* (lit. erotic love, dalliance, coition) is the name of the wife of Kama, the god of erotic love. Since Kama, owing to a curse, is invisible, Rati is the visible embodiment of erotic pleasure.

3. The term used here is *svayamvara sakhi. Svayamvara* (lit. self-chosen lover/bridegroom) is generally used for the ceremony in which a woman selects her husband from a group of suitors. Here it is unexpectedly joined with *sakhi* (female friend).

6.3.1. The next morning, Somaprabha packed a number of marvelous wooden dolls and toys in a basket for Kalingasena's pleasure, and flew through the air to meet her once more. Seeing her, Kalingasena wept with joy, rose, threw her arms around her neck, and, making her sit next to her, said: "O friend, the three watches of the night have seemed like a hundred without a glimpse of your moonlike face. If you know what our relationship [*sambandha*] was in the previous birth, of which this is the consequence, do tell me." Somaprabha replied: "I do not possess this knowledge, nor do I remember my previous birth." (6.3.6)

6.3.23. Kalingasena was so pleased seeing the wonderful toys brought by Somaprabha that she lost her appetite and refused food. Seeing this, her mother grew worried, thinking she was ill, and called a physician, named Ananda [joy] who examined her and said: "She has lost her appetite because she is pleased with something, not because she is sick. Her smiling eyes and face suggest this is the case." On hearing the physician, her mother asked her what the matter was, and she told her everything. Then her mother was happy that she was in the company of a worthy friend, and made her eat properly.

The next day, when Somaprabha arrived, she found out what had happened, and told Kalingasena in secret: "I have told my wise husband about my friendship with you, and have obtained his permission to visit you every day. Now you should obtain your parents' permission, so that you can enjoy yourself with me without fear, and at will."[4]

When she had spoken, Kalingasena immediately took her by the hand and went to her parents. She introduced Somaprabha to her father, King Kalingadatta, and mentioned her name and family. She also introduced her to her mother, Taradatta, and they, on hearing their daughter, greeted Somaprabha. Charmed by the beauty of the great Asura's wife, and from affection for their daughter, they said: "Dear child, we give Kalingasena into your hands. Now both of you can enjoy yourselves as you wish."

Both Kalingasena and Somaprabha were happy to hear this. They took the basket of magical toys and went to play in a monastery built by the king. (6.3.37)

6.3.49. Then, requesting the king for appropriate food, Someprabha took Kalingasena on her celestial vehicle with his permission. Somaprabha set off, with Kalingasena, through the sky, to meet her sister who was in her father's house. They reached her father's house, which was near the Vindhyas, in a moment, and Somaprabha took Kalingasena to her sister, Svayamprabha [self-irradiated]. There, Kalingasena saw the celibate Svayamprabha, with matted hair and a long rosary. She was dressed in white, smiling like Parvati, and engaged in a severe penance to overcome the pleasures of desire. On being introduced by Somaprabha to the princess who knelt before her, she offered hospitality and a meal of fruits.

---

4. The term used for "at will" is *svairam,* from the same root as *svairini,* the term for the self-willed, autonomous woman in the *Kamasutra* (see pp. 48–49).

Somaprabha said: "O friend, if you eat these fruits, your beauty will not wither with age, unlike the lotus which is blighted in winter. This is why I brought you here, out of love." Kalingasena then ate the fruits and felt as if her limbs were bathed in the water of immortality.

Inspired by curiosity, she wandered through the garden of that city, with its ponds full of golden lotuses and trees with fruit as sweet as nectar. It was full of golden and variegated-colored birds, and pillars that appeared to be studded with gems. There seemed to be walls where there were none, and the walls themselves seemed invisible. Water appeared like solid ground and land resembled water; it seemed to be another world created by the powers of Maya. The monkeys who were searching for Sita had entered here and, by the grace of Svayamprabha, were able to find their way out after a long time. (6.3.61)

6.3.65–67 Once, while they were spending their days thus, Somaprabha told Kalingasena: "As long as you are not married, my friendship with you can continue. Once you are married, how can I enter your husband's house? A woman friend's husband should not be seen or recognized."

6.4.1. Then, out of affection for Somaprabha, Kalingasena stood on the roof of the palace near the highway to follow her path with her eyes. At that very moment, a young king of the Vidyadharas, named Madanavega, saw her. (6.4.2)

[Madanavega performed severe penances to propitiate Shiva and win Kalingasena as his bride. Meanwhile, Somaprabha convinced Kalingasena that Udayana, the king of Vatsa, was the ideal man for her. Kalingasena was eager to meet him, and requested Somaprabha to use her magical powers to accomplish a meeting. Somaprabha consented, but cautioned her.]

6.5.6. "But take everything with you, including your own servants, for once you see the king of Vatsa, you will not be able to return. You will not see or even remember your parents any more, and having obtained your beloved, you will forget even me, who will be at a distance. For, O friend, I will not enter your husband's house."

Hearing this, the princess cried and said: "Then, O friend, bring the king of Vatsa here, because I will not be able to live without you even for a moment." (6.5.9)

[Somaprabha took Kalingasena to Kausambi, the capital of the king of Vatsa, but warned her that she ought not to try to meet the king on her own. Kalingasena disregarded her advice and sent a messenger to the king. The king treated her with respect, but, for various reasons, the marriage was postponed for six months. Somaprabha then took leave of her friend.]

6.6.193. "O friend, I will never return to you who are installed in your husband's house. Good women do not visit a friend's husband's house. Besides, I have been forbidden by my husband. As he is omniscient, I cannot even come to you in secret, drawn by my great love. Even today, he reluctantly granted me permission to come. O friend, there is nothing more I can do, so I will return home; if my husband permits, I will come again, overcoming my modesty." Somaprabha spoke tearfully to the princess

Kalingasena whose face was washed with tears, and, embracing her, the daughter of the Asuras returned to her own home as the day waned. (6.6.196)

[Kalingasena's plan to marry King Udayana was foiled by Madanavega who seduced her by pretending to be the king. Unwed, Kalingasena raises her daughter. When the girl is married to Udayana's son, Naravahanadatta, Somaprabha attends the wedding.]

Padma Purana: *Arjuni (Sanskrit)*[1]

Introduced by Ruth Vanita

The *Padma [Lotus] Purana* is a Vaishnava text (ca. twelfth century) devoted to the worship of Shri Krishna, incarnation of Vishnu. The Shri Krishna of this text is the god of full-blown medieval Vaishnavism, he whose erotic sport in Braja with Radhika and her friends, the cowherd women, represents the union of the divine with the human spirit.

However, the appearance of Arjuna in the *Padma Purana* brings about a rare and surprising conjunction between this Krishna and the Krishna of the *Mahabharata*. Arjuna's appearance here has gone unnoticed by most scholars, perhaps because of its anomalous nature.[2] The section extracted below is narrated by Sanatkumara to Krishna's friend Uddhava. Sanatkumara says he will narrate Arjuna's "experience in loneliness" and warns Uddhava not to divulge it freely to others. The section ends with repeated injunctions by Krishna to Arjuna and by Sanat to Uddhava not to let out this secret. The following chapter relates the similar experience of Narada, the divine sage, who also was transformed into a woman and sported with Krishna in that form for a year. Narada tells his disciple Gautama: "This is a great secret, the secret of secrets," and recounts how Krishna enjoined secrecy on him. Narada also tells Saunaka and other sages that this secret is to be guarded like the secret of one's mother having a paramour. The text also states that whoever reads or listens to it with devotion will obtain Krishna. It would seem that Vaishnava devotees were eager to guard their secret texts from anti-Vaishnavites who would misinterpret them as licentious.

---

1. Text used for this translation: *MahaPadma Puranam,* Part II (Delhi: Nag Publishers, 1984, reprint of Bombay: Shri Venkateswara Press, no date).
2. For instance, Robert P. Goldman, "Transsexualism, Gender and Anxiety in Traditional India," *Journal of the American Oriental Society* 113: 3 (July-September 1993): 374–401, mentions various accounts of Narada's transformation into a woman in his exhaustive list of sex change stories in ancient mythological texts but fails to mention Arjuna's sex change.

Arjuna's transformation into a woman in order to fulfill his desire to know the secret of Krishna constitutes a medieval reading of an ancient text—the *Mahabharata*. In the *Mahabharata*, Arjuna is represented as Krishna's loving friend whose devotion is expressed through *sakhya*, "loving companionship." In some branches of medieval Vaishnava devotion, *madhurya*, or "erotic love," becomes the dominant form of devotion.

The sections preceding this one (5.72–73) describe in detail how a series of male sages devoted to Krishna performed austerities and achieved rebirth as cowherd women. The Vaishnava rewriting of the idea of rebirth posits a woman's form as the highest human form attainable because it makes possible union with the divine, embodied in Krishna. Like any symbol, it has multiple dimensions—the cowherd women are said to be embodiments of the hymns of the *Vedas*, thus assimilating Vedic ritual tradition to popular devotion (*Padma Purana*, 5.73.31–36). The stories of Arjuna and Narada temporarily becoming women are both similar to and different from those of the sages being reborn as women. Since they return to their male form, Arjuna's and Narada's experiences remain, in one important sense, the experiences of men, whether we choose to read these as mystical, imagined, fantasized or disguised experiences.

Translated by Kumkum Roy

[Arjuna asks Krishna about the secret of his divine sport and how it can be witnessed. Krishna says Arjuna should not desire to witness it. Arjuna falls on the ground in despair. Krishna raises him lovingly in his arms and tells him that he will experience it if he worships the goddess Tripurasundari. Arjuna does so and is granted a sight of Krishna's *rasaleela*, or dance of love. Having seen the "great secret," Arjuna is overcome with love and loses consciousness.]

5.74.60 The goddess said: "After taking a bath in this lake, go to the eastern one, and having bathed in its waters, fulfill your desire."

She disappeared as soon as Partha [Arjuna], on hearing her words, plunged into the lake which was tinged with pollen from white, red, and blue lotuses, as well as lotuses that bloomed in the moonlight, whose waters were fragrant with drops of honey, which were agitated with the sound of swans, whose banks were decorated with jewels, and which rippled in a gentle breeze.

Emerging from the water, and looking all around, the one with the charming smile was confused. She found herself with an incomparable, pure, radiant form emanating golden rays, with the sparkle of youth and a face like the autumn moon. Her hair was dark, curly, and shining with jewels, the rays of an auspicious vermilion mark glowed on her forehead. Her raised, creeperlike eyebrows eclipsed the bows of the god of love.

Her playful eyes were like dark clouds; her cheeks shone with the luster of her jeweled earrings. Her wonderful arms resembled delicate lotus stalks; her exquisite hands seemed to have robbed the autumn lotuses of their beauty. A skillfully crafted band of gold adorned her waist, her hips shone with a tinkling girdle. Her vulva was covered with shining cloth, her lotuslike feet were adorned with tinkling, jewel-studded anklets. She possessed all the skills in the art of love and all good qualities, besides being adorned with every kind of ornament. This epitome of beauty looked at herself in wonder. She had forgotten everything about her previous body owing to the illusion created by the beloved of the cowherd women. She stood there, bewildered, not knowing what to do. (74)

[Arjuni meets the cowherd women, who give her a bath and help her to worship the goddess Radhika.]

135. She worshiped the goddess whose limbs shone with molten gold, who was adorned with all kinds of ornaments, whose form and beauty were marvelous, who was pleased and could grant boons.

144. Then the goddess, the granter of boons, who was compassionate toward her devotees, spoke. She said: "The words of my female friend are true. You are my dear friend. Get up and come with me, I will fulfill your desire." Hearing the words of the goddess, which were what her heart desired, Arjuni's hair stood on end, her eyes filled with tears, and she fell at the goddess's feet. (146)

162. Then the lord, the son of Yashoda, pleased with [her] devotion, smiled, glanced at the goddess Radhika and said: "Bring her here quickly." Thus commanded, the goddess sent her friend Sharada, who brought her [Arjuni] before the playful one. She, on coming before the lord Krishna, was overwhelmed with love and, wonderstruck by all that she saw, fell on the golden floor. She raised herself with difficulty and slowly opened her eyes. She broke into a sweat, her hair stood on end, and she trembled. She saw that the place was wonderful and charming.

171. . . . It was enchanting with flowers of all seasons. Their fragrance was more powerful than that of the aloe. Showers of honeydrops made it charmingly cool. . . . It resounded with the calls of cuckoos, pigeons, female parrots, and other birds hidden amongst the leaves. The dance of intoxicated peacocks heightened passion. It glowed darkly like collyrium produced from nectar.

She saw Krishna whose shiny, dark, curly, fragrant hair was tied with the finest plume of an intoxicated peacock. His ear ornament of flowers attracted swarms of bees, his cheeks shone like mirrors, bright with beelike locks of hair. His expansive forehead was decorated with a lovely auspicious mark. His nose resembled the flower of sesame or the beak of the king of birds. His beautiful smiling lips, red like the bimba fruit, inflamed desire. He was charming on account of his necklace, which resembled a wildflower. His broad shoulders were covered with a garland of the divine tree, and attracted thousands of female bees. . . . His beautiful waist resembled that of a lion, and his navel was very deep. His knees were like a good tree, rounded, and not too far apart. He was adorned with excellent ornaments—bracelets, armlets and anklets. His penis was covered with a part of his yellow garments. His beauty and charm excelled that of a choir of love gods. Enchanting were the charming melodies produced by his flute. He enchanted the three worlds and immersed them in the ocean of happiness. His every limb seemed to be that of the god of love, satiated with the pleasure of *rasa*.

189. On seeing Radhika humbly offering a betel leaf to the one with the charming smile, who seemed to be to her left, Arjuniya was overcome with desire. Seeing her in that state, the all-knowing Hrishikesa [Krishna] took her hand and indulged in all the sports in the forest. The great lord sported with her secretly, at will. Then putting his arm on her shoulder, and coming to Sharada, he said: "Quickly bathe this slender, gently smiling lady, who is exhausted with play, in the western lake."

The goddess Sharada took her to the western lake and said: "Bathe here," and the tired one did as she was told. She who entered the water was transformed once again into Arjuna, and rose at the spot where the lord of the gods and of Vaikuntha stood. Krishna, seeing that Arjuna was depressed and heartbroken, touched him with his magic hand, so that he became aware of his nature.

Shri Krishna said: "O Dhananjaya, I bless you, my dear [male] friend. There is none equal to you in the three worlds, as you know my secret. O Arjuna, you will curse me if you talk to anyone about the secret which you wanted to know and have experienced." (198)

Ayyappa and Vavar:
Celibate Friends

Ruth Vanita

Ayyappa, also known as Aiyanar, Sastha, and Hariharaputra, who is today the focus of a major devotional tradition, emerged from the fusion of a Dravidian god of tribal provenance with the Puranic story of Shiva's sexual interaction with Vishnu.[1] For the story from the *Bhagvata Purana*, see p. 69.

What is noteworthy about the story is that Shiva is not deluded in the way the demons are. Shiva asks Vishnu to assume the Mohini form for his own viewing pleasure, his "delight," as one text puts it, and Vishnu acquiesces. There is no external pressure, only their own volition. Shiva is eulogized both in the *Mahabharata* and the *Puranas* as neither god, demon, mortal nor animal, neither man, woman nor eunuch. As Wendy O'Flaherty remarks, "without any feeling of contradiction, the devotee sees in Shiva the realization of all possibilities."[2]

In the Ayyappa legend Vishnu as Mohini becomes pregnant from intercourse with Shiva, and produces a child. Ashamed, Vishnu drops the baby to earth, where it is found and adopted by the Pandyan king Rajasekhara of Pantalam.[3] This account of the god's birth is not found in the three Puranic narratives. The medieval legend invents it and refers to the child as *ayoni jata* (born of a not-vagina). The term *ayoni* is the same term used in texts like the *Manusmriti* and the *Arthashastra* to refer to nonvaginal sex of all kinds.

---

1. For a discussion of dating the growth of the Ayyappa legend, see Radhika Sekar, *The Sabarimalai Pilgrimage and Ayyappan Cultus* (Delhi: Motilal Banarsidass, 1992), 19–27. Sekar inclines to placing the historical Ayyappan in the eleventh century but other scholars favor a somewhat later date.
2. Wendy Doniger O'Flaherty, *Siva: The Erotic Ascetic* (Oxford: Oxford University Press, 1973), 253.
3. Sekar, *Sabarimalai Pilgrimage,* 18.

The child grows up to become a renowned warrior. In some versions he destroys a demon. He also gathers an army and fights the bandit chieftains who are ravaging the countryside. One of them is the Muslim pirate Vavar. Overcome in battle, Vavar becomes a close friend of Ayyappa and joins forces with him. It would appear that this story unites the local cult of a deified warrior chieftain with the Puranic account of Hariharaputra. Hariharaputra, whose name literally means "the son (*putra*) of Vishnu (Hari) and Shiva (Hara)," in his embodiment as Ayyappa (lit. father), represents the reconciliation of Vaishnavites and Shaivites who had often come into conflict in the South. Endowed with the immense powers of both the preserver and the destroyer gods, he embodies the power to protect.

The Ayyappa tradition incorporates Vavar as the inseparable companion of the god, thus symbolizing also a Hindu-Muslim rapprochement. The main Ayyappa temple at Sabarimalai, believed to have been originally constructed by Ayyappa's foster father on Ayyappa's instructions before the latter ascended to heaven, has a shrine for Vavar. All pilgrims, whether Hindu or Muslim, are supposed to carry an offering of pepper for Vavar along with other offerings for Ayyappa. The shrine is managed by Muslims who claim to be Vavar's descendants. Pepper perhaps commemorates the fact that Arab traders had come to the Malabar coast in search of pepper and other spices. Other Ayyappa temples elsewhere duplicate this pattern. Vavar is represented in his shrine not by an image but by a sword.

Vavar is a Robin Hood figure in the legend: "Since Vavar distributed the major portion of his plundered goods among his followers and the poor people, he had a large number of followers."[4] Thus, he and Ayyappa, both benevolent protector figures, are suited to one another.

Vavar is also part of the ritual in other ways. There are several songs in his praise, and all-night dance dramas performed by devotees before they set out on pilgrimage, include a dance performed by two men, representing Ayyappa and Vavar. One carries a knife and the other a sickle. Ayyappa is said to have instructed his foster father to build the shrine for Vavar, saying: "Consider Vavar as myself." This phrasing recalls Krishna's many statements in the *Mahabharata*, that Arjuna is inseparable from himself.[5] The Ayyappa Sewa Sangam, established about three decades ago to help the pilgrims, which has developed into a huge all-India organization with 600 branches and conducts many activities, including maintenance of forty temples, holding conventions, working for Harijan welfare, running religious classes, and producing literature and music cassettes, claims that Vavar wanted to become a Hindu but Ayyappa told him not to.

---

4. P. T. Thomas, *Sabarimalai and Its Sastha: An Essay on the Ayyappa Movement* (Bangalore: The Christian Literature Society, 1973), 11.
5. It is interesting that K. R. Vaidyanathan, *Pilgrimage to Sabari* (Bombay: Bharatiya Vidya Bhavan, 1978; 1992), 152–53, compares Ayyappa devotees to Arjuna who was chosen by Krishna as his special friend.

This closeness with Vavar is enacted in the context of celibacy. Ayyappa took a vow of celibacy and refused the marriage proposal made to him by Leela, a woman who had been imprisoned in a monstrous buffalo form, Mahishi, as the result of a curse and whom he had freed by slaying the buffalo. Ayyappa agreed to let Leela live as his companion, or Shakti, and instructed his father to build a shrine for her as well. Thus, the Ayyappa temples also have shrines to her in the form of the goddess Mallikapurathamma. Her shrine stands to the left of Ayyappa's image and Vavar's to his right. Vavar too is represented as unmarried in all narratives. The image of Ayyappa riding the tiger, an animal normally associated with the goddess in her fearful form, and killing the buffalo demon, also a task usually accomplished by the goddess, may suggest that in addition to the powers of Vishnu and Shiva, he has the goddess's powers or himself has female energies.

Ayyappa's celibacy is mirrored in that of his brothers, the other two sons of Shiva, Ganesha and Kartikeya, who are bachelors in many traditions and also leaders of all-male armies. All his temples have a shrine to Ganesha and some also have a shrine for Kartikeya. Ayyappa's celibacy is imitated by his devotees who take a forty-one day vow to refrain from sex and other indulgences such as animal food while preparing for and undergoing the pilgrimage. During this period, they live a simple life, sleeping on the floor and trying to be courteous and helpful to everyone.[6] Women of reproductive age are not permitted to go on the pilgrimage, which means that the pilgrims are almost all male.

Many students of medieval Europe, such as John Boswell, Janice Raymond, and Bernadette Brooten, have pointed out that in societies where marriage and parenthood were near universal and were arranged by families for young people, a religious vow of celibacy was almost the only way a person could refuse heterosexuality and choose to live in a same-sex community. In ancient and medieval Indian texts too, a similar opposition between city dweller and forest dweller is evident. Unlike the organized monasticism of Buddhism, the forest *ashram* was nevertheless a space in which people could choose not to marry, if they so desired. Both epic and Puranic texts construct the forest simultaneously as a space of celibacy and as a space of mystery and magic, where sex change, illicit types of sexuality and miraculous birth occur.

It is therefore significant that Ayyappa is characterized as a forest dweller. The Sabarimalai temple is situated on a mountain in the midst of dense forests, and the journey to it, conducted barefoot, leads the pilgrim away from the amenities of domesticity and civilization, into the forest where he may encounter wild beasts, bandits, and other hardships.[7] He performs this jour-

---

6. Accounts of the versions of the Ayyappa legend and of the temples, pilgrimage, and rituals are drawn from Sekar, *Sabarimalai Pilgrimage,* and Vaidyanathan, *Pilgrimage to Sabari.*
7. While these hardships have been considerably ameliorated in recent years, some of them still remain. As recently as three decades ago, A. Sreedhara Menon in his account of the

ney in same-sex community and finally reaches a temple where god is represented, unlike most Hindu gods, not with his consort but with his celibate friends, male and female.

A Kannada song in praise of Ayyappa explains why Ayyappa had to return from heaven to earth and take up his abode in the forest. The song narrates how Ayyappa replaced Brahma in heaven and decided to change the order of the universe by decreeing that human beings should not die. This change makes sense in the context of Ayyappa's own refusal to participate in reproduction—as many commentators have noticed, that the Hindu goddesses do not bear children is in part related to the idea that those who have children to replace them must themselves die and that heterosexual sex is thus innately related to death. The story continues with the gods, alarmed at Ayyappa's innovation, asking the divine mischief-making sage, Narada, to come to their rescue. Narada, pretending to praise Ayyappa, asks him how he is related to Parvati, Shiva's wife, and Lakshmi, Vishnu's wife, since Shiva is his father and Vishnu his mother. Puzzled, Ayyappa leaves Brahma's throne and withdraws into the forest where he stands to this day, still trying to figure out an answer to this unanswerable question. The song shows a wry awareness of the tension between normative heterosexuality and the person of the god, a tension that animates Ayyappa devotion.[8]

Female presence is incorporated in the tradition in a nonconjugal way through the shrine of the goddess Leela who also took a vow of celibacy after Ayyappa refused her proposal of marriage. Ayyappa is said to have told her that he would marry her only when devotees stop coming to his temple. In one version, he referred to fresh young devotees. Therefore, each devotee who goes to the temple buys a small wooden arrow. On the way to the temple, devotees stick these arrows in a large peepal tree to signal their presence. Thus, the devotees actively participate in keeping the god free from marriage. Their presence is crucial to enable him to remain unmarried.

After the pilgrimage season, there is a ritual wherein the goddess's image, decked in bridal finery, is carried in a procession to the tree. The bridal procession has to return disappointed after witnessing the evidence, in the form of the arrows in the tree, that the devotees are still coming to the temple. This ritual is reported by one observer to cause "amused delight" among the spectators, although another remarks that the spectators commiserate with the goddess.[9] Given the defining centrality of the bridal procession to the personal and social lives of most Indians, this inversion, whereby the frustration of marriage expectations is construed

---

cult, in *The Kerala District Gazetteer* (Quilon: Government of Kerala, 1964), described the forests as "inhospitable" and "infested by elephants, tigers and other wild beasts" (178).

8. The song was transcribed by N. Chinnappa and published in Kannada by the Institute of Kannada Studies, University of Mysore, 1924. Sekar published an English translation of the song in *Sabarimalai Pilgrimage*, Appendix A, 117–26.
9. Sekar, *Sabarimalai Pilgrimage*, 68; and P. T. Thomas, *Sabarimalai*, 46–47.

as auspicious, is highly suggestive. It may function as therapeutic and also as a critique, albeit limited, of the compulsory force of the institution of marriage.

The all-male pilgrimage to Sabarimalai, which excludes women of reproductive age, can be seen as providing temporary freedom to men from the burdens of compulsory heterosexuality and reproduction. One woman researcher who did go on the pilgrimage describes the pervasive atmosphere of elation and joyous camaraderie that begins to dissolve only on the return journey. In her words: "One can sense an air of reluctance to leave. One elderly devotee informed me that he felt carefree here at the holy summit—like a young lad."[10] It is significant that each devotee who takes the vow is himself addressed as Ayyappa throughout the period of preparation as well as on the pilgrimage. Thus, he temporarily shares the freedom and bliss of the god's unmarried state.

A very large number of devotees have been making the pilgrimage every year for decades. It may thus function as an annual safety valve for men to get relief from the pains of compulsory and organized heterosexuality. Of course, this relief is only temporary and is non-threatening since it is not expressed as a direct critique of marriage, nor does it require the devotee to choose between marriage and asceticism. It allows him to have the best of both worlds.

Ayyappa devotion, which is primarily south Indian, has been growing by leaps and bounds in recent years and drawing devotees from other parts of the country and also from abroad. The devotees are from all castes, and many Muslims and Christians also make the pilgrimage. Their presence has been ascribed by some commentators to the tradition's syncretist features. It reconciles differences between Shiva and Vishnu, local tribal deities and the pantheon, and perhaps even Hinduism and Buddhism. One of Ayyappa's names is Sastha, and the main chant of the pilgrims "*Swamiye Saranam Ayyappe*" seems to echo Buddhist phrasing. Some scholars argue that Buddhist influence in south India is evident in these and other features of the tradition, such as its openness to all castes and its emphasis on simple egalitarian living during the pilgrimage.[11] In this context, one of the god's names, Manikantha, ascribed by the legend to his having been found as a baby wearing a bell round his neck, may connect to the *Manikantha Jataka* (see p. 37).

Some evidence suggests that with the phenomenal growth of Ayyappa worship in recent decades and its institutionalization through such organizations as the Ayyappa Sewa Sangh, there is a move to domesticate the god. He is now increasingly being worshiped in homes in towns and villages instead of only in the forest. Many pilgrims are not aware of the significance

---

10. Sekar, *Sabarimalai Pilgrimage,* 85–86.
11. For a discussion of the syncretist features and the possibly Buddhist elements of the cult, see Sekar, *Sabarimalai Pilgrimage,* 20–24; Vaidyanathan, 9–10, and *The Kerala District Gazetteer,* 179–80.

of Vavar. Many go on pilgrimage in order to ask for progeny or the resolution of other family problems.[12] With the drawing of the whole family into the ambience of worship and the demands from some quarters that women be allowed to participate in the pilgrimage, which has become much easier and safer than it used to be, the god and his tradition may well be on their way to domestication.

---

12. See Vaidyanathan, *Pilgrimage to Sabari,* for these developments. He reports many instances of devotees whose problems were solved after they went on the pilgrimage. The problems range from homesickness, childlessness, baldness, financial worries, to their own, a wife's or a child's sickness. He also describes other devotees who make the pilgrimage repeatedly merely because it makes them feel happy, without seeking any material benefits from it.

Krittivasa Ramayana:
The Birth of Bhagiratha (Bengali)[1]

Introduced by Ruth Vanita

This text, which even today is the most popular Bengali version of the *Ramayana*, is ascribed to the fourteenth-century poet Krittivasa; however, additions to it continued to be made well into the eighteenth century.[2] The sage Bhagiratha is famed for having succeeded in bringing the river Ganga down to earth from heaven. Three of his forefathers had tried and failed to perform this task. Even today, in many Indian languages, the term *Bhagiratha prayatna* is the equivalent of a "Herculean enterprise."

In the *Puranas*, Bhagiratha is born when his parents worship Surabhi, the wish-fulfilling divine cow. However, the medieval text extracted below ascribes Bhagiratha's birth to divinely blessed sexual intercourse between two women. This text draws on the ancient medical text *Sushruta Samhita*, which declares that a child born to two women will have no bones (see p. 26).

Translated by Kumkum Roy

Adi Kanda

Dilipa ruled like Indra, the king of the gods, but was sad as he did not have a son. Leaving behind his two wives in the city of Ayodhya, Dilipa went in search of the Ganga.

---

1. Text used for this translation is *Sachitra Krittivasi Saptakanda Ramayana,* ed. Chandrodaya Vidyavinod Bhattacharyya (Calcutta: Manoranjan Bandopadhyaya at Hitavadi Pustakalaya, 1914). The extract is from the *Adi Kanda,* tracing the ancestry of Rama, incarnation of Vishnu.
2. For the dating problem with regard to the *Krittivasa Ramayana,* see Sukumar Sen, *History of Bengali Literature* (New Delhi: Sahitya Akademi, 1960, 1979), 67–69.

He performed a severe penance for countless years, living on water and fasting, but he neither found the Ganga nor became free of his sorrow. King Dilipa died and went to Brahma's world. On his death the city of Ayodhya was kingless. In heaven, Brahma and Indra were worried: "We have heard that Vishnu will be born in the family of the sun. How will this be possible if the line comes to an end?"

All the gods consulted together and decided to send the three-eyed god, Shiva, to Ayodhya. Riding his bull, Shiva went to Dilipa's two queens and said to them: "By my blessings, one of you will have a son." Hearing Shiva's words, the two women said: "We are widows, how can we have a child?" Shankara replied: "You two have intercourse with one another. By my blessings one of you will have a lovely child." Having bestowed this boon, the god who destroys the three worlds went his way.

The two wives of Dilipa took a bath. They lived together in extreme love. After some days, one of them menstruated. Both of them knew one another's intentions and enjoyed love play, and one of them conceived.

Ten months passed, it was time for the birth. The child emerged as a lump of flesh. Both of them cried with the son in their lap: "Why did the three-eyed one bless us with such a son? He has no bones, he is a lump of flesh, he cannot move about. Seeing him, the whole world will laugh at us." Weeping, they put him in a basket and went to the bank of the river Sarayu to throw him into the water.

The sage Vashistha saw them and understood everything through his powers of meditation. He said: "Leave the child on the road. Someone will have compassion on him, seeing him helpless."

The two of them left their son on the road and went home. Just then the sage Ashtavakra came along for his bath. Bent at eight places, the sage walked with great difficulty. Seeing the child from a distance, Ashtavakra thought: "If you are mimicking me in order to make fun of me, may your body be destroyed by my curse. If, however, your body is naturally as it appears, may you, by my blessing, become like Madanmohan, the god of erotic love."

Ashtavakra was as powerful as Vishnu, so neither his curses nor his blessings failed to bear fruit. He was a sage endowed with great and miraculous powers. The prince stood up. Through his powers of meditation, the sage came to know that this son of Dilipa was an auspicious one, a great man.

The sage called the two queens, who took their son and returned home, delighted. The sage came too and performed all the sacred rituals. Because he was born of two vulvas (*bhagas*) he was named Bhagiratha. The great poet Krittivasa is a recognized scholar. In this Adi Kanda he sings of the birth of Bhagiratha.

[When the child was five years old, he was sent to study with the sage Vashistha. One day, when the children were quarreling, another child called him a bastard. The child was deeply hurt and did not return home. His mother grew worried and went in search of him. She wiped his tears and asked what ailed him. He told her that he had been insulted, and asked to what caste he belonged and whose son he was. His mother then told him the truth that he was named Bhagiratha because he was born through divine blessing, of two *bhagas,* or vulvas, that his father had died before his conception, while trying to bring down Ganga, and that he belonged to the race of the sun, in the city of Ayodhya. At this, Bhagiratha laughed with pleasure and said that if he wished, he would definitely be able to bring the goddess Ganga down. He declared his intention to set out the very next day to perform austerities. At this, his mothers grew anxious and tried to dissuade him, but he disregarded them, took Guru Vashistha's blessing and set out.]

Jagannath Das *(Oriya)*

Sumanyu Satpathy

Jagannath Das, fifteenth-century poet-mystic, author of the Oriya *Bhagabata*, and disciple of major mystic Shri Chaitanya, is a household name in Orissa. Scholars tend to agree that Das was born in 1490 and died in 1550. Hagiographical biographies of him date from about a century after his death. Commentators have seen Das's relationship with Chaitanya as a mystical love based on Krishna-Radha love and on the repudiation of conventional marriage and worldly life. In India the relationship between *guru* and disciple has for centuries institutionalized a shared, almost familial, life for men. I present here the least controversial aspects of the legend.

Of the extant biographies of Shri Chaitanya, the most important is the early seventeenth-century *Chaitanya Charitamrita* by Krishna Das. Shri Chaitanya, who is viewed by his followers as an incarnation of Krishna, was born at Navadip in Bengal in February 1486. As a baby he would stop crying only when Krishna's name was chanted. He was gold-complexioned, so people said his inner self was that of Krishna and his outer that of Radha. Chaitanya's mother arranged his marriage but his wife died young. His second wife, Vishnupriya, who was thirteen when they married, witnessed his transformation as he became increasingly devoted to Krishna. Chaitanya was often absent and engaged in all-night sessions of praising Krishna, in which only his close associates were allowed to participate. As Chaitanya's message of love spread, he became very popular and also met with opposition. Finally he renounced the world, taking the name of Chaitanya (Consciousness). Within a month of his initiation in 1509, he took leave of his mother and wife and left for Puri, the coastal abode of the Oriya tribal deity Jagannath, identified with Krishna.

Oriya Vaishnavism received a fillip at this time from five men known as *Panchasakha* (five male friends)—Balaram Das, Jagannath Das, Achyuta Nanda Das, Ananta Das, and Yashobanta Das, who lived in all-male monasteries.[1] Although they were very popular, the

---

1. See K. C. Mishra, *Orissi Vaishnava Dharma* (Bhubaneswar: Orissa Sahitya Akademi, 1980).

king Prataprudradev is said to have been hostile to them, especially to Jagannath Das, whom he ordered out of the monastery. Das resisted his father's attempts to marry him when he was twelve. He had mastered the scriptures at this early age and was able to translate complex Sanskrit into transparent Oriya. Many devotees were attracted by the young scholar who explicated the Sanskrit *Bhagabata* in Oriya under a holy banyan tree in the Jagannatha temple premises.

Das was nineteen when he met Shri Chaitanya. Biographers describe the encounter with varying details. Dibakar Das describes it thus in his *Jagannath Charitamrita:* "At this time Shri Chaitanya arrived at the banyan tree with his friends and was delighted to hear Jagannath Das's rendition. Overwhelmed with love he held Das in a tight embrace. They stayed in this posture for two days and a half."[2] The following explanation of their attraction was offered, in one version of the legend, by Das, and in another version, by Chaitanya. In a mystic vision Radha and Krishna exchanged looks of love, and then Krishna laughed. Chaitanya was born from that laughter. In response Radha smiled, and Das was born from her smile. Chaitanya told Das, "You are a partial manifestation of Shri Radha and the supreme object of Krishna's love." He then took off his colored wrapper and tied it round Das's head, saying "You have spoken great words and you will henceforth be known as very great."

Jagannath became Chaitanya's constant companion. According to hagiographer Ishwar Das, Chaitanya used to address Jagannath as *sakhi* (female friend). In Gaudiya Vaishnavism, male devotees identified with the cowherd women who were Krishna's lovers and Radha's friends. In *Chaitanyaganoddedipika*, Jagannath is said to have been known by female names Bilasakya, Tinkini, and Kamalatika in previous births. Jagannath identified with Radha and her handmaids. Seeing Krishna in Chaitanya, he thought of himself as Chaitanya's maidservant. As part of devotional ritual, he would massage Chaitanya's legs and wear the clothes Chaitanya had taken off, including his loincloth. This intimate relationship continued till Chaitanya's death.[3]

Chaitanya's Bengali followers were so piqued by his feelings for Das that they left Puri, never to return. Chaitanya strictly shunned the company of women yet some people accused him of immorality. His fondness for an Oriya Brahman boy was analyzed thus by an associate, Damodar: "You show affection to the son of a Brahman widow. She may be a Brahman widow and a chaste anchoress, but she is young and fair. You too, O Lord! are young and fair, and by your affection to the boy, you give people opportunity for whispers."

---

2. Quoted in Prallhad Charan Mohanti, "The Literary Value in the *Bhagabata* of Jagannath Das," in Brajamohan Mohanti, ed., *Bhaktakabi Jagannath Das* (Cuttack: Orissa Book Store, 1990), 49.

3. Brajamohan Mohanti, *Jagannath Das and Oriya Bhagabata Sanskriti* (Cuttack: Orissa Book Store, 1990).

But Chaitanya's love for the boy was so intense that he disregarded Damodar's advice.[4] Rival Vaishnava cults also leveled charges of promiscuity against Das, but these were effectively repulsed by Das's followers.

In his *Bhagabata*, Das negatively depicts various practices of Kaliyuga:

"Maidens will choose and marry
Whoever they fancy.
The wicked and the villainous will prosper.
None will care for the upright and truthful.
Women will cohabit with women,
Men will know men.
Men, once they find whores, will desert their wives. . . ."[5]

4. Quoted in Jagannath Patnaik, "Chaitanya's Visit to Orissa as depicted in *Chaitanya Charitamrita* of Krishna Das Kaviraj," in H. C. Das ed., *Sri Chaitanya in the Religious Life of India* (Calcutta: Punthi Pustak, 1989), 137.
5. Jagannath Das, *Granthabali* (Bhubaneswar: Sahitya Akademi,1972), passage translated by me.

Part III

Introduction: Medieval Materials
in the Perso-Urdu tradition

Saleem Kidwai

During the early medieval period there are a few scattered references to same-sex love while in the late medieval period a huge body of literature on same-sex love develops. The information available overwhelmingly concerns men.

In the closing years of the tenth century armed migrants began to move into India from west of the Hindukush mountains. These raiding forays, initially led by Sultan Mahmud, ruler of the small principality of Ghaznah in northern Afghanistan, started a process of invasion that culminated in the establishment of kingdoms ruled by Muslims in India. These new rulers, their armies, and others who followed in their wake impacted Indian society in many ways.[1]

The new migrants carried Perso-Turko-Arabic cultural traditions into India. Originally this ruling elite and their cultural traditions were confined to military centers but soon got disseminated over large areas through the activities of the Sufis. Both courts and Sufis affected medieval literature but the latter influence was farther reaching.

Homoerotically inclined men are continuously visible in Muslim medieval histories and are generally described without pejorative comment. One very important reason for this visibility

---

1. For the social and political impact of these invasions and the resultant Muslim rule, see M. Mujeeb, *The Indian Muslims* (London: George Allen & Unwin, 1967), and M. Habeeb, *Politics of Society during Earlier Medieval India,* 2 vols. (New Delhi: People's Publishing House, 1981). For a useful survey of the economic impact, see T. Raychaudhari and I. Habib, eds., *Cambridge Economic History of India,* vol. 1 (Cambridge: Cambridge University Press, 1984).

is the cosmopolitanism of urban Islamic culture.[2] The new ruling elite had inherited the sophisticated mores of the Abbaside caliphate. Although the original conquerers of north India were slave troops or mercenaries from the fringes of the caliphate, the Muslim population was constantly supplemented by the migration of scholars, poets, and administrators from other kingdoms. These immigrants sought refuge in Delhi from the depredations of the Mongols who ravished most of Asia through the thirteenth and fourteenth centuries.

Two important features of this period concern us. First, the new ruling elite tended to settle in urban areas; increasing urbanization is a marked feature from the thirteenth century onward. The flourishing towns and markets created a culture of the streets based on interaction between men. In these bazaars men from different classes, castes and communities mingled; here homoerotically inclined men met and established relations. In urban marketplaces communal eating, drinking and social intercourse gradually eroded caste distinctions. For the poets the city was also the ideal place to be: "Because Majnu was crazy he headed for the jungle / Clever is he who enjoys his time in the city." (Abru)[3]

Second, the paper-making industry developed rapidly, resulting in a marked increase in texts from this period onwards. From the very beginning, the state funded the spread of literacy. By the fourteenth century, the book trade was established in bazaars. We also know that book dealers ordered books they thought would be more popular. So most of the texts we extract were available to people of different classes.

Medieval poetry depicts romantic and erotic interaction between men across class and religious divides. In Mir's *ghazals* (love poems) different male youths, including the sons of Sayyids, Brahmans, Mughals, Turks, gardeners, soldiers, masons, firework makers, washermen, moneychangers, boatmen, flower sellers, musicians, singers, goldsmiths, physicians, perfumers, and even sons of judges (*qazis*) and law-givers are included among "bazaar boys." Mir's narrative poem *Shola-i Ishq* is an example of a love affair between two males, one Muslim, one Hindu. Muslim mystic poets Madho Lal Hussayn (see p. 144), Ras Khan, and Sarmad were in love with Hindu boys.

In addition to meeting in the bazaars, men attracted to men also met at taverns, houses of entertainment, and brothels. Although a comparatively late account, Dargah Quli Khan's description of Delhi shows the tombs of saints and religious shrines as sites of festivals where liquor was drunk and homoerotically inclined men congregated (see p. 175). Despite Islamic injunctions against liquor, wine-drinking played an important part in city life. Rulers like Alauddin Khalji and, later, Akbar did prohibit or regulate social drinking, but their motiva-

---

2. Many historians have commented on the greater visibility of homosexuality in urban cultures. See, for instance, John Boswell, *Christianity, Social Tolerance and Homosexuality* (Chicago: University of Chicago Press, 1981), 207–41.

3. All translations are by Saleem Kidwai unless otherwise indicated.

tions were political rather than religious. The tavern (*maikhana*), the wine server (the *saqi*), the cup and the wine flask (*jaam* and *mina*) appear regularly in poetry. So do the the tavern keeper (*pir-i Mughan*) and the boys serving in these drinking establishments (*mugh bachche*). There is plenty of evidence to show that today's popular conception of the wine server as always a woman is inaccurate. Barani (see p. 131) states that in his youth he attended gatherings where both male and female wine servers and singers entertained the guests. Male brothels seem to have a long history, as Dargah Quli Khan's descriptions of highly organized ones indicate. Urdu poets often mention boys who grant favors only for a price.

Other institutions that grew substantially in the medieval period are slavery and harems. Domestic slavery existed in pre-Islamic India, but slavery took a different form now. Slave troops led by slave generals founded the Sultanate of Delhi.[4] The early Sultans were heavily dependent on slaves as soldiers. Alauddin Khalji (1296–1316) owned 50,000 slaves, and Firuz Shah Tughlaq (1357–1388) owned 180,000.[5] The Sultans patronised slave traders who provided them with slaves, mostly young boys, from all parts of the world.[6] Although the dependence on slave troops declined and became negligible by the sixteenth century, slaves continued as a major presence in urban areas.

Included among these slaves were a large number of eunuchs. Eunuchs were a prized commodity because they were considered the most reliable slaves. Since they had no progeny they had no reason to siphon away money. Their links with their owners were the closest personal links they had. They were therefore often entrusted with the most responsible positions.[7] Eunuchs were guardians of the harem, the institution that defined the relationship between the sexes in the ruling elite.[8] Harems grew phenomenally in size as the elite prospered.[9] Since endogamous marriages were allowed, women had to be secluded even from close male relatives. No sexually functional man could be entrusted with guarding and controlling the women, so eunuchs were given the job.

---

4. For a brief survey of the role that slaves played in Islamic history and in other states ruled by Muslims, see "Ghulam" in *Encyclopaedia of Islam* vol. 2 (Leiden: Brill, 1983), 1079–91.
5. Shams-i Siraj Afif, *Tarikh-i Firuz Shahi,* ed. Maulvi Vilayat Hussain (Calcutta: Royal Asiatic Society, 1891), 271–72.
6. Minhaj-al Siraj Juzjani, *Tabaqat-i Nasiri,* trans. H. G. Ravarty, vol. 2 (London: Gilbert and Rivington, 1881), 766, 796.
7. For an insightful study of the role played by eunuchs in kingdoms ruled by Muslims, see Indrani Chatterjee, *Gender, Slavery and Law in Colonial India* (Delhi: Oxford University Press, 1999).
8. See Saleem Kidwai, "Sultans, Eunuchs and Domestics: New Forms of Bondage in Medieval India," in M. Dingwaney and U. Patnaik, eds., *Chains of Servitude* (Madras: Sangam, 1985), 76–96.
9. M. Mujeeb remarks, "The *haram* of the Sultan was so far removed from family life that often the mothers of the sultan's sons could not be identified." *Indian Muslims* (London: George Allen & Unwin, 1967), 206–07.

Although Muslim traders had settled on the western peninsular coast soon after Arabia converted to Islam, Islam's presence as the religion of the conquerors had a different impact. Many consider the Quran unequivocal in its condemnation of homosexuality, which it addresses in connection with the Hebrew prophet Lot and the destruction of Sodom and Gomorrah. Lot said to the sinners of his city: "Do ye commit lewdness,/ Such as no people/ In creation (ever) committed before you?/ For ye practise your lusts/ On men in preference to women:/ Ye are indeed a people transgressing/ Beyond bounds."[10] (VII:80–81) And when they did not heed him, God "rained down on them a shower of brimstone:/ Then see what was the end/ Of those who indulged/ In sin and crime!" (VII:84). At least seven other passages in the Quran condemn the sin of Lot's people. The Quran also says: "If two men among you are guilty of lewdness,/ Punish them both./ If they repent and amend, leave them alone: for God is Oft -Returning, Most Merciful" (IV:16).[11] It is from Lot that the Arabic word for sodomists, *Luti*, is derived.

The *Shariah*, the unwritten law of Islam that is derived in part from *hadith* (traditions), the sayings attributed to the Prophet Muhammad, also defines homosexuality as a crime. Several pronouncements about same-sex acts are attributed to the Prophet. One of these is: "Doomed by God is he who does what Lot's people did." The Prophet is also supposed to have said: "No man should look at the private parts of another man, and no woman should look at the private parts of another woman, and no two men sleep [in bed] under one cover, and no two women sleep under one cover." In his last speech to the community, the Prophet is supposed to have said about anal sex: "Whoever has intercourse with a woman and penetrates her rectum, or with a man, or with a boy, will appear on the Last day stinking worse than a corpse; people will find him unbearable until he enters hell fire and God will cancel all his good deeds."[12] Al-Nuwayri, who compiled all the hadith of the Prophet, put the ones on sodomy together. According to him, both the active and passive participants should be killed by stoning. Al Nuwayri also reported that the first Caliph Abu Bakr ordered a sodomite to be buried under the debris of a wall and also advocated death by burning as punishment.[13] Other punishments prescribed were stoning, and throwing the offender headfirst off a minaret.[14]

---

10. From Abdullah Yusuf Ali's translation and commentary on the Quran.
11. The translator in his commentary adds "as the crime is most shameful, and should be unknown in well regulated society, the maximum punishment would of course be imprisonment for life," fn. 525.
12. Khalid Duran, "Homosexuality and Islam," in Arlene Swidler ed., *Homosexuality and World Religions,* (Valley Forge, PA: Trinity Press International, 1993), 182.
13. The former hadith was cited by the Taliban recently when they stood two men against a wall and drove a tank against it, causing it to fall on the men and crush them.
14. "Liwat," *Encyclopaedia of Islam* vol. 5 (Leiden: Brill, 1983), 776–77.

Of the jurists, Ibn Hambal prescribed the severest penalty, death by stoning. Others prescribed flagellation, the number of strokes varying from ten to one hundred. The Hanafi school, which came to be the predominant one in India, was far less severe. In any case, these legal provisions were rarely implemented since guilt was very difficult to establish. The Shariah demands incontrovertible evidence, such as confession or four faithful eyewitnesses confirming that they saw penetration occur, both for sodomy and adultery.[15] This suggests that anal sex alone is punishable as sodomy, and not other forms of sex between men. The difficulty of finding eyewitnesses to confirm instances of penetration in effect removes private acts between consenting individuals from the realm of punishment.

Orthodox Muslim theologians in India insisted that the Prophet recommended the harshest of punishments for homosexual sodomy. Shaikh Abdul Haq Muhaddis Dehlavi and Shah Waliullah, in the seventeenth and eighteenth centuries, on the basis of both the Quranic injunction (IV:16) and the reported hadith traditions, severely condemned sodomy and advocated extreme punishments for those who engaged in the act.[16] Many others hold that the Quran's injunction to forgive lewd men who repent and the Prophet's constant plea to sinners to repent indicate that punishment should not be too harsh. Compared to Christian Europe, trials and punishments for homosexuality are rare in the history of Muslim peoples in medieval times.

Some modern commentators insist that there is enough support in the Quran to make the orthodox position untenable. They cite passages from the Quran where beautiful boys and houris are promised to the virtuous in heaven (LII: 24; LVI: 24; LXXV:19). Wafer, in a recent study, has also pointed to the contradictions within reported hadith.[17] He quotes one tradition wherein the Prophet allowed an invert, whose wit pleased him, to be in the same room as his wives. He also quotes the hadith, variants of which have been quoted by Corbin and Schimmel, that the Prophet saw God as a beautiful youth with long hair and cap awry.[18] This picture of the beloved with his hair escaping from his headgear is one of the most popular images in Urdu and Persian poetry at least till the middle of the nineteenth century.

15. See Jehoeda Sofer, "Sodomy in the Law of Muslim States," in Arno Schmitt and Jehoeda Sofer, eds., *Sexuality and Eroticism among Males in Moslem Societies* (New York: Harrington Park Press, 1992), 1–24.
16. Cited by Mufti Zafiruddin, *Nasl Kushi* (Deoband, Uttar Pradesh: Mustafa-i Kutubkhana, 1965), 34, 37, 41–42, 101–2. Zafiruddin adds that no specific punishment was mentioned in the Quran because the Arabs were originally free from this "vice" (33).
17. Jim Wafer, "Muhammad and Male Homosexuality," in Stephen O. Murray and Will Roscoe, eds., *Islamic Homosexualities: Culture, History and Literature* (New York: New York University Press, 1997), 87–96. The authenticity of these traditions was debated by many generations of early Muslims.
18. Henri Corbin, *Creative Imagination in the Sufism of Ibn 'Arabi* (Princeton, NJ: Princeton University Press, 1969), 272; Annemarie Schimmel, *As Through a Veil: Mystical Poetry in Islam* (New York: Columbia University Press, 1982), 67–68. The Mughal prince Dara

Despite the severe position taken by the orthodox, homoerotically inclined Muslim males have been visible within the community from its inception. The Muslims who migrated to India were inheritors of a literary tradition that included not just pre-Islamic poetry but also *The Thousand and One Nights* and a large body of literature wherein male beauty and love between men were celebrated. Examples are the explicit poetry of Abu Niwas and the body of mystical poetry in Arabic and Persian.[19] In political discourse, relationships between rulers and their male lovers had been treated as a matter of practical politics.

Barani's attitude, for instance, seems to be in the tradition of the advice given in the *Qabus Namah*. In this text, Kai Ka'us ibn Iskandar, Prince of Gurgan, advises his son that even though falling in love with a male is natural for a man of "sensuous disposition," he should not "perpetually be in pursuit of your desire." He also advises against "any open display of passion" and warns his son to be careful when choosing a favorite. He cites the example of Masud, son of Mahmud of Ghaznah:

> Sultan Masud had ten slaves, Keepers of the Royal Robes, of whom one, named Nushtagin, was especially favoured by him. Several years passed without anyone's realizing who the Sultan's favourite was, because the gifts he distributed were all alike. Then, after five years, in a fit of drunkenness he said: "Register in Nushtagin's name everything that my father granted Ayaz." Thus it became known that the object of his affection was Nushtagin. . . . If [nevertheless] there is someone of whom you are passionately fond, let it be a person worthy of love; although the object of one's affections cannot always be a Ptolemy or a Plato, he should have some endowment of good sense. Although I know, too, that not every one can be Joseph,[20] son of Jacob, yet there must be in him some pleasing quality which shall prevent men from caviling and allow indulgence to be readily accorded to you.[21]

For Barani, as for most other medieval chroniclers, a homosexual attachment was condemned when its political implications were undesirable.

However, a brief departure from this tolerant attitude appears in the reign of Akbar (1556–1605). Projecting himself as the ideal ruler whose duties included overseeing his subjects' morals, he tried to regulate his courtiers' private lives.[22] He ordered that all of them

---

Shukoh also quoted this hadith in his *Sakinatul Awliya*. According to Naim, this hadith is not mentioned in A. J. Wensinck's *Concordance*. See C. M. Naim, "The Theme of Homosexual (Pederastic) Love in Pre-Modern Urdu Poetry," in Muhammad Umar Memon ed. *Studies in the Urdu Ghazal and Prose Fiction* (Madison: University of Wisconsin, Madison, Publication Series, #5, 1979), 120–142; 134 fn. 8.

19. For a recent analysis of such literature see J. W. Wright Jr. and Everett K. Rowson, *Homoeroticism in Classical Arabic Literature* (New York: Columbia University Press, 1997).
20. The Prophet Yusuf, known for his beauty.
21. Reuben Levy, trans., *A Mirror for Princes; The Qabus Nama* (New York: E. P. Dutton & Co, 1951), 171–76.
22. See Stephen P. Blake, "The Patrimonial-Bureaucratic Empire of the Mughals," in *Journal of Asian Studies* 39 (1979): 77–94.

should marry, and do so at a mature age so that the union would be fruitful. Marrying a barren woman was forbidden.[23] Homosexuality had no place in this concept of the empire as a family ruled by the perfect patriarch. Love between men was described as "the wicked ways of Transoxiana, which are neither consuming nor melting, neither love nor friendship."[24]

Even Akbar's disapproval could not stop many of his nobles becoming attached to other males. This tradition had been well established among the elite since the inception of Muslim rule in India. Sultan Mahmud of Ghaznah, often projected as the ideal Muslim ruler by medieval Muslim political theorists such as Barani, was in love with his slave Ayaz.[25] Mubarak Shah Khalji was in love with Khusro to the point of distraction (see p. 133). Terry, an Englishman who visited India in the early part of the sixteenth century, wrote about the Emperor Jahangir's personal establishment where he kept "little boys" for "a wicked use."[26] Jahangir, son of Akbar, discussed with another visitor the relative attractions of fair and dark slave boys (see p. 143). Sexual relations between eunuchs and their masters were frequent. Alauddin Khalji was enamored of Malik Kafur (see p. 132). A Mughal nobleman, Mira Nathan, was enamored of a couple of eunuchs and besotted by a beautiful one called Khwaja Mina.[27] According to Abu'l Fazl, the ruler of Bijapur, Adil Shah, who was "continually straining the skirt of chastity," had acquired two beautiful eunuchs. In 1580, when, "in the darkness of a private chamber, [he] stretched out the arm of improper lust against one of them," the eunuch stabbed him.[28] Some eunuchs operated as pimps and ran brothels, as described by Dargah Quli Khan (see p. 180).

The Muslim soldiers who carved out independent principalities were mostly recent converts to Islam. Although with the proselytising zeal that typifies new converts, they claimed to be waging a holy war on infidels or ruling according to the dictates of holy law, their adherence to the Shariah was in most cases extremely tenuous. Nothing could be more indicative of this than their acceptance of a female ruler, Razia (1236–40), even though all theologians and jurists deemed females unfit to rule.[29] Their position as a minority in India was not the only reason why the Muslim elite did not find it necessary to live according to the

23. Abu'l Fazl, *Ain-i Akbari,* trans. J. H. Blochmann (Calcutta: Royal Asiatic Society, 1873), I: 277–78.

24. Abu'l Fazl, *Akbarnamah* trans. H. S. Jarret (Calcutta, Asiatic Society, 1949), II: 121.

25. J. Matini, "Ayaz" in Ehsaan Yarshater, ed., *Encyclopaedia Iranica* (London: Routledge & Kegan Paul, 1989), III: 133–34.

26. William Foster, ed., *Early Travels in India* (London: Oxford University Press, 1921), 311.

27. M. I. Borah, trans., *Baharistan-i Ghaybi* (Gauhati: Narayani Hindiqui Historical Institute, 1936), 228.

28. Abu'l Fazl, *Akbarnamah,* 440–41.

29. Among many obvious examples of accommodation to indigenous traditions of the newly conquered lands is early Muslim rulers' continuing use on their coins of the image of the Hindu goddess Lakshmi along with Arabic inscriptions.

dictates of the orthodox. The other reason was the crucial role played by the Sufis, the Muslim mystics, in the growth and definition of Islam in India.

Islamic mysticism had developed a full-fledged institutional structure and become a movement by the time it spread in India. Muslim mystics had come into contact with mystics of other religions and absorbed gnostic and neo-Platonic influences. Unlike the orthodox who believed that adherence to dogma and conformity with the Shariah ensured salvation, Sufis believed that personal experience of divine love was the true way. The early history of Sufism in West Asia is one of persecution by the orthodox. Mansur Hallaj (858–922) proclaimed his metaphysical leanings in the statement "*ana'l Haqq*" (I am the Truth) and was executed. He became the ideal martyr for all Sufis. The early Sufis were viewed with suspicion by the orthodox. However, renowned scholars and theologians like Imam Ghazzali (1058–1111) and Muhiuddin Ibn al Arabi (1165–1240) argued for acceptance of "sober" Sufism, and by the thirteenth century Sufism was no longer considered subversive.

Sufis tended to be classified into two main streams—the *ba shara* (within the Shariah, also referred to as the "sober" Sufis) and the *be shara* (without the Shariah, also called the "intoxicated" Sufis). The former did not challenge the Shariah, even if they did not strictly follow its tenets. The latter, on the other hand, led defiantly independent lives on the margins of mainstream mysticism.[30] Naturally, the former made a larger impact on society. They were organized into orders (*silsillas*), each order having its own spiritual lineage of masters, and lived in monasterylike establishments called *khanqahs*. The pivot of this institutionalized Sufism was the *pir* (master). Each spiritual aspirant had to be accepted as a *murid* (disciple) by a pir, often referred to as the "Shaikh," who became the intercessor between the murid and the divine. The pir was considered a *wali* (friend of God). The murid's submission of his life and ego to the pir was the predominant feature of Sufism by the time it impacted India. When the pir felt a murid had graduated spiritually, he would appoint him his *khalifa* (viceroy) and assign him a spiritual territory where he would establish his own khanqah and enroll his own murids. This chain of spiritual masters with their own territories made for the organized and rapid dissemination of Sufism in India.

Sufism was attractive to newly converted Muslims and to non-Muslims because it foregrounded personal devotion, as opposed to the regimen of a dogma.[31] The method of devotion

---

30. An interesting example is Aftab Rai Ruswa (died 1747), whose corpse is said to have smelled of roses even after it was bathed in liquor in conformity with his will. He is said to have fallen in love and then left home to wander around naked. He had never met his beloved. One day when he came face to face with him, he kissed his face. The boy could not bear this and stabbed him in the stomach. The Sufi refused any help from bystanders. *Shab Khun* vol. 32, no. 218 (July 1998): 79.

31. For useful studies of Sufism see A. J. Arberry, *An Introduction to the History of Sufism* (London: Longmans, 1942); R. A. Nicholson, *The Mystics of Islam* (London: G. Bell,

adopted by the Sufis was not the prescribed prayer but *zikr*, or the mention of God's name as a meditative exercise. The zikr of the Sufis tended to stress the beauty of God and his nurturing quality. Music and dance were introduced as means of zikr, which made it more attractive to those unfamiliar with Arabic, the language of high Islam. These mystic concerts (*sama*) became a marked feature of Indian Sufism and were forums for cultivation of music and poetry. In the early centuries of the Sultanate (1206–1526) the Sufi establishments, not the royal courts, patronized poetry and music.

Love is the core of Sufi spiritualism, music, and poetry. The figure of the beloved in mystical poetry influenced the beloved's depiction in other types of poetry. Early mystical poetry in west Asia addressed God directly as the beloved.[32] By the twelfth century the notion had gained ground that God's essence was unfathomable and his beauty could be realized only by contemplating his creations who were the witnesses (*shahid*) of his magnificence. Schimmel says that Arabic mystical poetry generally used metaphors suggestive of a beautiful female while Persian poetry used those suggestive of a beautiful boy.[33]

In Sufi literature the relationship between divine and human was often expressed in homoerotic metaphors. Many Sufis insisted that only same-gender love could transcend sex and therefore not distract the seeker from his ultimate aim of gnosis. Worldly love (*ishq-i majazi*) was only a bridge to reach divine love (*ishq-i haqiqi*), so the loving gaze at the worldly beloved (*mashuq*) was pure. He was only a metaphor for either God's loving gaze or the Sufi search for a vision of the divine. On the other hand, "this highly spiritual art" sometimes "could also degenerate into more or less crude homosexuality," according to Schimmel.[34]

The idea of *shahidbazi* (literally, witness play) has been traced by Corbin to the Mandean and Manichean doctrine of heavenly twins.[35] It was particularly galling to the orthodox who branded it heretical. The Hanbalite theologian al Jauziyya said: "The immoral among the mystic lovers commit a more serious sin than either the idolators or sodomites. They combine the

1914); Annemarie Schimmel, *The Mystic Dimensions of Islam* (Chapel Hill: University of North Carolina Press, 1982). For Sufism in India, see S. A. A. Rizvi, *History of Sufism,* 2 vols. (New Delhi: Munshiram Manoharlal, 1978, 1983); Richard M. Eaton, *Sufis of Bijapur 1300–1700; Social Roles of Sufis in Medieval India* (Princeton, NJ: Princeton University Press, 1978); and Eaton, *The Rise of Islam and the Bengal Frontier 1204–1760* (Berkeley, University of California Press, 1993).

32. Margaret Smith, *Rabi'a the Mystic and Her Later Fellow Saints in Islam* (Cambridge: Cambridge University Press, 1928), 55.

33. Schimmel, *As Through a Veil,* 151.

34. Schimmel, *As Through A Veil,* 68.

35. Every individual in the universe is supposed to have a matching heavenly twin who not only protects him but is also a witness because in him the individual can see reflected his soul's beauty. Henry Corbin, *The Man in Light of Iranian Sufism* (Boulder, CO: Shambala, 1978), 33–37.

trangression of the two groups—worshiping their minions and copulating with their idols."[36] Many important Sufis condemned it too. Ali Uthman al-Hujwiri (tenth to eleventh centuries), one of the earliest Sufis to settle in the subcontinent, declared that those who believe in shahidbazi are not Muslims: "Looking at youth and associating with them are forbidden practices and anyone who declares this to be allowable is an unbeliever. The traditions brought forward in this matter are vain and foolish. I have seen ignorant persons who suspected Sufis of the crime in question and regarded them with abhorrence. . . . But God knows best what is the truth."[37] In the eighteenth century, criticism of mystic poetry was voiced again in India by the reformer Shah Waliullah, who warned that Sufi works and poetry could be poison for the illiterate masses.[38]

The arguments of theologians like Abu Hamid al-Ghazzali, that since all beauty was derived from God it could not be a sin to admire it, helped counter this criticism.[39] To further protect themselves from attacks by the orthodox, Sufis tended to "put a heavy philosophical and theological coat of mail over their (often charming) verses."[40] Nevertheless, the recognition of the beloved as a male in mystic poetry was established and was to have a profound impact on later Urdu poetry. Some mystical poetry acquired the status of sacred literature for Indian Muslims. The *Diwan* (collected works) of the Persian poet Hafiz, replete with metaphors of liquor and the beauty of shahids, was often used as a divinatory text.

Persian poetic traditions influenced Persian and, later, Urdu poetry in India.[41] Most of this poetry was produced by writers influenced by the Sufis. In this poetry, the shahid (beloved) was invariably male. Schimmel describes the ideal beloved of Persian poetry as having a "round, light coloured moon face, a mouth like a *mim* or a dot, and slightly slanting eyes,"[42] and, ideally, being a boy of fourteen.[43] Consistently used tropes were the adoring gaze, the rose, celestial wine, and heavenly cupbearers. The beloved was described as a young male with the stature of a cypress, wayward tresses, and cap awry. The overpowering and cruel beloved was compared to a Turk, both in Persian and Urdu poetry.

36. Quoted in Joseph N. Bell, *Love Theories in Later Hanbalite Islam* (Albany: SUNY Press, 1979), 143.
37. R. A. Nicholson, trans. *Kashf-Al-Mahjub of al-Hujwiri* (1938; Delhi: Taj Co., 1982), 416–17.
38. Ghulam Jalbani, *Shah Waliullah jo Talim* (Hyderabad, Sindh: Shah Waliullah Academy, 1961), 114.
39. Bell, *Love Theories,* 144–66.
40. Schimmel, *As Through a Veil,* 41.
41. According to Schimmel, more Persian poetry was composed in India than in Iran (55).
42. Annemarie Schimmel, "Hafiz and His Critics," *Studies in Islam,* 16 (1979): 1–33; 30.
43. Schimmel, *As Through a Veil,* 67.

Even though Gesudaraz, the mystic poet of the fourteenth and fifteenth centuries, continued to argue that the beloved was only a means to a higher aim,[44] and modern commentators assert that the Sufis were not interested in the beloved per se,[45] much of the language of the poetry is decidedly this-worldly in its homoeroticism. For instance, it is difficult to attribute profound mystical or metaphysical meaning to Amir Khusro's couplet: "If the spring were to compare itself to the verdure on your face/ The buds would clutch their stomachs and the flowers roll with laughter," or to his claim that the Prophet Khizr would break his fast if he received the water of life from the beloved's lip.[46] The use of the plural in the following confirms that it is not a divine beloved being addressed: "While they are submerged in the vanity of their beauty/ Their lovers have staked their lives for them."[47]

The pirs' establishments were all-male fraternities for, according to the Chishti saint Jamaluddin Hanswi (died 1260), "He who seeks Lord is male. . . ."[48] The Quran criticized monasticism (57:27) and made marriage incumbent on adult Muslims.[49] Although the early Sufis obeyed the Quranic injunction and got married, many later Sufis remained celibate, following the example of the celebrated Chishti saint Nizamuddin and his successor, Nasiruddin Chiragh-i Dihli.[50] The beloved in much Indian Sufi poetry can be identified as the pir, the agent without whose love the seeker would be lost. In Khusro's Hindvi (early form of Urdu) poetry his pir, Shaikh Nizamuddin, is named as the beloved.[51]

The Sufis preferred to teach in the indigenous Indian languages, which they found more emotive than Persian. Indian Sufi poetry was thus influenced by ancient Indian poetics and traditions such as the Radha-Krishna tradition of mystical love poetry. One indicator of the latter influence is the adoption of a female persona by the poem's speaker. Images and genres were also borrowed from the Hindu tradition. Domestic images carried into Sufi poetry included the well from which water is drawn, the fire, the spinning wheel, the loss of virtue, shame, the suffering of social ridicule for the lover's sake, and the abandoning of the world for

---

44. "You look at the beautiful one and see the stature and the figure—/I do not see in between anything but the beauty of the work of the Creator." Quoted in Schimmel, *As Through a Veil,* 67.
45. Mir Valiuddin, *Love of God: A Sufic Approach* (Farnham, Surrey: Sufi Publishing Company 1968; 1972), 171.
46. Andalib Shadani, "Iran ki Amrad Parasti ka Asar Urdu Shairi par" in *Tahqiqat* (Bareilly: Jaleel Academy, no date), 193–222; 200. Khizr was the prophet who discovered the fountain of eternal youth.
47. Zoe Ansari, *Khusro ka zahni safar* (New Delhi: Anjuman Taraqqi Urdu Hind, 1987), 122, couplet 4.
48. Quoted in Schimmel, *As Through a Veil,* 155.
49. F. Rahman, *Islam* (Chicago: University of Chicago Press, 1979), 132.
50. For Sufis and celibacy, see Schimmel, *Mystical Dimensions of Islam,* 426–35.
51. See Schimmel, *As Through a Veil,* 135; Mujeeb, *Indian Muslims,* 167, 170. Nizamuddin himself is said to have identified his own pir as the beloved; see C. M. Naim, fn. 9.

his sake. Most of the pseudonymous Hindvi poetry by Amir Khusro is in this tradition as is the Punjabi poetry of Madho Lal Hussayn who wrote: "If I play [thus] with the Beloved, I am ever a happy woman."[52]

Indigenous legendary love stories like those of Heer and Ranjha or Sohni and Mahiwal, were retold along with West Asian ones like those of Laila and Majnu, Shirin and Farhand, Yusuf and Zulaikha and Mahmud and Ayaz. When retelling indigenous love legends male poets assumed the voice of the heroine. Madho Lal, in his retelling of the Heer-Ranjha love story, lamented: "Ranjha is a Yogi and I his Yogini, what has he done unto me?"[53] Incidentally, the Mahmud-Ayaz romance, the only one involving two men, was also the only one with a happy ending.

Urdu, which replaced Persian as the high literary language, came to fruition toward the end of the seventeenth century.[54] It evolved from a mixture of many dialects in use in northern India in the early medieval period and was initially given other names, such as Hindvi and Rekhta. Persian, Arabic, and even Turkish words were included in its vocabulary. Eventually the Perso-Arabic script was adopted for its written form. Urdu was also written in other scripts, such as Gurmukhi and Devanagari. Although from the nineteenth century onward Urdu came to be considered the language of Indian Muslims, its antecedents lay in local languages and their interaction with Persian, and it was widely used by non-Muslims until well into the twentieth century.

The first important Urdu literary works appeared in south India, where Urdu was carried by migrants from the north and by the spread of Sufism. The Sufis, mostly from orders already established in the north, communicated in the evolving languages of north India. Wali "Dakkani" (1668–1744), his pen name indicating that he belonged to the Dekkan in the south, is considered the first major Urdu poet. The beloved as a male can easily be identified very frequently in his poetry. The influence of Persian was marked not just by vocabulary, poetic traditions, and genres but also the tropes in which physical and spiritual realities were interchangeable as were divine and human lover.

The *ghazal*, when it first appeared in south India, followed the indigenous tradition of using a female voice and addressing a male as the beloved.[55] Once it moved north, it evolved toward the Persian style in which the poet assumes a male voice to address a male beloved.

52. Lajwanti Ramakrishna, *Panjabi Sufi Poets* (London: Oxford University Press,1938), 43.
53. Ramakrishna, 44.
54. For a history of Urdu, see Mohammed Sadiq, *A History of Urdu Literature* (1964; Delhi: Oxford University Press, 1995); Annemarie Schimmel, *Classical Urdu Literature from the Beginning to Iqbal* (Weisbaden: Otto Harrossowitz, 1975).
55. Carla Petievich, "Making 'Manly' Poetry: The Construction of Urdu Golden Age," in Richard B. Barnett, ed., *Rethinking Early Modern India* (forthcoming, New Delhi: Manohar, 2000), 154–55.

Early Urdu contains a large body of homoerotic poetry. According to one critic, Urdu poetry was franker in its expression and closer to life in the period before Indian rebellion against British rule in 1857.[56] The homoeroticism of this poetry has largely been ignored by modern commentators.[57] A large number of homoerotically inclined poets can be identified individually and collectively through their own writings and the writings of others, rather than through informed conjecture or stray remarks, as was the case during earlier periods. From Dargah Quli Khan's travelogue, it is clear that homosexually inclined men were well integrated into the culture of cities such as Delhi. Contemporaries who mention the sexual preferences of these poets indicate that the poets formed networks with other men who were so inclined.[58] The names of some of their beloveds are known and the poets sometimes addressed their beloveds by name in their verse (see Taban, pp. 173–74). They even competed for the same beloved.[59] These poets were highly regarded by their contemporaries and successors. None of the terms used for them is derogatory. They were mostly referred to as boy worshipers (*amrad parast*), worshipers of beauty (*husn parast*), professional lovers (*ashiq pesha*) or of colorful/amorous temperament (*rangeen/ashiq mijaaz*).

Among those whose poetry represents homoeroticism, Abru (see p. 161) and Mir Taqi Mir (see p. 188) are the most prominent. Abru was unequivocal about his preference. A modern critic has described him as the chief of boy-worshipers,[60] and contemporaries indicated the sexual preferences of other poets, such as Naji and Ahsan, by knowingly labeling them "Abru's friends." Mir and Abru, along with other poets, developed a discourse of erotic commentary on young males. They openly discussed their attraction to males, dwelt on what they found attractive in young males, and recounted their experiences of pleasure, longing, and heartbreak. They narrated events that may or may not be autobiographical but are rich in detail.

---

56. Nurul Hasan Hashmi, *Dilli ka Dabistan-i Shairi* (Lucknow: Urdu Academy,1992), 124.
57. C. M. Naim was perhaps the first modern scholar to deal with the subject in a nonjudgmental way. See "The Theme of Homosexual (Pederastic) Love." Others have tended to ignore or gloss over the most obvious homoerotic emotion. See, for instance, the complete heterosexualization of the poet Mir's biography by Khurshidul Islam and Ralph Russell, *Three Mughal Poets* (1969; Delhi: Oxford University Press, 1991). Mir's homoerotic poems have been explained away in a footnote: "Inevitable consequence of the parda system was the prevalence of homosexual love" (104, fn. 1).
58. "One morning I went to the house of Salamullah Khan/ There I saw many fairy-faced boys—O wow, O wow, wow!" Mir Soz (Tariq Rahman, "Boy-Love in the Urdu Ghazal," *Annual of Urdu Studies*, #7, [1990]: 1–20; 15).
59. The poet Shaiq warned his beloved Shuja'at against the intentions of the poet Nasikh. "Do not fall into his trap, O Shujat/ About Nasikh we hear that he is a great boy-fucker," quoted in Tariq Rahman, "Boy-Love," 8.
60. Nurul Hasan Hashmi, *Dilli ka Dabistan-i Shairi*, 123.

In this poetry, the beloved might be smooth-faced or might have down appearing on his face. Some found this down (sabz-i khat) most enchanting. His hair was long and curly. Often it escaped his cap, which was placed carelessly on his head.[61] Some preferred the fair-faced, others the wheatish or dark complexioned.[62] Some found foreign boys irresistible.[63] The boys' stature reminded the poets of cypresses and they had narrow waists.[64] Eye contact was crucial to this commentary.[65] The beloveds were cruel and indifferent. Some were easily available,[66] others were more difficult.[67] Some were extremely mercenary.[68] Some lovers were attracted to the wayward.[69]

One of the terms used for homoerotically inclined men, amrad parast (boy lovers) has been the basis of much misconception. Orientalists as well as modern commentators have cited it to categorize all male-male relationships as age stratified.[70] That same-sex relationships involved men of different ages seems to overpower all discussions of medieval same-sex love. Naim discusses the theme of homosexual love only in the context of pederasty. Rahman insists that "the ghazal rests on the assumption that the lover is a man (mard) whereas the beloved is a boy (amrad)."[71] It is true that the beloved is usually young. The fetishizing of

---

61. The boys of Delhi with their caps awry/Have destroyed their lovers," Z. A. Abbasi, ed., *Kulliyat-i Mir* (Delhi: Taraqqi Urdu Bureau, 1983), couplet 1003.

62. "At the sight of your wheatish complexion and your velvet skin/ A man loses his senses, his manners, and his sleep." Naji, *Diwan-i Shakir Naji,* ed. Iftikhar Begum Siddiqui (Delhi: Taraqqi Urdu Hind, 1990), 177. "When the boy is so wheat complexioned/ Why wouldn't Adam become a sinner." Abru, *Diwan-i Abru,* ed. Muhammad Hasan (Delhi: Taraqqi Urdu Bureau, 1990), 177.

63. "Today, the stone-breaking glance of the English boy/Passed through my heart like a dagger." Be Jaan, quoted in Rahman, "Boy-Love," 19.

64. " Mohan, on seeing your waist/ Mani [the renowned painter] returned home." Naji, *Diwan-i Shakir Naji,* 245.

65. "Why pull out your sword, I'm already defeated/the secret look of yours is a hidden weapon." Yak Rang, quoted in Hashmi, 201.

66. "The boys of Jahanabad might put on airs/But give them a signal and they are by your side" Mir, in *Kulliyat-i Mir,* couplet 7887.

67. "That Brahman boy the whole night through/kept me pining for just one kiss." Bejaan, quoted in Tariq Rahman, "Boy-Love," 17.

68. "How long can one keep this greedy boy/His demands of get me this, get me that, are endless." Abru, *Diwan-i Abru,* 120.

69. "The lover who is crooked is the one who is most attractive/A sword which is not curved is never pleasing." Shaikh Sharfuddin, quoted in Hashmi, *Dilli ka Dabistan-i Shairi,* 193.

70. An exception is Muhammad Zakir, who defines *amrad parasti* not only as attraction for boys but also the "declaring of men as the object of desire for other men." *Intikhab-i Ghazliyat-i Abru* (Delhi: Urdu Academy, 1991), 14.

71. Rahman, however, adds, "It should however be kept in mind that exaggeration is a part of the ghazal and that there is no evidence to suppose that the beloved was a small child. Generally he was between fourteen and twenty years of age . . . it could have been a part of the poet's sexual fantasy to represent the beloved as a pubescent boy or girl." Tariq Rahman, "Boy-Love," 14.

youth is common to most cultures, and exaggeration of the beloved's beauty and celebration of youth is a feature of much heterosexual love poetry too. However, the ghazal does not rest on the assumption of disparate ages, and the beloved is not always a boy. What "boys" meant and whether all boys were adolescent is open to question.[72]

Shadani, a scholar who has discussed homosexuality in Urdu and Persian poetry at great length, argues that the pederastic poetry of most classical Persian poets gave the ghazal its main theme of a painful, unrequitted, and suicidal love, and that this tradition, along with boy love, was transplanted into India and into Urdu poetry.[73] He attributes the angst he finds in these Urdu verses to the "assumption" that all such love was between older men and boys. He argues that such attachments were intrinsically futile. While accepting that the attraction of these poets to "fairy-faced" youths was natural, he wonders why any "boy" would be attracted to older men. The cruelty, indifference, and mercenary attitudes which these "beloveds" exhibited, were, according to him just ways to deflect unwanted attention.[74] This simplistic and homophobic argument ignores the facts that the "'boys" were not always very young, that many of these boys were attracted to older men as well as to other boys, that not all poets were "old and unattractive" and that often other young men were attracted to them.[75] It was possible for the same man to be desired as a beloved and to desire as a lover. Such was the poet Taban, renowned for his beauty and desired by many, who yet wrote of rejection, jealousy, and heartbreak.

Furthermore, the ghazal was contemporaneous with the Radha-Krishna genre of mystical love poetry in Sanskrit and other Indian languages. This type of poetry celebrated separation, or *viraha*, in heterosexual love, with the pining female symbolizing the human soul yearning for the divine beloved. Anguish in love poetry is by no means confined to man-boy love; it is a convention in much love poetry the world over.

Other evidence reveals further that not all beloveds were so young as to be smooth-faced or have down apppearing on their faces; some were soldiers in the army as is the case in Siraj's

---

72. This is in part the result of literary convention and in part of an erotics that constructs the beloved as youthful or even childlike, which Boswell has explored in other contexts. See Boswell, *Christianity, Social Tolerance and Homosexuality,* 28–30.

73. Frances W. Pritchett points out that "the suffering lover theme antedates medieval Persian pederasty by some centuries." "Convention in the Classical Urdu Ghazal: the Case of Mir," *Journal of South Asian Studies,* 3:1 (Fall 1979): 71.

74. Andalib Shadani, "Farsi Ghazal aur Jafa-i Mehboob," *Tehqiqat* (Bareilly, Jaleel Academy, no date), 223–65. He uses the same argument while discussing Mir's poetry in "Mir Sahab ka ek Khas Rang," *Tehqiqat,* 143.

75. For example, in Mir's couplet the lovers are other young boys: "The pert beautiful boys of the city,/ What cruelty they inflict on young men;/ The ways of my street boy are so deadly/ A hundred young die for each one of them;/ This fairy born is an affliction to the heart/ Wide is his fame among the young and the old."

Masnawi Bustan-i Khayal. In this poem, the young soldiers pursue the narrator, an older man (see p. 169). In Mir's narrative poem, *Shola-i ishq* the narrator is in love with a married man. In his autobiography, Mir describes the attraction between his father and a young man about to get married (see p. 185). Mir also alludes to erotic relationships between boys: "The moon-faced one met another moon face/ This is a complicated tale for it has wheels within wheels."[76] The poet assumes the persona of a lover, irrespective of the age of the beloved.

Those who argue that all same-sex relationships at this time were age-differentiated assume that these relationships were transient and ceased when the "boy" grew up. But there is evidence that some attachments were permanent. An example is the long relationship between the poet Maulvi Mukarram Baksh and Mukkarram. Mukarram observed *iddat* (the period of sexual abstinence and mourning prescribed for a widow) when the Maulvi died. Mukarram also inherited his property.[77] Abru advises the young boy that once his facial hair has fully grown, he should seek out youths of his own age (see p. 168). Mazhar's yearning suggests that reciprocity is possible: "If someone were to care for my heart as if it were his/When a friend becomes a lover, how wonderful it is."[78]

The sexual roles assumed by lover and beloved within this literature are very rarely stated explicitly. Nevertheless, modern commentators presume that if the beloved is male, he is automatically passive in sexual relations because he is the replacement for a woman in a heterosexual relationship. According to Rahman, the boy belongs, as it were, to the category of women: "those who take the penis in the orifices of their body."[79] This assumption is problematic, particularly when we consider Rahman's own definition of the ghazal as "the only form of literature which makes the love of boys something which can be mentioned in an erotic, aesthetic, romantic and spiritual context."[80] It also ignores the fact that sexual contact need not necessarily mean anal intercourse.

The issue of sexual activity and passivity does not appear frequently in the ghazal. In most cultures, it is considered shameful for men to play a passive role, and therefore it is unlikely to be openly admitted. Mazmoon comments on the inappropriateness of this subject: "Even in the tavern such talk is inappropriate/ but then in the school too I heard talk of 'active' and 'passive.'"[81] That these categories are changeable is suggested by an oft-repeated story about Mahmud's distress when told that in the next life, the sodomized would have to carry their sodomizers across a narrow bridge to escape hell. The story continues that he was reassured when reminded that the sodomized would in turn be carried by those they had sodomized.

---

76. Mir, *Kulliyat,* couplet 7479.
77. Tariq Rahman, "Boy-Love," 8.
78. Hashmi, *Dilli ka Dabistani-i shairi,* 214.
79. Tariq Rahman, "Boy-Love,"3.
80. Tariq Rahman, "Boy-Love," 20.
81. Quoted in Tariq Rahman, "Boy-Love," 15.

Within the spiritual-mystical framework in which the ghazal was constructed, frankness of sexual expression was restricted. Almost as a challenge to this there appeared in the eighteenth century a trend known as *iham goi*—poetry with multiple meanings. These meanings were created by playing on words, inventing new meanings for words, using alternative spelling or using words from other dialects. Abru and Hatim are considered its chief votaries. Even after a conscious distancing from iham goi started in the nineteenth century, many poets occasionally continued to display their skill in this genre.[82] A modern critic, while dismissing iham goi as the product of a decadent period, mentions that most of the *iham go* poets were homoerotically inclined.[83] The denigration of iham goi as serious poetry coincides with the time when homoeroticism in Urdu poetry begins to disappear.

It will be clear from just a few examples that through iham goi homoerotic subtexts were introduced into the ghazal. In the couplet *Dhamkate ho jo hum ko kamar band baandh baandh/ Kholen abhi to jaye miya ka bharam nikal*, Abru plays on the two words *band* and *baandh*. *Kamar band* means a drawer string and *kamar baandhna* is getting ready for a fight. The couplet's hidden meaning is: "You who threaten me by getting ready to fight, If I were to open your drawer strings, your reputation would be mud." Sajjad's couplet, *Gar tuk zamin pe launde ki peeth ko lagawen,/Jaanen hum apne dil men Rustom ke ta'in pichaada*, simply means: "If I were to beat the boy for a moment in a wrestling bout/ In my heart I would think that I had beaten Rustom." However, the first line of the couplet read by itself translates literally as: "If I could get the boy on his back on the floor for a moment." Mir Hasan's couplet, *Aye lalchi tu keesa ghairon ka mat tatole/Jo kuchch tu chahe ek shab mujh paas aake so le*, appears to simply mean: "O greedy one, don't feel the pouches of strangers./ Come one night and take what you want from me." *Keesa* is a pouch tied to the waistband but one word in the second line could change the meaning of this couplet. *So* can mean "anything" or "sleep." Therefore a possible rendition of the second line could be "Whatever you want get it by coming one night and sleeping with me." Abru, in an interesting twist on the word *sabz* which means "green" but is also conventionally used to describe the down on a pubescent face, says: *Har ek sabz hai Hindustan ka mashuq/ Baja hai naam ki balam rakkha hai khiron ka*. One simple meaning would be that all greens, that is, vegetables, are beloved in Hindustan so it is appropriate for "lover" to be another name for "cucumber." The second possible reading is more risqué: "Every Hindustani beloved is so verdant/ That it is right for the cucumber to be named 'lover.'"

There was less self-conscious embarrassment about such material prior to the nineteenth century. Sadi's classic *Gulistan*, containing stories of attraction between men, was considered

82. Hashmi, *Dilli ka Dabistan-i Shairi,* 118–22.
83. Jameel Jalibi, *Tarikh-i Urdu Adab* (Delhi: Educational Publishing House,1989), vol. 2, part 1, 217–18.

essential reading for Persian students. Ghanimat's *Nau rang-i ishq*, a seventeenth-century *mas-navi* describing the love affair between the poet's patron's son and his beloved Shahid, was a prescribed text in schools (see p. 159).[84] "The Urdu poets," according to Rahman, "neither celebrate nor denigrate homosexual love to the exclusion of other types of passion. They accept it as one natural outlet for erotic feelings, and are quick to use pseudo-mystical arguments against any religious minded detractor. In short they do not feel stigmatised at all."[85] According to Naim, society seemed to have "a non-negative" attitude toward homosexuality, consequently "homosexuality never developed into "a way of life" or to the adoption of a "minority" status by homosexuals.[86]

In this society marriage was considered the legitimate sphere of sexual activity but not necessarily of erotic energies. Homoerotically inclined men could be conveniently accommodated within the framework of heterosexual patriarchy. As long as a man fulfilled his duties as a householder, he was free to seek emotional involvement anywhere he pleased. Romantic attachments outside the family were not only widespread but considered legitimate. Procreation was considered a social duty, but since procreation did not necessitate erotic commitment, erotic commitments were not seen as threatening to marriage. This is evident in the conventions prevailing among the heterosexually inclined male elite—they were allowed not only multiple wives and concubines but also liaisons with ever-present courtesans.[87] Hence it was either courtesans or other males who became the focus of such attention.

The roles of the wife and the lover, irrespective of the sex of the latter, were defined and distinguished. What is also clear is that sexual alterity was not generally considered a form of resistance to social control. In fact, it is debatable whether it was considered an alterity at all.

Sufism continues to be a powerful presence in modern India. The saints' tombs are still important gathering places for both Muslims and Hindus, and Sufi influence on music and poetry is immeasurable. The historical record has often been obscured or disguised, but popular memory frequently diverges from it. An example is that of Jamali and Kamali. Jamali (died 1535/6) was a popular Sufi poet in Delhi. The remains of his *khanqah* and of the mosque attached to it suggest a large establishment and generous patronage. Jamali is buried in a small tomb which has ornate yet attractive tile work on the inside. The tomb is supposed to have been built a few years before he died. In its chamber there are two graves. According to oral tradition the other grave is that of his beloved disciple Kamali. This is very unusual as typically it is family members who are buried together. The official cover-up at this popular tourist

84. Shadani, "Iran ki Amrad Parasti ka Asar."
85. Tariq Rahman, "Boy-Love," 124.
86. C. M. Naim, "The Theme of Homosexual (Pederastic) Love," 128.
87. Abru, in his unequivocal rejection of heterosexuality, remarks on the alternatives available to men: "He who prefers a slut to a boy/ is no lover, only a creature of lust." Muhammad Hasan, ed., *Diwan-i Abru*, 283.

site is embarrassing. The notice at the site says that the other grave is that of an unknown person and that Kamali was the nom de-plume of Jamali. The official guide says: "Since there are two graves in the tomb, one believed to be that of Jamali and the other that of Kamali, an unknown person, the monuments go under a double-barreled name."[88]

88. Y. D. Sharma, *Delhi and Its Neighbourhood* (New Delhi: Archaeological Survey of India, 1974), 66.

Amir Khusro (Persian and Hindvi)

Introduced and translated by Saleem Kidwai

Amir Khusro (ca. 1253–1325) is today known as the mystic poet-musician par excellence.[1] He is also venerated as a saint, with the suffix Hazrat (Honorable) attached to his name. His annual *urs* (death anniversary) is among the most popular of Sufi religious celebrations.

Amir Khusro grew up in the house of his maternal grandfather who was employed by the Sultans of Delhi to recruit for their army. It was probably in this military environment that he learned the many languages he knew. Although not disciplined enough to undergo the rigors of formal education, Khusro was a well-known poet by the age of eighteen. His poetic skills and charm earned him the position of a courtier-poet, a position he held under six Sultans, some of whom had replaced the previous ones through violence. He wrote elaborate and skilful panegyrics to all of them.

His Persian poetry is a voluminous and valuable source for the history of the thirteenth and fourteenth centuries. However, today he is more famed for his Hindvi mystical poetry developed through his association with the Chishti saint Shaikh Nizamuddin Aulia than for his court poetry.

Khusro seems to have come under Chishti mystic influence around 1272. He soon became a favorite of Nizamuddin whose extremely popular hospice was particularly conducive to Khusro's poetic and musical skills. Nizamuddin was partial to the use of music in devotional exercise and had a clearly stated preference for Hindvi over Persian poetry. He encouraged Khusro to compose Hindvi poetry in many genres—devotional songs, couplets, and riddles.

There is no written document containing Khusro's Hindvi poetry dating earlier than the eighteenth century. But Khusro in his Persian books does say that he loves writing in Hindvi

---

1. For further reading, see Wahid Mirza, *The Life and Works of Amir Khusrau* (Lahore: University of Punjab, 1935; Mirza, *Life and Times of Amir Khusrau Dehlavi* (New Delhi: National Amir Khusrau Society, 1975).

and has distributed Hindvi works among his friends. Unlike his Persian poems, Khusro's Hindvi poems were not compiled. They were transmitted orally, particularly by *qawwals*—musicians who sang *qawwali*, Sufi devotional music. It is almost impossible to establish the authenticity of any of Khusro's Hindvi poems. An enormous body of Hindvi poetry, much of it probably composed centuries later, is pseudonymously attributed to him. This kind of accretiveness is entirely typical of the oeuvres of most medieval devotional poets, both Bhaktas and Sufis.

Qawwals also sing many different versions of the same poem. A consistent feature of the poems is the theme of Khusro's great love for Nizamuddin. His poetry continues to be the staple of qawwali concerts today, even when these are held on nonreligious occasions. The Hindvi poems translated here represent the tradition of vernacular devotional poetry with which Khusro is identified. They have all the features of this genre as it is found in Bhakta poetry in other languages: folk idiom, the use of the female voice to address a male beloved, and images drawn from the domestic lives of women. All verbs for the "I" in these poems are gendered female. In most poems the beloved is gendered male. The use of the signature name in each couplet is common to both Urdu and other Indian language traditions. Khusro died a few months after the death of Nizamuddin.

Persian Poetry

Tonight I heard that he whom I want to see will come—
May my head be sacrificed to the road you will take.
The gazelles in the desert carry their heads in their hands,
Hoping that you will come hunting them one day.
The attraction of love will not leave you unaffected—
If you don't come to my funeral you will come to my grave.
My soul has reached the edge; come so that I may live.
Once I am no more, what use will it be if you come?[2]

Delhi—Oh, its unadorned beloveds
Wear turbans but their tresses are loose.
They openly kill with their pride
Though they drink liquor in secret.
The Muslims have become sun-worshipers
Because of these simple sprightly Hindu boys.
I am desolate and intoxicated

---

2. Translated from Masood Qureshi, ed., *Khusrau-i Shireen-i Sukhan* (Islamabad: Lok Virsa Isha'at Ghar, n.d.), 160.

Because of these pure Hindu boys.
Tied up in their locks,
Khusro is like a dog with a collar. (123)[3]

That pert one drinks and then denies it to me—
What am I to do for I dare not smell his breath?
I saw him once in a dream, and now for years
Every night and day I remind myself of that dream.
Only the wind can now carry my feelings to the beloved's abode
For no caravan bearing solace passes this way any more.
Alas, I am too weak to inquire about him—
Enough that I am lying at his door. (129)

You know that Khusro is famed for his sweet words
If not for my heart's sake, come for my tongue. (136)

"Sugar is that which is under your tongue"
And these are the words that I say. (136)

The language of my beloved is Turkish, and Turkish I do not know
Would it not be wonderful if his tongue were in my mouth. (139)

Beloved, if at night I put my lips to yours,
Pretend to be asleep—don't ask whose mouth this is.(139)

Oh lord, is this me with my shoulder next to my beloved?
Have I been in bed sleeping by his side? (139)

The sun that is his face scorched me from afar—
It was a relief when I found the shade of his tresses.(140)

Don't tie a band around your waist,
Let me wrap my hands around instead. (140)

Oh cruel one with your cap askew, whose beloved are you?
With your words of love whom are you seducing now? (142)

Pseudonymous Hindvi Poetry

The beauty sleeps on the bridal bed, her tresses all over her face;
Come, Khusro, let's go home, for darkness settles all around.[4]

---

3. Translated from Z. Ansari, *Khusrau ka Zahni Safar* (New Delhi: Anjuman Taraqqi Urdu
   Hind, 1986).
4. This famous couplet is generally considered an epitaph Khusro wrote for himself on hearing of his master's death. It is exceptional in that the beloved here is gendered female.

Looking at the empty bed, I weep day and night
Every moment I yearn for my beloved, cannot find a moment's peace.

He has gone, my beloved has crossed the river,
He has gone across, and I am left behind.

I adorned myself before I went to my beloved,
But when I saw his beauty, I forgot my own.

Khusro, I play the game of love with my beloved—
If I win, he will be mine; if I lose, I am his.

Khusro, I spent the wedding night awake with my beloved—
My body is still mine, my heart his, both dyed the same color.

When our eyes met you took away my tilak,[5]
When our eyes met you gave me a love potion,
When our eyes met you intoxicated me,
When our eyes met you seized my arms,
My fair arms, my green bangles.
I give you my life, O cloth dyer,
For you dyed me your hue when our eyes met.
Khusro has given himself to Nizam—
You made me your bride when our eyes met.

The path to the well is hard—
It's hard to go fill my pot with that wine.
When I went to fill my pot with water
It got broken in the mad rush,
The path to the well is hard.
Khusro has given himself to Nizam—
Protect my honor, keep me veiled,
The path to the well is hard.

I exchanged amorous glances with my beloved.
Let the women and girls say what they like—
I exchanged amorous glances with my beloved.
His beautiful face, his charming form
I absorbed into my innermost heart.
Khusro has given himself to Nizam.
He declared me his matchless female disciple.
Let the women and girls say what they like.

I am sold on your beautiful face, Nizam,
I am sold on your beautiful face.

---

5. The mark indicating religious, caste or marital status.

Of all the girls' veils, mine is most soiled,
The women look at me and laugh, Nizam . . .
This spring, dye my veil afresh,
Preserve my honor, beloved Nizam,
For the sake of Baba Ganj-i Shakar,
Preserve my honor, Nizam . . .
Qutub and Farid have come in the groom's procession,[6]
Khusro is the bride, Nizam . . .
Some women fight with the mother-in-law, some with the sister-in-law,
But my hopes are set on you, Nizam . . .
I am sold on your beautiful face.

My blossoming youth is red with passion
How can I spend this time alone?
Will someone persuade Nizamuddin Aulia,
For the more I coax him, the more he acts coy,
My blossoming youth . . .
I'll break my bangles and throw them on the bed,
I'll set fire to this bodice of mine.
The empty bed frightens me
The fire of separation scorches me.

Color lights up the world today, O mother, color lights up the world—
My beloved's color lights up the world.
I have found my lover,
Found him in my courtyard,
I have found my Pir, Nizamuddin Aulia.
I searched this land and other lands—
Only your color pleases my heart.
The world is alight, the universe is alight—
I've never seen such color before
It's with me wherever I look
Color lights up the world today, O mother . . .

---

6. Refers to Baba Farid Ganj-i Shakar and Shaikh Qutubuddin Bakhtiar Kaqi, two earlier
saints of the Chishti order.

Ziauddin Barani:
The Khaljis in Love (Persian)[1]

Commentary and Translation by Saleem Kidwai

Barani was employed as a companion to the Sultan Muhammad ibn Tughlaq (1325–51) and had this job until the Sultan's death. In the change that followed he was briefly imprisoned, his property was confiscated, and he ended his last days in penury, living off charity at the *dargah* (shrine around the tomb) of Shaikh Nizamuddin Chishti. His burial expenses were paid from charity.

In the following extracts, Barani does not condemn male attachments on grounds of either *shariah* or *zawabit*.[2] He condemns Sultans who lost their better judgment over male lovers and thus surrendered the crucial instruments of power—fear, grandeur, and majesty. He also blames them for losing their senses to the point where they would not listen to warnings of wise counselors. The beloveds of the Sultan are reviled not just because they were murderers but also because they belonged to other groups that Barani hated. In this section of Sultanate history, Barani added two more groups—eunuchs and those involved in anal sex—to those he already blamed (the "low-born," the converts, the Hindus, rationalists, merchants, and others who were not "true-born Turks") for the misfortunes of the original elite.

The following extracts refer to events in the reign of two rulers of the Khalji dynasty. Alauddin Khalji (1296–1316) was one of the most powerful Sultans. He was despotic, created a huge and successful army, enforced wide-ranging economic reforms, and expanded the Sultanate southward. During an early invasion of Gujarat, he captured a eunuch slave, Malik

---

1. Translated from Zia ud Din Barani, *Tarikh I Firuz Shahi*, ed. Saiyid Ahmad Khan, Bibliotheca Indica series (Calcutta: Asiatic Society of Bengal, 1862). All page numbers refer to this edition.
2. The state-promulgated secular laws that Barani agreed were necessary for effective rule since the institution of kingship was itself un-Islamic. For a study of Barani's thought, see M. Habib, *Political Theory of the Delhi Sultanate* (Allahabad: Kitab Mahal, 1960).

Kafur, among other booty. Malik Kafur joined Alauddin's army and came to be called *Haz-ardinari* (one who cost 1,000 gold coins). It has been suggested that the merchant from whom he had been taken had paid that price for him. This price is very unlikely and the description was obviously a metaphorical compliment to Malik Kafur.

Alauddin Khalji appointed Malik Kafur deputy ruler (*Malik Naib*). Describing the last years of Alauddin's life, Barani says: " In those four or five years when the Sultan was losing his memory and his senses, he had fallen deeply and madly in love with the Malik Naib. He had entrusted the responsibility of the government and the control of the servants to this use-less ungrateful, ingratiate, sodomite." (337)

Malik Kafur tried to remove all nobles from important positions and imprisoned or blinded all of Alauddin's sons, mostly with the Sultan's knowledge. Enumerating the four factors he thinks were responsible for decline of the Khalji state and dynasty, Barani says: "The third rea-son was that the Sultan loved the Malik Naib very much. He made him the commander of his army, a minister. He raised him above all the others. The heart of this sodomite beloved of his was soon corrupted." (368)

Describing the last days of Alauddin, Barani says: "It was now that Alauddin was sum-moned and he began his journey from this world. Some people even say that the Malik Naib, chopped in front and torn at the back, killed him during his illness." (369)

Malik Kafur raised a six-year-old son of Alauddin to the throne and in spite of being a eu-nuch, married the boy's mother, a widow of Alauddin, and became the regent. Malik Kafur was assassinated a few months later. As an obituary, Barani comments: "This ignorant man did not know that to be castrated, to be addicted to the vice of being sodomized and to be faith-less are the worst vices. He did not know that the necessities and rules of kingship require a person to be exceptional, independent, fearless, generous and strong. The few days of power intoxicated him" (375).

Qutubuddin, another son of Alauddin, became the next ruler at the age of seventeen in April 1316. The end of Alauddin's reign also ended the fear that the late emperor had created in the city. According to Barani, people started enjoying themselves again in an atmosphere of freedom, unwatched by Alauddin's efficient spy system. "Beloveds and liquor" and "slaves and boys" reap-peared in the life of the city (383). The new emperor wrote poetry and was interested in music.

The whole world became given to leisure. The ways of the world changed. Fear of the monarchy began disappearing from the hearts of the people. Many people gave up their abstinence and said farewell to virtuous lives. The interest in worship that people had developed also lessened. Even obligatory duties began to be ignored. Mosques began los-ing their congregations. Since the emperor was constantly and flagrantly involved in impiety and immorality, the people followed his example. New young men began to make their appearance. All the beautiful singers returned to the city. The price of young male slaves, beautiful eunuchs and beautiful slave-girls went up to five hundred, a thousand, two thousand tankas. (383–84)

⌖ ⌖ ⌖

Among these new beloveds who made their appearance was Hasan, whom Ibn Batuttah, the Moroccan traveler, described as a "fine looking man."[3]

⌖ ⌖ ⌖

There was a boy called Hasan, from the people of Barwar, who had been brought up by one of Alauddin's important nobles Malik Shadi. The emperor became crazy about him and within a year of his enthronement, gave him special and high honors. He also gave him the title of Khusro Khan. In the indifference and recklessness of youth he even handed over Malik Naib's troops and lands to this son of the Barawars. He went further in his giddiness and temerity. He even made him a minister. In spite of his youth and his lustfulness, he had become so enamored by Hasan, the son of a Barawar, that he did not want to be parted from him for a moment. (381)

He gave Khusro Khan [Hasan's new title] a *chhatar* (an insignia of royal favor) and he raised him to a higher position than that of the Malik Naib in terms of giving him proximity and rank. He was more in love with Khusro Khan than his father Alauddin had been with the Malik Naib. (390)

⌖ ⌖ ⌖

Barani bemoans that Qutubuddin had not learned from his father's fate. He too entrusted this untrustworthy and vile person with an army and sent him on an expedition to the south. Like Malik Naib before him, Hasan too began plotting against his royal lover. According to Barani:

⌖ ⌖ ⌖

He often wanted to put a sword through the Sultan and kill him while he was doing the immoral act or publicly kissing him. This vile murderer of his father was always thinking of ways to kill the Sultan. Publicly he offered his body to the Sultan like an immoral and shameless woman. But within himself he was seething with anger and choking on a desire for revenge at the way the Sultan forced himself upon him and took advantage of him. (391)

---

3. A. M. Hussain, trans., *The Rehla of Ibn Batuttah* (Baroda: Oriental Institute, 1953; 1976), 45.

⬒⬒   ⬒⬒   ⬒⬒

Mubarak Khilji dispatched Khusro Khan to Ma'abar just as his father had done with Malik Kafur. The onset of the monsoons forced the armies to stay on in the south. According to Barani, Khusro Khan and his cohorts spent their time plotting rebellion. The king's faithful nobles were aware of this and were keen that the army return as soon as possible to the capital so that they could expose Khusro Khan's treachery to the emperor.

⬒⬒   ⬒⬒   ⬒⬒

But Sultan Qutubuddin was so overcome by lust and so eager to invite these delicate-bodied ones back that he ordered their recall. Hence Khusro Khan was put into a palanquin and with great speed was brought to the capital within seven or eight days. Palanquin-bearers were stationed at all stages of the route so that the journey was uninterrupted. This illegitimate traitor, while being sodomized by the Sultan, which is a strange state, would complain about other faithful nobles. He would say that they were defaming him as a traitor and falsely slandering him. In fact, as far as he could, he turned the Sultan against the faithful nobles. The Sultan was so enraptured by him and so much in love with him that he accepted and believed all the calumnies of this ingrate against his faithful supporters. Therefore, even before these faithful nobles and their troops could reach the capital, the Sultan had already turned against them and he was very pleased with the hundred elephants and the wealth [of Khwaja Taqi] that Khusro Khan had brought with him, and his love for Khusro Khan knew no bounds. (400)

⬒⬒   ⬒⬒   ⬒⬒

Those nobles who complained about Khusro Khan were demoted, punished, and their grants appropriated. It became clear to everyone that whoever complained about the royal favorite would be punished. The Sultan's well-wishers began to keep their distance as the Sultan's love for Khusro Khan continued to increase. The wise could foresee an imminent rebellion:

⬒⬒   ⬒⬒   ⬒⬒

Before he rebelled, Khusro Khan told the Sultan that he had risen in the reign of his majesty and had been sent on distant campaigns. All the nobles had their families and friends but he had no one. If his Majesty permitted he would send his brother to Bhiwal and Gujarat so that he could assure a few of their relatives of his majesty's kindness and bring them here.

⬒⬒   ⬒⬒   ⬒⬒

The love-stricken Sultan, according to Barani, granted Khusro his wish, and he summoned his supporters to Delhi. He passed them all off as his relatives and honored them with wealth and

appointments. They gathered in the house of the former Malik Naib and planned the emperor's death. They decided to murder him in his residence, the palace of a "thousand pillars."

⊠   ⊠   ⊠

In the state that he and the Sultan often were, Khusro Khan told the Sultan that after
spending the night with him he could leave the palace only in the morning. Till then
the doors of the palace were locked. Those relatives of his who had left their homes and
come to be with him were unable to come to him or meet him. If the key of the back
door were given to his men, then he could invite his relatives to the palace at night. The
Sultan, intoxicated as he was with lust, ordered that the keys of the doors be given to
Khusro Khan's men. He was so indifferent to his own safety that he did not comprehend
the implications of delivering the keys of the back door to Khusro Khan. (403)

⊠   ⊠   ⊠

Qutubuddin did not heed those who tried to warn him. Once Ziauddin warned the Sultan,
who reacted angrily. Just then Khusro Khan came in and

⊠   ⊠   ⊠

went to the Sultan's side. This unfortunate Sultan who was submerged up to his neck in
sexual desire, in his foolishness and with great carelessness, told this father-murderer that
Qazi Ziauddin was telling me such and such about you. He, who was used to lying
under men, in order to deceive, pretended to cry and wail. He told the Sultan that since
he had been so kind to him and because he had raised him above the senior nobles, all
the nobles and the members of the royal household hated him and were trying to get
him murdered.

A surge of passion engulfed the Sultan at the coquettish crying and wailing of the delicate one. He took him in his arms and hugged him, kissed him on the lips and threw
him on the floor and did what he had to do. In this state when it is easy to risk one's
life, the Sultan told him: "Even if the entire world is turned upside down, and if all those
who are close to me say things against me, I am so much in love and maddened by you
that I will sacrifice all of them for one hair of yours. Believe me, I will not believe a word
against you no matter who says it." (407)

⊠   ⊠   ⊠

One night, when the Sultan was alone with Khusro Khan, the latter's accomplices entered the
palace and the Sultan was murdered by his lover. Barani concludes: "The roots of the Alai
state were shaken. The unfaithful world destroyed the family of Alauddin. In the way Alauddin and Qutubuddin were destroyed by Malik Naib and Khusro Khan, the wise and those
looking for lessons will see the results of pampering young men and catamites" (409).

The Mirror of Secrets:
"Akhi" Jamshed Rajgiri (Persian)

Commentary and Translation by Scott Kugle

Jamshed Rajgiri was born in eastern Uttar Pradesh in the late fourteenth century. His story was recorded by Abd al-Rahman Chishti in his collection of stories written in Persian about Indian Sufi saints of the Chishti lineage, *Mir'at al-Asrar* (The Mirror of Secrets).[1] Although this account was written more than two centuries after Akhi's death, the author mentions that an account of Akhi's life was written by his own nephew, Shaykh Qiyam al-Din. This later account is therefore based on narratives written in Akhi's own time. It has been published in an Urdu translation, which omits many details, such as the description of the cross-dressed youths.[2] My translation has been rendered from the Persian manuscript, which is far more vivid and detailed than the Urdu version.

In his youth, Jamshed experienced much "inner turmoil," so he decided to renounce the world and dedicate himself to mystical devotions. He devoted himself to serving his spiritual master, Makhdum Jahaniyan, who, when he saw that he had reached spiritual maturity, sent him to live in the capital of Jaunpur with the nickname "Akhi," meaning "my brother." However, to escape the crowds who flocked to receive his blessing he went to Rajgir, a small town on the river Ganga. He did not accept the standard social role of the Muslim saint: to marry, set up an extended household, train disciples and bless followers. Instead, Jamshed chose to live alone, in anonymity. At Rajgir, he remained in contemplation. He negated worldly love by imagining God as his true beloved and negated worldly beauty by attributing true beauty only to God.

---

1. Abd al-Rahman Chishti (1596–1685), *Mir'at al-Asrar,* (manuscript in Hyderabad: Andhra Pradesh Oriental Manuscript Library and Research Institute, 306 Tazkirah Farsi). Akhi Jamshed's life is summarized in English in S. A. A. Rizvi, *Revivalist Movements in Northern India* (Lucknow: Balkrishna Book Company, 1965), 59.
2. Captain Vahid Bakhsh Siyal, *Miratulasrar* (Lahore: Sufi Foundation, 1982).

One spring, at the festival of Holi (associated with the amorous play of Krishna and the cowherd women, this festival is the occasion for carnivalesque play in north India), he had a strange experience:

◈ ◈ ◈

In the land of Hindustan, Hindus celebrate the new year with the ritual of Holi. In every town and city, from house to house and lane to lane, they wander singing, playing instruments, dancing with joyful abandon, flirting and stealing each others' hearts. They recite poems of longing and arousal and from their complete delight, they dance with abandon as if in drunken ecstasy.

. . . Akhi Rajgiri was sitting alone in his world of spiritual delight, absorbed in contemplating the scintillating beauty of ultimate reality. Suddenly a large band of handsome Hindu youths came wandering through his courtyard. They were decked out in jewels and sporting the alluring clothing of brides. They were singing and dancing, teasing each other and playing with each other. They were all singing melodies of longing and passion, dancing with all manner of delicate and beguiling gestures, languorous winks through half-closed eyes, and beseeching nods. They came bobbing along the road from the city, as if they were the bridesmaids of passion set to rout the self-control of ascetic discipline.

On laying his eyes upon these waves of passionate love, Akhi Rajgiri let slip the reins of self-control that he had once imagined to be in his command. He was gripped by a state of blissful unselfconsciousness. He rose up intoxicated by the onslaught of desire, and joined their joyful band dancing among them with total abandon, spreading ecstasy and reciting poems of love. Three days and nights passed while Akhi Rajgiri stayed with these young men, engrossed in tasting love and falling into trances.

At this point, the whole city fell into disarray and confusion. All the people from Kanauj and the surrounding towns poured out of their homes and gathered at that place to catch a glimpse of the beauty of Akhi Rajgiri's sainthood. Each one who saw him dancing and singing with the youths was struck by the sight, and tearing his clothes would rush to join that gathering that pointed the way to real love.[3]

◈ ◈ ◈

The situation soon turned explosive as the assembly gathered momentum and drew in more participants, presumably from both the Muslim and Hindu communities, perhaps including women as well as men.

---

3. *Mir'at al-Asrar,* 570–71.

When the tumult reached a peak, the Qazi met with the Mufti, the elders of the town and those who pretended to be Sufis. They wrote up a *fatwa* saying that Akhi Rajgiri had stepped outside of the boundaries of Islam and that he, along with all his followers, must be punished so that this civil disorder could be put to rest and the fabric of religious law saved from being rent. Then the fatwa was sent to each of these hypocrites for his signature and seal.

In those days, the head of all the town scholars and religious leaders was Mir Sayyid Ahmad Munjhali. They went to him to request his signature on the fatwa. However, since Mir Sayyid Ahmad was also a saintly man with spiritual insight, he refused to sign and criticized the others. He said, "I am a man trapped in the worship of my own selfish desires, so how can you expect me to dispute with those who are intimate friends of God?" So the progress of that fatwa was halted by the efforts of Mir Sayyid Ahmad.

Each of those hypocritical pretenders without exception was afflicted with calamities and disasters to the end of his days. Even their offspring to this day remain afflicted with trials; most of them who married and had families have been robbed, looted and pillaged.[4]

It is not clear what exactly the religious elders objected to—the eroticism of the cross-dressed young men, the tumult in the town, or a Muslim Sufi celebrating a Hindu festival. However, the text praises Syed Munjhali for recognizing that apparently respectable elders too have selfish desires, perhaps expressed in their married lives, and goes on to say that his family flourished in Kanauj, as his sons and grandsons rose to preeminence as scholars and nobles. The text stresses that the other elders who were married and had children but hypocritically denounced Akhi suffered divine retribution.

These hypocrites tried to get Akhi executed by poisoning, but the king accepted the mystic's explanation that real men accept true love in all its forms:

Later, those pretenders presented that biased fatwa to some of the nobles of the Sharqi Sultan of Jaunpur, who was the ruler of Kanauj at the time. They tried to forge blame against Akhi Rajgiri, but without any success. They then wrote a letter to all the religious scholars of the capital at Jaunpur, demanding that they bring the matter to the attention of the Sultan: to place before him his tray with medicines arrayed upon it that will cause Akhi Rajgiri to lose his life and leave this worldly existence, for there is no other way but

---

4. *Mir'at al-Asrar,* 571.

to have him killed. But Akhi Rajgiri wrote a letter to the Sultan, full of humility and in accord with the teachings of the great Sufis, in which he displayed his total sincerity.[5]

❖❖❖   ❖❖❖   ❖❖❖

Akhi wrote: "I do not want a crown, I do not want a throne. I want only to rub my forehead in the dust and dance with abandon over the earth. If the Sultan would show me favor, then I might be allowed to dance even upon the winds. . . . Because those who denounce me are not real men in the spiritual sense, they cannot accept love with all its consequences in their hearts. Oh my love, there are a thousand snares in every form; oh my love, one who is not a real man can never experience true love!" The Sultan appreciated these expressions and exonerated the mystic, giving thanks that such a holy man lived in his kingdom to bless his rule. This royal sanction presumably protected Akhi Jamshed from any further attacks until his death, some time after 1440.

---

5. *Mir'at al-Asrar,* 574. The full text of this letter is preserved at the end of the Persian narrative, 574–79.

Baburnama *(Turkish)*[1]

Introduced by Saleem Kidwai

Zahiruddin Muhammad, the first Mughal ruler of India, was born on February 14, 1483. His successors took far grander titles than his nickname Babur (tiger). His father Umar Sheikh Mirza was the ruler of Farghana, a small principality in northern Afghanistan. When he was eleven years old he succeeded his father to the throne.

He was the paternal great-grandson of Timur. His mother's father was a thirteenth-generation descendant of Chengiz Khan.[2] His maternal grandmother Aisan Daulat Begum was obviously a strong influence on him. He writes: "Few amongst women will have been my grandmother's equals for judgement and counsel; she was very wise and far sighted and most affairs of mine were carried through her advice."[3]

In 1497, when he was fourteen years old, he captured Samarqand, the fabled capital of his ancestor Taimur. He lost it three months later. "It came very hard on me, I could not help crying a good deal." Babur lost Ferghana too, and wandered homeless till he took Kabul in 1504. In 1526 he defeated the ruler of Delhi. He died in 1530.

Babur wrote poetry in Turkish. He also wrote an autobiography, parts of which have survived. It is referred to as the *Tuzuk-i Baburi*.[4] Some periods went unrecorded due to his personal circumstances, and some sections were lost during his eventful life as a warrior-adventurer. This extract is placed in the period between August 1499 and July 1500.

1. *Babur-Namah: The Memoirs,* trans., from the original Turki text of Zahiru'd-din Muhammad Babur Padshah Ghazi, Annette Susannah Beveridge (London: Luzac & Co.,1921), 120–21.
2. *Babur-Namah,* 19.
3. *Babur-Namah,* 43.
4. It became better known as Baburnama after it was translated into Persian on the instructions of his grandson Akbar in 1589. Babur's daughter Gulbadan Begum also wrote an account of the times.

⬖ ⬖ ⬖

Babur's First Marriage

Ayisha-sultan Begim whom my father and hers, i.e., my uncle, Sl. Ahmad Mirza had betrothed to me, came [this year] to Khujand and I took her in the month of Sha'ban.
Though I was not ill-disposed towards her, yet, this being my first marriage, out of modesty and bashfulness, I used to see her once in 10, 15, 20 days. Later on when even my
first inclinations did not last, my bashfulness increased. Then my mother Khanim used
to send me, once a month or every 40 days, with driving and driving, dunnings and
worryings.

A Personal Episode and Some Verses of Babur

In those leisurely days I discovered in myself a strange inclination, nay! as the verse says,
"I maddened and afflicted myself" for a boy in the camp-bazar, his very name, Baburi,
fitting in.[5] Up till then I had had no inclination for any-one, indeed of love and desire,
either by hear-say or experience, I had not heard, I had not talked. At that time I composed Persian couplets, one or two at a time; this is one of them:

> May none be as I, humbled and wretched and love-sick;
> No beloved as thou art to me, cruel and careless.

From time to time Baburi used to come to my presence but out of modesty and bashfulness, I could never look straight at him; how then could I make conversation and
recital? In my joy and agitation I could not thank him [for coming]; how was it possible for me to reproach him with going away? What power had I to command the duty
of service to myself? One day during that time of desire and passion when I was going
with companions along a land and suddenly met him face to face, I got into such a state
of confusion that I almost went right off. To look straight at him or to put words
together was impossible. With a hundred torments and shames, I went on. A [Persian]
couplet of Muhammad Salih's came into my mind:

> I am abashed with shame when I see my friend;
> My companions look at me, I look the other way.

That couplet suited the case wonderfully well. In that frothing-up of desire and passion
and under that stress of youthful folly, I used to wander, bare-head, bare-foot, through

---

5. Baburi literally means "belonging to Babur" or "Babur's."

street and lane, orchard and vineyard. I shewed civility neither to friend or stranger, took no care for myself or others.

> Out of myself desire rushed me, unknowing
> That this is so with the lover of a fairy-face. [Turkish verse]

Sometimes like the madman, I used to wander alone over hill and plain; sometimes I betook myself to gardens and the suburbs, lane by lane. My wandering was not of my choice, not I decided whether to go or to stay.

> Nor power to go was mine, nor power to stay;
> I was just what you made me, O thief of my heart. [Turkish verse]

"Mutribi" Samarqandi:
The Fair and the Dark Boys (Persian)[1]

Translated by Saleem Kidwai

"Mutribi" (musician) was the pen name of a poet-scholar from Samarqand who visited the Mughal court in the last year of the emperor Jahangir's reign (1605–1626). He recorded his conversations with the emperor. This is the account of the tenth meeting between the two.

I presented myself before the throne. After I had expressed my submission, the vicegent of God showed me a great deal of kindness. Then [his majesty] said: "Preacher, is a fair young man better or is the dark color more beautiful?"

I said: "Different people have different temperaments. Some prefer the dark and some are attracted to the fair. However, the wise have said:

'The lover will find out all about his beloved
Whether the beloved has a beautiful or an ugly form.'"

His majesty said: "I have asked you what you feel. Of what concern is it to us what others feel?"

I said: "O Qibla of the universe,[2] I can only say when I see for myself."

He said: "Look to your right and to your left. Maybe then you will know."

1. Abdul Ghani Mirzoyef, ed., *Khatirtat-i Mutribi by Mutribi Samarqandi*, (Karachi: Institute of Central and West Asian Studies, University of Karachi, 1977), 39–40.
2. Qibla is the direction of the Kaba. Like "Viceregent of God," it is a title often used for Muslim rulers in India.

As he spoke, to my right stood a dark-complexioned Hindu youth and what a danger to one's life he was! As soon as I saw him, I lost my heart.

> A Hindu boy stole my wretched heart
> He stole its tranquillity and its calmness
> My reason, my judgment, my endurance, my patience
> All of these he stole with his laugh.

To my left stood a fair-complexioned youth, so beautiful and elegant that I could not believe my eyes.

> O moon-faced beauty in this beautiful night
> So astonishingly desirable in the light of the candle
> You have stolen Mutribi's heart altogether
> With a wink, guilelessness, playfulness and amiability.
> Do not tell me to look at the splendor of the perfumed plants
> My heart is your captive, what do I need from there?

My endurance exceeded rational boundaries. I once again looked to my right and to my left. I said: "O Qibla of the universe, first I have been attracted to the dark and then to the fair one. From these two colors has emerged another color and I can no longer tell whether the fair youth is fair and the dark one dark. In fact it seems it is the color of verdancy that is most beautiful."

He replied: "Then we must say that it is the verdant color which is attractive." He recited this quatrain:

> "He who is altogether attractive—
> His attractive vitality
> Infused with life
> Has created this wonderful appearance."

I said: "That confirms what the great ones have reported that the refuge of Prophecy [the Prophet Muhammad], peace be upon him, had said: 'Although my brother Yusuf [the Prophet Joseph], peace be upon him, was a beauty, I have charm.'"

His majesty said: "That's exactly what I meant."

I said:

> "O God, as long as the sun and the moon be,
> May Jahangir, son of Akbar, remain the emperor."

Haqiqat al-Fuqara:
Poetic Biography of "Madho Lal" Hussayn (Persian)

Commentary and translation by Scott Kugle

with Hussayn's Poems (Punjabi)

Translated by Aditya Behl

Sufi mystic Shah Hussayn was born ca. 1539 into a Muslim weaver family. When he was about ten years old, he was initiated into the Qadiri Sufi lineage by Shaikh Bahlul Darya'i, who lived in Chiniot, a village outside Lahore. He lived as a mendicant student, wandering in the empty lands outside the city walls by day and returning to stay at the shrine of Lahore's patron saint, Ali Hujwiri, by night. At the age of thirty-six he had a profound spiritual experience while studying the Quran, when his teacher Sa'dullah recited the verse, "the life of the world is nothing but play and pleasurable distraction."[1] Hussayn immediately resolved to throw off all constraints of piety and instead to live like a child at play, abandoning hypocrisy and ambition as well as fear of social disrepute.

Hussayn's biography is preserved largely in one source, a lengthy Persian poem entitled *Haqiqat al-Fuqara* (The Truth of those Impoverished by Love), written by Shaikh Mahmud ibn Muhammad Pir, ca. 1662, just sixty-two years after Shah Hussayn's death. The author's father had been a companion of Shah Hussayn, while the author himself was a close attendant

---

1. *Ma Hayyat al-Dunya ila Lab wa Lahw.* Quran: Surat al-Anam 6: 32. The Quran contains two separate verses that echo this phrase closely in *Surat al-Ankabut* 29: 64 and *Surat Muhammad* 47: 36.

of Hussayn's companion Madho. Although this source is quoted by all subsequent biographers in Persian and Urdu, biographers in English have ignored it. Passages are translated here for the first time into English.[2]

The poem recounts how Hussayn met and fell in love with Madho, a Brahman youth:

⬦   ⬦   ⬦

> Madho was wondrous in his beauty and his grace,
>   A young man refined, noble Brahman by descent,
> Tender and delicate—from the liquor of this youth's wink
>   the worshiper of grace would fall down flat drunk.
> Raised as a Hindu, his faith was pure haughty infidelity—
>   stone-hearted, he flaunted beauty to oppress those ensnared.
> Madho went out one day to steal hearts for sport,
>   riding through the streets with alluring arrogance and captivating pride.
> On that same street Hussayn was reeling,
>   drunk with wine, surrounded by his loving companions.
> In that state of ecstasy, he saw Madho's glowing face
>   and his heart wailed with a cry of delicious pain.
> My friends, he cried out, look over there—
>   that young man has just stolen away my heart!
> He lifted everything I had from me with a glance
>   he snatched my heart from my soul, swiped my soul from my body.
> I'm dazzled with passion for this youth,
>   my friends, what should I do, I'm helpless in his grasp,
> I'm a captive to the sorrow of being separated from him
>   I can't bear the burning fever of not seeing him for an instant!
> When his companions heard him reveal this secret
>   they replied by revealing another secret:
> O God, our friend Hussayn doesn't even know
>   who this boy is who is playing with his heart.
> I know, insisted Hussayn, that my heart's curse
>   is a young infidel, who will raze the house of my faith to the ground.
> With the graceful curls of his hair, this bare-chested idol
>   has tied up my heart, hung it from the sacred thread on his shoulder.[3]

⬦   ⬦   ⬦

He soon began to follow Madho wherever he went, and spent nights on his doorstep:

---

2. *Haqiqat al-Fuqara,* folio 30. The Persian manuscript is housed in Pakistan in Punjab University Library, number 3253/248 Farsi.
3. *Haqiqat al-Fuqara,* folio 38.

From longing to glimpse his beloved
  Hussayn would stand weeping before Madho's door.
Crying with passion he would remain immobile
  standing day and night in Madho's alleyway.
Even when his tears ran dry Hussayn stayed restless,
  without sleep, without patience, without sense, without peace.
Since he dropped the reins of self-control
  this open passion ruined his reputation throughout Lahore.
Vitality vacated his soul, tranquility slipped his mind—
  he writhed in the searing flames of passion.
Burning day and night in the fire of yearning,
  his heart fevered in the heat of longing,
He wandered restless with this incendiary love
  yet Madho never once glanced his way.[4]

The spring celebration of Basant temporarily lifted these constraints and gave the two a chance to interact. This holiday was one of the few times that people of different backgrounds could meet. The biography relates:

Basant arrived, the day the world is flooded with joy
  Hindus play Holi with colors: music and wine, flirting and teasing.
Everyone gathers together that day without a care—
  the honorable mingle freely with the shameless,
Drinking wine surrounded by cup-bearers with bodies like silver,
  Drinking with vigor, at a lively pace, engrossed in beauty,
Dancing limbs, plucking strings, wine, tales, melodies,
  luscious forms finely arrayed, color and fragrance mingled.
Everyone on the street takes up the intoxicated play,
  joy struts stately and seductive in each alleyway.
Finally, on that day Madho stooped to show
  sincere kindness and a courteous face to Hussayn
For the buoyancy of spring had arrived
  the season that sparkles like dusky wine in crystal pitchers.
In that season all energies become restful,
  Indians lay aside their concerns, relax and play.
So Madho, too, was playing Holi on Basant,
  handsome and graceful, winsome and coy,
Playing with everyone, immersing himself in frolic,
  teasing everyone and dallying seductively.
He strode up to Hussayn very shyly

---

4. *Haqiqat al-Fuqara,* folio 39.

and threw colors over his head and his shoulders
And as he poured colors over his hair and clothes
  he sang and his body arched in a dance before him.
Hussayn, in his longing, took on a lively air—
  his feet suddenly nimble, his steps answered Madho's dance.
To his haughty grace Hussayn's every gesture implored
  and Madho himself became Hussayn's game of Basant.
His friends gathered around in support
  playing and clapping around them in concert.
From that joyous day onward Hussayn devoted
  himself to play as if each day were Basant.[5]

The ice of social convention broken, the two became intimate, but Madho's family disapproved. They tried to hinder their meetings, and even tried to assassinate Hussayn. It is not
clear how the two managed to overcome this conflict with the Brahmans of Lahore. The biography recounts that Madho's family tried to take him away on a pilgrimage to the Ganga at
Hardwar. Madho defied them and stayed back in Lahore, but Hussayn promised the family
that Madho would be in Hardwar on the day they reached there. He asked Madho to close his
eyes and the boy found himself on the riverbank in Hardwar. After the bath, he opened his
eyes and found himself back in Shahdara. On their return, the parents confirmed that Madho
had indeed been with them in Hardwar.[6] This miracle may hint at a reconciliation between
Hussayn and Madho's family.

    Hussayn then invited Madho to spend a day or two with him in private in a hut in the vil-
lage of Babupur, far from Lahore:

One day Hussayn said to Madho
  My head reels with desire to take you to Babupur.
We will travel together, just you and me
  We will drink in intimacy the wine of our heart's desire.
What I truly long for is the pure delight
  of sitting alone with you and sipping your wine.
We could be alone together there for an ample time
  and drink, lying in each other's embrace.
Madho asked, Tell me, what's your obsession
  with drinking wine in my intimate company?
If for one moment I leave wine, Hussayn replied,
  I collapse into sorrow and despair.

---

5. *Haqiqat al-Fuqara*, folio 42.
6. *Haqiqat al-Fuqara*, folio 44.

Since your liquor is the very spirit of my life
   you are my livelihood and you alone are my joy.
My dear friend, at that moment I'll drink from your hands
   and gaze at you in ecstasy in my arms.
Speak the truth now, Madho contested,
   and to hell with what will come of all your obsessions.
Who am I to you? Why am I the object of all your desires
   that I should let you ruin my good name?
What if, as we stay together in intimacy,
   someone should spy me lying on your breast?
Tell me yourself, where would I end up
   when people across the world begin to insult me?
They will inflict merciless blame on me
   and toss my honor and reputation to the winds.
A youth, simple and innocent, who sits among drunkards
   may be seen as a sinner just like them.
You know what all the people will do—
   they will go to any lengths to destroy my name.
Enough, you arrogant man, for God's sake,
   don't ruin me with these inclinations of yours!
Hussayn coaxed him, you're playing hard to get,
   how I'll weep upon the blade of your teasing.
When you sit with me alone in intimacy
   who will have bravery enough
That they could stand up to denounce me
   or stain my clothes with their accusations?
Nobody has the boldness to face me
   or soil your reputation on account of me.
Madho at this time didn't know
   that Hussayn had a secret way to lead him to God.
Madho didn't understand Hussayn's real intent
   that these seductions were for his own salvation.
He didn't know that Hussayn really desired
   to raise his star up to the zenith of salvific bliss.
He couldn't have known Hussayn's secret—
   how brightly he would kindle his star.
He knew nothing of those who are united with God
   how they can convey to others such rapture.
For this reason Madho remained so anxious
   and worried since his heart was not yet ripe.[7]

---

7. *Haqiqat al-Fuqara*, folio 49.

Eventually, Madho agreed to meet Hussayn in private at this secluded house, although he insisted on traveling separately in order to avoid suspicion:

> Hussayn and Madho sat together in one room,
>   together they laid aside the sorrows of separation.
> Hussayn was kneeling in respect,
>   his eyes and his heart focused only on Madho.
> Madho took from his hand a glass of deep-hued wine—
>   he drank from it, and Hussayn kissed his wine-sweet lips.
> Then Madho gave him a glass filled to the brim
>   and kissed Hussayn in answer on his reddened lips.
> Hussayn rose tranquilly from his place
>   and Madho rose as well, answering his call.
> Holding his hand, Madho sat down, crossing his legs,
>   his face illumined with bright joy.
> Hussayn handed him a goblet of sparkling wine
>   as if burning in a fever of ardor.
> He took a sip from the goblet and gave one to Hussayn,
>   he accepted a kiss and gave one to Hussayn.
> Hussayn rose again to give of himself more generously
>   and Madho graciously accepted his advances.
> In this way, the lovers engaged in a play of passions,
>   demanding and acceding, teasing and refusing.
> Each enticed the other, stirring his desire,
>   mingling wine and kisses like sugar dissolved in milk.
> One passes the goblet like the very shape of delight
>   while the other accepts the gift with humble supplication.
> When the other holds the cup, imploring,
>   he accepts the tribute, begging for even more delicacies.
> In this duet of beseeching and tenderly replying
>   the two friends made love with each other.[8]
> Each of them in each act is captivated by the other
>   loving each other with the kindest intimacy.
> One kisses the other with an ecstatic breath
>   moving from his wrist to his hand, his strong arm, his shoulder,
> Then he kisses his forehead and then his cheek,
>   gently kisses both his eyelids and then his brows,
> Then with sweet affection he kisses his lips,
>   with love he kisses the smooth skin beneath his chin.[9]

---

8. *Haqiqat al-Fuqara,* folio 50.
9. *Haqiqat al-Fuqara,* folio 52.

The poet notes that some of Hussayn's followers observed the lovers' play through the keyhole and were troubled for a time by doubts about its propriety. The poet defends their play as a spiritual initiation in which Hussayn passed on to Madho the spark of divine love through touch, which conveyed to him mystical knowledge more holistically and powerfully than words could. It is a persistent theme in Sufi tradition that mystical insight can be passed on through bodily contact, especially through a shared drink or saliva. Initiatory visions often contain the image of a spiritual master passing a bit of his saliva to a follower's mouth with his finger or through a kiss. Shah Hussayn himself is reported to have met the perennial spiritual guide, Khidr, in his boyhood. Khidr poured out some water from his jug into his own palm, and Hussayn drank from his hand.[10] This transmission of spiritual blessing allowed him to finish memorizing the Quran with ease, and eventually pushed him toward sainthood in his adult life. The poet-biographer explains:

When you look at these two true men embracing
  don't think that you are witnessing a sin.
They don't drink wine to excite their selfish natures—
  they put wine to a much better and more subtle use.
Their play of kisses are ripples from the ocean of guidance,
  not from selfish lust—their aim is greater than that.
When Hussayn takes Madho's lips in his own
  he transmits his blessing in the most intimate way.
When Madho answers his lips with shy delicacy
  he coaxes from each blessing many more blessings.
Hussayn is training Madho from the depth of his soul
  how to pass along the mystic path to truth.
He wants to burnish within Madho the passion for God—
  he plays this love off against that love, intensifying each.
When Hussayn sips from Madho's goblet of wine
  he burns with the longing passion for Madho's beauty.
In this burning, his soul rises from its place—
  he can kiss then directly from his heart.
Madho kisses Hussayn's lips until his breath like a cool breeze
  ripples over the heart of Madho, stirring his passion.[11]

10. *Haqiqat al-Fuqara*, folio 22.
11. *Haqiqat al-Fuqara*, folio 50.

Madho then began to live with Hussayn at Baghabanpura on the outskirts of Lahore. (The neighborhood is now within the expanding city just next to the Shalimar gardens). So inseparable were they that Hussayn himself became known as "Madho Lal" Hussayn. Although Hussayn initiated many other followers, there is no evidence to suggest that such erotic play was part of any other initiation. Neither Hussayn nor Madho ever married.

In his commitment to a spirituality of play, Shah Hussayn found a Sufi equivalent to the Bhakti practice of Rasaleela, the amorous play of Krishna with his devotees. Such a synthesis of Hindu and Islamic ideas was natural since Hussayn's weaver community had converted to Islam only a few generations before.[12] His poetic outpourings in Punjabi continued to explore the theme of divine love manifested in the passion between two people. He often cited the Punjabi romance of Heer and Ranjha, identifying himself with the woman, Heer:

> I wander the forests looking for him,
> but my Ranjha is always with me.
> My heart demands my princely Ranjha!
>
> The cows come home, but not the cowherd,
> so Heer is in tears in Jhang.
> I wander night and day in the wilderness,
> enduring the sharp acacia thorns.
>
> Says the poor faqir Hussayn,
> how can I ever meet Ranjha?[13]

At this time the Mughal emperor Akbar was on the throne in Delhi and Lahore was his second capital. It was reported in the royal court that Hussayn "wears red clothes, drinks wine openly, sings and plays music, and is surrounded by smooth-faced young men as beautiful as the moon. He dances with them in the street in front of his home. He shaves his beard off but lets his mus-

---

12. The weavers who converted to Islam in the medieval centuries were most likely low-caste Shudras. Some later Urdu sources claim that Hussayn was an upper-caste Dahda Rajput. But Rajputs did not engage in weaving, and conversion rarely affected a caste's means of livelihood. These stories are later accretions to make Hussayn more socially acceptable, as are the stories of Madho's conversion to Islam.

13. Translated by Aditya Behl from Abdul Majid Bhatti, ed. *Kafiyan Shah Husain* (Lahore: Punjabi Adabi Academy, 1961), poem no. 9. Subsequent parenthetical numbers refer to Bhatti's verse numbers.

tache grow long."[14] The police chief of Lahore, Kotwal Malik Ali, was told to keep a watch on Hussayn. One day the chief was administering punishment to a criminal in the marketplace, when Hussayn on the roadside was exchanging glances with a handsome young man, who happened to be the police chief's son. When told that this amorous man was Shah Hussayn, the police chief arrested and imprisoned him, charging him with being a heretic. Miraculously, the chains kept falling from Hussayn's ankles no matter how the police chief struggled to secure them. The chief did not take this warning to heart but resorted to violent threats:

When Hussayn saw that he was to be chained like a criminal,
   he addressed the police chief, laughing like a woman:
For what reason are you treating me like this,
   what sin have I committed, you stupid ass?
He said, look closely at yourself and think it through—
   admitting your own crime is better than such insults.
You commit debauchery and drink wine
   and always stare at beautiful young people.
With the beat of a kettle drum and your wild song
   you smash the mirror of religious law against a stone.
What kind of sainthood is this? What kind of holiness?
   Why are you so blind to your own obvious faults?
Hussayn assured him, Yes sir, you speak the absolute truth
   but tell me, why bother with such an inquisition?
I may be a sinner in respect to the religious law
   but how have I injured you or the king who sent you?
If my actions are a sin, then I sin against God
   but I commit no crime against anyone, you or your king.
Said the chief with a groan, As rebuke and punishment
   yours will be a disgraceful death, driven through with a spike—
A spike that will go into you from behind
   so that your soul will leave you from behind.
Such a long spike I will use to impale you
   that will go in from behind and come out your side—
On this very day I'll do it, not a day later
   I'll sit you on a spike that opens the seam of your side![15]

---

14. *Haqiqat al-Fuqara,* folio 72. In the later Urdu translation, the allegation about dancing with young men is omitted. See *Tahqiqat-i Chishti* (Lahore: Koh-i Nur Press, 1993), 322.
15. *Haqiqat-i Fuqara,* folio 72–73 and *Tahqiqat-i Chishti,* page 327. Rebel nobles murdered the thirteenth-century British monarch Edward II by anal rape with a hot iron rod. They also killed his male lover Gaveston. See the play *Edward II* (ca. 1594) by Christopher Marlowe.

Hussayn was not flustered by this threat that hinted at an unconventional execution by anal rape. However, before the police chief could carry out his threat, the emperor Akbar grew angry with the police chief and had him punished instead; by miraculous coincidence, he was impaled up the backside with an iron spike.

Hussayn's triumph over his persecutors seems to bear out the faith expressed in his Punjabi poems:

Sway in ecstasy in your dance in the courtyard,
  the Lord is near those who chant his Name!
In this courtyard flow many streams,
  each with thousands of boats—
I've seen many sink in the water,
  and some cross over to the other shore.
This courtyard has nine doors,
  and the tenth is always locked.
No one knows the door of the Prince—
  he comes and goes as he pleases.
There's a lovely alcove in the courtyard,
  with a beautiful window in it—
I spread my bed in this niche,
  to enjoy the night with my bridegroom.
A wild young elephant roams the yard,
  and breaks his chains to pieces.
It could never harm
  those who are truly awake,
says Hussayn the faqir of God. (61)

Hussayn also confronted the chief religious scholar of Akbar's court, Makhdum al-Mulk, whom he criticized for being wealthy and greedy. Later Hussayn confronted the emperor Akbar himself. Akbar questioned why he drank wine in public while claiming to be a saint, but did not question his sexuality.[16] The encounter ended with Akbar acknowledging Hussayn as a great saint and one of the pillars of Lahore's spiritual well-being. Thereafter, religious scholars' protests quieted down. Nobles began to seek his blessings. As one of Akbar's chief nobles, the Hindi poet Abd al-Rahim Khan-i Khanan, was traveling with an army toward Sindh, he stopped in Lahore to receive Hussayn's blessing. The army successfully conquered Thatta in Sindh, and Hussayn's reputation spread. Prince Salim, who later became the em-

---

16. *Haqiqat al-Fuqara*, folio 74.

peror Jahangir, ordered an account of Hussayn's life to be recorded by Bahar Khan. Hussayn was also held in high esteem by later Mughal nobles, including Dara Shukoh, who mentions Hussayn in his book on spiritual boasts of the saints, *Shathiyat*, and in his memorial to the saints, *Hasanat al-'Arifin*.

Madho stayed with Hussayn and his companions for a few years, then asked permission to join the military service. He left Lahore in the service of Raja Man Singh for a three-year stint in the army, fighting in Bengal and the Dekkan. Then he returned to live with Hussayn until the saint's death in 1599 at the age of about sixty. Hussayn had prepared his own grave next to their home. Madho was inconsolable and grew weak with mourning. He wished to die in order to be reunited with Hussayn.[17] After some time, he joined the army again, journeying for twelve years throughout Hindustan. Finally, he returned to Lahore to live at Hussayn's tomb for thirty-five more years. He lived in isolation and become known as the spiritual successor of Hussayn's saintly authority. Upon his death Madho was buried directly beside Hussayn, and their tomb is a shrine today, the focus for a riotous celebration on the anniversary of Hussayn's death, accompanied by frenzied drumming, ecstatic dance, and blazing fires.

In stark contrast to the explicitly erotic terms used in this medieval biography, modern commentators both in Urdu and in English are extremely uncomfortable with the life of Shah Hussayn. Lajwanti Ramakrishna, who has written the definitive book in English on Shah Hussayn, states that "many people had become suspicious of the un-natural [sic] relationship."[18] She further reveals her misunderstanding when she writes that "Hussayn tried for sixteen years to possess the lad" although the sources show that Hussayn was not interested in possessing Madho, only in loving him. Ramakrishna deviates from the sources in speculating that Madho moved in with Hussayn not for love but only for shelter, since he had been "excommunicated" by his parents and the Brahman community after having eaten with Hussayn and his companions. She adds that a man loving a youth "is opposed to the Indian concept of Divine Love." She does not explain why a very Indian Sufi like Hussayn whose family had no claim to Persian ancestry or education and whose poetic output is so clearly Punjabi did in fact love a young man. It is clear that Ramakrishna knew of the existence of the poetic biography I have translated but chose to ignore it although she consulted other manuscript sources at the same archive. She claims that

---

17. *Haqiqat al-Fuqara,* folio 102.
18. Lajwanti Ramakrishna, *Punjabi Sufi Poets: AD 1460–1900* (New Delhi: Ashajanak Publications, 1973), 32–46. Other studies which focus on Shah Hussayn as a poet include Ramakrishna and A. Rauf Luther, *Madho Lal Hussayn: Sufi Poet of the Punjab* (Lahore: Shaykh Mubarak Ali, 1982), and Najm Hosain Syed, *Recurrent Patterns in Punjabi Poetry* (Lahore: Majlis Shah Husain, 1968).

"as far as [Hussayn's] poetry can help us, we can find no immoral flaw in Lal Hussayn's love for Madho."

Shuja al-Haqq is a bit more frank in his assessment when he writes that "Hussayn became enamored of his [Madho's] beauty at the first sight of him. From then onward he could not rest without seeing him. He had to live in separation from him for some time until the youth also began to be attracted to him."[19] Yogi Sikand's essay shows how Shah Hussayn's love for Madho was an important part of his spirituality. He writes that "It is possible and indeed very likely that Hussayn's greatly unconventional involvement with Madho had a deep impact on his own thinking, his mystical poetry and most of all his religious life."[20]

Modern Urdu writers also bowdlerize the Persian sources that they claim to be translating. Nur Ahmad Chishti writes a long description of Shah Hussayn and Madho in which he claims to be quoting this biography I have translated, *Haqiqat al-Fuqara*. Yet when he describes the scene of intimacy between Hussayn and Madho at Babupur, he writes in one line only "So the saint, while drinking wine, embraced Madho and made him arrive at the Truth [wasl bi-Haqq], making Madho into a complete and perfected saint himself without any rigors or strenuous labors."[21] The erotic encounter, with its play of kissing and embracing, has been erased. Most contemporary Urdu sources are based on this early translation and repeat the erasure.[22] Other Urdu sources do not even mention Madho.[23] This process began early, for even in the Persian collection of saints' stories composed in 1865, Madho is mentioned only once, in passing.[24]

Similar types of distortion occur in the biographies of other Sufis, for example, that of Shaikh Makhu, a Gujarati Sufi who was a contemporary of Shah Hussayn. The biographical compendium, *Gulzar-i Abrar* (Blooming Garden of the Righteous), in its original and unpublished Persian, states that the saint, at the age of forty, fell in love with a handsome young man named Hansu. Yet in the Urdu translation that is published and widely quoted, the Urdu translator records that Hansu was a beautiful young woman.[25]

19. Shuja al-Haqq, *A Forgotten Vision: A Study of Human Spirituality in the Light of the Islamic Traditions,* 2 vols. (New Delhi: Vikas, 1997) 2: 219–34. Rizvi also cites the love of these two men, without analyzing the phenomenon or assessing its importance, in S. A. A. Rizvi, *History of Sufism in India* (Delhi: Munshiram Manoharlal, 1978, reprinted 1986) vol. 2: 64–65 and 437–38.
20. Yogi Sikand, "Martyr for Gay Love," *Bombay Dost,* 4: 4 (1998): 8–9.
21. *Tahqiqat-i Chishti,* 307–61.
22. See Muhammad Latif Malik, *Auliya-i Lahore* (Lahore: Sang-i Meel, no date): 145–74.
23. See Aijaz al-Haqq Qudusi, *Tazkirah-i Sufiya-i Punjab* (Lahore: Salman Academy, 1962); M. Habibullah Faruqi and Mohan Singh Diwana, *Halat o Kafiyan Madho Lal Hussayn* (Lahore: Malik Ahmad Taj Book Depot, no date).
24. Ghulam Sarwar Lahori, *Khazinat al-Asfia* (Lucknow: Munshi Nawal Kishore, n d): 141–46.
25. See Fazl Ahmad Jiyuri, trans., *Azkar-i Abrar: Urdu Translation of Gulzar-i Abrar* (Lahore: Islamic Book Foundation, 1975), 458.

Sarmad (Persian)[1]

Introduced and translated by Saleem Kidwai

Sarmad (eternal, inebriated) was born a Jew in Kashan, around 1590.[2] He became a trader and acquired knowledge of mystic traditions and of Arabic and Persian poetry. Before he arrived in the port city of Thatta in 1632, he had converted to Islam. In Thatta he met a Hindu boy named Abhai Chand. The attraction was mutual and soon after meeting him, Sarmad abandoned his trade and became a naked faqir.[3]

According to the official biography of Sarmad published by the keepers of his shrine, Sarmad first saw the young Abhai Chand when he was singing a *ghazal* at a poets' gathering. Sarmad was smitten by his beauty. Abhai Chand responded warmly: "For some days this attraction continued from afar. Eventually the sparks of this fire were fanned by the flames of love and it began to blaze and Abhai Chand began staying with Sarmad." Both the governor of the province and Abhai's father tried to separate them, but eventually they gave in when they realized how pure this love was. Sarmad soon taught Abhai all that he knew. The author of the seventeenth-century *Dabistan-i Mazahib* (Compendium of Religions) is said to have gotten his information on Judaism from Abhai Chand.

---

1. Poems translated from Nawab Ali Saulat, ed., *Rubiyat Sarmad Mahmud* (Delhi: Shahjahani Press, 1921).
2. Biographical details from M. G. Gupta, *Sarmad the Saint* (Agra: M. G. Publishers, 1991). Also see the book published by the official keepers of Sarmad's shrine, *Sayyid Muhammad Ahmad Sarmadi, Tazkirah Hazrat Sarmad Shahid* (Delhi: Kutub Khana Sarmadi, no date). See also I. A. Ezekiel, *Sarmad, the Jewish Saint of India* (Beas, Punjab: Radha Soami Satsang, 1996).
3. Other naked faqirs were Shaikh Badhni and a eunuch named Rahat (M. Mujib, *The Indian Muslims,* London: George Allen & Unwin, 1967), 157–59. There were (and are) orders of naked Hindu ascetics too, such as the Nagas, and of Jains, the Digambaras. Some individual Bhakta mystics threw off all clothing when they renounced the world. Among them were the women poets Mahadeviakka and Lal Ded.

Sarmad and Abhai traveled from Sindh to the Dekkan and then to Delhi. In Delhi Sarmad found an admirer in Dara Shukoh, eldest son of the Mughal emperor Shah Jahan. Prince Dara was a philosopher, interested in mystical traditions of all religions. Dara's younger brother Aurangzeb won the war for the throne and executed Dara and Sarmad in 1660. The stated reason for Sarmad's execution was that he refused to abandon his nudity, which the orthodox considered reprehensible. The more important reason may have been that Sarmad was a partisan of Dara.

Sarmad was buried at the foot of the Jama Masjid in Delhi. Today he is considered a martyr. His tomb is a much-frequented shrine and he is popularly known as Hare Bhare Shah (the Colorful Saint). Sarmad's poetry follows the classical pattern of Persian mystic poetry where the Divine and the earthly are often addressed as the same and where love of a human is the way to love of the Divine.

O veiled one, why don't you reveal yourself
How long shall I search for your dwelling?
I yearn to embrace you, hold you by my side,
How long will you stay hidden from me? (4)[4]

My beloved does not even glance at me—what shall I do?
The heart's wail he does not hear, what shall I do?
In my heart he is forever present
But is unaware of its state, what shall I do? (192)

I am crazy for the luster of my beloved who is different
I am amazed by his beautiful form which is different.
The rest are involved in cares and woes which are different,
My fears and grief are about something that is different. (196)

I have been saddened by that curly ringlet—
I had not planned it, it was my luck.
I am now a prisoner of that curl
As if it was a fetter around my foot. (200)

I am in sorrow, having sowed the seeds of lust
I now pluck flowers discolored a thousandfold.
I must extinguish these flames
Before they become a blazing fire. (204)

---

4. Translation from *Naghma-i Sarmad*, ed. Arsh Malsiyani (Delhi: Markaz Tasnif Was Taalif, no date). Quatrain numbering according to this text.

Muhammad Akram "Ghanimat" Kanjohi: Love's Sorcery (Persian)

Summarized by Saleem Kidwai

Poet "Ghanimat" (Good Fortune) wrote in the second half of the seventeenth century and was employed by a provincial chieftain during the reign of the Mughal emperor Aurangzeb (died 1707). His reputation is based on *Nai Rangi i-ishq*, the *masnavi* (narrative poem) summarized below, which continued to be used as a text in *madarsas* (Muslim schools) until the nineteenth century. The latest edition we could find was published in 1870 by Navalkishore Press, Lucknow.[1]

Dedicated to God, who is referred to as the *Shahid* (beloved) of the brokenhearted, the poem begins with the poet's confession of his transgressions. He prays for a beloved whom he can hold in his lap, embrace and make his own, and also prays that God make him God's lover.

Following Sufi conventions, the poem recounts the love story of the metaphorically named Aziz (Lover) and Shahid. The poet remarks that a relative of his was in love with a boy called Shahid and, after much pain, found the path to divine love. Shahid was born to a poor family in Punjab, land of love and beauty. When he was ten, he shone like the full moon and had innumerable admirers. He joined a company of wandering Hindu mystics and sang with them. One day they performed at the house of a provincial chief. His son Aziz's heart was set ablaze and the smoke formed a screen across his face. Many in the city also lost their hearts to Shahid, alarming the official censors. Recording this conflict between Muslim religious orthodoxy and Muslim mysticism, the poet warns the custodians of public morality not to challenge lovers who are ready to fight and die for love.

An officer set out to confront Shahid but the moment he saw him, he too fell in love so madly that he forgot the rituals of compulsory prayer. It was said in town that the rod of the

---

1. This edition was used for the summary. I am grateful to Muhammad Asfar Faridy and Muzaffar Alam for their help in translating the poem.

censor had blossomed into a vine branch. The Qazi, the chief Muslim judicial officer, chided his subordinate for worshiping an infidel and went to report to the chieftain. As the Qazi argued against Shahid, Aziz, sitting next to his father, felt every mention of Shahid's name as a stab in the heart.

On the chieftain's orders, Shahid was arrested and was about to be banished, but Aziz pleaded that he be allowed to host Shahid for one night. Aziz organized a huge gathering where Shahid's singing and dancing sent everyone into ecstasy. Aching to make Shahid his own, Aziz offered him his whole fortune and begged him to move in with him. Shahid, however, missed his fellow mystics and left with them.

After leaving, Shahid was in pain and remembered the suffering Aziz. Deciding to be kind to his lover, he returned and told Aziz that he had chosen him over his own people. Aziz built Shahid a house and gave him his best servants. At night when all was quiet, he would invite Shahid to his room, but except for a few confidants, no one knew of this. Gossipmongers, whose tongues should be cut off, took Aziz's father to the room and showed him Aziz and Shahid lost in each other. Furious, the father banished Shahid once again, whereupon Aziz lost his sanity and wandered about, looking for his love. On the advice of his counselors, the father brought Shahid back, apologized and begged him to stay, adding that even though Aziz was his lover, his own heart too had been wounded by looking at Shahid. He also assured his son that he could live with Shahid like two flowers in a garden.

Shahid started going to school, where he caused chaos. The teacher of the school, a lover by temperament, lost his heart and so did all the other schoolboys. Shahid would have made the philosopher Aristotle a lover like Majnu had they met. Once, when Shahid went to visit his mother, Aziz could not bear the separation and followed him, disguised as a messenger. Shahid recognized him and returned.

Once, while out hunting, Shahid met a beautiful peasant girl Wafa (Faith) and fell in love with her. After some adventures, Shahid eloped with Wafa and disappeared. Aziz searched for him in vain. Waiting endlessly, he lost his senses. By thinking of nothing but Shahid, he was led to contemplate the beauty and majesty of Shahid's creator, and thus he progressed from earthly love to divine love.

Najmuddin Shah Mubarak *"Abru"*:
Advice to a Beloved *(Urdu)*[1]

Translated by Saleem Kidwai,
versified by Ruth Vanita

Najmuddin Shah Mubarak, who used the pen name "Abru" (Honor) was among the earliest well known Urdu poets of north India. He came from a family of Sufi saints and scholars. He was born in Gwalior in central India, ca. 1683, and migrated to Delhi for employment. He died in December 1733 after being kicked by a horse.[2]

During Abru's lifetime, important Urdu poetry first appeared in the literary gatherings of Delhi, and Abru influenced the early development not only of the language but also of its best known genre, the *ghazal*. Contemporaries describe him as a "worshiper of beauty" and speak of his "romantic temperament."[3] Few biographical details are available except that Abru had only one eye and was attached to another poet, Mir Makkhan, who used the pen-name "Pak Baaz."[4]

Abru contributed much to the evolution of Urdu as well as the formation of the ghazal. He is considered foremost of the *ihamgo* poets who played on words (see p. 123). Abru used words from Persian, Hindvi, Khari Boli, Punjabi, Haryanvi, Rajasthani, and Dekkani Urdu in his poetry. All subsequent ihamgo poets are judged by the standard of Abru.

Not much attention has been paid to the preservation of Abru's work. Only one manuscript of the untitled *masnavi*, translated below, survives. However, this poem was well-known in Abru's own time. Contemporaries referred to it as "Advice for the Adornment of a

1. Mohammad Hasan, ed., *Diwan-i-Abru* (New Delhi: Taraqqi Urdu Bureau, 1990), 298–308. Our translation is a somewhat condensed version and the numbers follow the order in Mohammad Hasan's edition.
2. Jamil Jalibi, *Tarikh I Urdu Adab* (Delhi: Educational Publishing House, 1977; 1989) vol. 2, part 1, 212.
3. Hasan, *Diwan-i-Abru*, 9–12
4. He was the son of Saiyyid Shah Kamal Bukhari. Abru mentions the name Mir Makkhan Pak Baz as his beloved in a few couplets. Jalibi, *Tarikh I Urdu Adab*, 211.

Beloved." The only published version is poorly edited. Many couplets are incomplete, some are incomprehensible and many are not properly deciphered.

All you who love the things I do and say,
Shall I tell you what happened the other day? (1)

Depressed at home that day I set out,
To take a walk, to wander about. (2)

Through Delhi's markets, gardens, canal street,
I strolled, wondering whom I'd chance to meet. (3)

All at once, I saw a real beauty—
I lost my heart to him instantly. (4)

How shall I paint his picture—with what art?
He was a dream to subjugate the heart. (5)

Those eyes, those brows, that softly glowing face—
Each part of him a captivating grace. (6)

His body soft, his face smooth and pure,
Magnetized me with a strange allure. (8)

But all oblivious of his own attractions
He was, in baggy clothes and clumsy turban. (9–10)

This waywardness enhanced the stripling's sway,
But all admirers he kept at bay, (11)

Warding off every enamored glance
With "Brother, kindly keep your distance." (12)

"What a waste," I thought, "what a pity—
Such pure notes bereft of melody." (13)

[14–28: The poet begins to talk to the boy, who is thrilled when he realizes this is
the famous Abru. When the boy expresses his admiration and begs that he continue talking, Abru facetiously remarks that as all his poetry is in praise of lovers,
the boy might be interested in it but is unlikely to be guided by it.]

He got my drift and eagerly replied,
"Sir, teach me love's art—I would have died

To meet you, to this end—please do advise
Me how to conquer hearts, please make me wise."(29–32)

I said, "Sure, I'll give it to you straight—
No fancy words but you must concentrate (33–34)

. . . .

Remember what I say—a lad like you,
So uninformed, must mold himself anew (35–37)

. . . .

First let your hair grow out and fall in locks
Around your face, but not run wild—that shocks

The connoisseurs of beauty; snip your curls,
But no shaving, no razors, no sideburns! [38–41]

Wash your hair with shampoo every morning,
Never skip this—oil it, comb it, adorning

It in braids, in buns, but please don't keep
Flaunting it to get stared at—that's cheap. (42–44)

A bit of oil and turmeric on your skin—
And when it's sunny, please, please, stay in! (47)

Saffron and jasmine oil with lemon juice
Gets rid of blemishes and acne—use (48–49)

It each night, and wash it off each morning.
Whiten your teeth, darken your gums; chewing

Betel will keep your lips red—smile a lot
But don't say much, and, my dear, not a jot

More collyrium than your eyes can take—
Too much of it looks dreadfully fake. (50–52)

Put henna on your fingers, not your palms;
If you like fingerbands, enhance your charms,

My beauteous fairy, with an amber ring—
A shining necklace too is quite the thing.

Be sure your sleeves don't hide your amulet,
Keep dust of *karbala* in your locket.[5]

---

5. The battleground in modern Iraq where the Prophet's younger grandson Husain lost his
   life fighting the Caliph Yazid in A.D. 680. It is a sacred site for Shia Muslims.

Wear golden bracelets on both your arms—(54–62)
If they look good on you, what's the harm?

If you wear a turban, wrap it carefully—
Untie and tie a hundred times if need be.

Stand at the mirror—take pride in your work,
Fold it neat, pile it high like local folk.

I've seen hundreds of turbans in my day—
Each fell short of perfect in some way. (63–68)

Study all styles of dress, and choose the kind
Which makes you look your best, and most refined.

A perfect fit, matching shades, none clashing,
A long kurta, creased at the waist, looks dashing.

Well starched and ironed clothes, sleeves neatly pleated,
Fabrics, not too thin or thick—try the blended.

Trousers neither too wide nor too narrow,
Everything in proportion's best, you know.

Shoes with embroidery or with sequins shine
But can look good too in a plain design. (73–87)

A sash has manifold uses for a charmer—
Trail it behind or use it like armor—

Cover your face with it (let eyes peep through!)
Or wrap it round your head and turban too,

Drape it on your right shoulder, to your left
Hang your dagger with gilt-carven heft. (88–93)

Dressed in such style, enter any room
Like a garden in full springtime bloom, (94)

Chewing betel, your lips red and rosy,
Your smile like pearls gleaming through rubies. (95)

Perfume yourself, sit down elegantly
To smoke a hubble-bubble—use your hanky

To dab your brow and cheeks from time to time.
Chirp like a nightingale and scatter smiles—(96–98)

Beauty without wit is tasteless fare,
What draws lovers is a playful air. (100)

A calm and graceful mien, good conversation,
Bright eyes and manners that provide diversion. [102–03]

Swaying as you walk is an attraction,
Don't overdo it—all things in proportion! (104)

If you enjoy mincing, swaying, prancing,
Do it in a way that proves entrancing. (105)

Even sitting down can be an art—
Sit delicately, grace in every part. (106)

Always smile before you start to speak,
Weave every gesture into your mystique. (107)

Forget even keen hunger when you're talking,
Express desire with playful amorous glancing—(108)

Learn the art of speaking with your eyes—
A lifted brow can smile, can weep, can sigh. (109)

Make every moment uniquely your own
That all may say: "What style! What grace! What tone!" (110)

Ignore someone, and smile on someone else,
Now a coquette, now subtlety itself. (112)

Look away, then let your eyes meet theirs,
A wounding glance; a blush; a knowing stare

As if you read the heart, then in a moment
Wide-eyed, and altogether innocent. (114–19)

Eyes on their own can do all acts of love—
Assess, seduce, encounter, and rebuff.

Talk to all, but look much more at one,
Send eye-to-eye epistles on the run,

Find ways to talk, or if he seeks you out,
Meet him halfway—that's pleasurable, no doubt. (120–28)

But, careful! don't become a laughingstock
For those who want to use you and then mock

You—the base, the vulgar, the dissolute
Who pose as noble lovers—be astute

And keep away from them—the heartless too,
Who envy beauty, will only ruin you. (130–40)

Look for a decent person—when you find
Your love is driving him out of his mind—

Restless by day and night, he roams around,
Only the sight of you can calm him down,

Such men are rare—a veritable treasure,
Do everything that will give him pleasure.

Love without shame; if he's possessive of you,
My dear, why wound the heart of one who loves you? (141–49)

I've seen hundreds of beauties of your kind—
Believe me, dear, true love is hard to find. (150)

Still searching, lonely through the world I wander—
They all want sex, but where is a true lover? (151)

Remember, beauty's virtue—search it out—
One worth loving can never be a lout. (153)

Beauty must know its worth, keep its good name,
Love dies when loved ones have no pride, no shame.

Brook no insults, behave with dignity,
Let none embarrass you in company. (154–59)

Beauty makes you a king, but who would be
A potentate at someone else's mercy? (161)

You are the king, those courting you the courtiers—
One hands out payments, one is chief minister, (162)

One spends the days and nights with you, his star.
One can only greet you from afar. (163). . . .

One's appointed to keep you entertained,
Another by the watchmen is restrained. (164)

Great is the kingly power of the fair—
While one exults, another's in despair.

But all must be obedient and polite,
Though they are rivals, don't let them ever fight. (165–169)

To be accomplished, virtuous, well framed,
Makes one beloved—the heart is claimed (171)

Not by beauty alone, but by the art
That's beauty's life, and breathes in every part. (172)

The wise are cautious, don't fall easily,
They check the beauteous ones out carefully, (173)

But beauty perfect in love's many arts
Trips up the wisest, makes him lose his heart. (174)

Beauty sans virtue and accomplishment
Is like a flower, all show, but lacking scent.

The charms of face and form will fade and flee
But virtue's beauty still the same will be. (176–77)

Don't drink with strangers, you'll get a bad name—
They'll take advantage of you, then defame

You—soon, the city starts to talk—beware,
Dear one, of scandal—it destroys the fair. (179–85)

Never be tempted by the lure of gold,
Or soon you'll find yourself being bought and sold.

Accept even one coin—you're in their debt—
A kiss is nothing, they'll take all they can get. (187–90)

Be self-contained, not greedy—this rare state
A well-bred person can appreciate. (192)

One who commits himself to loving you
Will give you all unasked—wealth, and life too. (193)

Don't fret—remember, what is in your fate
Must come to you, whether early or late. (195)

When on your cheeks the down begins to show
Don't shave at first, let God's handiwork grow.

Let all be maddened by these signs of spring
But when hairs coarsen, you must start shaving. (196–204)

When you know you've lost your loveliness,
The delicate bloom is gone, the youthful grace, (206)

Then all you've heard of beauty's fickle ways—
You'll see it happen; the admirers' gaze

Is turned elsewhere; spring has come and gone:
Where flowers blossomed, now there sprouts the thorn. (207–09)

Then give up the desire to be adored,
Don't overdress or act coy any more.

Love your friends with no ulterior aims,
Mingle with lovers, make no special claims.
 Enjoy the company of beauteous ones."
Now I'd said all I had to say—enough

To teach him how to mold himself and win
The hearts worth winning, so let him begin. (210–18)

Now may all lovers get their hearts' desire,
May those who yearn be blessed with love's sweet fire. (219)

All I want is your happiness, dear readers,
I aim to please—my art adds to your pleasures. (220)

Immersed in love's sweet pain, if you should pray,
Remember me too in your prayers today. (221)

Let me not be deprived, in this world
Or the next—let Abru's honor be preserved. (223)

Siraj Aurangabadi:
The Garden of Delusion *(Urdu)*

Translated by Saleem Kidwai

ayyid Sirajuddin, "Siraj Aurangabadi" (ca.1715–1763) was a Sufi poet, who wrote first in Persian and then in Urdu. He compiled his poems in 1738 and stopped writing poetry when he was twenty-four, on the advice of his *pir*.

The following is a summary of his narrative poem, *Bustan-i Khayal*, which contains 1,162 couplets.[1]

O friends, listen to my strange tale for all my sorrows revolve around just one ache.

My heart no longer blooms when I am in a garden nor is it distracted when I stroll in the streets. Would it matter if I were given a kingdom or if I were taught alchemy? My lover has left my heart inconsolable, my world desolate. Each sigh is a flame and each breath the end of life's game. This is how I fare each day, and every night is the same nightmare. I feed on the night, and by day my heart bleeds.

There was a time when I was with my flower-faced beloved and life felt divine. Always together, hand in hand, we would talk and drink wine. The nights were moonlit, every gesture was an embrace, and together we would recite *ghazals*. We did what we wanted, the drums of pleasure beating in our ears. Even silence was a treasure for life was brimming with pleasure. With my beloved beside me, I had no fear of the future. This sounds like a fairy tale from the past. That happiness unfortunately did not last.

Yes, there were many others, all lovely, each one nature's brilliant gift. A flowing tress, a frown, a swing of the hips or a sparkle from their eyes left lovers dumb. The brush would swoon if it had to paint their likeness. Their words were nectar to the soul, their

---

1. *Kulliyat-i Siraj*, ed. Abdul Qadir Sarvari (Delhi: Qaumi Council Barai Farosh-i Urdu Zaban, 1998), 149–246.

looks could put a mirror to shame. With hair sprouting on their faces, they were like a thousand Yusufs—delicate, smooth, pink, and heavenly.

With turbans of brocade, strings of flowers wrapped around their wrists and necks, sashes round their waists, scarves around their necks, they carried swords or daggers in velvet scabbards.

They targeted the well known and famous with their sweet talk and wiles. To be the beloved of someone with a name was their way to fame. They knew me as a Darvesh, a heart-pleasing poet with a shattered heart, well spoken and kind. And when they found that I had many devotees, that I'm known far and wide, toward me they came. They tried to win my heart with respect. But I wasn't to be distracted and they took it as a challenge. When we can have any of thousands, how is it that we fail to attract him? they wondered.

They were wise in the knowledge of seduction. They changed their tactics. Respect and devotion they replaced with intimacy and flirtation; they'd hold my hand, bring their faces close to mine, touch my hair, put their heads on my shoulder or creep under my shawl. They wanted me to be the seeker and themselves the sought. Their wiles could have driven the most abstemious to madness. My heart however was no longer mine to lose. Their antics made me even sadder, for all I could think of was my own Mohan.[2]

Among them, the finest was the son of a Sardar.[3] He had wealth, his own forces, elephants and standard bearers. Were I to describe his beauty I'd be speechless for life. When half asleep, he yawned, my heart would ache to be by his side. He was beautiful and generous and won everyone's heart. Everything one could want, he had. To me he was exceptionally kind.

He said to me, I know lovers have no home, but will you come to mine? If you do, I'd welcome each step of yours.

To his home I went. He was loving and hospitable. He claimed to be my slave. If I didn't eat, neither did he. When I couldn't sleep, he sat up with me. He would tell me stories or sing me a song, asking me what I wanted to hear. But the pain would not leave my heart for long. Look at the clouds, he said one day, let's go out and maybe you will forget your ache. He took me by the hand and would not let me refuse. Going to the garden was a mistake. Everything was beautiful, peacocks were dancing and it was raining. And he was perfect. But I was cursed by a sorrow which only someone who has been through it would know. I missed my beloved even more.

Then I saw a cypress and imagined it was my lost beloved. I ran to it crying and fainted. I ruined the day for everyone as well as my companion. He took me home and when we were alone, he said: Are you in love that you have lost your mind? Who is he? Talk, for the pain might go away. Tell me his name—what did he do?

---

2. Enchanting one; a name of Krishna, the divine lover.
3. A military commander.

He had been so kind, I did not want to make him sad. When he insisted, I had to tell him all, and it wasn't easy:

O beautiful one, I have been the victim of another faithless one. One who did not know what promises meant, yet for the dust of whose feet I still crave. I was seven, had just discovered poetry, when I first saw him. Seven years passed, and I learned the ways of life. I became renowned for my knowledge and he for his beauty. Suddenly he appeared before me like a vision, perfect from head to toe. Speechless, I managed to ask him his name, and said: Why don't you come this way more often? You can bring your books and I can teach you what I know.

He started coming frequently and I was in love. He started spending all his time with me for he too couldn't do without me. If he went home I couldn't sleep and he too would return immediately. We were one, by passion engulfed. People talked and the envious were incensed. His people were outraged. It's inappropriate, this friendship with a Muslim, they said. We will cast you out of the community,[4] they threatened.

I don't care, he said, as long as I have my Siraj. That's all that matters to me. When he related this to me I was aghast. You should have kept quiet, I said at last. We can still be friends and you needn't be defamed. He insisted he was mine forever. People saw the truth, this welding of hearts. The gossip died and so did the strife.

I was lucky and felt like a king. I had found a beloved with the heart of a lover. We were going to be together, forever. I had no idea what fate held for me. I did not know that this friend would become my enemy.

An accursed individual, inspired by envy, turned my world topsy-turvy. He turned my beloved against me. He left and I was bereft. He avoided me, and before his house I would stand and fall at his feet when he appeared. I would remind him of our love. In return he would throw abuse and stones at me. Seven years have passed and still it is only he I can think about.

The Sardar's son was moved by my tale of sorrow and said: This person was not worthy of you. Forget him, I too am beautiful and would do any thing for you. If you called the dawn evening, and the earth the sky, so would I. I will make you forget the past.

Those who have been hurt by lovers fear lovers the most. My pain is incurable. Why should you suffer for something for which you are not responsible? I said. How can Heer cure the injury done by Laila? Nala who suffers for Damyanti, cannot be cured by Chandrabadan. I have already lost my heart, how can I give it to you? Begging his forgiveness I left and went to Hyderabad where my tormentor lived.

Reaching the city felt like a balm to the soul. My heart was bursting in my chest. I headed straight toward the street of my beloved. I saw him step out, smiling and intoxicated by his own beauty. He headed straight toward me and I fainted. He held me and hugged me and claimed he had suffered just as I did. What I did was the fault of

4. The boy was a Hindu. For a similar situation in the life of Madho Lal Hussayn and Sarmad, see p. 148.

an accursed one, he said. I forsake the past and swear my love again. Take hold of your-self, your state is not appropriate for a public place. Go now and rest, and come back in the morning.

The ways of the beautiful are fake and their words untrustworthy. I found that out again the next morning when he behaved as if nothing had happened the day before. He was his cruel self again. I lost my mind, banged my head on stones and wandered off again into the wilderness. Death seemed the only solution and much as I tried, it wouldn't come.

Then it struck me that the only solution was to turn my heart to God. And to him I turned and prayed: Free me from the snare of those tresses, save me from those pointed eyelashes. Save me from the chains of their beauty, let me not taste the honey from their lips. Save me from the beautiful ones so that I may see your beauty.

Mir Abdul Hai "Taban": A Lover Who Looked like a Beloved (Urdu)[1]

Introduced and translated by Saleem Kidwai

Mir Abdul Hai "Taban" (Luminous) lived in Delhi. He was born some time between 1718 and 1722 A.D.[2] All contemporaries, including Mir Taqi Mir, describe him as extremely good looking and often refer to him as Yusuf-i sani, the second Yusuf.[3] He always dressed in black. A story frequently related is that the Mughal emperor Shah Alam, on hearing of Taban's beauty, wanted to have a look at him and arranged to pass by his house. Taban heard of this and made sure he was sitting in front of his house when the royal cavalcade passed.[4]

Taban was attached to a male friend called Sulaiman whom he mentions by name in a few couplets.[5] He was also very close to the famous poet Mazhar Jan-i Janan (1700–1781). Muhammad Hussain describes Taban's familiarities with the senior poet of whom others were in awe. Taban would take the liberty, in public, of whispering into Jan-i Janan's ears' remarks that would make him laugh. In a recent edition of Taban's poems, the editor is at pains to stress that despite the various rumors about their relationship, the real relation between them was that of a master and a disciple.[6] Tariq Rahman, on the other hand states that Taban was

1. Translated from Abdul Haq, ed., *Diwan-i Taban* (Aurangabad: Anjuman Taraqqi Urdu, 1935). As the couplets are not numbered in the original, I have numbered the couplets on each page separately. In parentheses, I indicate the page number followed by couplet numbers.
2. Ismat Malihabadi, ed., *Intikhab-i Abdul Hai Taban* (Lucknow: Uttar Pradesh Urdu Academy, 1997), 5.
3. The biblical Joseph, traditionally considered the epitome of irresistible male beauty.
4. Muhammad Hussain Azad, *Aab i-hayat* (Calcutta: Usmaniya Book Depot, 1967), 170–71.
5. Malihabadi, *Intikhab-i Abdul Hai Taban*, 7.
6. Malihabadi, *Intikhab-i Abdul Hai Taban*, 5.

"actually the beloved of the poet Jan-e Janan."[7] Taban drank a lot; while still in his twenties, he died of a drink-related illness (ca. 1750).[8]

> My nemesis, as you deal the worst you've ever dealt,
> Have you any thought of how I feel, or have you not?
> With trepidation, when I told the dandy how I felt
> He snapped, do you want to live, or do you not?
> Some say it's nonexistent, others that it's very svelte—
> You can tell us, dear one, is that a waist, or is it not?
> Wonder why, today, he asked Taban how I feel—
> He must know a bit of how he feels, or does he not? (123: 6, 9, 10; 124: 1)
>
> All the nights that he with others spends—
> By telling me of them what does he gain?
> When anguish echoing through this world ends,
> My heart, even then do not tell your pain.
> Wounds as keen as my beau extends
> Even the Rustum-hearted cannot sustain.[9]
> Taban, your strange state none comprehends—
> Night and day you weep, yet silence maintain. (26:1, 3, 4, 5)
>
> When I sleep all night with my flowerlike beloved,
> Next day, I'm steeped in fragrance from his clinging.
> Sweet one, since your lover has been from you severed,
> He is never seen laughing, only lamenting.
> Dear one, drink less, don't get so intoxicated,
> When you swoon, you leave my senses swooning.
>
> These drops of sweat, in your locks scattered,
> Appear to me as pearls threaded on a string.
> All the world knows how your Taban is agitated,
> All are woken at night by the sound of his weeping. (150: 2–6)
>
> My longing has drawn my Yusuf to me—
> Your love, Taban, can achieve the impossible. (3: 9)
>
> You, who were displeased when Taban gazed,
> Must be glad now the spring has fled from his face. (5:6)
>
> What if I cannot see you, my Sulaiman—
> Your image dwells and moves in my eyes. (153:5)

---

7. Tariq Rahman, "Boy Love in the Urdu Ghazal," *Annual of Urdu Studies,* 7(1990): 1–20; 8–9.
8. Malihabadi, *Intikhab-i Abdul Hai Taban,* 10.
9. Tough as the legendary Persian warrior Rustum.

Dargah Quli Khan:
Portrait of a City (Persian)[1]

Commentary and translation by Saleem Kidwai

D argah Quli Khan belonged to a family of Persians who migrated to India in the first half of the seventeenth century. He was born in 1710 A.D. in Aurangabad and, at the age of fourteen, joined the service of Nawab Nizamul Mulk Asaf Jah I, autonomous Mughal governor of Dekkan Province. Later appointed official chronicler, Quli Khan was a part of the retinue of Asaf Jah l when he traveled to Delhi. They were in Delhi from June 1738 to July 1741 and witnessed the sack of Delhi by Nadir Shah in 1739.

Dargah Quli Khan kept a record of his visit, known as the *Risalah e Salar Jung* (The Treatise of Salar Jung). In 1926 the sections concerning Delhi were extracted and published as *Muraqqa i Dehli*. Since then Dargah Quli Khan's journal has been known by this title.

Dargah Quli Khan was an enthusiastic chronicler of the life of Delhi and its people—the nobility, the common folk, musicians, dancers, poets, artistes, and sex workers—as well as the social occasions that marked the calendar of Delhi. He vividly sketched the bazaars and *dargahs* (shrines), two of the most important, predominantly male, social spaces of the city. His work is a useful description of the metropolis and some of its remarkable inhabitants.[2]

---

1. This text has been re-edited three times and translated four times, once into English. This translation is from *Muraqqa i Dehli*, Persian text with Urdu translation, edited and translated by Khaliq Anjum (New Delhi: Anjuman Taraqqi Urdu [Hind], 1993). The page references are from this edition. This editor seems to have collated the largest number of extant manuscripts. The English translation, *Muraqqa-e-Dehli: The Mughal Capital in Muhammad Shah's Time,* by Chander Shekhar and Shama Mitra Chenoy (Delhi: Deputy Publication, 1989), is rife with bowdlerizations.
2. For example Stephen Blake, *Shahjahanabad: The Sovereign City in Mughal India 1639–1739* (Cambridge: Cambridge University Press, 1991), depends entirely on Dargah Quli Khan for re-creating the "popular culture" of the city; see 153–60.

The commercial life of the city centered around two markets—Chowk Sa'adullah Khan and Chandni Chowk. Both were near the main mosque, Jama Masjid, and the royal palace, the Red Fort. A variety of goods imported from distant Indian provinces as well as from the Middle East and Europe were on sale here, and the squares were full of storytellers, astrologers, pavement doctors, and hawkers of all sorts. Men from all classes visited these bazaars, some to patronize the coffee and tea shops where poets recited their compositions. Aristocrats had to pass through the milling crowds on their way to the mosque or the palace, and many lingered to enjoy the sights. As Quli Khan described it: "Young good-looking men danced everywhere and created great excitement. . . . Young men and pubescent boys are at the fringes of the crowds. Whenever one lifts one's eyes, the gaze glides over the beauty of a moon-faced one and if one extends one's arm it seems to become entangled in some young man's tresses." (20–21)

There were other places too where crowds gathered. Reti Mahabat Khan, the ruins of a riverside home on the sandy banks of the Yamuna, had become a wrestling arena popular with the aristocracy as well as the common people. Huge crowds gathered to watch the wrestlers display their skills. According to Quli Khan, "this place is full of attractions. Many beautiful men too come here, much to the pleasure of the spectators."[3] (77–79)

Popular faith centered on the saints' shrines. The belief that the *barakka* (grace) of the saint lingered around his grave led many to seek a saint's intercession. The popularity of shrines encouraged commerce around them. The most important ritual associated with the dargah was the *urs* (lit. marriage, celebrated on the day of the saint's death anniversary when he was wedded to his divine beloved in eternal union.)

The Urs of Khuld Manzil

The widow of Bahadur Shah[4] made elaborate arrangements for his urs. The mood was set for indulgence. Young men and their admirers gathered on these occasions.

In every corner lovers embrace. In every lane and street pleasure seekers search for carnal pleasures and dance with joy. Those who drink do so without worrying about the public censor. The enamored show devotion to their lovers without fear of public rebuke. The crowd of pubescent young men is enough to break the resolve of hermits. These young deer, brimming with unparalleled ardor, could shake the foundations of propriety and rectitude. Wherever the gaze falls you see lovestricken faces . . . [There are

---

3. Shekhar and Chenoy make "men" into "beautiful ladies," 52.
4. The Mughal emperor who ruled from 1707 to 1712.

so many distractions that] when a person comes back to his senses a youth winks at him and by the time his eyes light up, some wretch sends her message. The bazaars and lanes are crowded with aristocrats and nobles and every nook and corner is abuzz with the rich and the poor. There are more singers than flies and more beggars than mosquitoes. (58)

〰 〰 〰

Basant (spring) was celebrated by the people of Delhi for a whole week with music and dance. On the first day the celebrations centered on the shrine, where a footprint of the Prophet was housed. Crowds waited for the appearance of the musicians and dancers who arrived "accompanied by beautiful people who sprinkled perfumes on the waiting spectators. The sight of these fairy-faced ones[5] with glass decanters in their hands drove those present out of their senses and caused them to lose their reason . . . at this holy shrine beautiful, young and pubescent singers, standing in separate rows, with great style and coquetry, pay homage to the blessed relic with their song."

During the next five days musical soirees were held at various shrines, homes, and in the palace.

〰 〰 〰

On the seventh day, dancers gather at Ahadipura at the grave of one of their dear ones. They bathe the grave with liquor and dance incessantly through the night, taking turns, for they believe this will bring peace to the soul of the departed one.[6] *Qawwals* [singers of devotional music] come in groups and colorful music sessions take place. Beautiful people gather here and since privacy is available it is possible to enjoy wonderful company. For six days visitors, spectators, and participants join in the revelry and in a week gather a treasure of pleasures to last them a year. How privileged are these people! (71–73)

〰 〰 〰

On the eleventh of each month, a soiree was held at the house of Miran,

〰 〰 〰

5. Shekhar and Chenoy translate as "women"(42) although the context clearly indicates that these were males.
6. This was most probably the shrine of a eunuch.

a humble man with impeccable manners. His hospitality is legendary and his parties are the envy of his peers. Since he is the chieftain of musicians and dancers, singers visit him frequently and some scorn him for this. Since the Wazir ul Mumalik [the prime minister] is fond of beautiful faces, has a taste for coquetry and likes to drink liquor, Miran is dear to him for he provides him with all these. Since he also has great skills in discovering new and pleasing faces and entrapping them with his charms, he is favored over the other courtiers. Large numbers of flower-faced ones make his house look like a garden in bloom and because of the profusion of fairy-faced ones, his dwelling appears to be the land of the fairy-born. Every beauty wants to be a part of his assemblies as does every connoisseur of beauty. The most alluring of the young *kalawants* [a caste of singers] crowd these gatherings, and these assemblies are full of young Hindu and Muslim boys. These sessions are organized on the eleventh of each month, and dancers gather from the morning onward and start dancing and entertaining to please the eyes and hearts of those who gather. . . . Many canopies are put up and the floor is covered with colorful spreads. The people of the city are invited and important people are present. . . . There is entertainment for everybody and it is all for free. (73–74)

⬲   ⬲   ⬲

The Prophet's birthday was celebrated at Arab Ki Sarai, where Arabs, mostly stipendiaries of the court, lived. The pious collected here. Eulogies to the Prophet were sung and the Quran read throughout the night. The Arabs were extremely hospitable to all visitors:

⬲   ⬲   ⬲

Some came to see the unpleasing Arab lads even though their dress is neither beautiful nor fashionable. They do not have coy ways nor are they charming. This couplet says it all:

> Confirmed seekers find in a camel
> the same beauty as in those from Chighil and China.[7] (74–76)

⬲   ⬲   ⬲

Among the fascinating characters mentioned by Dargah Quli Khan is Azam Khan, son of Fidwi Khan,

⬲   ⬲   ⬲

---

7. Chigil: city in Turkestan famous for handsome men and expert archers. See F. Steingass, *A Comprehensive Persian-English Dictionary* (New Delhi: Asian Educational Services, 1992).

one of the great nobles. He is colorful by temperament, knowledgeable in ragas and is recognized by the musicians of India. By nature he likes boys and is enamored of smooth, shaven faces.[8] . . . The fortunes of the world are laid at the feet of these boys. Whenever he hears of a good-looking one he wants him as a companion and snares him with favors. . . . These boys, with indescribable dignity and authority, ride around on fast horses. Whenever you see a fresh youth it can be presumed that he is connected to the great noble Azam Khan. With the beauty of these flower-faced ones he seems to be masking his own age. He knows that there is little time left for him and is therefore eager to indulge all his sexual desires.

Mirza Munun is one of the nobles of the times who has perfected the art of seduction.[9] Many other aristocrats learn these arts from him. He is the one best suited to organize these gatherings of *ghilman* [beautiful boys who will be found in heaven]. Azam Khan's residence is like a paradise, populated by the progeny of fairies. Any young man unconnected with these gatherings is spurious and any charming youth who has not been at them is not to be trusted. The boys are scrutinized at these gatherings and these occasions are the touchstone by which the flower faced ones are tested. Coins that have not been minted at these gatherings are counterfeit. Silver may be silver but it will never be considered so till it is melted in this furnace, no matter how pure the silver be. (69–70)

☒ ☒ ☒

Mir Abdullah was

☒ ☒ ☒

a great reciter of the *marsiya*. When he lamented the death of Husain, the martyred grandson of the Prophet, listeners were driven into a frenzy of sorrow. . . .

He always had many attendants with him. He used to move around with good-looking and beautiful young men. Except on the day when Hussain was martyred, his house was full of fine young men. They usually came to learn the art of reciting the marsiya or to understand its finer points. (87)

☒ ☒ ☒

Another great marsiya reciter was Jani Hajjam[10] who had great beauty and distinction and used to be the lover of a nobleman from whom he had managed to acquire a lakh of rupees.

---

8. The English translation unnecessarily adds "lasses" here.
9. Shekhar and Chenoy assume that it is "the art of sodomy" he has perfected.
10. His second name indicates that he was a barber by caste.

Since he was fond of liquor, he had lost all his wealth and his fortunes had changed. Young aristocrats invited him to their gatherings where there was liquor and dance (88–89).

Taqi is

the head of a troupe of boys who mime, dance and perform conjuring tricks. He is a favorite of the king and has access to his private chambers. The great nobles desire to know him and treat him with great respect. . . . Like flowers of many colors, young men are always present in his gardenlike home. In that verdant meadow there are beautiful dark boys blooming like tender flowers. On one side are beautiful boys, hair just sprouting on their cheeks, throwing out the webs of their down, and on the other there are those hunting their prey with arrows that pierce the heart. Fair boys, like the purity of their emerging dispositions, are bright and pleasing and the dark ones are like salt in the manna that nature has bestowed. His dwelling is like a vision of fairyland and his establishment would be the envy of a house of wonders. Dainty waists sway like the petals of a flower and tresses are envied by the scented hyacinth. The slender, well-proportioned beauties capture hearts with their graceful strutting, and the dark-eyed send out messages with their looks. Wherever there is a boy who is unhappy with the male garb, Taqi's searching eyes spot him and wherever he sees a soft and tender boy, the gardens envy his discovery. He is the master and patron of all sorts of catamites because they know that he has carried this art to new heights. He is the leader of all the eunuchs and they feel proud to be his disciples. In short he is the leader of the eunuchs and a patron of pimps. (97–98)

Khwasa and Anutha[11]

are among the well known mimes of Delhi and are attached to the imperial court. Their performances are unique and their skills of imitation unparalleled. They sing the *khayal* very well and are great dancers too. They come into their element in those soirees where courtesans are present for then they excel themselves, particularly in their conversation.

Two boys Sabza and Mazza are new saplings and are the fresh flowers of their garden. They dance as if to summon doomsday and their movements are astonishing. Such is their sauciness and their efflorescence that one wants to meet them. They are worthy of

---

11. The first name means "special" and the second "unique;"both appear to be stage names.

being kept as close companions. Their long tresses are better than long life and a look from their eyes is longer than the length of a man's vision. They are built perfectly and their conversation is entertaining.

> Wherever I look I see such spectacles
> May god give me the chance to enjoy them. (98–99)

To try and describe the beauty of Bari Naqqal's blooming beauty one would have to invent a pen made from the feather of a parrot that can write on the petals of scented flowers.[12] Instead of ink one would have to use verdigris:

> I was unaware that budding youth is such a calamity,
> that verdant looks hide such a deadly snare.

His magnificence and dignity are such that the eye cannot look at him unblinking. His complexion is clear and each part of his face attractive. His gait is like a bunch of flowers swaying in fragrant air. With his hands he evokes images beyond metaphor. Whoever meets him is bewitched. Whoever was close to him even once spends the rest of his life wanting to be with him for ever. Spring is no match for his blossoming youth and all the flowers in the garden pale before his beauty:

> His beauty or his voice, either is enough for the heart,
> and when they are together they wreak havoc for lovers.

His entire troupe is excellent and well versed in mime. A few promising saplings are sprouting among them. May the envious heavens give me a chance to see them. (99)

⬖ ⬖ ⬖

Allah Bandi

⬖ ⬖ ⬖

is a well proportioned comely young man. He makes sure to look very beautiful at night. His father used to be a well known qawwal. He too sings the *khayal* very well and adds a great deal of color to it. Many are attracted to him and desire his company. (101)

⬖ ⬖ ⬖

The devastating youth Miyan Hinga has a

---

12. Shekhar and Chenoy presume that he is a woman (99).

complexion like porcelain and a dress white as jasmine. Every day he collects crowds in front of the imperial fort. He entertains as the crowd desires. On the pretext of strolling or shopping for rarities, well known people come to the square to see him dance and enjoy his beauty. Some of his admirers, riding their steeds, self-consciously gather to watch this miracle of nature. . . . Instead of buying the things that they had come to buy, they get lost in enjoying themselves. All the money they have, they spend on him instead of buying the things they had come for. His graceful walk and delightful movements are enough to wreak havoc, and whoever he pays attention to is destroyed.

The dusk contributes to his fairness and the garden pays tribute to the growing down on his face. He looks so dazzling in his white dress that it seems as if the day is breaking at dusk, and that flowers made of moonbeams are being scattered. Till sunset he displays his charms, gathers a lot of wealth and goes home. Though many of his admirers invite him he never visits their homes, but the ones to whom he is attracted visit him and enjoy the pleasures of his company. (102)

Sultana[13]

is a twelve-year old dark-complexioned youth. When he dances his gestures and movements are enchanting, and when he sings, he charms the universe and drives his listeners crazy. He is young but musically very skilled. He is just a bud but can match any flower in full bloom and even though he is only the flame of a candle, he can claim equality with the sun. His admirers can never have enough of his singing and those who want to gaze at him forever are embarrassed at the misfortune of the limits of their vision. One evening a friend of mine organized a concert of his and I got the opportunity to be in his company for a long time. The whole night was one of pleasure and joy. The yearning for his company still lingers in the heart of my friends. In fact, desire itself yearns for that evening. (102–03)

Visions of desire light up on seeing Saras Rup's[14] bewitching elegance. When he walks, the heart blooms like a garden. His songs are like fresh breeze and his scented voice spreads the perfume of his melodies. His dance is attractive and colorful and his songs

---

13. Sultana is the feminine of Sultan.
14. The name, which seems to be a stage name, is from the Sanskrit. *Saras* means one who is replete with all types of aesthetic emotion (*rasa*) and *Rup* means beauty or form.

delightful and lovely. He is appreciated by the rich and powerful as well as by the mystics. The brightness of his beauty dazzles the eyes and his brilliance blinds rationality. It is impossible to meet him without a proper introduction or without sending him appropriate gifts. May God give those who yearn for him, the opportunity to gaze to their hearts' content and may their desires be fulfilled. (103)

Mir Taqi "Mir": Autobiography (Persian) and Poems (Urdu)

Introduced and translated by Saleem Kidwai

Mir Taqi "Mir" (ca. 1723–1810) is generally considered the greatest Urdu poet. He is also an originator of much in Urdu literary tradition. It was during his time that Urdu replaced Persian as the more popular literary language.

While he wrote in almost all genres of Urdu poetry, he was master of the *ghazal*. Alhough he wrote in refined Persian too, his genius lay in creatively articulating the language of the streets of Delhi and incorporating classical tropes therein. A large part of Mir's poetry is addressed to or is about other males.

His father, Mir Muhammad Ali (died 1733), was a Sufi saint living in Akbarabad (modern Agra), the former Mughal capital. After his father's death, Mir shifted to the current Mughal capital, Shahjahanabad (modern Delhi), where he lived until about 1782, when he migrated to Lucknow, the emerging cultural capital of the newly independent province of Avadh.

Mir is the only classical Urdu poet to have written an autobiography. This work, *Zikr-i-Mir*, is in Persian. In the introductory episode, translated here, Mir recalls the relationship between his father, Mir Muhammad Ali (also known as Ali Muttaqi because of his piety), a Sufi teacher, and one of his disciples, Amanullah. At the time when the events described occurred, Mir was not quite eleven. He wrote about these events nearly forty years later. This is the only portion of the work that deals at length with a member of the author's family, and therefore it has special importance.

The editor of a recent edition of *Zikr-i-Mir* dismisses Mir's claims about his father's spiritual achievements as exaggerated and adds that the events described lack historicity.[1] Yet this

---

1. N. A. Faruqi, *Mir ki Aapbiti: A Translation of Zikr-i-Mir into Urdu,* with the Persian text (New Delhi: Anjuman Taraqqi-i-Urdu [Hind], 1996), 223–33. My translation is from the Persian text in this edition.

is how the events appeared to Mir when he was reconstructing his life. His father had suddenly left home in Agra and had wandered to Delhi and then to Bayana where he sat down on
the steps of a mosque, exhausted:

⬖ ⬖ ⬖

There he saw a good-looking, rosy-cheeked young man, the son of a Saiyyid.[2] One look
at the boy and his spiritual gaze drew the boy to him. The fairy-faced shy boy was suddenly transformed. He went into a trance and fell at my father's feet, in a faint.

⬖ ⬖ ⬖

Mir's father revived the boy, Amanullah, and when the boy was able to, he pleaded with the
Sufi to stay with him for a few days. Mir Muhammad Ali resisted but was eventually persuaded
by the people who had gathered around. The day he moved in with Amanullah was also the
day the young man was to be married. When asked to join in the festivities Mir Muhammad
Ali commented that marriage was a hindrance to the spiritual quest, and that he was lucky to
have been "freed from this trap." When Amanullah and his party left for the bride's home,
Mir Muhammad Ali disappeared without informing anybody. When Amanullah returned, he
immediately set out to look for the wandering Sufi. He suffered tremendously in the search
but his prayers were answered when he was told that Mir Muhammad Ali would be found in
Agra.

⬖ ⬖ ⬖

He entered the city at midnight, asked about the mystic and the way to his home, and
finally earned the pleasure of kissing his feet. Tears of happiness rolled down his glowing cheeks. The fear of loss was replaced by the pleasure of having his wishes granted unexpectedly.

The wounded-hearted *Darvesh* looked at him.[3] Just this one pure look at his beauty
transformed the beautiful youngster into a perfected one. I cannot describe how lovingly
my father behaved toward him. His demonstration of affection was beyond words. He
drew his head to his bosom and said "Oh Mir Amanullah. You have been through hell
and you've seen the ups and downs of life. Now you'll no longer miss your family. This
house is yours as are the servants. Be grateful that you have merged your stream with

---

2. One who claims to be of the Prophet's lineage, therefore, the highest-born among Muslims.
3. Darvesh, a wandering ascetic; literally, one who is at the door. "Wounded-hearted": conventional appellation for a mystic, wounded by the love of God.

this wonderful river. Be thankful that like the cypress which stands beside the river and yet doesn't get wet, you too have saved your purity. Now, relax, go to your room, lock yourself in and get lost within yourself. That is what attracts the divine.

The Darvesh advised the new disciple on the basics of the mystic path: how the soul is more important than the body, how it is necessary to pray and meditate, to negate the ego and pride, and always to remember that one is mortal and to trust God completely. Along with meditation and prayer, the body had to be kept clean and attractive because only in a tidy home can one have visitors. He asked Amanullah to go and get the rest he needed. He instructed a servant to show him the way and to be in constant attendance on him.

Mir's father, Ali Muttaqi, began calling this disciple "dear brother" and began leading him rapidly along the spiritual path. Amanullah served his pir night and day, caring for all his needs. Soon he had become a saint himself and was performing miracles. He became famous and even his relatives came to pay their respects. Meanwhile Amanullah's wife had withered away and died. Amanullah wanted to withdraw from his devotees but his pir convinced him to continue to bless others. Amanullah constantly expressed his admiration for his pir who had mastered all his desires. Mir proceeds to write about his own relationship with Amanullah.

I was seven years old then. I was very close to him. He had adopted me as a son and never left me with my parents. I spent all my time with him and he even taught me how to read the Quran.

One day he [Amanullah] went for a stroll in the Friday bazaar. There he saw the son of an oil manufacturer and vendor, a rich young man.[4] Instantly, he lost his heart and his natural poise. He grew visibly agitated but when he got no response he returned home with an aching heart. He tried very hard to regain his self-control but he had no power over his yearning heart.

He was reduced to leaning on an attendant's shoulder in order to walk. He would constantly reprimand his heart: "Beloved, how did you play this trick on yourself? How could you get yourself embroiled in a scandal which involves streets and bazaars? I, who had reached the stage of detachment, am now in the throes of longing. Even a child wouldn't play such a cruel trick. The path on which you have led me is one that even the blind avoid. My heart, you are too precious to be sacrificed for a boy from the bazaar. You burn for one who doesn't even step out into the sun. You have fallen in love with one who does not know how to take a single step along the path of love. It seems as if

---

4. The term used to denote this young man's caste, Teli, suggests that he was a Hindu.

my eyes have been waiting for a chance to weep, and my heart has been longing to ache. How shall I deal with this? Even in my youth I was never enamored so. Now, when my face is wrinkled, my heart is creating havoc. If I suffer silently, my eyes cause a flood. I am lost, what shall I do—how shall I untangle this knot? There seems no other way than to go to the master for help."

Close to the time of the sunset prayer, he entered [my father's presence], leaning on the shoulder of the attendant, completely distraught, tears in his eyes and sighs on his lips. Those present at the gathering paid him respects. The Darvesh beckoned him to sit beside him. Father asked, "Where have you been—it's been a long time since you showed your face."

He replied: "I went for a walk in the Friday bazaar."

The Darvesh said: "Have you heard this couplet?:

> 'Only those afflicted by love know the passion and scandal
> That arises from looking at boys in the bazaar.'

"Go to your room and do not leave it for eight days. Don't think about this. Allah may be kind and send him to you to save you from dishonor."

What a coincidence! The same week, the moon-faced one, restless at home, came and sat at his shop. The hawker at the stall next to his shop asked him: "What's the matter with you? You look worried." The boy replied, "How can I tell you what happened to me? It is so difficult to talk about. Yet, since you are my friend, I will tell you. Six days ago, a Darvesh passed this way and he saw me and my beauty. He stood still for some time, lost and transfixed. I, in my arrogance, pretended to pay him no attention. Wounded, the Darvesh sighed deeply and left. Now it is I who am constantly thinking of him, and his face stays with me all the time. What shall I do? How should I distract myself? Where do I go, whom shall I ask who he was, where he lives?"

The hawker said that he knew the Darvesh—he was the brother of the famous saint Ali Mut-taqi who himself had hundreds of followers. The hawker took the youth to meet the saint.

Thus, that lowly man brought the youth to my father who heard them and then said: "Finally, heedless love has triumphed over indifference." He called a servant and told him to tell his dear brother to come to him, since what he sought had come looking for him. When this good news reached the broken-hearted one who had been languishing in a corner, he emerged from the hell hole of his misery, dancing.

First he bent his head to kiss his master's feet and then extended a welcoming arm toward the boy and drew him to his side. True to his heart's yearning he hugged him to his bosom, and his deep desire was fulfilled.

The pir allowed them to go and sit by themselves and talk. They started talking and when the subject came up, the Darvesh said: "Beautiful one, I am a faqir [mendicant] and my heart is already possessed, and free from desire. Don't think I will become a prisoner of your tresses. God knows that my heart is caught up with Him. So don't be under any illusions and don't put on airs or you will regret it. We Darveshes, unlike other people, do not live under this inverted dome of the sky, yet like other people our states are unpredictable. Go now, you must have suffered a lot."

The boy replied: "Yes, I have suffered but have now found a treasure. I know the privilege it is to be even the sweeper of this abode. I hope you will not turn me away—do not withdraw your benevolent gaze from me."

He used to come every day and did everything to serve his pir.

One day the Darvesh was in a state of contemplation. The boy turned up and the pir called to him: "dear young man" and made him sit next to him. He looked at him in such a way that the youth found his answers. He graduated to enlightenment. He became famous. The powerful of the city began to respect him and the other advanced murids became jealous of him. Soon he was to become one of those unparalleled on the mystic path.

It is a fact that when the gaze of the Darveshes works, it transforms dust into gold.

Mir's Poetry[5]

My mind has been tossed like a ball in the playing field of love
Since the days when I too roamed around, tossing a ball. (138)

The verdant spring stares at you, O newly bearded one—
Are you the mirror in which spring sees its reflection? (176)

From Yusuf to the flower; from the flower to the flame—
Whom does not beauty carry to the marketplace? (732)

Your face with down on it, is our Quran—
What if we kiss it—it is a part of our faith. (836)

When hair appears on your face, my dear, you will learn kindness.
Helplessly you will offer your lovers betel leaves as tokens of parting. (860)

When another turban-fold of the intoxicated one came undone,
It seemed as if a whip lashed across the ocean of beauty. (881)

His life passed amongst amorous young men—
The tavernkeeper was a wonder of an old man. (970)

---

5. All translations are from Z. A. Abbasi, ed., *Kulliyat-i Mir,* vol. 1 (Delhi: Taraqqi Urdu Bureau, 1983). Numbers of couplets follow this text.

The boys of Delhi with their caps askew
Were the nemesis of all lovers,
No lovers are now to be seen—
The ones wearing caps have carried out a massacre. (1003–04)

Yesterday while strolling in the garden I lost my heart
When a smooth-faced flower seller came with his wares
And as the spring disappeared from my sight,
Today, without him, my heart mourns in darkness. (1562–63)

Do not bend to lift my head from your feet—
Sir, you have a well-covered sword tied to your waist. (1588)

If you have to come to these boys of the tavern, O Shaikh[6]
Be prepared to lose your gown and turban. (1735)

When the beautifully statured mount horses
The cypress and the moon fall victims. (2071)

His beard has appeared, but his indifference survives—
My messenger still wanders, waiting for an answer. (2740)

There was no one like him in those schools—
How shall I descibe that perfect face of his? (3017)

Mir, why bemoan the fate of your crushed heart—
These boys have created havoc in the entire city. (3998)

Finding him inebriated, I pulled him into my arms last night.
He said "So you too have become intoxicated tonight." (4556)

I stood before his horse
Like weakened prey. (5426)

God having given these boys such beautiful faces
Should have given them a bit of compassion too. (6678)

It would be strange if an angel could hold its own—
The fairy-faced boys of Delhi are far ahead of them. (7016)

Even though the sprightly one is still at school
He can teach just about any one a few tricks. (7424)

After I kissed him, I too slipped away—
Say what you will, I care only for myself. (7668)

---

6. A holy or learned man.

Gaze at the grace with which he moves—
See how delicate each movement is. (9890)

The ways of my street boy are so deadly
A hundred youths die at each gesture. (9971)

His steed flashed by like a thunder clap—
The hearts of lovers pounded, their chests burst. (10293)

I will not write to him for he is very mischievous—
He will make my letter into a kite to test the wind. (10941)

My classmates have acquired knowledge and gone—
I, still ignorant, want to hang around schoolboys. (11442)

If not him, there is his brother—
Mir, are there any restrictions in love? (12446)

These pert smooth-faced boys of the city,
What cruelty they inflict on young men. (12810)

These boys have a strange sense of honor
Let's see, Mir, if you can save your own. (13395)

Part IV

Introduction: Modern Indian Materials

Ruth Vanita and Saleem Kidwai

For the purposes of this book, we define modern India as nineteenth- and twentieth-century India. Two significant phenomena develop during this period—first, the minor homophobic voice that was largely ignored by mainstream society in precolonial India (see pp. 112–13) becomes a dominant voice; and second, sexual love between women is depicted increasingly explicitly while such love between men is almost entirely silenced.

Love between Women in Rekhti Poetry

The history of Rekhti poetry (see p. 220) embodies both the last vestiges of medieval freedoms and the new voices of modernity. Rekhti is a kind of Urdu poetry written in the female voice by male poets, including some major poets, in Lucknow, capital of the princely state of Avadh, in the late eighteenth and early nineteenth centuries. Twentieth-century critics labeled Rekhti obscene for its explicit depiction of female sexuality, especially lesbian sexuality, and systematically eliminated it from the canon of published works of the poets concerned.

T. Graham Bailey calls Rekhti the language of "women of no reputation" and the poetry "a debased form of lyric invented by a debased mind in a debased age."[1] Ali Jawad Zaidi says it catered to those "who sought decadent pleasures." He adds that though it is "vulgar" it provides insight into the "evils that feudal order bred in the lives of women."[2] Recent critics have

---

1. T. Graham Bailey, *A History of Urdu Literature* (1928; Delhi: Sumit Publications, 1979), 56.
2. Ali Jawad Zaidi, *A History of Urdu Literature* (London: Oxford University Press, 1964), 122, 137.

condemned it as misogynist: " aimed at entertaining its male audience by making gross fun of women, its enhanced appeal lying in that it also pretended to be a view from inside, in fact, the very objects of ridicule."[3]

These critics assume, without evidence, that Rekhti was never heard or read by women. They also assume that no man could ever be an intimate friend of women or take a sympathetic view of sexual love between women. However, Bailey and Zaidi suggest that Rekhti poets picked up this language from "debased" women, by which they mean courtesans (*tawaifs*), who were the definers of culture in Lucknow at this time. The courtesan-poet network was well established. As independent women, courtesans were free to associate with men socially, and they used to sing the compositions of the poets.

Modern critics ignore the possibility that men could be intimate friends of homoerotically or bisexually inclined women. In Siraj Aurangabadi's poem *Bustani-i Khayal* (see p. 169), the narrator, heartbroken over the loss of his male beloved, seeks solace in the company of courtesans who understand his plight and try to cheer him up.[4] These women dancers are referred to as *aliyan* (female friends of each other). The editor says that this word may connote that the women are *rangin mijaz* (of colorful temperament), a term often used to described homoerotically inclined men.[5] Veena Oldenberg has examined the close emotional relationships between courtesans who referred to themselves as *chapatbaz* (given to sex between women) and also analyzed their repertoire of satirical songs mocking marriage and heterosexual relations.[6]

To dismiss Rekhti poetry a priori on the grounds that men can never be sympathetic to romantic or sexual attraction between women and can only ridicule or be titillated by it is to beg the question. Even if the representation of sex between women does titillate some men, that does not necessarily mean that it may not also titillate women. In any case, it is impossible to measure the effect of a poem on individual readers, male or female. If some are titillated, others may be moved, and still others delighted. As we shall see, at least one male reader mistook Jan Saheb for a woman poet writing under a masculine pen-name (see p. 193).

Another strategy used by critics to dismiss Rekhti poetry is comparing it unfavorably to the Urdu *ghazal*, saying that the ghazal depicts mystical love between ungendered persons, while Rekhti depicts sexual love between women, so Rekhti is degraded. We have demonstrated that the ghazal often genders both lover and beloved as male, and also refers to explic-

---

3. C. M. Naim and Carla Petievich, "Urdu in Lucknow/Lucknow in Urdu," in Violette Graffe, ed., *Lucknow: Memories of a City* (Delhi: Oxford University Press, 1997), 171.
4. Abdul Qadir Sarvari, ed., *Kulliyat-i Siraj* (Delhi: Qaumi Council Barai Farosh-i Urdu Zaban, 1998), 151–53.
5. Sarvari, *Kulliyat-i Siraj*, 151, fn. 2.
6. Veena Talwar Oldenberg, "Lifestyle as Resistance: The Case of the Courtesans of Lucknow," in Graffe, ed., *Lucknow*, 136–54.

itly sexual love (see pp. 119-122). But even if this were not so, the norms set up in one genre cannot be used to condemn poetry in another genre. Rekhti, unlike the ghazal, is written in colloquial, not Persianized, Urdu and is heavily influenced by the traditions of heterosexual Hindi love poetry in the Reeti tradition, where love is explicitly sexual and the lovers are gendered. Reeti poetry also came to be compared unfavorably to Bhakti poetry by modern Hindi literary critics, precisely because of its eroticism.

Whatever the intentions of the authors, Rekhti poetry was not altogether removed from the lived reality of some women, as is indicated by its use of words such as chapatbaz, which Oldenberg has found twentieth-century courtesans still using to refer to female same-sex activity. Pioneering sexologist Havelock Ellis, in his study of homosexuality worldwide, quoted a statement sent to him by an officer in the Indian Medical Service, which gave five Hindustani words for homoerotically inclined women: *dugana, zanakhe, sa'tar, chapathai,* and *chapat-baz.*[7] Four of these words occur in Rekhti poetry (see p. 221 for elaborations). The officer went on to say that two women who lived together were referred to as "living apart," and gave examples of such women whom he had come across, including an inter-caste couple living in a town, a widow who had relations with her three maidservants, a couple in prison, and a pair of widowed sisters. Some of these women were said to practice tribadism (rubbing) and others to use dildoes or phalli made of clay. The officer referred to the Hindu medical text which indicated that two women could produce a boneless child (see p. 26) and also referred to Rekhti poetry: "The act itself is called *chapat* or *chapti,* and the Hindustani poets, Nazir, Rangin, Jan Saheb, treat of Lesbian love very extensively and sometimes very crudely. Jan Saheb, a woman poet, sings to the effect that intercourse with a woman by means of a phallus [dildo] is to be preferred to the satisfaction offered by a male lover" (208).

Rekhti represents women clearly stating that they prefer women to men (see p. 224) when they have access to both. The preference for women is represented not as only sexual but also as emotional and romantic. The erotic encounters in these poems are not presented as mimicking heterosexual lovemaking. Although the dildo is mentioned, there is greater emphasis on kissing, petting, passionate embraces, and clitoral stimulation. It is more than likely that courtesans provided the poets with details of their romances, which the poets then versified and recited to the women as well as in all-male gatherings. Whatever their sources, these male poets accurately portray sexual details in contrast to Western nineteenth-century fictions on lesbianism written by men—such as Gautier's *Mademoiselle de Maupin* (1836)—which pretend ignorance regarding the details of lesbian lovemaking. In one poem, the poet Insha says that since the voice of the woman who loves women is being quenched, he has to speak for

---

7. Havelock Ellis, *Studies in the Psychology of Sex* (1900; New York: Random House, 1942), vol. 1, 208–09.

her (see p. 228). The poets did indeed give sexual love between women a voice—they introduced it into the realm of literary discourse from which it had been almost completely absent.[8]

Rekhti may have been labeled obscene partly because it emerged in Avadh, which was the last kingdom to be annexed by the East India Company before widespread rebellions broke out against the Company in 1857. Avadh was also the site of the stiffest resistance to colonial rule. Indian nationalists accepted British representation of Avadh culture as decadent. But Amresh Mishra argues that Avadh culture was the "last impulse of Asiatic modernity" before the imposition of Western modernity.[9]

Aristocratic men of Avadh subverted the notions of Indo-Persian masculinity they had inherited from Mughal high culture. The king Nawab Nasirudin Haider (1827–37) added his own religious innovations to those of his mother, who had maintained, in great style, eleven beautiful girls to represent the wives of the last eleven Shia Imams. Her son decided to adopt the female gender model to further these innovations. On the birth date of each Imam he would pretend to be a woman in childbirth. Other men imitated him, dressing and behaving like women during that period.[10] British Victorian men viewed this kind of transgendered masculinity as unmanly decadence.[11]

Empire and New Law

Arguably, the crushing of the 1857 rebellion, followed by the official incorporation of India into the British Empire with Queen Victoria replacing the East India Company, signaled the violent end of medieval India. For same-sex love, that end was signaled by the 1861 law that criminalized homosexuality.

The texts we have compiled thus far indicate a set of generally tolerant traditions in precolonial India. As far as we know, not a single person has ever been executed for homosexual behavior in India. On the other hand, for centuries, in many parts of Europe, men found en-

---

8. An interesting parallel is a poem from medieval Iberia in which a man teasingly envies a woman as "desirous of cunt" as himself but more successful than himself in getting it. See Josiah Blackmore, "The Poets of Sodom," in Josiah Blackmore and Gregory S. Hutcheson, eds., *Queer Iberia: Crossing Cultures, Crossing Sexualities* (Durham, NC: Duke University Press, 1999), 195–221.

9. Amresh Misra, *Lucknow: Fire of Grace. The Story of Its Revolution, Renaissance and the Aftermath* (New Delhi: Harper Collins, 1998).

10. Juan I. Cole, "Shi'ite Noblewomen and Religious Innovation in Awadh," in Graffe, ed., *Lucknow.*

11. Ashis Nandy argues that Victorian notions of masculinity were subverted from within by Oscar Wilde and from without by Gandhi. See *The Intimate Enemy: Loss and Recovery of Self under Colonialism* (Delhi: Oxford University Press, 1983), 42–48. Arguably, Avadhi men, before their culture was crushed, represented a similar kind of challenge.

gaging in homosexual acts were vilified, tortured, or legally executed.[12] There were also cases of women being executed for homosexuality as late as the eighteenth century. In early nineteenth-century England, men found engaging in sex with one another were put in the pillory and pelted with rubbish until half dead. Other men, such as the famous Jewish painter Simeon Solomon (1840–1905), were legally penalized and socially ostracized for the same "crime."[13]

The British antisodomy law of 1860 was progressive in Britain insofar as it reduced the punishment for sodomy from execution to ten years' imprisonment.[14] However, when introduced in India in 1861 as Section 377 of the Indian Penal Code, it was a retrogressive step.[15] This law, which remains in place today in India, even though homosexuality between consenting adults was decriminalized in England in 1967, reads: "Whoever voluntarily has carnal intercourse against the order of nature with any man, woman or animal, shall be punished with imprisonment for life, or with imprisonment of either description for a term which may extend to ten years, and shall be liable to fine." The attached "explanation" says that "penetration is sufficient to constitute the carnal intercourse necessary to the offence." The absence of the word "penile" with "penetration" could conceivably lead to the section being used against lesbians. Although the law has very rarely been invoked to punish anyone for consensual homosexual activity (of the thirty-six recorded cases since inception, most concern anal rape), police routinely use it to harass and blackmail men in parks and public places. It has been invoked to whip up antagonism against homosexuals in the context of trials for other offenses, such as murder and rape. Thus, in 1998 a rape case in Delhi's Tihar jail was prosecuted under Section 377 and reported in the papers "Tihar inmate held for sodomy," when the issue should have been rape, not sodomy (that is, the raped man's lack of consent, not the fact that he and the rapist were both male). In 1998 the Population Service International was charged under Section 377 with "promoting homosexuality" on an All India Radio sex education program, even though neither this nor any other Indian law mentions such an activity.

In 1895, in Britain, poet Oscar Wilde was convicted under a new law that criminalized "indecency" between men (as distinct from "sodomy") and his sufferings in prison led directly to his death. This widely reported case functioned to instill fear into homosexually inclined men in England and could not but have similar effects in India, where newspapers in English and in other Indian languages picked up reports of the case. However, the Wilde case also made homosexuality widely visible in the West. The years following his conviction saw increased

12. See Alan Bray, *Homosexuality in Renaissance England* (1982; New York: Columbia University Press, 1995).
13. See Ruth Vanita, *Sappho and the Virgin Mary* (New York: Columbia University Press, 1996), 74–79.
14. For the history of British law on homosexuality, see Stephen Jeffrey-Poulter, *Peers, Queers and Commons* (London: Routledge, 1991).
15. Similar laws were introduced in other colonized countries in the same year.

research and writing in Europe, both attacking and defending homosexuality. Even in England, several of Wilde's contemporaries, such as Edward Carpenter, an admirer of Gandhi, continued to live openly as homosexuals and write about homosexuality, without incurring persecution. Indian society too entered a transitional phase as older indigenous discourses of same-sex love and romantic friendship came into dialog with the new Western legal and medical discourses of homosexuality as an abnormality or an illness.

British educators and missionaries often denounced Indian marital, familial, and sexual arrangements as primitive—demeaning to women and permissive for men. Arranged marriage, child marriage, dowry, polygamy, polyandry, and matriliny were treated as evidence of Indian culture's degeneracy. Hindu gods were seen as licentious, and Indian monarchs, both Hindu and Muslim, as decadent hedonists, equally given to heterosexual and homosexual behavior but indifferent to their subjects' welfare. Brahmans came in for similar stereotyping as greedy sensualists. In contrast, British monarchs, especially Queen Victoria, were held up as models of family propriety. These overgeneralizations were intended to justify the imperial enterprise. Educated Indians, defending Indian culture, did not altogether reject Victorian values but rather insisted that Indian culture was originally very similar to Victorian culture and had been corrupted during the medieval period. They tended to accept British stereotypes as adequate depictions of Indian princely rulers and priests.

All of these views of Indian sexual practices, propagated in the context of colonial rule and Victorian puritanism with its deep antipleasure and antisex bias, had a major influence on the social reform movements that developed in many Indian communities in the nineteenth century and later on nationalist movements as well. While doing laudable work for women's education and against women's oppression, social reformers tried to form an ideal Indian man, woman, child, and family, largely on the model of the British Victorian nuclear family. Monogamous heterosexual marriage came to be idealized as the only acceptable form of sexual coupling, within which the woman was to be the educated companion of the male head of the household. It is not fortuitous that such movements as the Arya Samaj opposed polytheism, idol worship, and polygamy, all of which were viewed by the British as indicative of Indian moral inferiority.[16] For example, the sexual arrangements of *devdasi* communities (promiscuous and matrilineal), of certain Vaishnava communities in eastern India, and the matrilineal inheritance systems of some communities in Kerala, which had been viewed with some suspicion and contempt even in precolonial India, came to be characterized as immoral in colonial India and finally to be outlawed after independence.

---

16. Ashis Nandy, among others, has described the efforts of such reformers as Vivekananda and Dayanand, and such novelists as Bankim Chandra to "Christianize Hinduism." See *The Intimate Enemy*, 18–29.

It is therefore no surprise that the new homophobia was also internalized by modern educated Indians. Their anxieties regarding female and child sexuality mirror British anxieties on these subjects. Such early twentieth-century warning tracts as Madhavacharya's introduction to the *Kamasutra* (see p. 236) and the pseudomedical *Do Shiza* (see p. 260) which instruct parents how to protect their children from masturbation and homosexuality, are clearly influenced by Victorian campaigns for sexual purity and by such attacks on India as Katherine Mayo's *Mother India* (1927).[17] Mayo claims that overpopulation, poverty, and disease in India have nothing to do with British colonization but are directly traceable to Hindus', especially Hindu men's, "sex-life" (22). Painting a horrific picture of licentiousness both inside and outside the family, Mayo states, without citing any evidence:

> In many parts of the country, north and south, the little boy, his mind so prepared, is likely, if physically attractive, to be drafted for the satisfaction of grown men, or to be regularly attached to a temple, in the capacity of prostitute. Neither parent as a rule sees any harm in this, but is, rather, flattered that the son has been found pleasing.
> This, also, is a matter neither of rank nor of special ignorance. In fact, so far are they from seeing good and evil as we see good and evil, that the mother, high caste or low caste, will practice upon her children—the girl "to make her sleep well," the boy "to make him manly," an abuse which the boy, at least, is apt to continue daily for the rest of his life (25–26).

She adds that the "devastation of body and nerves" by the routine practice of masturbation "will scarcely be questioned" (26). In another chapter, in the course of her attack on various types of indigenous leadership (Brahmans, princes, English-educated youth), she connects political militancy with deviant sexuality:

> Bengal is the seat of bitterest political unrest—the producer of India's main crop of anarchists, bomb-throwers and assassins. Bengal is also among the most sexually exaggerated regions of India; and medical and police authorities in any country observe the link between that quality and "queer" criminal minds—the exhaustion of normal avenues of excitement creating a thirst and a search in the abnormal for gratification. (122)

Justifiably outraged, Indian nationalists and Western Indophiles unfortunately reacted to such claims with counterclaims that homosexuality and masturbation were unknown in Hindu society and as strongly disapproved of as in the Christian West. A related reaction (see p.249) was to acknowledge the existence of homosexuality in India but to claim that it was imported from somewhere else.

---

17. Katherine Mayo, *Mother India* (New York: Harcourt, Brace & Co., 1927).

Marriage and Family versus. Same-Sex Spaces

Tensions produced by the need simultaneously to open up and to guard domestic space were compounded by similar tensions around extradomestic spaces. British rule greatly expanded some all-male spaces in India, such as the standing army, the large urban jail, the organized police force, the largely male bureaucracy, and single-sex schools, colleges, and dormitories, while forming new all-women institutions. Thus if the court and the all-male communities around it disappeared in independent India, such communities reappeared in different guise elsewhere. And if the women's quarters began to meld into a shared family space (a process by no means complete today), women's schools, colleges, and hostels provided new all-women environments into which men were not allowed. Older same-sex spaces, framed by the assumption of religious celibacy, such as the *ashram* and *khanqah*, continue to flourish in modern India. Older institutions, such as male prostitution and domestic servants as sexual partners also persist in modern India.[18]

There is also an uneasy coexistence of old and new within family and marriage—the modern Euro-American ideal of heterosexual romantic coupledom with older patterns of filiation. Most Indian marriages today are family-arranged rather than self-arranged. Individuals, while aspiring to companionate love in marriage, do not generally expect it to constitute their sole source of emotional support. It is taken for granted that individuals will spend much of their leisure time with persons of their own sex. This often allows homoerotically inclined individuals to develop ties of varying closeness with one another.

Indian cultures tend to be more of the type anthropologists call shame cultures than guilt cultures. Reputation is familial rather than individual, and even harmless behaviors that cause others to gossip about one's family are considered shameful.[19] Having a child outside marriage is heavily disapproved of, unmarried parenthood is almost unknown, and premarital pregnancies almost always end in abortion or giving away the child in adoption. In this social context, same-sex friendships and spaces are generally more approved by parents than cross-sex friendships and mixed-gender spaces.

---

18. On male prostitutes in army brothels in Karachi, 1845, see Richard Burton, "Early Days in Sind," in N. M. Penzer, ed., *Selected Papers on Anthropology, Travel and Exploration* (1852; London: A. M. Philpot, 1924), 13–22. On male prostitution, concubinage, and coupledom in Bihar today, see Kanhaiah Bhelari, "Male Concubines," *The Week,* July 19, 1998, 16–18.
19. Sudhir Kakar, *The Inner World: A Psycho-analytic Study of Childhood and Society in India* (Delhi: Oxford University Press, 1981) argues that " . . . although Indians publicly express a staunch commitment to traditional moral codes, privately in relation to himself, an individual tends to consider the violation of these codes reprehensible only when it displeases or saddens those elders who are the personal representatives of his communal conscience" (135–36).

This situation leads many to argue that homosexuals actually have an easier time than heterosexuals in India, because they can more easily be alone together without social suspicion. However, this invisibility also has a downside. A same-sex relationship is tolerated and approved only as long as it masquerades as nonsexual friendship and does not conflict with marriage and parenthood. Even lifelong same-sex relationships never get full-fledged public acknowledgment, and a tremendous effort of will is required on the part of both partners to sustain such a relationship without any overt support from family.

Since sexuality is almost never discussed in public or even in the family, refusal to marry generally becomes the site for the declaration of difference. Men and women who refuse to marry usually face enormous emotional pressure from their families, especially their parents. In many cases, especially for unemployed daughters and for only sons, violence and restraint are applied to force consent.

Even in urban India, the parental family remains a major locus of social and emotional interaction for adults. There are few public places where people can comfortably interact, so friends are entertained at home and absorbed into the family or turned into fictive kin. The family is also the only form of social security and old-age insurance available to most people. This means that heterosexual marriage and parenthood hold many attractions even for homosexually inclined people. Many deal with the dilemma by marrying and then leading a double life. But the double life that was more socially viable in earlier periods now has to be more hidden since the domestic space has become more fiercely contested.

The contestation is evident both in fictional and nonfictional representations of homosexuality. Older traditions of romantic friendship continue in relatively uninhibited expressions of love in private documents, such as letters, but love between men disappears almost completely from poetry and is very rarely depicted in fiction. The correspondence between Bengali writers Banaphool (Balaichand Mukhopadhyay) and Parimal Goswami reveals a romantic relationship. In many letters written during the 1930s, Banaphool sends Parimal "unending, numberless, limitless kisses," "liquid kisses," "rain-drenched kisses," and many other types of kisses (*Pravartak*, July-December, 1994). Josh Malihabadi addresses Saghar Nizami as "my bride" (see p.279). The painter Amrita Sher-Gil's letters reveal her lesbian involvements (see p. 257), and Sunil Gangopadhyay has fictionally re-created the romances of Michael Madhusudan Dutt on the basis of extant letters (see p. 336).

Biographies and autobiographies tend to depict romantic and sexual interactions in nonjudgmental terms. Such is Nirala's good-humored autobiographical tale of advances made to him by a villager who later became a good friend (see p. 270). In his autobiography K. P. S. Menon mentions different types of homosexuality, including flirtations between schoolboys. Menon had "an amorous attachment" to a boy with whom he exchanged ardent love letters. The two remained good friends in later life.[20] In his autobiography, Akhtar-ul-Imans describes,

20. K. P. S. Menon, *Many Worlds Revisited: An Autobiography* (Bombay: Bhartiya Vidya Bhavan, 1965), 16.

in mildly pejorative terms, romances between schoolboys around the 1930s, relationships between older and younger men he witnessed when working as a tutor in Delhi, and *hijra* prostitution in old Delhi.[21]

Very much in the tradition of medieval mysticism, the assumption of celibacy enables men to express passionate attachments to other men. Shri Ramakrishna (see p. 229) is the direct heir of Shri Chaitanya and the Sufis in this respect, and the poems of Gopabandhu (see p. 241) are also in the same broad tradition.[22]

Travelogues by Euro-American homosexuals who visited India in the early twentieth century and found it less homophobic than their native countries also bear witness to tolerant traditions that survived in the face of the new homophobia. On his first visit in 1912–13, E. M. Forster met Maharaja Vishwanath Singh Bahadur (1866–1932) of Chhatarpur, the passions of whose life were "philosophy, friendship and beautiful boys."[23] On his second visit in 1921, Forster worked for six months as secretary to the saintly Maharaja of Dewas. In writings published only after his death, Forster described the affairs he had at Dewas and the range of reactions, from the Maharaja's friendly tolerance, to the gossip mongering of servants, to the hostility of some staff who conspired to banish a young Indian homosexual man from the kingdom.[24]

The New Homophobia

Although we are aware of the limitations of an analysis that blames all modern ills on colonialism, the evidence available to us forces us provisionally to conclude that a homophobia of virulent proportions came into being in India in the late nineteenth and early twentieth centuries and continues to flourishes today. This is particularly evident in twentieth-century Indian attitudes to male homosexuality and is best exemplified in the twentieth-century heterosexualization of the Urdu ghazal. The British consistently attacked Muslims as particularly prone to the "abominable vice," a stereotype adopted by an important section of Hindu nationalists. Ugra and his friends' writings and the debate around them (see pp. 249–50) clearly show how the idiom of Western sexologists and psychologists was used to further indigenous agendas.

21. Serialized in *Saughat,* Vols. 1–6 (September 1991-March 1994).

22. For a controversial psychoanalytic study of Shri Ramakrishna in the context of Tantric goddess-worship, see John Jeffrey Kripal, *Kali's Child: The Mystical and the Erotic in the Life and Teachings of Ramakrishna* (Chicago: University of Chicago Press, 1995).

23. P. N. Furbank, *E.M. Forster: A Life,* 2 vols. (Delhi: Arnold Heinemann, 1983; 1977), 1: 235.

24. See Furbank, vol. 2, chap. 4. *The Illustrated Weekly of India* (April 29-May 5, 1984) published "Kanaya," in which Forster describes how his affair with a young barber, Kanaya, although arranged by the Maharaja, caused some scandal. See also E. M. Forster, *Indian Essays and Journals* (Delhi: Arnold-Heinemann, 1984).

In reaction, speakers of Urdu, particularly Muslims, became increasingly uncomfortable with homoeroticism in Urdu poetry. In 1882 Altaf Hussain Hali planned a campaign to purify Urdu poetry. As part of this campaign, he argued in 1893 that Urdu poetry on the theme of "boy-love" was inconsequential and should be purged from the canon.[25] Andalib Shadani, a scholar who spent immense energy combing Urdu and Persian literature for homoerotic verses, declared that referring to "boy-love" as love "is an insult to that pure emotion. Wouldn't it be great if all well wishers of Urdu destroy whatever they can of such poetry so that this ugly blot on Urdu's reputation is washed away."[26] In his polemical tract *Nasl Kushi* (Race Suicide), which was translated into several languages, Mufti Muhammad Zafiruddin blames the Persians as well as the Shias for spreading this vice. He asserts that Satan appeared as a beautiful boy in Sodom and introduced the vice to mankind.[27] Warning that it is spreading like a plague in educational institutions, he emphasizes the need for watchfulness over self and others—adolescent boys should be watched; friendship between men and boys is dangerous; and men should not even look at beautiful boys' faces.

Some apologists try to explain away same-sex desire in the ghazal by arguing that the beloved was gendered male in earlier times because it was considered improper to refer to women in love poetry. The most common explanation, however, was that the beloved in the ghazal was really God, hence his masculine gender. The quest to explain away homoeroticism led some critics to desperate measures. One suggests that Mir turned to boys after frustration in a heterosexual love affair. Another concurs and adds that this was a defense mechanism.[28] The effect of this was that the well-established convention changed, and in the twentieth century the beloved in the ghazal is gendered female (for a change in the 1990s, see p. 212).

Even poets like Josh and Firaq, widely reputed to be bisexually inclined, went out of their way to gender the beloved female in their verses. If Josh's letters tell a different story (see p. 274), Firaq's defense of homosexuality in literature (see p. 264) shows that he was an assiduous reader of Western writings on the subject. Writing in 1932, he displays a wide-ranging and up-to-date knowledge of Western literature, from Plato to the 1928 *Well of Loneliness*, but seems to deliberately omit the most famous homosexual of all, Oscar Wilde, because his name had become associated with infamy.

---

25. Altaf Hussain Hali, *Muhammad-i Sher o Shairi* (Lahore: Kashmir Kitab Ghar, 1983), 12. For a detailed account of Hali's campaign, see Frances W. Pritchett, *Nets of Awareness: Urdu Poetry and Its Critics* (Berkeley: University of California Press, 1994), 179–83.

26. Andalib Shadani, "Iran ki Amradparasti ka Asar Urdu Shairi par," *Tehqiqat* (Bareilly: Jaleel Academy, no date) 193–222. In this homophobic polemic, Shadani focuses particularly on the poetry of the best known Urdu poet, Ghalib.

27. Muhammad Zafiruddin, *Nasl Kushi* (Deoband: Mustafa-i Kutub Khana, 1965), 24–29.

28. Cited by Tariq Rahman, "Boy-Love in the Urdu Ghazal," *Annual of Urdu Studies*, no. 7 (1990), 2.

The shadow of Wilde hung heavy over early twentieth-century modernists in England including homosexually inclined ones such as Forster and Virginia Woolf, and may have something to do with the paucity of representation of male homosexuality in twentieth-century Indian fiction. Until the late twentieth century, male homosexuals are depicted, if at all, as denizens of the underworld, and are constantly confused with *hijras*. Hijras include castrated, transgendered, and transvestite men, many of them homosexual, as well as persons born intersexed who live in well-organized communities in modern India. While it is true that becoming a hijra often seems the only option available to working-class homosexual men, the conflation of hijras with homosexual men in fiction, nonfiction, cinema and popular imagination is also a product of a homophobic refusal to acknowledge homosexual men as full-fledged "men" living in mainstream society.

The hijra phenomenon has attracted a lot of attention in recent years with a couple of documentary films and Serena Nanda's *Neither Man nor Woman* (Belmont, CA: Wadsworth, 1990). These studies show that some hijras identify as women and undergo castration or, more recently, sex-change operations, while others say they joined the community only for male sexual companionship. Some men neither cross-dress nor get castrated—they simply spend time with hijras.

In 1947 Vaikom Muhammad Basheer's Malayalam novel *Shabdangal* (Voices) was condemned as immoral because it depicted male homosexuality. In this novel, a discharged soldier, now a vagrant, recounts how he fell in love with a woman but, after sleeping with her, found she was actually a man who had joined the hijras after being homosexually assaulted by his schoolteacher. Although nauseated, the soldier, like the prostitute, becomes addicted to homosexual sex in the underworld, and contracts both gonorrhea and syphilis.[29] So taboo had the subject become that Kamleshwar's Hindi novel *Ek Sadak Sattavan Galiyan* (first published in literary journal *Hans* in 1956; the film *Badnam Basti* [1971] was based on it) created a furore merely because it depicts a truck driver and part-time bandit keeping a young man. The relationship is wholly subsidiary to the heterosexual involvements of both men in the underworld they inhabit, and is visible in the novel mainly in the young man being derided by others as effeminate and a hijra. In Chandrakant Khote's Marathi novel *Ubhayan Vai Avyaya* (1970), Dinkar is addicted to liquor and dope and also to anal sex with men, women and hijras. When he tries to force it on his wife, the marriage breaks up, and he falls into the underworld and dies of cancer. Homosexuality is entirely conflated with anal sex, which is depicted as a bad habit like liquor and drugs.

Depictions of male homosexuality in magazine fiction also tend to homophobia. Vivek Tandon's "Why I Am Gay" shows the narrator being humiliated by a woman who analyzes his homosexuality as stemming from his "inferiority complex" as a mediocre painter (*Illustrated*

---

29. Translated into English by V. Abdulla in *Poovan Banana and Other Stories* by Vaikom Muhammad Basheer (Hyderabad: Orient Longman, 1994).

Weekly, April 8–14, 1984). Partha Basu's surrealist "Take One" explores the psyche of a man traumatized in boyhood by his father's homophobia (*Illustrated Weekly*, June 23, 1985).

After Bankim's charming depiction of romantic emotion between two women (see p. 233) and the unembarrassed expression of such emotion in the barely fictionalized schoolgirl story "Farewell" (see p. 267), most Indian fiction we have found that depicts love between women does so with different degrees of homophobia, usually influenced by Western psychiatric discourse. Thus, lesbianism is often depicted as situational—caused by lack of access to men. Sometimes the women are neglected wives, as in Chughtai's story "Lihaf" (The Quilt). In Siddiqa Begum's Urdu story "Taare Laraz Rahe Hain," a married woman makes a pass at her husband's unmarried sister, and although both enjoy it, it is ascribed to their domestic confinement.[30] More often, lesbianism is shown as an adolescent phase in an all-women institution (see Chughtai, p. 283, and Nandakumar, p. 311) or a sheltered environment (see Deshpande, p. 327) which ends with marriage. Mumtaz Shireen's Urdu story "Angrai" depicts an affair between a student and a teacher as a phase and says: "I too passed through the stage that Gulnar did."[31]

An interesting variation is introduced when the married woman is shown yearning for her girlhood lesbian romance. In K. C. Das's story "Sarama's Romance" (see p. 298) this yearning is ambivalent, framed in the characterization of the older girl as abnormal and morbid, but in Shobhana Siddique's story "Full to the Brim" (see p. 304), it is sympathetically depicted as also in "The Sandal Trees" by Kamala Das. Kamala Das (born 1934) is one of India's best known writers in English, and her autobiographical *My Story* (1976) shocked readers with its explicitness about sex, including lesbian sex. In her Malayalam story, "The Sandal Trees," the elderly married narrator, Sheela, recounts her girlhood affair with a friend, Kalyanikutty, who was her illegitimate half-sister, and their lifelong mutual obsession. When Sheela's husband tells her that their apparently successful marriage is a sham because she has always been in love with Kalyanikutty, she realizes that she has ruined her life by not eloping with her lover:

> After this I felt ashamed to look at his face. That moment I thought my reflection in the mirror was the face of a stranger. Was it I, that woman with the glowing cheeks, hair clearly displaying the silver strands and the yet-to-be effaced vermilion spot on the forehead? Never. I was transformed into a young lass who embraced her girlfriend and sought the blissful rapture of her kiss. A girl who found heavenly pleasures in the bodily touch of her beloved—her beloved who, having swum and bathed in the pond for hours together, smelt and tasted of weeds and mosses, water lilies and medicinal herbs. "Oh, my love, how can I live now?" I whispered to the darkness that slowly spread in the car.[32]

---

30. For an English translation, see Susie J. Tharu and Lalita K., eds., *Women Writing in India* (Delhi: Oxford University Press, 1993), vol. 2.
31. S. Akhtar, *Urdu Afsanon mein Lesbianism* (Gaya, Bihar: Cultural Academy, 1977), 97.
32. Published under her Malayalam pen name Madhavikutty. English translation by V. C. Ummer Harris and C. K. Mohamed in *The Sandal Trees and Other Stories* (Hyderabad: Orient Longman, Disha Books, 1995).

When lesbians are depicted as adult women with choices available to them, they often appear frustrated, sad, and unloved, doomed to suicide (see Tendulkar, p.332) or loneliness (see Yadav, p. 289). In more homophobic depictions, they prey on, beat, or even murder one another (see Sood, p. 301). The use of a stereotyped "West" or Westernized character in these stories shows how xenophobia and communalism fuel homophobia, which is formulated in categories imported from the West. Bani Ray's Bengali short story "Sappho" describes the relationship between two schoolteachers, one "masculine" and ugly, the other "delicate" looking.[33] The "manly" one, Mondira, is labeled "Sappho" by the female narrator's relatives. Her kind of love, described as "unnatural" and "evil," is said to be spreading in girls' hostels. She is compared to a spider swallowing a helpless cockroach. Finally, the narrator's brother-in-law deliberately seduces Mondira, much to her lover's distress. He then spurns her, mocking her attempts to feminize her appearance and she stabs herself to death.

Perhaps the most horrific of these fictions is Rajkamal Chaudhuri's Hindi novel *Machhli Mari Hui* (Dead Fish), first published 1965, reissued in 1994 by Rajkamal Prakashan. In his foreword entitled "About dead fishes . . ." the author proudly claims to have published two short stories on the subject in 1959 and 1961, and also to have read a number of English books, ranging from *Female Sex Perversion* by Dr. Morris Sidekel to Donald Webster Cory's eloquent defense, *The Homosexual in America* (1951), de Beauvoir's *The Second Sex*, and Kinsey's writings. Complaining that while male homosexuality is punishable in most parts of the world, lesbianism is not, he adds that while Western lesbians claim freedom of sexual expression, Indian women practice homosexual acts without knowing what they are doing, "in sleep, in intoxication, unconsciously." In this novel, lesbianism is depicted as the result of frustrated heterosexuality and as unsatisfying because the women involved are really obsessed with men: "The fishes swim in the darkness, they leap up to hold each other. But they have no arms. They throb to embrace each other, but they have no feet. . . . Two blue fishes and darkness, the void."(121) Finally, one woman is cured when her husband returns to her. He then brutally rapes and impregnates the other woman, whose father writes to thank him for curing her! Interestingly, a short story by the same author represents homosexual relations between two schoolboys in a much more nuanced way.[34]

This trend continued into the 1990s, with best-selling English novelist Shobha De's soft-porn novel *Strange Obsession* (Delhi: Penguin, 1992), in which the heroine is rescued from a lesbian affair by marriage. Her lover, nicknamed "Minx" and described as ugly and "reptilian," a rich, Westernized, gun-toting, chain-smoking, hard-drinking member of Bombay's underworld, stalks,

---

33. In Enakshi Chatterjee, ed., *An Anthology of Modern Bengali Short Stories* (Calcutta: Prayer Books, 1977).
34. "Bhugol ka Prarambhik Gyan," in Devshankar Navin and Neelkamal Chaudhuri, eds., *Rajkamal Chaudhuri: Pratinidhi Kahaniyan* (New Delhi: Rajkamal Prakashan, 1995).

abducts, and nearly murders the heroine, but finally dies in a lunatic asylum. Feminist Punjabi novelist Ajeet Kaur's story "Aak Ke Phool" (1995) is equally homophobic with its depiction of a rich spinster living in a working women's hostel, preying on and violently abusing girls who are thirty years younger than she is, who take advantage of her and then abandon her for men.[35]

Academics and Politics

The homophobic attitudes evident in fiction find their counterpart in the studied silence maintained by the Indian academy on the subject of homosexuality. While avidly picking up other kinds of critical theory generated in the Western academy, such as Marxism, feminism, deconstruction, and postcolonial theory, the Indian academy has by and large avoided lesbian and gay studies. With a few exceptions, South Asianists both in India and outside have contributed to the myth that homosexuality is unknown in India by ignoring it completely or relegating it to footnotes.

Political parties, both on the Right and the Left, maintained the same sort of silence, as did women's and feminist organizations through the 1980s. A few pioneering books on the subject have been written outside the academy. One such early book is *The World of Homosexuals* (Delhi: Vikas, 1977) by mathematical wizard Shakuntala Devi. It opens with an interview of a South Indian Brahman company executive, recounting his discovery of his homosexuality, and the double existence he proposes to lead, with his male lover and the wife his parents have selected for him. The book goes on to survey the scholarship on homosexuality in history, in relation to law, psychiatry, different religions, and different cultures, with a detailed account of various surveys conducted in the West, including the *Kinsey Report*. Representation in literature and film is also surveyed, with a useful reading and viewing list. The author describes the origin and progress of modern gay liberation movements in the West, and interviews a male couple in Canada who have married each other and are suing the state for the right to register their marriage legally. This is followed by an interview with a young Indian who has told his parents why he cannot marry a woman and a fascinating interview with S. Raghavachariar, priest of the Shri Rangam temple (see p. 216). The book ends with a call for decriminalization as well as "full and complete acceptance—not tolerance and not sympathy" (155) by the heterosexual population, which will enable homosexuals to come out of hiding and lead dignified, secure lives.

In 1991 the AIDS Bhedbhav Virodhi Andolan (Anti-AIDS Discrimination Campaign), known as ABVA, conducted a study on homosexuality in India and published the findings in a booklet entitled "Less than Gay."[36] They noted the indifference and even hostility they faced

---

35. In Ajeet Kaur, *Kaley Kuen* (New Delhi: Kitabghar, 1995), 36–64.
36. A number of other reports have appeared in recent years. Perhaps the most comprehensive is Bina Fernandez, ed., *Humjinsi: A Resource Book on Lesbian, Gay and Bisexual Rights in India* (Mumbai: India Centre for Human Rights, 1999).

when trying to interview government and medical authorities and civil liberties, leftist, and feminist organizations. Their report contains interviews with a number of homosexuals, most of them under assumed names; surveys the Indian legal, social, medical, and cultural context of homosexuality; attempts to answer prevalent myths about homosexuality and AIDS; and also presents summaries of Western scholarship on these subjects. After listing the many problems faced by homosexuals in India, such as pressure to marry the opposite sex, opposition to their marrying or living with their lovers, misinformation and prejudice, lack of places to meet each other, and enforced silence and invisibility, the booklet concludes with a charter of demands, which includes decriminalizing of consensual homosexuality, inclusion of homosexual rape in the antirape provisions of the criminal code, inclusion of "sexual orientation" in the antidiscrimination section of the Indian Constitution, amending of the Special Marriage Act to allow same-sex marriage, noncoercive anonymous HIV testing facilities, nonheterosexist sex education, and AIDS education. ABVA was forbidden to distribute condoms in Indian all-male prisons on the ground that it amounted to a violation of Section 377. In 1994 ABVA filed a writ petition, still pending, asking for the section to be repealed as unconstitutional.

In 1995 lawyer Rajesh Talwar published his play *Inside Gayland* in the form of a pamphlet. The play depicts the visit of a married Indian lawyer to a planet where homosexuality is considered the only natural form of intercourse while heterosexuality is outlawed. He is apprenticed to a famous lawyer, herself a lesbian, who is defending two film stars accused of having a heterosexual affair. He gets arrested for holding a young woman's hand, and, when he returns to Earth, is frightened to sleep with his wife. The play comically depicts the effects of social pressure on people's view of what is normal or moral and what is not.

Rakesh Ratti's *A Lotus of Another Color* (Boston: Alyson, 1993) is an anthology of diasporic South Asians' autobiographical accounts. In 1996 Giti Thadani's *Sakhiyani: Lesbian Desire in Ancient and Modern India* (New York: Cassell, 1996) appeared (see p. 2). Ashwini Sukthankar's *Facing the Mirror: Lesbian Writing in India* (Delhi: Penguin, 1999) is a collection of fiction, poetry, and autobiographical accounts by a wide range of lesbians, bisexual, and transgendered women. Interestingly, these writings suggest that the fictional representations we have gathered, from the Krittivasa Ramayana and Rekhti to modern novels, which depict the family and women's institutions such as schools, colleges, and hostels as the main sites of love and sex between women, are not far from real life. One account in Sukthankar's book, by a domestic servant (transcribed and translated from her oral narrative), describes her happy lifelong relationship with her cowife. *Yaraana: Gay Writing from India* (Delhi: Penguin, 1999) is a collection of contemporary writings on gay male experience, edited by Hoshang Merchant.

In the 1990s journals such as *Economic and Political Weekly* and *Seminar* have carried essays about homosexuality in India. One such essay, Vimal Balasubrahmanyan's "Gay Rights in India" (*EPW*, February 3, 1996), points out that the Right and the Left seem equally opposed to homosexuals' rights and calls on civil liberties organizations to support ABVA's petition for repeal of Section 377. Instead, it elicited a one-and-a-half page response "Natural Is Not Always Rational" by H. Srikanth. He states that homosexuality is "backward and reactionary," just like sati, polygamy, and the caste system; he argues that like incest, homosexuality may be ancient and widespread but is nevertheless immoral.[37] Combining this homophobia with xenophobia, he goes on to condemn the media for reporting on gay liberation movements in the West, which he labels "decadent bourgeois . . . encouraging all deviant forms of sexual relations." He concludes: "Marxists . . . stand for heterosexual, monogamous relations and proscribe all deviant forms of sexual relations, including homosexuality. . . . Marxists try to change sexual behaviour through education,. . . . if some people, much against public conscience, take to the streets on the plea that they have the right to gratify their sexual urges in any way they like, Marxists do not hesitate to use force against such homosexual activists" (*EPW*, April 13, 1996, 975–76).

Srikanth finds an unlikely bedfellow in right-wing intellectual Swapan DasGupta, who makes exactly the same argument in the aftermath of the *Fire* controversy. Criticizing demonstrators who carried placards stating that "lesbianism is part of our heritage," DasGupta writes: "Thievery, deceit, murder and other IPC-defined offences have a long history. That doesn't elevate them to the level of heritage. . . . Homosexuality may have found mention in some ancient manual and even depicted [sic] in a temple carving or two, but as in the pre-promiscuous West, it was a preference that was greeted with tolerant disapproval. It was always an alternative to marriage and family but never a socially acceptable option" (*India Today*, December 21, 1998, 83).

English Language Press

In the 1980s, the negative valence of Freudian discourses was often offset in the English media by news of the advances made by gay liberation movements in the West. Today the national-level Indian media in English continues to pick up both positive and negative discourses on homosexuality from the West, and to interpret contemporary Indian phenomena in the light of both. One factor influencing the English media's attitude is its desire to keep abreast of the secular media in the West and not to appear retrogressive. The women's movement in India has received relatively positive coverage in the English media, and so has the nascent gay movement as well as gay individuals and their activities. On the other hand, the regional-language newspapers tend to be much more overtly hostile to anything they label "Western" and also to be more explicitly antisex and homophobic.

---

37. Sati, literally a woman who embodies truth, originally was used as an honorific for great women like Sita and Draupadi, but later came to refer to widows who were burned alive on their husbands' pyres, sometimes voluntarily and often under social pressure.

Through the 1970s and early 1980s, English-language Indian newspapers' reportage on gay-related topics mostly referred to the West. There were reports on such stars as Martina Navratilova, Billie Jean King, Rock Hudson, and other celebrities, feature-length articles on the secret lives of famous personalities ranging from Tchaikovsky to Michelangelo, and occasional brief mentions of achievements of gay liberation in western countries, such as rallies, changes in law, and same-sex unions.

With regard to Indian society, the reports that appeared were about sensational events, particularly completed or attempted joint suicides by young women who left notes saying that they chose to die together because their families forbade them to live together. These reports were usually sympathetic to the plight of the women and not homophobic in tone, but were brief and rarely followed up. This has begun to change, with civil rights and gay organizations following up the most recent cases (see p. 215).

Reviews of Western novels and of films or plays produced in Indian cities that had homosexual content also appeared, and varied in tone, generally maintaining a liberal tolerance without connecting the phenomenon to anything Indian. Very occasionally an essay appeared on an Indian historical figure, such as Babur, under such titles as "A Youthful Folly" (*Hindustan Times*, February 27, 1983).

Contemporary figures such as the novelist Aubrey Menen were reported on in euphemistic terms. A reader wrote to protest when an article on Menen after his death described Graham Hall, his partner of twenty years, as a "friend." The magazine published the letter with a photo of the two men captioned "Hall and Menen: Friends and Lovers" (*Illustrated Weekly*, March 5 and 19, 1989). In a contrasting case, when a small press report mentioned Madame Blavatsky's possible lesbianism, an indignant theosophist wrote in to protest against such "slander" (*Hindustan Times*, August 1 and 17, 1981).

Another kind of writing was found in so-called agony aunt columns, published in women's magazines as well as Sunday supplements to dailies, in which some usually unqualified counselor or celebrity, such as a TV star, responded to readers seeking advice regarding personal problems. Here the biases of pseudo-Freudian homophobia are much clearer, with the person who reported homosexual feelings or desires usually being advised to seek medical help or to actively resist such desires and seek out the company of the opposite sex.

After the mid-1980s, these areas of writing continued but the proportion and emphasis changed. New areas of writing also appeared. Reports on lesbian suicides were complemented by relatively in-depth reports on Indian lesbian weddings. The wedding of two policewomen, Leela and Urmila, in 1987, caught the public imagination and was widely reported, with front-page photographs. After the two women's suspension from the police force, one reporter went to Urmila's parental home in rural Madhya Pradesh and reported in detail how Leela, dressed as a bride, was living there like any new daughter-in-law. In another case, where the young women had met as college students in Delhi and one of them underwent a sex-change operation in order to marry the other, again reports were largely sympathetic and papers carried romantic stories and photos of the two as well as interviews with their families who were accepting of the relationship (*Times of India*, March 3, 1989). The Hindi press took a similar tone, reporting the wedding of Neeru and Meenu in Faridabad, under the title "The Interesting Wedding of Two Girls" (*Madhur Kathayen* 49, October 1993). The report pointed out, as did many others, that this kind of wedding is fairly common in the West.

In all cases where photos appeared of the wedded couples, one was dressed in conventional male and the other in conventional female attire. In the couple of cases where photos appeared of women who committed suicide together, however, both were dressed in female attire. Interestingly, while in many cases the women's families forcibly separated them, leading them to attempt suicide, there has been no organized religious or political opposition to these weddings of the kind that there is to interreligious and intercaste marriages. In a couple of cases, women were reported to have followed up a Hindu religious ceremony by attempting to file an affidavit under the Hindu Marriage Act, whose ambiguous language ("an Act to regulate the marriage of two Hindus") makes it difficult for the authorities to refuse permission. There were also reports of women in Gujarat filing "friendship contracts" (generally used by men to endow their extramarital female partners) to bestow partnership and inheritance rights on one another.

In cases such as these, the women are portrayed sympathetically by the press both because they are perceived as courageously resisting social injustice and perhaps because their romantic love for one another appeals to a general Indian delight in weddings and sympathy for besieged young love. The press takes a much less sympathetic view of other kinds of "odd weddings" that are not paralleled by Western phenomena. The wedding of *devdasis* or temple girls to the goddess Yellamma, which allows them the status of married women and their children, born of liaisons and prostitution, the status of the goddess's children, is condemned, even though the reporter acknowledges that the social reformers' replacement of this kind of wedding by child marriage of devdasi girls to adult men is substituting one evil for another (*Times of India*, January 25, 1998). The annual mass wedding of hijras to the deity Aravan in Tamilnadu is also linked to homosexuality and condemned as "a useless lifestyle" (*Deccan Herald*, April 19, 1998).

Advice proffered in agony aunt columns has also changed somewhat in the 1990s. While some counselors continue to take a homophobic tone, others encourage the questioner to explore his or her sexual identity and to accept it if it is homosexual, explaining that this orientation is no longer considered abnormal or sick.

Also new are interviews with Indian celebrities who discuss their homosexuality openly. These include gay journalist Ashok Row Kavi, a founder of *Bombay Dost*, who was one of the earliest to make such a statement (*Savvy*, April 1986); the famous painter Bhupen Khakhar (*Indian Express*, March 10, 1996); Delhi theater personality Barry John; and Sylvie, a cross-dressing hairdresser in Delhi whom the media projects as brave and odd.

In the 1990s there are many reports on Indian sexual behavior, including homosexuality. These reports attempt to portray the everyday life of ordinary people, not just the sensational and extraordinary. Typical recent examples: *Sunday* magazine's excellent cover story "Women in Love" (May 17–23, 1998), which sold out overnight, and *Bangalore* magazine's cover story "Gay in the Garden City"(September 1998). These articles carry addresses of organizations gay people can contact.

Some individuals as well as magazines have conducted sex surveys and reported the results. One of the earliest, by sexologist Narayana Reddy, conducted in Madras, mainly among men, was reported in *India Today* on December 31, 1982. Thirteen percent of the males said they preferred sex with men. *Outlook* magazine conducted a survey among urban English-reading married couples in eight cities and reported the findings in a cover story titled "Sex in the 90s: Uneasy Revolution" (September 11, 1996). Thirty percent thought homosexuality was normal, 54 percent thought it was not, and 16 percent did not answer. Fifteen percent admitted to having had homosexual experience. Lucknow scored the highest both in experience and acceptance of homosexuality, with 34 percent admitting to experience and 46 percent considering it normal. The methodology used in these surveys has been questioned.

Activities of the nascent lesbian and gay movement have been favorably reported. Such was the first-ever protest against police entrapment of gay men held outside the Delhi police headquarters on August 11, 1992, after the police arrested eighteen men from a park. From 1993, a group in Delhi has been holding an annual Siddharth Gautam film festival in memory of a young lawyer activist, member of the anti-AIDS group, ABVA. These festivals, held in the "safe" premises of European cultural consulates, show lesbian, gay, and AIDS films.

The newly emergent gay print media has heavily influenced the mainstream media in a positive direction. Perhaps the oldest of these was the newsletter *Gay Scene*, published from Calcutta in 1980; it folded after a couple of numbers. *Trikone*, founded in 1986 in California by two Indian men, is now a professional-looking magazine carrying reflective essays, news reports, fiction, poetry, letters, artwork, photography, and lots of personal ads, including many from India. *Shakti Khabar* was founded in London in 1988. *Bombay Dost*, the longest-running lesbian and gay magazine in India, was founded in 1990 and is still going strong. *Pravartak* was founded in Calcutta in 1991; *Friends India* from Lucknow and *Good as You* from Bangalore, newsletters produced by groups of the same names, appeared intermittently in the 1990s. Organizations and groups have come up in many cities and towns. Most of these groups and magazines were registered and thinly camouflaged as anti-AIDS organizations, which protected them legally. This has begun to change at the turn of the century with the establishment of openly lesbian and gay support groups, helplines, listserves, and websites in some cities.

Some of the most imaginative representations of homoeroticism have appeared in advertisements and in the world of film entertainment and fashion magazines. Even in the 1970s and 1980s, many advertisements used a tongue-in-cheek suggestiveness to speak simultaneously to two audiences, a larger one that may miss the point and a smaller one that will get it at once. This involves creative play with the unspoken subtext of romantic friendship in urban Indian culture.

In the last two decades, gay movements in the West have produced a large, openly lesbian and gay section of consumers who are now acknowledged by the corporate world.[38] The effects of this are felt in contemporary India, not only through the availability of Western products but through the training of advertising personnel. Calvin Klein and Newport Jeans have ads showing groups of men, some dressed, some undressed, posing together and smilingly admiring one another. Chelsea Jeans had large billboards in Delhi showing two girls in jeans and leather boots embracing and looking over their shoulders to say "F— off and leave us alone." A Bombay Dyeing ad for bedsheets showed one woman, lying in bed, the sheet pulled up over her, another stepping off the bed with the other sheet draped around her unclothed body.

Radio, TV, and Films

Radio and television, being under government control, have lagged behind the print media. Following the liberalization of the airwaves that began in the early 1990s, the appearance of independent channels as well as foreign channels, and the rapid spread of cable TV and video in urban areas, much more representation and analysis of sexual behavior has appeared. This has generated a moral panic in urban areas regarding the "corrupting" influence of the West on youth.[39] Perhaps the only demand on which the Indian Right and Left, including most religious groups and women's organizations, agree is that the State should censor sexually explicit material in cinema, radio, and TV. But despite increasingly draconian laws forbidding explicitness, so far the surge has not been dammed.

Foreign films with lesbian and gay content that are otherwise unavailable in India are regularly screened by cable TV networks, and Indian talk shows have held several discussions on homosexuality. A few people actually have come out on these talk shows; others have spoken on condition that their faces would not be broadcast.

Precolonial narrative traditions have carried over into Indian cinema, which, from its beginnings, has displayed an overwhelming interest in same-sex bonding. The heterosexual romantic interest in numerous films, from the 1940s to the present, is very often accompanied by an equally intense or even more intense same-sex romantic friendship. Same-sex friends often sing songs swearing undying love and fidelity to one another, risk their lives for one another and go through all the ecstasies and agonies associated with romantic passion and jealousy. On an all-India level, Hindi films are probably the single most powerful common cultural denominator, cutting across gender, class, caste, religious, regional and

38. For an account of this development in the United States, see Charles Kaiser, *The Gay Metropolis* (San Diego: Harcourt Brace, 1997), 339.

39. See Shohini Ghosh, "The Troubled Existence of Sex and Sexuality: Feminists Engage with Censorship," in Christiane Brosius and Melissa Butcher, eds., *Image Journeys: Audio-Visual Media and Cultural Change in India* (New Delhi: Sage, 1999).

even linguistic boundaries. The same-sex component in cinematic tradition is thus a crucial shaping factor in the way Indians view same-sex love. It may also explain why an acute fascination with Hindi cinema and film music is so central a part of gay culture in India today. This fascination has centered more on an identification with the protagonist of the opposite sex (i.e., gay men with intrepid film heroines such as Meena Kumari, Nargis or Helen, and some lesbians with charming heroes like Rajendra Kumar and Dev Anand) than on romantic bonding in films such as *Dosti*.

There are various kinds of vibrant play with gender and sexuality in the Indian performing arts and fine arts and in the worlds of fashion and design. Several theater personalities, dancers, fashion designers, and hairdressers are openly gay. Many plays with lesbian and gay themes have been staged in the big cities.

The 1990s

While homophobic fiction continues to be produced in the 1990s, it is countered by a spate of new positive representations of homosexuality. Among these are Ambai's Tamil story (see p. 352) and Nisha da Cunha's English story "La Loire Noire" in which a woman sympathetically recounts her friend Varun's grief as his French lover is dying of AIDS.[40] These are the only two positive representations we have found in twentieth-century Indian fiction of long-term male couples; interestingly, both depict interracial couples. In 1996, S. Rengarajan, writing under the female pen name Sujatha, published a Tamil story in the series "Thoondil Kathaigal" in the magazine *Ananda Vikatan* about a relationship between male colleagues.

A new genre of openly gay writing has emerged, including Mahesh Dattani's plays, produced in many cities and recently published by Penguin; Merchant's poetry (see p. 349); and R. Raj Rao's collection of stories, *One Day I Locked My Flat in Soul City* (Delhi: Rupa 1992), and poems, which formed the basis of a film by Riyadh Wadia. Bhupen Khakhar's Gujarati stories and plays depict the everyday lives of working- and middle-class homosexual men, many of them married (see p. 294). Leslie de Noronha's English novel *Dew Drop Inn* (Calcutta: Writers' Workshop, 1994) depicts the successful lives and loves of three young men in Bombay and Delhi, two of them Catholics and one a Jew. Most recently, P. Parivaraj's English novel *Shiva and Arun* (Norfolk, England: Gay Men's Press, 1998) depicts young men discovering their homosexuality in a small town in south India.

In 1995 Khalid Suhail, inspired by Pakistani poet Iftikhar Nasim's brave efforts to reclaim the convention of male-male love in the ghazal, wrote an Urdu book *Har Daur mein Maslub: Lesbian aur Gay, Adab wa Zindagi* (Crucified in Every Age: Lesbian and Gay Life and Literature) (Calcutta: Sharjil Arts, 1995). The publishers withdrew the book when the Urdu liter-

---

40. In Nisha da Cunha, *Set My Heart in Aspic* (Delhi: Harper Collins, 1997).

ary establishment in the city reacted against it. The book examines the historical and scientific background and the legal and medical debates around homosexuality, has a section of literary writings in Urdu and in translation, and argues for the acceptance of the World Human Rights Guide for gay rights.

Among the earliest to write consistently about lesbianism in English was feminist fabulist and poet Suniti Namjoshi, whose works were first published abroad and then republished in Indian editions. Another even earlier writer on this theme is Inez Dullas (see p. 347). From the new wave of Indian writing in English emerged openly gay Parsi writer Firdaus Kanga, whose autobiography *Trying to Grow* (London: Bloomsbury, 1990) was made into the film *Sixth Happiness* by Waris Hussein. Homosexual episodes occur in novels by other writers, such as Vikram Seth, Salman Rushdie, and Arundhati Roy. Among the most brilliant of these is Vikram Chandra's densely imagined story "Artha" wherein a Muslim computer jock embarks on a search for his long-term Hindu lover who, it turns out, has been murdered by the mafia in riot-torn Bombay.[41]

Perhaps the earliest full-length film to feature a homosexual South Asian was *My Beautiful Launderette* (1985), based on Hanif Kureishi's novel. In the late 1990s, some Hindi films have begun to directly portray nonheterosexual characters instead of merely using coded language. The best such portrayal was that of a hijra in *Tamanna* (1997). The protagonist is a man who, the film suggests, was born a hermaphrodite. He has a close male companion who is unmarried, and with whom he raises two adopted children. The film portrays him as morally the best "man," better than his daughter's biological father who threw her out to die.

Marriage/Family versus Same-Sex Underworld

It is no accident that *Fire* (1998), the film which sparked off the first public debate on homosexuality in independent India, depicts lesbianism in an ordinary household. Depictions of homosexuality in domestic spaces in Rekhti poetry, in Chughtai's story *Lihaf* and Ugra's *Chocolate* (see p. 246), were also labeled obscene and suppressed, while depictions of homosexuality in the underworld or in same-sex environments were not attacked with the same virulence. As long as homosexuality is seen as infrequently occurring between unmarried persons, or as frequently occurring in same-sex spaces or among people who look entirely different from average men and women, it is possible to view it with pity as a perversion caused by an unfortunate situation rather than an active preference. However, the reality is that most homosexually and bisexually inclined people in India are married at some time in their lives, live in the everyday world—in ordinary families, workplaces, and neighborhoods—and look indistinguishable from heterosexually inclined people.

---

41. Vikram Chandra, *Love and Longing in Bombay: Stories* (Delhi: Penguin, 1997), 163–228.

Fire depicts this reality through powerful traditional symbols, some of which we have explored in this book. The title evokes an ancient Indian symbol for energy that is not only purifying but also passionate, creative, and itself created by female forces (see p. 15). The film uses tropes of female intimacy such as oiling each other's hair, tropes of marriage such as exchanging bangles, feeding each other cardamom, and pressing each other's feet, and explores in a masterly fashion the eroticism of exchanged glances. Tropes of romantic love from mainstream Hindi films are used when the women exchange glances, dance together, or get soaked in the rain together. Their visiting, and finally meeting in, a Sufi *dargah* (a medieval space of same-sex community) frames them in yet another Indian tradition. With its not very credible depiction of Radha going through a fire ordeal and of her husband practicing celibacy on the advice of his guru, the film also launches an unnecessary and ill-conceived critique of Hinduism.

Beautifully shot and well acted, *Fire* had won many international awards when it was finally released in India after protracted consideration by the censor board. The censors made only one change—the heroine's name Sita was changed to Nita in order to avoid hurting Hindu sensibilities. When the film was screened to packed houses, activists of the Hindu rightwing organization Shiv Sena vandalized theaters in Delhi, Bombay, and Calcutta. The film was withdrawn and resubmitted to the censor board amid huge uproar and public debate. Despite the Shiv Sena's attempts to turn the debate into a Hindu versus Muslim issue, by slandering Muslim actors Shabana and Dilip Kumar, the debate was clearly about homosexuality, not about religion. This is evident even from the petition by the Shiv Sena women's wing's to have the film banned: "If women's physical needs get fulfilled through lesbian acts, the institution of marriage will collapse . . . reproduction of human beings will stop" (*Indian Express*, December 2, 1998). This is not a Hindu but a nonreligious authoritarian position.

Some feminists who opposed the tactics of the Shiv Sena nevertheless damned the film.[42] In a blatantly heterosexist analysis, Madhu Kishwar, editor of women's magazine *Manushi*, claims that though the film should not be censored, it is "boring,"(3) anti-Indian, and does "a big disservice to the cause of women"(11) by depicting the women's relationship as explicitly sexual instead of "ambiguous" as, she claims, most Indian women's love relations are.[43] In a self-contradictory argument, she states, on the one hand, that Indian society always has been and still is tolerant and nonhomophobic in contrast to the homophobic West, and, on the

---

42. Mary John and Tejaswini Niranjana in "Mirror Politics: 'Fire,' Hindutva and Indian Culture," *Economic and Political Weekly*, March 6–13, 1999, argue that the film is classist, casteist, and inadequately feminist. For a counterargument, see Ratna Kapur, "The Cultural Politics of Fire," *Economic and Political Weekly*, May 22, 1999. See also Shohini Ghosh, "From the Frying Pan to the Fire," *Communalism Combat*, 6:50 (January 1999): 16–19, for a more nuanced analysis.

43. Madhu Kishwar, "Naive Outpourings of a Self-Hating Indian: Deepa Mehta's *Fire*," *Manushi* no. 109 (November-December 1998): 3–14.

other hand, that explicit depiction or discussion of lesbian sex will inhibit Indian women from "expressing physical fondness for fear of being permanently branded as lesbians" (11–12). Why such a "brand" should be feared if society is so tolerant remains unexplained.

Kishwar fails to mention the numerous homophobic texts we have discussed above and also the frequently reported suicides by lesbians in India, of which the most recent is the subject of a report by ABVA. This report (*For People Like Us*, 1999) on the suicide in rural Orissa of Monalisa, a nineteen-year-old, and attempted suicide of her lover Mamta, twenty-four, now being accused of murder by Monalisa's family, takes its name from the deed of agreement for life partnership that the two women had registered in court four days before their suicide attempt. The report also contains a fairly comprehensive list of lesbian joint suicides reported in the media from the 1980s onwards.

A recurrent myth cited in the *Fire* debate is that gay liberation is a Western import into India. Thus Deepa Mehta, a Hindu who grew up in India, is dismissed as Westernized because she now lives in Canada. It is impossible and entirely futile to try to separate "Western" from "Eastern" in the modern world and in modern India. This inseparability is demonstrated in the paradoxical fact that all the Indian lesbians whose weddings have been reported so far are non-English-speaking lower-middle-class women, unconnected with the supposedly "Western" phenomenon of feminist or gay movements in Indian cities. Furthermore, while lesbian and gay marriage is increasingly prevalent in Western countries, the modern critique of patriarchal marriage as an institution emerged from feminism in those same Western countries and is partially shared by many feminists in India today.

Dan Detha's story (see p. 318), based on a folktale, brilliantly rewrites ancient Indian tropes of sex change, same-sex marriage, and cross-dressing, to celebrate love and marriage between women. The wonderful lyricism of Detha's Rajasthani and his evocation of literary tropes that have a long history in Indian literature, combined with his trenchant critique of patriarchal marriage and family systems, which he elsewhere ascribes to the influence of writers like Chekhov, demonstrates the impossibility of separating Eastern from Western influence in a text.

The Continuity of Tolerant Traditions

Despite the new homophobia, tolerance seems to have persisted in those Indian religious and philosophical traditions that have remained outside the purview of party politics. Thus the famous spiritual leader Jiddu Krishnamurti, himself a great example of East-West synthesis, when asked to comment on homosexuality, argued that all desire, whether heterosexual or homosexual, is the same and that religions have caused unnecessary suffering by trying to suppress it. According to him, celibacy is not the answer. Rather, we should inquire why desire becomes a problem: "Not condemn one or the other or approve one and deny the other, but inquire why sexuality has become so colossally important?" The problem arises not from acting on desire but rather when instead of admiring or enjoying the beautiful, we desire to possess it. The aspirant to liberation should enjoy the beautiful without identifying with or trying to possess it.[44]

American novelist Christopher Isherwood, follower of Shri Ramakrishna, describes the non-judgmental way his Indian guru Prabhavananda received him, his male lover, and their gay friends. The guru's view was that all lust, whether heterosexual or homosexual, is the same, and the aspirant must try to become celibate by seeing god in the beloved, thus purifying love of lust.[45] So he advised Isherwood to try to see his male lover "as the young Lord Krishna" (25). While Isherwood was struggling to do this, Prabhavananda did not condemn him for sexual behavior, but encouraged him to pray and try to become pure. Much more recently, gay activist Ashok Row Kavi describes a similar experience when he ascribes his "coming out" to the advice given him by two monks of the Ramakrishna mission.[46] Gandhi, who saw all sexual desire as basically sinful, also placed homosexual and heterosexual desire on the same plane (see p. 253).

Maulana Abu'l Kalam Azad, a respected Muslim theologian, places heterosexual and homosexual desire on the same plane when writing of Sarmad (see p. 157):

> Sarmad's experience was not unique. No one is worthy of being called a human unless he has crossed the Rubicon of love. He who has not experienced the intensity of desire or the deluge of tears is less than human. When the ascetic in the mosque bows the head in Namaz, despite all his piety and devotion, he cannot help enjoying thoughts of smiling Houris and Ghilmaans of Paradise. Even the super-ascetics who seek the truth in the recesses of the mosques are not free from these alluring images.[47]

In contrast to the Shiv Sena women's ridiculous fear that India will become underpopulated is a position more definitely rooted in Hindu philosophy—that of Srinivasa Raghavachariar, Sanskrit scholar and priest of the Vaishnava temple at Shri Rangam. Happily married, with thirteen children, he was interviewed by Shakuntala Devi, and remarked that same-sex couples must have been cross-sex lovers in previous births. The sex may change but the soul remains the same in subsequent incarnations, hence the power of love impels these souls to seek one another. He continued:

> Homosexuality is also a design of Nature. Earth is overpopulated by the human species and the Earth Mother—Bhooma Devi—is no longer able to carry the burden. So this is one of Mother Nature's way [sic] of combating the population explosion. Nature will not allow any species to

---

44. From Krishnamurti's second public talk in Ojai, California, May 3, 1981.
45. On reading about Wilde's conviction, Prabhavananda commented, "Poor man. All lust is the same." Ishwerwood, *My Guru and His Disciple* (New York: Penguin, 1980), 254.
46. Ashok Row Kavi, "The Contract of Silence," in Hoshang Merchant, ed., *Yaraana: Gay Writing from India,* (Delhi: Pengiun, 1999), 12–15.
47. Introduction to *The Rubayyat of Sarmad,* trans. Syeda Saiyidain (Delhi: ICCR, 1991), 24–25.

dominate completely. . . . It's only man who has acquired the ability to prolong his life span . . . the sly human is exterminating vitally important insect, plant, and even mammalian life in order to make life for himself more luxurious. This, of course, you understand, creates an unnatural imbalance in the life pattern. . . . There's also mankind's pressing and overriding desire to reach out to other planets. These are all Mother Earth's plans to relieve herself of the burden of the mass of humanity. All we can do is to sit back and wonder at the divine tricks of the Almighty![48]

The Shiv Sena attacks on theaters screening *Fire* elicited opposition from many quarters. In Calcutta, theatergoers fought off the arsonists, and a number of political parties and human rights organizations, including Communist parties and feminist groups, came out in support of freedom of expression. For the first time, lesbian and gay groups publicly protested in Delhi, calling for the right to "our way of life." Thus a public debate explicitly on the subject of same-sex love has finally been initiated in India, and it is to be hoped that *Fire* is only the first of many films on the subject. The Indian polity's commitment to democratic values was demonstrated when, after the furore, the censor board again released the film without any cuts and the Bharatiya Janata Party government endorsed this position on February 14, 1999.

One positive effect of the debate is that lies about homosexuality—for example, that it was unknown in ancient India and that it is a foreign import—are now being combated by many, who point to ancient texts and temple sculptures as also to folk songs and everyday life to demonstrate the opposite. Every homophobic response to *Fire* was amply countered by numerous groups and individuals.[49] Even as we write, this debate is leading to an upsurge of research along the lines of the present book, to demonstrate that same-sex love has a long and complex history in the Indian subcontinent and cannot be eradicated by violence or wished away by neglect and derision.

48. Shakuntala Devi, *The World of Homosexuals,* (Delhi: Vikas, 1977), 146–47.
49. Thus Madhu Kishwar's article sparked off a big debate on the SAWNET website; some of the responses disagreeing with her were published in *Manushi,* nos.112, 113 and 114 (1999).

Nazir Akbarabadi (Urdu)[1]

Introduced and translated by Saleem Kidwai

Nazir Wali Muhammad (ca. 1735–1830) wrote under the pen name Nazir "Akbarabadi" (meaning, a specimen from Akbarabad, modern-day Agra). He was born in Delhi, the thirteenth but only surviving child of his parents. His survival was attributed to the blessings of a *faqir*, his nose and ears were pierced to save him from the "evil eye," and as a child he was always dressed as a girl. Unlike other Urdu poets who migrated to Delhi or Lucknow looking for court patronage, Nazir stayed in Agra and made a living as a teacher.

Critics have dismissed him as a bazaar poet, thereby condemning his voluminous works as pedestrian. He has also been charged with using obscenities; often his published poetry is punctuated by ellipses. He wrote poetry about street people in their language, and it was among them that he was most popular. He often wrote verses at the request of performers, vendors, and even beggars who then used it in their trade. Much of his poetry, therefore, has been left unrecorded. It is said he knew eight languages: Arabic, Persian, Urdu, Punjabi, Brij Bhasha, Marwari, Purbi, and Hindvi. He was also a musician, which explains why his poetry lends itself so easily to song. Nazir worked in close collaboration with musicians of his time. He has been referred to as Hind's Shakespeare. Often the beloved in his poetry can be identified as male.

> Almost everyone carries around a baby squirrel,
> Every master has to have his own baby squirrel,
> But so special is this my baby squirrel—
> Any boy who saw my baby squirrel
> Would immediately be enchanted by my baby squirrel.

---

1. Abdul Ghafoor Shaharbaz, ed., *Kulliyat-i-Nazir*, (Lucknow: Naval Kishore Press, 1901).

Black stripes woven delicately into whiteness,
As on the cheek of a boy, a serpentlike tress,
A collar with lace, on it many little bells ringing,
A necklace, bangles around its paws and a nose-ring—
  Head to toe covered in jewelry is my baby squirrel.

Listen friends, one day a whim struck a chieftain
To watch the skills of master seducers, to have some fun.
He ordered, let all the masters be brought—
Thus suddenly by his servants I was sought.
  I was unprepared, but I did have my baby squirrel.

I looked disheveled, my clothes a disgrace,
My eyes watery, stubble on my pale face,
My turban dirty, my shirt coming apart,
But even dressed in rags, I was master of my art—
  For occasions such as these, I saved my baby squirrel.

And when he saw my state, when he saw my lost look,
He wondered, " A boy how would he manage to hook?"
I knew what he was thinking, I did not have to be told.
Not in my pockets or in my waistband but in my turban's fold,
  After much searching, I found my baby squirrel.

Sitting near and watching was his twelve year old boy,
Fairy-faced, a piece of the moon, a fair, plump toy—
Friends, the moment he saw my baby, on sight of it,
He was enchanted and demanded : "I want it, I want it,
  Come on quick, I want it in my hands, that baby squirrel."

Anxious, desire driving him into an eager mood,
Friends, he came running, right to where I stood—
A hundred pleas, he begged: "Give it to me, give it to me!"
His father screamed: "Throw out the man immediately!"
  How extraordinary the magic of this, my baby squirrel.

Rekhti Poetry:
Love between Women (Urdu)

Introduced and translated by Saleem Kidwai, versified by Ruth Vanita

*R*ekhti is the feminine of *Rekhta*, which is what Urdu was originally called. But "Rekhti" usually refers to poetry written by male poets in the female voice and using female idiom in Lucknow in the late eighteenth and nineteenth centuries.

Although the poet Rangeen is supposed to have coined the term "Rekhti," the tradition of men writing mystic poetry in the female voice and idiom was well established in the various northern Indian languages and dialects from which Urdu emerged. Many poems attributed to Amir Khusro (see p. 129) are devotional poems in the female voice.

In the twentieth century Rekhti was labeled obscene and systematically eliminated from the Urdu canon (see pp. 191–94 for an account of this process). Rangeen's poems, translated here, have been selected from the very small body of his work that is available. The two poems that poet Jur'at called *chaptinamas* have been excluded from editions of his collected works published in India. Critics exclude Jur'at from their account of the Rekhti poets in order to avoid citing his chaptinamas.

In Rekhti recitation at *mushairas* (poets' gatherings), poets often mimicked the feminine voice to stress the female persona in the poem. Poet Insha assumed different personae while reciting,[1] and Jan Saheb (1817–1896) used a veil as a prop during mushairas. Several poets seem to have dressed as women at nineteenth-century mushairas.[2] Many Rekhti poets also took feminine pen names, including *Dogana*, one of the terms used in Urdu to refer to homo-erotically inclined women.

---

1. Muhammad Hussain Azad, *Aab-i Hayat,* (1907; Lucknow: Urdu Academy, 1997), 221.
2. See Farhatullah Beg, *Dilli ki Aakhri Shama,* trans. *The Last Mushaira of Delhi,* (New Delhi: Orient Longman, 1979).

Rekhti poetry is remarkable for its use of terms to indicate sexual activity between women as well as women given to such activity. One of these terms, *chapti*, is still in use today. *Dogana*, from the root *do* (two), refers to doubling or twoness, and is a noun that refers to lesbian activity as well as women given to such activity. Chapti means the activity of sticking, clinging, or rubbing together. Like dogana, it is used to indicate this activity between women as well as the women engaging in it. Thus, the speaker may refer to her lover as "my dogana" and to her own predilection for "dogana" as an activity. The poem's genre, Chaptinama, derives from this word, as do several other words in the poem, as when the women say in the last stanza that they are famous as *chapatbaz*, or "given to the activity of chapti." The notion of lesbian activity as rubbing is close to the French (and English sixteenth-century) term for a lesbian, "tribade" from Latin *tribas*, Greek *tribein*, (rubbing) as well as to the Arabic term for lesbian activity, *Sahq* (rubbing). Compare also the metaphor of friction generated by rubbing the firesticks in ancient Indian texts (see p. 15).

Shaikh Qalandar Baksh, who used the pen name "Jur'at" (Audacity) (1748–1810), was born in Delhi but moved to Lucknow looking for patronage. He lost his sight due to smallpox. A musician, known for his frivolous antics, he has been called the first Urdu erotic poet.[3] He was a good friend of Insha.

Sa'adat Yar Khan, "Rangeen" (Colorful, see p. 119) (1755–1835), was a mercenary, a horse trader, and a poet. Zaidi describes him as "a gay, dissolute and handsome young man."[4] As a poet he found patronage in Lucknow. Rangeen was a prolific writer. Apart from his poetry, which includes long poems on weapons and on horse diseases, translations from Arabic, and religious poetry, he also wrote four works in prose, one in Persian. He organized his poems into four volumes: two of *ghazals*, one of obscene poetry and one of Rekhti.

Insha Allah Khan, "Insha" (1756–1817), was a good friend of Rangeen. He grew up in Bengal and later settled in Lucknow. A polyglot, he was known for his versatility with words and for his humor. He wrote poetry in many genres and languages. A large part of his poetry was in Rekhti. He also wrote *Darya-i Latafat*, a Persian book about the Urdu language. This is the first Urdu grammar written by an Indian. In it he argues in favor of the common Indian pronunciation of Arabic and Persian words as opposed to their pronunciation in their original lands.[5] In another work, *Kahani Theth Hindi Mein* (Stories in Pure Hindi), he did not use any Arabic or Persian word.

3. Nurul Hasan Naqvi, ed., *Kulliyat-i Jur'at,* (Aligarh: Muslim University, 1971), 15.
4. Ali Jawad Zaidi, *A History of Urdu Literature* (London: Oxford University Press, 1964), 142.
5. T. Graham Bailey, *A History of Urdu Literature,* (1928; Delhi: Sumit Publications, 1979), 54.

Jur'at: "Chaptinamas"[6]

1.
Yesterday Sukkho and Mukkho started a strange litany:
　　These wretched husbands have made our lives a mess and misery.[7]
How can the heart's bud blossom until one wanders the garden?
　　How can the glance but stray till one roams from alley to alley?
　　Come, let's play at doubled clinging, why sit around, better labor free.[8]

Let's invite all the women in town who are given to clinging,
　　Welcome them to our house with flowers and betel, embracing,
Perfuming each other; when of their husbands they start to complain,
　　That's when you and I begin our chant, teach them our refrain:
　　Come, let's play at doubled clinging, why sit around, better labor free.

This play, my love, is better than all others in the universe,
　　It's worth staking your life on, in thoughts of it yourself immerse—
When some old woman comes and starts doling out her thoughts adverse,
　　Laughing, we'll say between ourselves each moment through gestures:
　　Come, let's play at doubled clinging, why sit around, better labor free.

To the enjoyment of this clinging what other pleasure can compare?
　　This rubbing above, below, is intercourse wondrously rare,
Making love with one's own likeness is a strange, delightful thing,
　　Even if you get entrapped, being so consumed is comforting:
　　Come, let's play at doubled clinging, why sit around, better labor free.

Sometimes you'll be on top of me, sometimes I, your slave, will be on top,
　　When the body's rubbed all over, the heart's delight is multiplied,
When passion overflowing swells the womb's mouth, how can I stop?
　　Let the whole family be my foe, enough to say this to me:
　　Come, let's play at doubled clinging, why sit around, better labor free.

To let the rains pass, sitting idle, is to brew a storm within,
　　Drink this hidden wine, get drunk, the time will fly happily.
If anyone's opposed to you, who cares, to hell with them,
　　Exchange a glance between yourselves that says this intimately:
　　Come, let's play at doubled clinging, why sit around, better labor free.

---

6. Iqtida Husain, ed., *Kulliyat-e Jur'at* (Napoli: Istituto Universitario Orientale, 1971), II: 261–62; 294–97.
7. The names are diminutives and not explicitly Muslim or Hindu, although other references in the poem create the ambience of a Muslim household. *Sukh* is "happiness" and *Mukh*, "mouth" or "face."
8. "Doubled clinging": in the original, the two words used are *dogana* and *chapti*.

When the heart is sorrowful, all space, all time, appear empty.
     To live with unfulfilled desire—such a life is burdensome.
All are absorbed in their own pursuits throughout the city—
     Waves arise in hearts that enjoy the river of beauty:
Come, let's play at doubled clinging, why sit around, better labor free.

We've been betrayed to the Mirza by that wretch of a Chameli—
     The saying has turned out true—Ravana's own brother destroyed his city—
Now he will confine us strictly, he's entered the house looking very angry.[9]
     Tell me, my dear, what else is there to do besides this remedy:
Come, let's play at doubled clinging, why sit around, better labor free.

What else can I write about Sukkho and Mukkho's daring acts?
     When their husbands forbade them to do what they were doing,
They said, We are now famous everywhere as clinging women—
     Why not act upon it then—when going out to dance, why wear a veil?
Come let's play at doubled clinging, why sit around, better labor free?

2.
There's no love lost between women and men these days—
New ways of being intimate are seen all around.
Everyone knows about women who love women—
At night these words are always to be heard:

The way you rub me, ah! it drives my heart wild—
Stroke me a little more, my sweet Dogana.

I'd sacrifice all men for your sake, my life,
I'd sacrifice a hundred lives for your embraces
How delightful it is when two vulvas meet—
This is the tale they tell each other all the time:

The way you rub me, ah! . . .

When you join your lips to my lips,
It feels as if new life pours into my being,
When breast meets breast, the pleasure is such
That from sheer joy the words rise to my lips:

The way you rub me, ah! . . .

---

9. Mirza refers to a man. *Chameli* is a flower, and often the name of a low-caste woman. Here, she is most likely a domestic servant. In the *Ramayana,* demon king Ravana 's brother Vibhishana defected to Ravana's enemy Rama. In the idiom, Vibhishana thus stands for a traitor.

How can I be happy with a man—as soon as he sits by me
He starts showing me a small thing like a mongoose—
I'd much rather have a big dildo
And I know you know all that I know

The way you rub me, ah! . . .

When I take your tongue in my mouth and suck on it—
With what tongue shall I describe the state I am in?
Long are the hours I wait for you, deprived of love—
Why then, my life, should I not lose myself and say:

The way you rub me, ah! . . .

What other companion or confidante do I have but you?
The truth is no one can match you in what you do,
All the other Chaptis should become your pupils—
Instead of coyness why shouldn't these words rise to my lips:

The way you rub me, ah! . . .

You are the best of all—to whom can I compare you?
Whoever I tell about your skills, starts desiring you.
Oh, oh, what kinds of pleasure your strokes give me—
To tell the truth, there is no delight greater than this:

The way you rub me, ah! . . .

Let my shoe go close to that wretched man.
Let her go to men who wants stakes hammered into her—
Can she ever get these hours and hours of pleasure?[10]
How can I persuade myself to find pleasure with men?

The way you rub me, ah! . . .

I'd give up anything for that moment when you come in,
Dressed pretty as a picture, and put your arms around my neck!
For that pleasure when our nipples touch and meet,
And when we caress each other any way we please!

The way you rub me, ah! . . .

I'm taken with your manner, your style is entrancing,
I from above, you from below, let's put in more energy,
When our bodies come together, we will lose ourselves—
Oh how much I enjoy this, why shouldn't I tell you:

---

10. The metaphor used here compares sexual intimacy between women to a medicine that is
taken to prolong pleasure in sexual intercourse.

The way you rub me, ah! . . .

Who can find words for the pleasure of this act?
For hours when we're together, I'm deaf to other voices.
How to describe the taste of sweets eaten in secret?
There's no pleasure in the world like clinging to a woman.

The way you rub me, ah! . . .

When you run your tongue over my lips,
My heart and being experience a myriad pleasures.
I think of men, young and old, as one thinks of a holy man—
I have forsaken the whole world for you:

The way you rub me, ah! . . .

What fools they are who run after men,
It's absurd to burn oneself up like a candle for men!
When one woman clings to another, such is the happiness
They never want to part or let their desire decrease:

The way you rub me, ah! . . .

That wretched man should feel ashamed of coming so soon—
It's sheer humiliation to be in that useless fellow's company.
Why in this garden of the world do women lovers not have pricks?
In any case, I would much rather have your fruit than that banana![11]

The way you rub me, ah! . . .

However much daring a man may have,[12]
However much energy and lustful desire,
I'd rather see a face that gives me pleasure—
I'd give anything for this intimacy which I much prefer.

The way you rub me, ah! it drives my heart wild—
Stroke me a little more, my sweet Dogana.

---

11. "Your fruit" is the *kamrakh* fruit in the original. It is an astringent green fruit with four angles and resembles a vulva.
12. The word "daring" is a play on the poet's name Ju'rat.

Rangeen: Couplets[13]

1.
O Zanakhi, ever since you heard the organ play,
You have become obsessed with a foreign woman.[14]

Come, let's go to Qutb Saheb,[15] put up a swing, and swing there.
Dogana! It's raining wine, this is the month of Sawan. (10:3)[16]

2.
Sleep does not come to me—crazy girl, come!
Tell me some story from your life, come.

These days of the new year are green
Buy green clothes for me, put them on me, come.

You have tied the hair on your brow with a string,
Today your face looks frightening, come. (11:4)

3.
When did the Zanakhi last come to my house?
When did I last have a bath?

The girl has been so annoyed for a long time!
When did she and I make up our quarrel?

That rascally girl was not at home
Whenever I sent the maid to look for her. (11:8)

4.
O Dogana, you have come to rob me again.
My purity will slip away, at home, again.

The maid I had thrown out has been brought back, Rangeen.
That mock cudgeling at home is written in my fate. (12–13: 14)

---

13. All translations of Rangeen's and Insha's poems are from S. S. M. Naqvi, ed., *Intikhab-i Rekhti* (Lucknow: Urdu Academy, 1983). Page numbers are followed by numbers of the ghazals from which the couplets are extracted.

14. *Zanakhi* is a term used in Rekhti to refer to a female lover of women. This is a rare verse where an Indian woman is shown to be in love with a Western woman.

15. The tomb of thirteenth-century mystic Qutub ud Din Bakhtiyar Kaki in Mehrauli, a village near the old city of Delhi. Residents of Delhi often went there to get away from the city.

16. This and the preceding verse are not in the 1833 manuscript, which is in Rangeen's own hand. It may be an attribution by editor S. S. M. Naqvi. We are grateful to Carla Petievich for pointing this out.

5.
This heart of mine hungers for Dogana
Like a fish in the sand thirsting for water. (13: 15)
6.
O God, may no one be inclined to desire,
And if they are, may they be inclined to commitment.

I am given to Dogana
As the moss is given to greenness.

The path of love is very rough
Why should anyone take to such a wretched path? (13: 16)

7.
Ah, my Dogana's style is quite unique—
She's cream-complexioned with a special magnetism.

The amulet on her head looks killing
Her hair perfumed, her plait with an unusual twist.

Her way of talking is different from all others', every detail of her appearance is unique.
Her teeth are a picture, marked with antimony.

If the world says anything, sparks fly from her tongue.
And when they stop, her way of stopping is special.

Everything about her is different from everyone else
She goes at her own unique pace.

Her way of dressing is unique,
Her way of adorning herself unique. (14: 22)

Insha: Couplets

Your plait is a wriggling serpent, O Dogana,
I take poison because of you, Dogana.

May people not be so keen to find one's house—
These Doganas have found out all the secrets of the city.

You and I sitting here like bride and groom,
Let's agree on a dower of a lakh rupees, O Dogana.

Do tell me who this Insha is—
O Dogana, you are a real firebrand made by God! (22: 5)

2.
In fear of your waving plait, I wake trembling at night,
Startled, I cry out "A snake, a snake!"
Don't keep blessing me all the time—
O Dogana, you are very naughty.

To tell the truth, when you are not here,
I can't find a moment's peace, whichever way I turn.

O Insha, my heart was wounded
When I first heard her footstep. (23: 10)

3.
O Dogana, your loose trousers are very fetching.
The waistband is pink and the drawstring blue! (24: 20)

4.
To take the name of love is to get one's face scorched,
How long can one burn in this heat of the heart?

Alas for this thought embedded in the heart,
How long to keep wringing these two hands?

The Dogana's voice is getting quenched today.
Tell Insha, someone, that he should voice these sorrows now. (27: 35)

Shri Ramakrishna Paramahansa

Ruth Vanita

Perhaps the greatest mystic of modern India, Shri Ramakrishna (1836–1886) was a legend in his lifetime and is considered a divine incarnation by his followers. His ashram at Dakshineshwar, built on the site of what was once a Sufi dargah, developed into a commune of devotees.

As a child, Ramakrishna was charmingly precocious and also went into trances, which led the village women to worship him as the boy Krishna. While spending time with these women and observing their behavior, he used to dress up as a woman for fun and played this role so well that none could detect him. The villagers said that if he were a girl, he would have married his close friend, a seventeen-year-old boy named Ram Malik. After moving to Calcutta as a priest at the Kali temple, young Ramakrishna had a vision of the goddess and of the universe as an "endless ocean of light." Over the next few years, he undertook many different kinds of spiritual exercises, including Tantric, Yogic, Vaishnava, and Vedantic. Identifying for some time as a handmaid of the goddess, he dressed and lived as a woman in the home of his friend and patron, Mathur. He saw the goddess in the whole universe, even in animals and trees.

Afraid that he was going mad, his family got him married when he was about twenty-three. When his wife was sixteen, Shri Ramakrishna performed ritual worship of his wife as the goddess Kali. Throughout their lives, the marriage remained completely sexless and expressive of a spiritual love.

Around 1861, Ramakrishna met a Bhairavi, a middle-aged Brahman woman renunciant, whom he saw as his spiritual mother and teacher. He went through different types of devotion, worshiping the child Rama in the company of a visiting devotee, identifying as a Muslim for a few days, and having a vision of Jesus as a white man who embraced him and disappeared into his body.

Although he was in communication with many fellow seekers and admirers, including Brahmo Samajis, around 1879 Ramakrishna began to feel a deep yearning for dedicated disciples who would renounce the world to follow his teachings. He describes how he would climb

230 Modern Indian Materials

to the roof of his hut and cry out in anguish: "Come to me, my boys! where are you? I can't bear to live without you!"[1] Soon after, the disciples began to come to him, one by one. The most momentous of these encounters was with the eighteen-year-old university student Narendra Nath Datta, known as Naren, who later became Swami Vivekananda (1863–1902). Recognizing him immediately as a great spiritual aspirant, Shri Ramakrishna caught hold of his hand as soon as they were alone and shed tears of joy. In Naren's words,

> he said to me affectionately, as if to a familiar friend, 'You've come so late! Was that right? Couldn't you have guessed how I've been waiting for you?'. . . . And then suddenly he folded his palms together and began addressing me as if I was some divine being, 'I know who you are, My Lord. You are the ancient sage, the incarnation of Narayana. You have come back to earth to take away the sufferings and sorrows of mankind.' I was absolutely dumbfounded. . . . I didn't answer him, and I let this wonderful madman go on talking as he chose." (194–95)

Shri Ramakrishna then fed Naren sweets with his own hands and made him promise to return soon, alone.

At their second meeting, Naren found the Master meditating on his bed. He made Naren sit on the bed and placed his foot on Naren's body. Naren then had a mystical vision of himself and the entire universe about to disappear into a void. By touching him with his hand, the Master brought him back to ordinary reality.

Shri Ramakrishna later said that he had had a vision of a sage who was Naren in an earlier incarnation, in the company of a child who was Shri Ramakrishna. The sage and the child were "eternal companions"—when the child was incarnated as Ramakrishna, the sage had to accompany him as Naren. Ramakrishna's devotion to Naren surprised all who witnessed it. If Naren stayed away from Dakshineshwar even for a few days, Ramakrishna would shed tears. "I can't bear it when I don't see him," he told the other young disciples. "I wept so much and still Narendra didn't come! He doesn't understand at all what I feel for him. . . . What will people think, seeing a man of my age weeping and pining for a boy like him! With you, I don't feel ashamed of it—you are my very own. But what must the others think? And yet I can't stop myself—" (202).

Some time later Ramakrishna's attitude changed and he began to ignore Naren. This apparent indifference continued for a month, yet Naren kept coming. Finally, Ramakrishna asked him, "Why do you keep coming here, when I don't speak a single word to you?" Naren replied,

---

1. Christopher Isherwood, *Ramakrishna and His Disciples* (Hollywood, CA: Vedanta Press, 1965), 167. From this point on, my account is based on this biography authorized by the Ramakrishna Mission. Isherwood, himself a devotee, based his narrative on the records of the Master's life kept by two disciples: *The Gospel of Sri Ramakrishna* by M (Mahendra Nath Gupta) (1907; New York: Ramakrishna-Vivekananda Center, 1992), and *Sri Ramakrishna the Great Master* by Swami Saradananda (1920; Hollywood, CA: Vedanta Press, 1984). Numbers in parentheses refer to pages in Isherwood's biography.

"Do you think I come here just to have you speak to me? I love you. I want to see you. That's why I come" (207–08). Ramakrishna was delighted and said he had been testing Naren's spiritual qualities. Naren's family urged him to marry, but Ramakrishna preached the virtues of chastity to him. His grandmother overheard this one day, and Naren's family then became opposed to Ramakrishna. But they could not dissuade Naren from going to Dakshineshwar.

Shri Ramakrishna had loving relationships with many devotees, married and unmarried, men and women. He encouraged his unmarried male followers to remain unmarried and celibate. His most intense emotional relationships were with the young men who were drawn to him, often against the wishes of their families. Although Naren was in some ways Ramakrishna's dearest disciple, there were several other dear ones too. Ramakrishna was able to recognize by certain physical characteristics which of them had spiritual potential. For instance, he said that eyes shaped like lotus petals indicated good thoughts while eyes like those of a bull indicated the primacy of lust. Some of the disciples remembered with vivid clarity their first encounter with the Master. Thus Hari Prasanna Chatterjee (Vijnanananda), who went to Dakshineshwar when he was about eighteen, was filled with delight when he heard Ramakrishna speak. When he was leaving, Ramakrishna asked him if he could wrestle and invited him to wrestle with him. Surprised, Hari thought to himself "What kind of holy man is this?" In Hari's words:

> Sri Ramakrishna came closer, with a smile on his lips. He caught hold of my arms and began to shove me. But I was a muscular young man, and pushed him back to the wall. He was still smiling and holding me with a strong grip. Gradually I felt a sort of electric current coming out of his hands and entering into me. That touch made me completely helpless; I lost all my physical strength. I went into ecstasy, and the hair of my body stood on end. Then Sri Ramakrishna let me go. He said, smiling, 'Well, you are the victor.' With these words he sat down on his cot again. I was speechless. Wave after wave of bliss was engulfing my whole being. After a while, Sri Ramakrishna got up from his seat. Patting me gently on the back, he said, "Come here often." Then he offered me some sweets as *prasad*, and I returned to Calcutta. For days the spell of the intoxicating joy lingered, and I realized that he had transmitted spiritual power to me. (237)

Another beloved disciple was Rakhal, who went to Dakshineswar as a seventeen-year-old, already married. Before he arrived, Ramakrishna had a vision of Rakhal as one of the cowherd companions of Shri Krishna. (Rakhal's mother had actually named him after one of these companions). Ramakrishna felt towards Rakhal as Yashoda felt towards her foster son Krishna. In Ramakrishna's words:

> In those days, Rakhal had the nature of a child of three or four. He treated me just like a mother. He would keep running to me and sitting on my lap. He wouldn't move a step from this place. He never thought of going home. I forced him to, from time to time, lest his father should forbid his coming here altogether. His father is a landowner, immensely rich, but a miser. At first he tried to stop his son from coming here, in various ways. But then he came here once and saw how many rich and famous people visit this place, and so he didn't object any more. . . . What a wonderfully childlike nature Rakhal had! Sometimes I fed him and played with him to keep him

happy. Often I'd carry him around on my shoulders. . . . And he was jealous too, just like a child. He simply couldn't bear it if I loved anyone but him.

Rakhal's wife Vishweshwari was accepted by Ramakrishna and his wife as their daughter-in-law. Shri Ramakrishna's wife, Sharada Devi (died 1920), also engaged in spiritual pursuits all her life, acting as mother to his followers, and came to be recognized as Holy Mother to the Ramakrishna Mission.

Bankim Chandra Chatterjee: Indira (Bengali)[1]

Introduced and translated by Shohini Ghosh

Bankim Chandra Chatterjee (1838–1894) is widely considered the greatest Bengali novelist of the nineteenth century. A deputy magistrate in the Indian Civil Services, he wrote one novel in English and thirteen in Bengali. Outside Bengal he is perhaps best known as the author of "Bande Mataram" (Hail Motherland), a Hindu patriotic anthem contained in *Ananadamath* (The Mission House of Ananda), a novel about the ascetic rebellion in Bengal in 1773.

While Bankim purported to provide moral education through his stories, he was attacked for depicting too many embraces, kisses and illicit affairs. Among Bankim's ardent aficionados were Bengali middle-class women.

Bankim first published "Indira" as a short story in the magazine *Bangadarshan* in 1873. In 1893 he wrote a new novella based on this story, from which the following extract is taken. Indira narrates the story of her friendship with Subhashini who, with her husband Ramen Babu, mentors Indira when she is accidentally separated from her husband soon after marriage. While the plot revolves around Indira's quest for reunion with her husband, the relationship between the two women remains pivotal to the novel. In the novel's closing lines, Indira, many years later, says: "I have not forgotten Subhashini. I will never forget her in this life. I have not met anyone else like Subhashini in this world."

. . . Subhashini took me in and bolted the door. I asked, "Why have you locked me in?" Subhashini said, "I want to dress you up."

---

1. This translation from *Bankim Chandra Granthabali* (Calcutta: Upendra Nath Mukhopadhyay at Boshumoti Steam Machine Press, 1892), Vol. 2, 411–14.

She wiped my face clean. Then, having massaged my hair with fragrant oil, she started to tie my hair into a chignon and said, "This hairstyle is worth a thousand rupees—when the time comes, you can return the amount to me." She then took one of her own clean and beautiful saris and started to drape it around me. She tugged at my clothes in such a manner that I gave in, for fear of being left naked. Then she proceeded to ornament me with her own jewelry. "I refuse to wear this," I said.

This led to more arguments—seeing the firmness of my refusal, she said, "All right, I've arranged for another set—you can wear that." Having said this, she proceeded to take *mollika* [jasmine] flower buds from a jardiniere and made me wear bracelets, anklets, and a necklace of these buds. Then, producing a brand-new pair of golden earrings, she said, "I've acquired these through R. Babu from my own money, and they're for you. Wherever you are and whenever you wear these, they will remind you of me. Who knows, dear, what if I never see you after today—God willing, I will see you—but that is why I will make you wear these earrings. Don't say no to this."

While speaking, Subhashini began to cry. I was near tears myself and could not refuse any more. Subhashini put the earrings on me.

After the dressing-up was complete, the maid brought in Subhashini's son. I sat him on my lap and started talking to him. After a while, he fell asleep. Then a sad thought crossed my mind and despite all the happiness, I could not but share it with Subhashini. "I am really happy but I am also secretly unhappy with him. I have recognized him as my husband so whatever I have done with him, to my mind, is not a problem. However, it is not possible that he has recognized me. I had seen him as an adult—that's how I suspected who he was—but he had only seen me as an eleven-year-old. I don't see how he could recognize me. Therefore, when he felt attracted to me, thinking I was someone else's wife, I could not help being critical of him. But he's my husband, I am his wife— it is not done to be critical of him—so I haven't discussed this matter. But I decided, if I ever got the chance, I'd rid him of such an attitude."

Subhashini said, "Monkeys like you can't be found on trees—he doesn't have a wife."

I: "Do I have a husband or not?"

Subho: "Heavens! Are men and women the same? Let me see you work at the commissariat and earn money!"

I: " Let them bear children in their wombs and bring them up—and I'll go to the commissariat too. People do what they can. Don't men have any strength of will?"

Subho: "Okay, first get a home and then you can set fire to it. Now, forget this talk. First tell me, how will you charm your husband—I'll test you on that. Otherwise, you are lost."

I replied with some concern: "But I've never acquired that skill."

Subho: "Then learn it from me. I am an expert in this art, did you know?"

I: "That is quite evident."

Subho: "Then learn. You are the man. See how I charm and bewitch you."

Saying this, the wretch pulled the sari slightly over her head and offered me a betel that she had prepared with her own hands. She usually prepares this kind of betel specially for Romen Babu. Never even has it herself. Romen Babu's hookah was lying there. She prepared the hookah—of course, the coal had turned to ashes—and then proceeded to smoke—pretend, rather. Then she picked up the flower-bedecked fan and began fanning me with it, her bangles making a sweet clinking sound.

I said: "My dear! This is slavishness—is it to show how slavish I am that he has been held captive?"

Subhashini asked: "Are we not slaves?"

I said: "When I know for sure he loves me, I am willing to be a slave. Then I'll fan him, massage his legs, light his pipe. No servitude till then."

Then Subhashini began laughing and moved closer to me. She reached out, held my hand in hers and started speaking sweet endearments. Then, laughing, chewing her betel and swaying her earrings, she started to praise my appearance that was, in effect, her own handiwork. But soon she forgot her performance, and began talking like herself, as my girl friend. That I would soon be leaving came up again. Her eyes were again moist with tears. To cheer her up, I said, "What you have taught me are certainly weapons that women use, but is this guaranteed to work on U. Babu?" Subhashini laughed: "I haven't shared my ultimate weapon as yet." Saying this, she reached out, held my face in her hands and kissed me on my lips. I felt a tear drop on my cheek. I swallowed, suppressed my tears and said: "Oh dear, you are teaching me to offer rewards without any commitment." Subhashini said: "Then you won't learn anything. Show me what you have learned—this is an exam. Imagine that I am U. Babu." Saying this, she settled comfortably on the sofa and tried to stifle her laughter behind her sari. She stopped laughing briefly—looked at me seriously—then dissolved into laughter yet again. Controlling her laughter she said, "Come on, you are being examined." I performed on Subhashini some of the skills with which the reader will be acquainted later. She pushed me off the sofa and said: "Go away! You are a regular snake."

I asked: "Why, dear?"

Subhashini said: "Can any man survive your doings? They will surely perish."

I: "You mean I pass?"

Subho: "You pass very well. Not one of the 169 men in the commissariat could survive either this look or this smile. If the fellows lose their heads, bring them back to their senses with an oil massage."

I: "All right. I can hear that the men have finished having their meal. Romen Babu will soon return to the room—and I will have to leave. Of all the things that you taught me, I loved the kiss the most. Come, let us learn it again together."

Then Subhashini clasped my neck again and I clasped hers. In an intense embrace, we kissed each other; then, holding each other, we both cried. Can there ever be love like this? Can anyone ever love like Subhashini? I will die but never forget Subhashini.

The Kamasutra in
the Twentieth Century

Ruth Vanita

Until Alain Danielou's 1995 translation, published in the United States, Sir Richard Burton's 1883 version was the only widely known English version of the *Kamasutra*.[1] Burton's version is not only inadequate (it omits many sections, misreads others, and condenses most parts) but also skewed by his tendency to exoticize Asian sexuality as more "primitive" than European sexuality.[2]

Pirated editions of Burton's version can be found in pavement stalls and glossy summaries in coffee table book form in India today, but scholarly editions of the *Kamasutra* are hard to find. As Kumkum Roy reports, librarians tend to keep the text under lock and key, with other erotica, and hesitate to allow readers access to it. One librarian asked her not to leave it lying on her carrel because girls had been seen leafing through it.[3] In India today, sex education is minimal or nonexistent in schools and colleges, and sexual matters are not considered subjects fit for discussion in most social, political or academic forums.

The standard Hindi translation of the *Kamasutra*, by Pandit Madhavacharya, used by scholars today, was published in 1911, reissued in 1934 with a 50-page introduction by the translator, and reprinted in 1995.[4] In the introduction, Madhavacharya argues that young people should study the text to learn the right forms of conjugal sex and to recognize and stay away from the wrong forms of sex. The wrong forms, according to Madhavacharya, are all noncon-

1. *The Kama Sutra of Vatsyayana,* trans. Sir Richard F. Burton (1883; Delhi: Penguin, 1993).
2. See *The Perfumed Garden of the Shaykh Nefzawi,* trans. Sir Richard Burton, ed. Alan Hull Walton (London: Granada, 1963). The second part of the text, dealing with homosexuality, was supposedly excised by Burton's wife. It was published later as *The Glory of the Perfumed Garden* (London: Neville Spearman, 1975).
3. "Unravelling the *Kamasutra,*" *Indian Journal of Gender Studies,* 3:2 (1996): 170, fn 6.
4. *Kamasutram* (Bombay: Venkateswara Steam Press, 1911, 1995).

jugal and all nonvaginal forms, including masturbation and oral and anal sex. And the epitome not only of wrong sex but of all society's ills is homosexual activity, especially between men.

Madhavacharya titles his commentary on the text "Purusharthaprabhakhya," which connotes manliness being brought to light through interpretation. Madhavacharya opens his introduction with an account of god. He describes god as a compassionate father who sends his sages to give a divine message to humanity. He attempts an uneasy blend of Hindu and Christian attitudes, distinguishing between those who are saved and those who are damned: "Those beings who obey his commands, believe the immortal sayings of the sages he sends, reform their ways, and follow the path laid down by them, . . . attain the highest. Those who disobey the teachings and disrespect the message, such men . . . fill places in hell" (1).[5] Madhavacharya says he is addressing those theists in the "west and the east" who believe that only one god created the world. Thus he tries to present Hindus as acceptably enlightened monotheists.

Madhavacharya argues in traditional style for the importance of desire as a driving force in the universe. This argument moves him in the direction of endorsing the multiplicity of desire. He cites the creation story in which Brahma does not make the universe but becomes it: "In the heart of that playful one the desire was born 'I am one, let me become many'" (11). In this account, of course, all desires are divine.

But Madhavacharya does not sustain this liberatory position. His next section is subtitled "Stopping improper tendencies in desire." Here he states that all the sages tried to control desire but few succeeded. He argues that it necessary to study desire in order to control "improper tendencies" (13). He adds: "Lord Krishna is the giver of Moksha; only one on whom he has compassion and whom he draws to himself can tread the path of liberation" (15). Denouncing adultery, he states that monogamous sex with one's lawfully wedded wife for the purpose of having a son is the only appropriate kind of sex. He cites Shri Rama as the prime example of this.

Interestingly, he refers here only to the Krishna of the *Gita*, and not to Krishna the lover of the cowherd women, who might seem more relevant to the *Kamasutra*. Instead, he remarks of Rama and Sita: "Foreigners constantly praise India for this conjugal love. When the world conqueror Alexander prepared to conquer India, his teacher Socrates said to him: 'O king . . . After conquering India, bring as a love-gift for me this story of Rama and Sita, so that I may repeatedly meditate on it. . . . It was this Kama that the sage Vatsyayana desired. . . . He thinks it is opposed to such love for one to marry a woman of a caste higher than one's own or to desire a woman who belongs to another" (17).

Madhavacharya's next subsection is entitled "Intimacy with a woman belonging to another is absolutely forbidden." Here he denounces modern fiction and romance that glorify nonmarital

---

5. All translations of Madhavacharya's comments are by me.

love. Medieval poetics in Sanskrit and other languages had developed *shringara rasa* or erotic emotion as primary in literature, with nonmarital eroticism as one of its chief forms. Many critics and mystics claimed that adulterous or *parakiya* love, being the most risky and the least possessive, was the appropriate symbol for the love of god. Madhavacharya disregards this tradition to hammer home his post-Victorian nationalist ideal.

Explaining Vatsyayana's devotion of an entire section to the way a man can carry on a relationship with a married woman, he fits it into his conception of the *Kamasutra* as a warning text: "The purpose of the section on adultery is only to warn good married people so that they can protect their families against sinners, for those who do not know these maneuvers cannot save themselves from falling prey to them" (18). Madhavacharya denounces modern women who do not want to become mothers, adulterous women, and prostitutes, and reads the section of the *Kamasutra* that deals with courtesans as designed to warn men against falling into the "net of deceit" (20) that prostitutes use to "sway wealthy men."

But the heart of Madhavacharya's argument is a section entitled "The Reason for the Present Disasters," where he writes:

> The present government has laid down severe penalties for unnatural fornication and the subjects fear these penalties, but who then are the immoral ones who practice unnatural immorality? We are not told how to recognize them, but in the section on oral sex, the author of the Kamasutra has drawn a portrait of their activities and has also introduced us to their identity, saying 'Usually, this act is performed by *shandas*' [a term for impotent men not used by Vatsyayana].

Madhavacharya then quotes verses on homosexual activity. The verses he quotes are not the ones on oral sex performed by persons of the "third nature" but verses II. 9:35–39, which describe oral sex between men and male servants and between consenting male friends. He issues a warning: "These evil practices are spreading among young men today like an infectious disease. If these tendencies were removed from their hearts by good education, they could become healthy, disease-free, good charactered heroes, who would adorn the country by their lives" (26).

Madhavacharya argues for sex education, but he wants the education to be anti-sex, not pro-sex. Madhavacharya's views are heavily influenced by post-Freudian Western sexologists and psychologists. His homophobia and fear of everything except vaginal penetrative sex in marriage clearly derives from a late nineteenth-century discourse that is an amalgam of Puritanism, heterosexism and paranoia. Although his stance is self-consciously that of an Indian nationalist, the Western sources of his fear and hatred of autoeroticism finally do emerge when he is arguing that laws such as the law against child marriage cannot be truly effective in controlling untimely sex since only education can teach people to control themselves:

> Mothers and fathers in Western countries, who are lovers of knowledge, are so careful of their children that at night they even tie the child's hands to their sides, so that during the night, the

child should not inadvertently touch its lower organs and spoil its health.[6] When one's own hand can be harmful for oneself, what use can a legal enactment or imprisoning the body be? . . . (31)

In II. 6:49, when the text mentions anal intercourse, and Yashodhara in his twelfth century commentary explains that it can take place with a man or a woman, Madhavacharya not only translates the term for "anus" as "bad path," but also adds his own footnote: "This is an unnatural fornication. Men who do such things become unfit to have sex with women and also lose their energy" (448, fn.1).

In II. 9, the chapter on oral sex and the third nature, when the text describes men of the third nature who take the form of women, Madhavacharya adds a footnote that has no basis either in the text or in Yashodhara's commentary: "A woman who is a *napunsika* [feminine of impotent] has all the organs like those of a woman, only does not have a vulva suitable for intercourse. The chest is also not very big. A *napunsaka* [impotent] man is without an organ or has a very small organ and is incapable of intercourse" (503, fn.1).

Sutras 35 and 36 present him with a problem because they clearly describe oral sex between two persons, both of whom are gendered male; in fact, in 36, both males are friends and have the full status of a citizen. Forced to acknowledge this as sexual activity between men, Madhavacharya adds a footnote to 35:

> Such boys do not engage solely in oral activity, they also engage in another type of unnatural fornication. People involved in theater commonly are puppets of that type of vice. They all pretend to be pure, though. On one occasion, a fight with daggers broke out between BA and MA students of a college over such an affair (522, fn.1).

Having said this, Madhavacharya seems released to translate 36 (about mutual sex between males and between females) without any pejorative comments.

This type of attitude is by no means unique to Madhavacharya or his ideological camp. As late as 1975, the Marxist scholar N. N. Bhattacharyya, in one of the few books on the subject, his *History of Indian Erotic Literature*, glorified the Indian past too, but a different part of that past. Unlike Madhavachaya, he does not revere Sanskrit texts, but like Madhavacharya, he wishes to homogenize them. According to him, "the sextravagance of Khajuraho and Konarak was mainly the reflection of the abnormal sexual desires of the dominant class."[7] The *Kamasutra*, like these temples, catered to the "crude, perverse and fantastic imagination" (x) of this

---

6. Madhavacharya does not exaggerate here. For an account of such policing in nineteenth-century campaigns in England against schoolboy masturbation, see Edward J. Bristow, *Vice and Vigilance: Purity Movements in Britain since 1700* (Totowa, NJ: Rowman & Littlefield, 1977).
7. Narendra Nath Bhattacharyya, *History of Indian Erotic Literature* (New Delhi: Munshiram Manoharlal, 1975), 28.

class of men. He argues that the subordinate classes who constituted 80 percent of the population were much closer to primitive "matriarchal values" (2) which are still prevalent among lower classes and tribes in India.

"Matriarchal values" identify woman with the fertility principle, the earth, and treat the sexual act ("sexual act" for Bhattacharyya is synonymous with the heterosexual penetrative sex act) as a sacrifice. Women who can have sex with more than one man are defined by Bhattacharyya as enjoying "sexual freedom," whether this freedom is expressed in Tantric rites or in customs such as those of the Badaga tribe: "It is also the etiquette among the Badagas that, when a woman's husband is away, she should be accessible to her brothers-in-law" (22).[8] The only erotic Sanskrit poetry Bhattacharyya finds worthwhile is that which praises newly wedded couples or monogamous romantic lovers (54): "Bhavabhuti has idealized conjugal love from the viewpoint of his social responsibility, and for this he deserves unreserved praise" (48). Bhattacharyya's view of the *Kamasutra* is that "as far as the purely sexual matters are concerned, it is frankly worthless" (69) and that "Vatsyayana had a purely patriarchal outlook" (82).

With his anticaste, anticlass claims, Bhattacharyya appears on the surface to be the diametrical opposite of Madhavacharya. But they agree on the basic point—sex for pleasure alone is perverse, while sex for procreation or fertility is pure.

---

8. It would appear that Bhattacharyya constructs many of his notions of "sexual freedom" from the "sexual revolution" in Euro-America in the sixties, which had a major impact in many intellectual circles in urban India as well. As Euro-American feminists realized, this kind of "freedom" often meant pressure on women to prove their liberation by being sexually available to whichever man wanted them.

Gopabandhu Das:
Poems Written in Prison (Oriya)

Introduced and translated by Sumanyu Satpathy

Freedom fighter, poet, lawyer, and journalist Gopabandhu Das (1877–1928) was educated in English at a school in Puri. When he was in the sixth grade, his guru, Ramachandra Das, introduced him to Basudev Rath, a student of Sanskrit, saying: "I have introduced you two to each other; I have joined East and West."[1] The two friends would go to their guru every evening and continue their discussions with him till midnight.

Das studied and practiced law, but devoted more time to social work until he became a full-time activist in the Gandhi-led movement for Indian independence. He instituted a boys' school with a new educational agenda at Satyabadi. When Gandhi saw this school where freedom fighters were in the making, he wrote: "No wonder if I believe that with such earnest men, *Swaraj* [self-rule] is possible to attain within the year."[2]

When Das was thirty, his wife died and he never remarried. In 1917 he became a member of the Bihar-Orissa legislative assembly. On one of the many occasions when he was sent to prison, Das told the grieving crowd: "Don't be saddened because they are taking me away. . . . Save the Congress, save the country. Spread Gandhi's message; . . . Fight injustice." When Gandhi heard of this, he was moved to write: "The *Tapasvi* [sage] of Orissa was arrested. . . . His words at the time of arrest are inspiring."[3]

The two poems excerpted here were written in 1922 while Das was in prison. The first of them is included in most school textbooks in Orissa even today. Das's poems deal with many themes, such as the freedom movement, the beauty of nature, and, as in these two poems, human love as well as how it leads to divine love. The words used in the poems make it clear

1. Radhamohan Gadanayak, ed., *Gopabandhu Rachanabali* (Bhubaneswar: Sahitya Akademi, 1980), Introduction, 3.
2. *Young India* April 13, 1921.
3. *Young India* June 8, 1922.

that Das is addressing a beloved male friend. Radhanayak Gadanayak comments that in these poems, "a friend has withdrawn himself from Gopabandhu's ways. . . . Gopabandhu is deeply hurt when jilted by his close associate."[4]

One of Gopabandhu's close associates, Rama Barik, who went to the Satyabadi school when he was fourteen, looking for work, described in an interview his life with Gopabandhu. Barik first lived with Pandit Nilakantha, the headmaster of the school, and afterward with Gopabandhu who was then thirty-four years old. Barik lived with him like a shadow for the remaining seventeen years of Gopabandhu's life: "I have cooked rice for him, I have washed him, I used to accompany him even when he was sent to jail. . . . The only day I wasn't with him was the day he passed away. He was very fond of the cattle. He loved the boys, carried them around, fondled them. . . . He was most concerned for the afflicted; and used to cry a lot."[5] When questioned about the gossip around his relationship with Gopabandhu, Barik expressed surprise; he also repeatedly emphasized that Gopabandhu always slept with his doors open or on the verandah, and that Barik himself used to sleep outside the cell whenever his master was in prison.[6]

The Last Tears of an Anguished Soul[7]

(for a lifelong coworker of mine)[8]

For whom shall I sing this song of my life?
Near whom shall I play this harp of my soul?
To whose ears shall I confide my soul's anguish?
My innermost thoughts, alas, are forever locked up in my heart.

The soulmate I chose at the dawn of life
As my life's friend, did not understand
The innermost thoughts of my heart.
He gave a cruel blow to my life, my being.
. . . .
Love, it is said, forbears,
And, forbearing, is beatified.
Love knows no apprehensions.

---

4. *Gopabandhu Rachanabali,* Introduction, 67–68.
5. Gopinath Mohanty, *Utkalamani* (Cuttack: Friends Publishers, 1989), 12–13.
6. Mohanty, *Utkalamani,* 13, 28–29, 33.
7. *Gopabandhu Rachanabali,* 96–99.
8. Gendered male in Oriya. Oriya does not gender either verbs or pronouns so nouns are the only indicators of gender. These are clearly male throughout both poems, for example, "lifelong coworker": *ajivana sahkarmi;* "life's friend": *prana-sakha;* "lover": *premiko.*

The lover never deserts the beloved,
Not even under the gravest distress.

Is my love a mere pretence?
Does it, unwittingly, seek its own ends?
Have I indulged in self-deception,
That I now suffer such extreme heartache?
. . . .
With poisoned eyes, my companion, if you see,
In my simple self the blackness of deception,
Wipe your eyes and see in my heart your heart,
And seeing yourself there, reproach me no more.

I do not heed your abuses and insults.
I am anxious only for you to regret them.
But if they make you happy, even your hard words
Will give me sweet ecstasy.

Does love too fade like flowers of the forest?
No, love is an endless, infinite stream.
By driving me away, can you distance me?
Are not you the prisonhouse of my life's love?
. . . .
Intimate embraces, delicate kisses,
Streaming tears—if these be the uses of love,
Red eyes, hard words, angry backward glances—
These are the abuses of love.

I have felt in my being[9] both moods of love
During my brief intimacy with you.
How often have I not felt secretly in my senses
Happiness, sorrow, laughter, and tears?

In your fiery ire this self of mine
Has smoldered and shone doubly bright,
Has apprehended in this world
Both the wrath and the gift of love
Of the Eternal Lover.

In His land of love is no ugliness,
Nor injustice, nor atom of impurity.
Have my emotions, has my life-stream
Met that ocean of love at long last?

9. *Angey*, literally "in this bodily self." The word is repeated in the third line, *Angey guptey*, literally "hidden in the body."

Is This Love's End?[10]

The two youths' molten vibrating hearts
Merged like two water drops flowing together.

Their love jelled in tender youth.
Neither could bear a moment's separation.

Eating, sleeping, bathing, conversing,
singing, thinking, studying, laughing, weeping—

In life's every act, two bodies in unison
Moved as if moved by one automation.

When one heart was hurt, injured or hit,
The other's eyes shed tears in an instant.

One soul, one life, one mind, inhabit bodies two,
The same tune plays in twin heartstrings too.

Somewhere in that charming musical instrument
Grew unseen a fine crack, of which neither had dreamt.

In a moment, the instrument split into two,
No more could be heard that melody true.

Whence sprang that drop of acid unseen
Whose selfish heat curdled love's milk-ocean?
. . . .
Will life follow this course for ever?
In this world, is man's love so brittle?

Like a flower garden on a thorny road is love,
Like a soothing fountain in the desert is love.

Love is an immortal spark in the mortal being,
Love is heavenly nectar on this earth.

Is this eulogy of love just a poet's fancy?
Is love merely a selfish fraud?

In youth love springs when life melds with life.
Should such love dissolve in later years?

Love broadens the heart in sweet youth.
In adult eyes, is love the mind's aberration?[11]

---

10. *Gopabandhu Rachanabali*, 152–55.
11. *Mastishka vikara. Vikara* derives from *Vikrit,* meaning "perversion" or "distortion."

. . . .

Be damned a hundred times the wisdom of middle age
Which kills the heart's spontaneous affection.

. . . .

Childhood is goal-free, pure, simple,
Youth liberated, lovely, tender, fluid.

Love blossoms in fresh sweet youth.
Oh, that human life ended with youth!

. . . .

"I won't leave you for an instant, even if you leave me"—
Will one say this to the other with a glance?

. . . .

Those silent conversations, that heartfelt speech—
Shall one embrace the other again?[12]

Love will then rise again, spread its new rays,
The two lotus buds will blossom with affection.

After separation, love is sweetest—
At winter's end, new leaves shine brightest.

---

12. The construction of the sentence is such that it could be translated as above or as "Will
you never embrace me again?"

The New Homophobia:
Ugra's Chocolate

Ruth Vanita

Pandey Bechan Sharma, better known by his pen-name "Ugra" (Extreme) was a nationalist, a social reformer and a Hindi writer and journalist. His fiction tends toward the didactic and generally has a social message. His writings champion the causes of nationalism, oppressed women, and lower castes, and critique corruption in high places, alcoholism, gambling, adultery, prostitution, and communalism. He remained unmarried all his life, had a reputation for inciting controversy, and edited a very large number of newspapers and magazines, most of which folded within a short time. In 1924 Ugra became associated with the Hindi weekly *Matvala*, which had been first published in Calcutta in 1923 under the editorship of the famous poet Suryakant Tripathi "Nirala" (see p. 270). *Matvala* was a nationalist paper whose style tended to the comical and satirical.

On May 31, 1924, Ugra published a story entitled "Chocolate" in *Matvala*. The story opens with an Urdu *ghazal* recited by the narrator Gopal's friend Dinkar Prasad. Dinkar's friends all ask him whom he is in love with, but he responds only by reciting more ghazals. In response, another friend, Manohar, recites Banarsi Hindi love poetry which Dinkar greatly appreciates. Just then, a beautiful boy in his early teens calls Dinkar out of the room. Manohar tells Gopal that this boy is Dinkar's "chocolate."[1] Gopal fails to understand the term so Manohar explains, offering a definition that was to be much quoted in the later controversy: "'Chocolate' is the name for those innocent, tender and beautiful boys of the country, whom society's demons push into the mouth of ruin to quench their own lusts" (100). He explains that in Uttar Pradesh these boys are called "chocolate" or "pocket book" and other names too indecent to be recorded. Gopal finds it hard to believe that an educated man like Dinkar can

---

1. All citations are from *Chocolate* (Calcutta: Tandon Brothers, 1953) and are translated from Hindi by me. The word is spelled and pronounced "Chaklet" in Hindi.

fall into such "sin." Manohar advises him to talk sympathetically to Dinkar on the subject: "You will then see what he has to say. He will scan history, shave the head of the *Puranas*, and prove that boy-love is also natural—not unnatural. The day I talked to him he told me, on the basis of an English book, that even Socrates was guilty of this offence. He said that Shakespeare too was the slave of a beautiful friend of his. He talked of Mr. Oscar Wilde too" (101).

The next day Manohar writes Gopal a letter in which he claims that homosexuality is spreading like an epidemic among young people: "There are few students who do not have a beautiful friend. They call them 'friends' or 'relatives' but what they do with these friends and relatives is impossible to describe"(103). Boys are becoming effeminate and spend their time beautifying themselves instead of studying. Their guardians are to blame for not guarding them better. Boarding schools, ashrams, company gardens, fairs, and festivals are the places where boys are seduced. Often, teachers themselves corrupt their students.

The same day, Dinkar and his young friend Ramesh come to visit Gopal. On the pretext of fetching refreshments, Gopal deliberately leaves them alone and then spies on them from behind the door. Dinkar asks Ramesh to come close to him but Ramesh is embarrassed to do so in another's house. Dinkar woos Ramesh with several ghazals including one by the famous eighteenth-century Urdu poet Mir Taqi Mir: " Mir dies a thousand times in one moment/ He has found a new way to live" (105). When he advances toward Ramesh, the boy picks up a pot of ink and pretends to throw it at him. His hand slips, the bottle opens and Dinkar gets soaked in black ink. Ramesh's anger and modesty enflame Dinesh's passion and he embraces and kisses the boy whose face also gets blackened. Gopal then emerges and escorts Ramesh to his father's house. Dinkar disappears and Gopal says that though six months have passed, no one knows where he is.

When the story was published, the *Matvala* office was flooded with readers' letters, both of praise and protest. Ugra was encouraged by this controversy to write four more stories on the theme. At this juncture, the British government imprisoned him for nine months under Section 124-A of the Penal Code for his nationalist writings in the newspaper *Swadesh*. He recounts that when he was released, his friends advised him not to publish any more such stories as he was being criticized, slandered, and accused of himself being a homosexual.[2] He proceeded to write three more stories on the subject and in 1927 published all eight as a collection entitled *Chocolate*. The book gave rise to a tremendous furore. Queues formed at Calcutta bookshops to buy it and it ran through several editions in the same year.[3]

Ugra's crusade against homosexuality was not appreciated by other nationalists. Hindi litterateur Pandit Banarsidas Chaturvedi, nationalist editor of *Vishal Bharat*, began a movement

2. Ugra's foreword "Kaifiyat" in *Chocolate* pages "ka" to "ja."
3. Ratnakar Pandey, *Ugra aur Unka Sahitya* (Varanasi: Nagaripracharini Sabha, Samvat 2026), 258.

against what he termed *Ghasleti* literature. *Ghaslet* literally refers to kerosene oil, widely used as cooking fuel in India, and metaphorically to inflammatory, that is, sensational and obscene, literature. As the term suggests, Ugra's opponents argued that while he claimed to be opposing homosexuality, the actual effect of his writings was to titillate and excite his readers and thus to encourage, not discourage, homosexual desire. They stated that such filthy topics as homosexuality should not be discussed at all.

Cartoons in Hindi papers depicted Ugra carrying a trashcan overflowing with his writings. Interestingly, these depictions of Ugra reveal the underside of the apparently non-communal and anticaste nationalists. In one cartoon, Ugra is wearing a *tehmad*, the dress of poor Muslims, while respectable men at a literary conference hold their noses at the stink; the image of his carrying a trashcan identifies him too with so-called untouchables. In another cartoon, he is being welcomed by a band of tribals, the implication being that only "savages" can appreciate his writings.

The controversy spread like wildfire. Almost every Hindi newspaper and magazine entered the fray, and almost every major writer and critic expressed an opinion. An incomplete list of essays and editorials on the subject runs into two pages in fine print.[4] While some of Ugra's other writings such as those on prostitution were also accused of obscenity, *Chocolate* was the main target. This was perhaps the first public debate in the Hindi literary world on homosexuality. It also rapidly became a debate on censorship.

Ugra's supporters claimed that his detractors were envious because his book had attracted a record number of readers. The question that cannot be answered definitively is: were all these readers actuated by the revulsion against homosexuality expressed both by Ugra and by his opponents, or were some of them merely eager to read fiction about homosexuals? Despite the overt homophobia, do elements of representation in these stories lend themselves to positive interpretation? Ugra's opponents thought so.

Except for one story set in jail, none of Ugra's protagonists are members of the underworld. They are respectable members of society; they include teachers, college students, writers, and men about town. Most of them are married—thus their desire for men cannot be explained away as due to a lack of options. When questioned, a married poet claims that he does not find his wife attractive. Unconvinced acquaintances wonder why he cannot satisfy himself with female prostitutes.

Furthermore, Chaturvedi pointed to those passages where Ugra allows his homosexual characters a voice and they use this voice not only to defend their practices but to claim an illustrious ancestry and history. Thus, in the story "Chocolate," Dinkar associates his desire with famous poets both in the English and in the Urdu literary traditions. Another such pas-

---

4. Pandey, 258–60.

sage occurs in the story "Paalat" (Kept Boy) when Mahashay, a man who falls in love with a boy, engages in the following dialog with his friend, the narrator:

> Narrator: Do you call this love? Love? Poor love must be wondering how it got involved with this activity. A man to fall in love with another man for his beauty! I think, brother, that just as "Woman is not charmed by woman's beauty" [quote from Tulsidas' medieval epic *Ramcharit-manas*] neither should man be charmed by man's beauty.
> Mahashay: But the world cannot run by your thinking alone. Truth must be respected wherever it is. Beauty is truth. Wherever beauty may be found, in a woman or in a man, I am the slave of love.
> Narrator: Your arguments may be correct. But this is a misuse of education.
> Mahashay: Search history. Raskhan fell in love with a boy and then became a devotee of Krishna. Surdas was madly in love with Krishna. Tulsi? Have you read the blazon of Rama's beauty in *Vinay Patrika?* What else is it but the portrait of an extremely beautiful boy?
> Narrator: Be quiet! You seem like an atheist. To justify boy love, you even drag in Lord Rama and Shri Krishna. Be thankful you are in your own room. If you present such arguments in an assembly, it will be impossible to protect the hairs on your head. (117)

Although the narrator denounces Mahashay's claims, Ugra's detractors were not satisfied that these claims were thereby sufficiently distanced by the author. Thus, Banarsidas Chaturvedi wrote: "It is the height of impertinence to discuss such fancies and ideas in the book. Any cultured person who reads the names of Socrates and Shakespeare, Surdas and Tulsidas, Rama and Krishna, in such a context will denounce the author a thousand times."[5] Chaturvedi's anxiety here clearly centers on the question of who owns culture. Almost all of the protagonists in Ugra's stories are highly cultured and educated men, familiar both with Indian and with Western literatures. Some of them are poets in their own right. In the passage quoted above, the homophobic narrator quotes a famous line from Tulsidas' fifteenth-century epic that is, even today, the most popular version of the Rama story in north India. What is unsettling, however, is that the bisexual Mahashay cites Tulsidas right back, thus confidently claiming a right to interpret a common literary heritage in his own way.

Almost all Ugra's homosexual characters are immersed in the world of Urdu love poetry. They recite ghazals, delight in hearing them recited, and also compose them. In his foreword, entitled "Scientific Analysis of Unnatural Fornication," Shri Ramnath Lal "Suman" attempts to blame homosexuality on Muslims. He claims that homosexuality spread from Greece through Europe, Arabia, and the middle East, to India. Acknowledging that there may have been isolated cases in India before the advent of Islam, he states that Arabs and Persians brought the practice with them to India. He then launches an attack on the conventional idiom of Urdu poetry: "The tendency of men to love men has been excessively awakened in Urdu and Persian poetry. . . . More than half the poets depict men's love for women but their

---

5. Pandey, 261.

form of expression is imprinted with male-male love. A man writing about love for a woman will refer not to his mischievous *mashuqa* (beloved feminine) but to his *mashuq*. Urdu is now changing but earlier it was full of this"(53). A character in the story "Vyabhichari Pyar" (Adulterous Love) supports this line of reasoning when he comments on a Hindi poet who has taken to writing in praise of his boy beloved: "the shadow of Muslim poets has fallen on this Hindi versifier. The fool has forgotten his own culture and pure religion and goes around pursuing idols [signifies beloveds in Urdu poetry]" (77).

However, the hybridity of Indian culture made it difficult for Hindus to simply identify the ghazal with Muslims and then denounce it. In north India, most Hindu litterateurs were (and are) given to quoting ghazals at the drop of a hat. In Ugra's stories all the ghazal-reciting protagonists are Hindus; Muslims appear only as minor characters. Ugra's young, educated men-about-town are a group comprising both Hindus and Muslims who are fluent in Hindi, English and Urdu. When Mahashay falls in love with a beautiful boy he sees at a cinema, all his friends, both Hindu and Muslim, applaud his good taste. The narrator is the only exception and thus may, for readers so inclined, emerge as a prude.

Similarly, Ugra denounces the western education system with its boarding schools and residential universities as encouraging same-sex desire; one character goes so far as to say that he would rather kill his son than allow him to be educated in this system. However, by the early twentieth century the western education system was too deeply entrenched in India for middle class Indians to see its eradication as either possible or desirable.

Ugra's and Suman's attempt to conflate homosexuality with pederasty also falls short of success. Six of the eight stories are about men falling in love with thirteen- to fourteen-year-old boys and the narrator attempts to whip up parental hysteria against homosexuals as predators by showing the boys succumbing to diseases like tuberculosis and asthma which physicians diagnose as stemming from their seduction. However, this picture gets somewhat confused when the boys and young men are shown as actively involved with others of their own age. In "Vyabhichari Pyar," for instance, the police catch the protagonist's boy beloved having sex with another boy in a park.

Although some of Ugra's protagonists commit suicide or are jailed, several others seem to thrive or simply disappear from the narrator's view. More important, a number of minor characters who are engaged in homosexual activity blend into the everyday world and their predilections are not seen to have any negative consequences. Such are the nameless but numerous college students described in "Chocolate Charcha" (Discussion of Chocolate) as pervasively given to affairs and flings with one another.

Several Hindi literary bodies formally denounced Ugra's writings at their annual meetings, as did many famous writers including the left-leaning nationalist Premchand.[6] These denun-

---

6. He opined that homosexuality should be combated by pamphleteering, not in literature whose ideals should be kept pure (Pandey, 266–67). Nirala seems to be one of the few

ciations display an interesting mix of attitudes towards the West. On the one hand, they associate homosexuality with the West: "This is a murderous attack on Indian culture and mores. Decent people should boycott such newspapers just as they do foreign cloth and intoxicating substances."[7] On the other hand, they draw on Western sources to legitimize their homophobia. Thus, *Vishal Bharat* (vol. 2, no. 1, August 1929, 264) published a translation of Professor Gilbert Murray's letter to the editor of the *Nation and Athenaeum* (March 23, 1929, 876). This letter had appeared in the course of a controversy generated in the aftermath of the 1928 ban in Britain on Radclyffe Hall's lesbian novel *The Well of Loneliness*. The controversy was ignited by Leonard Woolf's remarks, in his column "The World of Books" on the American puritan Anthony Comstock who had led a crusade against "indecent" writings.[8] The controversy raged for six months until the editor called a halt to it. Such eminent writers as Leonard Woolf, Lytton Strachey and E. F. Benson ably argued the anticensorship case from a nonhomophobic perspective. In the Indian debate, however, the eminent writers who became identified with an anticensorship position were avowedly as homophobic as their opponents.

The Ghaslet controversy temporarily ended when Banarsidas Chaturvedi took the issue to Mahatma Gandhi and triumphantly reported that the national leader was opposed to Ghasleti literature. So upset was Ugra that he withdrew from the Hindi literary world and became involved with the cinematic world in Bombay. However, in 1951, much after Gandhi's death, Chaturvedi published a note Gandhi had written to him over twenty years earlier. Gandhi had read *Chocolate* on Chaturvedi's bidding, and remarked that the aim of the book is "pure" since the author generates "revulsion against inhuman behavior."[9] Chaturvedi claimed that in his subsequent discussion with Gandhi, he read to him passages from various other obscene books, which convinced Gandhi that Chaturvedi's position was correct.

However, Ugra was outraged by what he saw as dishonesty on Chaturvedi's part in having suppressed Gandhi's letter about *Chocolate*. In 1953 Ugra published a new edition of *Chocolate*, with several lengthy forewords by himself and others, that recount the whole controversy and portray Ugra as a selfless nationalist crusader out to expose and eradicate the "plague" of homosexuality afflicting Indian youth. However, even these texts work against themselves—thus Suman's foreword first defines sodomy as pederasty, then as any nonvaginal sex with women or men, and finally expands the definition to include all same-sex desire.

---

writers who retained a sense of humor; he remarked that Chaturvedi had introduced originality into his paper by inventing *Ghaslet* as well as *Chhayavad* (the latter was the movement of which leadership was ascribed to Nirala among others).

7. Padma Singh Sharma quoted in editorial, *Vishal Bharat* vol. 2, no. 1, July-August, 1985, 132.
8. "What We May Be Coming To," *The Nation and Athenaeum,* December 15, 1928, 415.
9. Quoted in *Chocolate,* 1.

He pejoratively cites case studies, from Havelock Ellis, J. A. Symonds, and others, in which boys or girls desire others of their own age.

The draconian safeguards advocated by Suman are designed to prevent sexual interaction not only between men and boys but also between boys of the same age. They include closing all boarding schools; forbidding boys to sit together on a bench in class, instead requiring a distance of two yards between desks; immediate expulsion of any teacher or student suspected of misbehavior; forbidding youths under twenty to see any films except patriotic ones; criminalizing the act of walking with one's arm around the neck of a boy under sixteen; and forbidding boys to dance and sing. So unrealistic are these proposals in the context of Indian society, that they inadvertently suggest that eradicating homosexuality is as impossible as eradicating a taste for chocolate among modern Indians.

M. K. Gandhi:
Reply to a Query (English)

Introduced by Ruth Vanita

Although most famous for leading the nonviolent struggle for national independence, Mohandas Karamchand Gandhi (1867–1948) defined independence not in merely political but in ethical terms, holding that *Swaraj*, or self-rule, would be viable only when Indians had learned the art of freedom expressed in nonviolent self-mastery. In the course of his leadership of the movement for Swaraj, which encompassed movements for the rights of all victims of violence including the urban poor, peasants, women, so-called untouchables, and nonhuman animals, thousands of people asked Gandhi questions on almost every aspect of existence. The answers he suggested, in his voluminous personal correspondence as well as in *Harijan* and *Young India*, the magazines he edited, frequently led to extended controversies, in the tradition of debate that structures so many ancient Indian texts.

The following letter appeared in *Young India* in 1929. Although it refers to male homosexuality as "unnatural vice," it interestingly complicates the issue by advising the questioners not to treat sex between men as a different category from sex between men and women. Like Jesus telling the male accusers of the adulterous woman to cast stones at her only if they themselves were free from sin, Gandhi tells his questioners not to self-righteously sit in judgment on others but to examine and purify themselves.[1] He suggests that there is no difference in kind between heterosexual and homosexual lust. Equally significant is his statement that the government cannot legislate in such matters, but change has to be brought about at the individual level.

---

1. The biblical resonance is clear in Gandhi's use of the phrase "we need not hug the comfort to ourselves that we are not like other men," a direct echo of the Philistine in Jesus' parable who self-righteously claims in his prayer that he is "not as other men."

His remarks must be read in the context of his oft-stated belief that all sexual activity, even within marriage, that is not directed toward procreation is "unnatural" and a "vice."[2] In fact, he viewed even procreative sex with suspicion, encouraged his followers to enter into celibate marriages and blessed some newly-wed couples by saying "May you have no children." He felt that love directed toward spouse and offspring could be more profitably directed toward the whole community. These apparently eccentric views acquire new meaning today, in the context of what one scientist has called humanity's "breeding binge," which is rapidly driving most other species to extinction and seriously threatening the earth's ecosystem.

Gandhi's reference to Roman Catholicism in this letter is significant. Traditions that make celibacy available as an option to men and women and view it as superior to heterosexual marriage allow nonsexual but passionate same-sex relationships to acquire primary importance in the lives of those so inclined. Ancient Indian ascetic traditions, both Hindu and Buddhist, were similar to the Roman Catholic tradition in this respect. Traditions that glorify marriage and procreation above celibacy and make the former way of life near compulsory tend to trivialize or be hostile toward same-sex relationships. Such was the tradition inaugurated by sexologists and psychoanalysts in post-Freudian Euro-America who were contemporaries of Gandhi. Gandhi's language here is obviously influenced by psychiatry. Although using the new terminology, Gandhi conveys his conviction, based on older traditions, that all sexual activity not directed toward procreation is "the same disease."

As one of his biographers has remarked, "when he had given up all sexual activity, Gandhi obviously was able to find a certain erotic-aesthetic gaiety in a kind of detached physical closeness to both women and men."[3] Having renounced phallic sexuality, which, from his own self-examination and his observations of married life, he associated with male violence and possessiveness, Gandhi was freed to express deeply passionate as well as flirtatiously playful feelings for friends, both male and female. For example, "Gandhi was able, in deep sorrow, to have engraved on a stone dedicated to the memory of [his nephew and coworker] Maganlal that the latter's death had widowed him."[4] In a letter to the ailing C. F. Andrews, the British Anglican priest who was his intimate friend and devoted follower, Gandhi wrote:

> . . . there is no doubt that you need a curator euphemestically called a nurse. And how I should like to occupy that post! If you cannot have a nurse like me, who would make love to you but at the same time enforce strict obedience to doctor's orders, you need a wife who would see that you had your food properly served, you never went out without an abdominal bandage and who would

2. See Jawaharlal Nehru's discussion of this opinion in his *Autobiography* (1936; Bombay: Allied Publishers, 1962), 512–13. Nehru calls Gandhi's attitude to sex between man and woman, which he sees as more extreme than that of Catholicism, "unnatural and shocking."
3. Erik H. Erikson, *Gandhi's Truth: On the Origins of Militant Non-Violence* (New York: W.W. Norton, 1969), 121–22.
4. Erikson, 402.

not allow you to overworry yourself about bad news of the sickness of relatives. But marriage is probably too late. And not being able to nurse you myself I can only fret. I can do better if I pray and that is precisely what I am going to do.[5]

▨▨▨ ▨▨▨ ▨▨▨

From *Young India,* July 26, 1929[6]

Some years ago, the Bihar Government in its education department had an inquiry into the question of unnatural vice in its schools, and the Committee of Inquiry had found the existence of the vice even among teachers who were abusing their position among their boys in order to satisfy their unnatural lust. The Director of Education had issued a circular prescribing departmental action on such vice being found to exist in connection with any teacher. It would be interesting to know the results, if any, issuing from the circular.

I have had literature too sent to me from other provinces inviting my attention to such vice and showing that it was on the increase practically all over India in public as well as private schools. Personal letters received from boys have confirmed the information.

Unnatural though the vice is, it has come down to us from times immemorial. The remedy for all secret vice is most difficult to find. And it becomes still more difficult when it affects guardians of boys which the teachers are. "If the salt loses its savour, wherewith shall it be salted?" In my opinion departmental action, necessary as it is in all proved cases, can hardly meet the case. The leveling up of public opinion alone can cope with the evil. But in most matters there is no such thing as effective public opinion in this country. The feeling of helplessness that pervades political life has affected all other departments. We therefore pass by many a wrong that is being perpetrated in front of us.

A system of education that puts an exclusive emphasis on literary equipment not only is ill-adapted to deal with the evil but actually results in promoting it. Boys who were clean before they went to public schools have been found to have become unclean, effeminate and imbecile at the end of their school course. The Bihar Committee has recommended the "instilling into the minds of boys a reverence for religion." But who is to bell the cat? The teachers alone can teach reverence for religion. But they themselves have none. It is therefore a question of a proper selection of teachers. But a proper se-

---

5. In *The Collected Works of Mahatma Gandhi* (Delhi: Publications Division, Ministry of Information and Broadcasting, Govt. of India, 1958–1994), XV: 3–4, Letter to C. F. Andrews, August 6, 1918.

6. This is the title and date of this letter as it appears in *Young India* (Navajivan Publishing House, Ahmedabad, 1931), Vol. XI, page 212. However, in *The Collected Works of Mahatma Gandhi* XLI (Delhi: Publications Division, Ministry of Information and Broadcasting, Govt of India, 1989), 84–85, this letter is dated 27 June 1929.

lection of teachers means either a much higher pay than is now given or reversion to teaching not as a career but as a lifelong dedication to a sacred duty. This is in vogue even today among Roman Catholics. The first is obviously impossible in a poor country like ours. The second seems to me to be the only course left open. But that course is not open to us under a system of government in which everything has a price and which is the costliest in the world.

The difficulty of coping with the evil is aggravated because the parents generally take no interest in the morals of their children. Their duty is done when they send them to school. The outlook before us is thus gloomy. But there is hope in the fact that there is only one remedy for all evil, viz., general purification. Instead of being overwhelmed by the magnitude of the evil, each one of us must do the best one can by the scrupulous attention to one's own immediate surroundings, taking self as the first and the immediate point of attack. We need not hug the comfort to ourselves that we are not like other men. Unnatural vice is not an isolated phenomenon. It is but a violent symptom of the same disease. If we have impurity within us, if we are sexually depraved, we must right ourselves before expecting to reform our neighbors. There is too much sitting in judgment upon others and too much indulgence towards self. The result is a vicious circle. Those who realize the truth of it must get out of it and they will find that progress though never easy becomes sensibly possible.

Amrita Sher-Gil: Letters (English)

Introduced by Ruth Vanita

One of twentieth-century India's greatest painters, Amrita Sher-Gil (1913–1941) was the daughter of an aristocratic Sikh scholar and a Hungarian socialite. She went to Paris in 1929 at the age of sixteen, where she studied art, and visited Hungary regularly. When she returned to India in 1934 she was powerfully drawn to ancient Indian art and to miniature painting.

Much sought after in elite circles for her beauty and vivacity, Amrita resisted familial pressure to marry and instead had a number of short-lived affairs with men. While in Paris, she developed an intimate friendship with another painter, Marie Louise Chasseny. Until the end of her life, she spoke affectionately of this friend, whose pictures she hung prominently in all her homes and of whom she painted a portrait. They shared a studio apartment, and rumors that they were sexually involved reached Amrita's mother who wrote to question her about it. In a February 1934 letter from Hungary, Amrita responded:

My dear Mummy,

Do you know that I am of age? So, please do respect me, my dear clever and understanding mother. Yesterday I received your letter that affected me like lightning from the clear sky. . . . I never had any relationship with Marie Louise, and will not have one either. And you can believe me. Knowing how unprejudiced, objective and intelligent you are, I am going to be very frank with you. I confess that I also think as you do about the disadvantages of relationships with men. But since I need to relieve my sexuality *physically* somehow (because I think it is impossible to spiritualize, idealize sexuality *completely* in art, and channelizing it through art for a lifetime is impossible, only a stupid superstition invented for the brainless), so I thought I would start a relationship with a woman when the opportunity arises, and to be quite frank I myself thought that Marie

Louise was of abnormal inclinations. Marie Louise is in fact not quite normal (it is enough to look at her art which is wonderful and interesting but sickly) but she is not a lesbian. She is a curious woman. I still do not know about her sexual life for she keeps on avoiding the subject or simply does not answer my questions. To sum up, we never had anything to do with each other in sexual terms, and I think that she does not have a sexual life (at least in the usual meaning of the word)! I think that she is the slave of some sort of odd intellectual masturbation and she also has exhibitionist inclinations which if you watched, you might have noticed. She keeps holding my hand whenever we have people around, and every five minutes, in a variety of ways, keeps on repeating how beautiful I am or how I excite her. But as soon as we are left to ourselves, she suddenly alters, her way of behaving with me immediately changes, as if she becomes a completely different person. That's that.[1]

◮   ◮   ◮

Shortly afterward, however, the opportunity to "start a relationship with a woman" did arise when Edith Lang, a Hungarian pianist who had won many awards, fell in love with Amrita. After Amrita's death, her widower, Victor Egan, told her biographer N. Iqbal Singh that Edith had "a great crush" on Amrita and "chased her around" while Amrita "only played a passive part" but was "very fond of her." Iqbal Singh characterizes Edith as "manly" but "attractive." He states that Marie Louise once walked in and surprised them in bed together, which made Amrita feel very remorseful.[2]

Vivan Sundaram has characterized Amrita's painting *Two Girls* as "a painting of the physical and emotional longing of two women for one another"[3] that is also about synthesis or confrontation between dark and light, East and West. In it a fair, nude woman stands upright, her hand on the back of a chair on which a dark girl wrapped in a cloth is seated.

In 1938 Amrita married her Hungarian cousin Victor. She saw marriage as the only way out of dependence on her parents. They were greatly opposed to her choice, but she emphasized that, although she was not in love with Victor, she was comfortable with him because he understood her. Soon after her marriage, she wrote to her parents to protest at their having read and burned her letters without her permission, among them those of Marie Louise and Edith:

---

1. Letter in the collection of Amrita's nephew Vivan Sundaram, reproduced with his permission, translated from the Hungarian for this volume by Margit Koves. A slightly different translation appears in Vivan Sundaram, *Amrita Sher-Gil* (Bombay: Marg Publications, 1972), 89.
2. N. Iqbal Singh, *Amrita Sher-Gil: A Biography* (New Delhi: Vikas Publishing House, 1984), 28–29.
3. Sundaram, *Amrita Sher-Gil*, 20.

Dearest Mummy and Daddy,

I must admit it was a bit of a shock to hear that all my letters are being perused and destined to the flames! I had already made a spring cleaning among them and burnt and destroyed a whole roomful of letters, some weeks before my departure. Those letters I had specially kept either because they were dear to me, amused me, or were important from an artistic point of view or otherwise. However it is no use crying over spilt milk. I merely *hope* that at least the letters of Marie Louise, Malcolm Muggeridge, Jawaharlal Nehru, Edith and Khandalawala have been spared. I had left them behind not because I thought them dangerous witnesses of my evil past but because I didn't wish to increase my already heavy luggage. . . .

However, now I suppose I have to resign myself to a bleak old age unrelieved by the entertainment that the perusal of old love letters would have afforded it.[4]

Amrita never experienced old age—she died suddenly in Lahore, aged twenty-eight, but her parents' destruction of her letters destroyed an important part of history.

4. Sundaram, *Amrita Sher-Gil*, 126.

Hakim Muhammad Yusuf Hasan: Do Shiza (Urdu)[1]

Translated by Saleem Kidwai

D*o Shiza* (A/The Virgin), edited by Hakim Muhammad Yusuf Hasan, is purportedly a book on sexual science. Although forgotten now, it probably was very popular in its time because the following extract is from the third edition. The preface consists of a discussion of the *Kokashastra* (erotic treatises in the Sanskritic tradition). Labeling Kokashastra unreliable, the editor argues that books based on it are salacious and corrupt the national morals. Hasan insists that his book is not a religious but a medical text. He adds: "This book should not be taken to be an erotic treatise. I write these words because I am not writing this book for debauched people. . . . Instead, by informing readers of human weaknesses, vices, the rules of nature which should not be broken, the book will save them from evil."[2] The following extracts are from the section on child rearing.

Hermaphrodites[3]

I have informed the readers of the necessary details about men and women, boys and girls. Therefore it is necessary to discuss those beings who are neither men nor women. Eunuchs[4] exist not only in India and in the East but also in Europe and America.

---

1. Hakim Mohammed Yusuf Hasan, ed., *Do Shiza* (Lahore: no publisher, 3rd ed.1934). The term *Hakim* indicates that Hasan practiced *Yunani* medicine (supposed to be Greek in origin).
2. *Do Shiza*, 31.
3. The term used is *khansa*. It is in this category that he discusses homosexuals and *hijras*.
4. The term used here is *khwaja sara*, the eunuch in charge of the seraglio/household. This was a term used in Mughal times for eunuchs in imperial service. Later it came to be used for all eunuchs. I use "eunuch" for khwaja sara in this translation.

In India the eunuchs are formally organized. There is complete agreement and unity among them and they are constantly intent on expanding their community. You can well ask what sort of wretched person would want to join the community of these *hijras* [see p. 202]. You might not know but there are countless such men who are counted as men but whose emotions are exactly the same as those of women. Some of these men are married and have children but in them is an inherent emotion which makes them love only other men. They might be with women for sexual needs or to fulfill the needs of being man and wife. However, they are not completely satisfied with this. Their desires are not fulfilled and they are not happy. In their hearts they wish that they were with an attractive man, one with large dark eyes, a rosy and glowing complexion, red lips and a beautiful mustache, one who would take them in his arms, hold them tight and make love to them. They are constantly in search of such a man. Sometimes they are successful in finding such a match. European doctors have mentioned such cases in their medical books. In India too, after some search, such men can be found. The moment they get the opportunity, men with such feelings join the community of hijras.

Since there are men who prefer to love men and who find satisfaction in it, there is no reason why there should not be women who dislike men and prefer other women. Therefore there are women who to all intents and purposes are free from the qualities of women and have manly qualities. Such women are well built and slightly fair with a muddy complexion. Desire and lust drips from their eyes. They laugh often and prefer masculine manners. They stride along with their heads held high and they try to make friends with beautiful women. Gradually they entrap them in their magic and get closer to them. Simple, respectable women, trusting them as other women, accept their love and friendliness as affection. Slowly they start kissing and petting. Finally they seduce them towards illicit relations. If by chance or in the course of joking and playing, a woman falls into their hands, we should take this as the end of that poor creature. These illicit relations develop so fast that in a couple of months the poor woman starts looking as if she suffers from tuberculosis. The simple one turns into the unbought slave of the manly, shameless one. She constantly waits for the moment when her husband leaves the house. She sacrifices her wealth, honor and health to the shameless one. She begins to hate her husband and wants to spend all her time with this shameless one.

If, by chance, the husband finds out, then such lewd acts are stopped. Otherwise, the woman loses her health and finds a place in the grave. The shameless one then starts to entrap some other woman. Even if such events are rare and unusual, it is necessary to mention them so that men can protect their homes from the poisonous atmosphere that can be created by those women who pay visits in order to get familiar [with the wife] while the husband is away. I have treated one such woman. This woman admitted to her crimes in detail but I cannot describe them here because they are obscene. Physicians and the intelligent will recognize the necessary symptoms.

Talking to hijras, the following was found[5]:

---

5. This might be one of the earliest records of conversations with hijras.

How the Hijras Feel.

1. I constantly feel that I am fully a woman.
2. I always feel that I have a woman's reproductive organs.
3. During the period of my menses I feel pain and am uncomfortable.
4. In my heart arise all the desires of women but I am not attracted to any one man.
5. Sometimes I feel I am pregnant.
6. When I see women, I feel I am one of their kind.
7. When I see men, I want to love them.
8. When I see children maternal feelings arise in me.
9. I feel happy doing housework.
10. If I am called by a female name, my heart leaps with joy.

The Existence of Eunuchs is Dangerous

Do not allow eunuchs or hijras to enter the house. If the existence of lewd women is a danger, so is the presence of eunuchs. Eunuchs may corrupt the thoughts of respectable women with their poisonous conversation. Therefore it is not wise to let them come into the house or to make them guard women. Instead, it is an invitation to the corruption of respectable women. . . . (132–35)

Ways of Protecting Young Boys and Girls[6]

1. Never let children sleep with maids, female servants or strange women.
2. Get children into the habit of sleeping alone on their beds.
3. Young girls should not be allowed to sleep together on the same bed.
4. Boys and girls should be stopped from sleeping on the same bed.
5. Boys and girls should be watched so that they do not go to the bathroom together and do not stay there alone for too long. It should also be ensured that they do not go the bathroom at odd times. In whatever way possible, a secret vigilance has to be maintained.
6. Young boys should not be allowed to sit in a room alone. Privacy is destructive for the young.
7. Keeping boys and girls busy in play, studies or housework protects them from bad habits.
8. Young girls who are friends often talk for hours alone in rooms or on the roof. It is essential that they be watched. However, there is no harm if they are alone for a short time.

---

6. The author uses the term *chhote bacche* (young children) and *naujawan* (young adults) interchangeably here.

9. It would be better if they were made to sit where the older women of the family could occasionally watch them.

10. Stories and novels about love and romance should not be available to them.

11. Husband and wife should not have intercourse in the presence of their children. In fact they should sleep on separate beds.

12. When you are awake after the young boys and girls have gone to sleep, you should have a look at them. If, in the morning, the young stay tucked in their quilts for a long time, then trouble is possible. Therefore they should be awoken early and made to rise from bed.

13. Do not always consider them as angels, innocents or "only a child." In the light of the true examples I have presented above, you should guard your children completely.(140–42)

"Firaq" Gorakhpuri: Poet vs. "Critic" (Urdu)

Saleem Kidwai

Born Raghupati Sahay in a Hindu Kayastha family, "Firaq" (Quest) Gorakhpuri (1896–1982) is among the finest Urdu poets of this century. Active in the Gandhi-led independence movement, he tried to combine Marxism, Gandhism and English Romantic thought with the classical traditions of Urdu poetry. From 1930 to 1957 he taught English literature at Allahabad University. Firaq's poetry is marked by its uninhibited depiction of heterosexual love and female beauty.

Firaq became a legend in his lifetime for his poetry, his erudition, his arrogance, his temper, his brilliance as a teacher, and his homosexual proclivities. Firaq's contemporaries were well aware of his sexual preferences. Dwivedi, a prolific chronicler of Firaq's life, mentions his "infamies" and "disrepute" and adds that any young man in Allahabad who associated with Firaq was bound to have "fingers pointed at him."[1] Notoriety dogged Firaq throughout his life. Stories about his crude passes at young men, his mistreatment of his wife, and hate mail written to him were in constant circulation both in literary and social circles. Even the suicide of his young son was attributed to Firaq's having molested the boy's friend.[2]

In 1936, Firaq wrote an essay on the *ghazal*, in response to an attack on the ghazal written by someone using the pseudonym "Naqqad" (the Critic), published in the May issue of *Kaleem*, a journal edited by Josh Malihabadi (see p. 274). Firaq's response was published in the journal *Nigaar*. According to Firaq, this created a major controversy.[3] In response to Firaq,

---

1. Ram Prasad Dwivedi, *Firaq Sahab* (Allahabad: Ramnarayanalala Arunakumar, 1987). Also see Gyan Chand Jain, *Parakh aur Pehchan* (Delhi: Educational Publishing House, 1990), 206–07.
2. Jain, *Parakh aur Pehchan*, 207–11.
3. This essay was published independently as *Urdu Ghazal Goi: Firaq Gorakhpuri* (Lahore: Idarah-i farogh-i Urdu, 1955).

Professor Andalib Shadani (see p. 201) wrote a series of articles, running into over 100 pages, in the journal *Saqi*.[4]

The basic contention of "the Critic" was that the ghazal, as opposed to the *nazm* (Urdu verse) did not encourage creativity and that it had no future as a poetic genre. His main criticism was that the emotions expressed in the ghazal were shallow and shameless. What irked "the Critic" most was that the ghazal represented men as boy lovers, which was disgusting and "unnatural." He even suggested that poets who praised boys' beauty deserved a fourteen-year prison sentence.

At the conclusion of his long essay in defense of the ghazal, Firaq addressed this "fear of homosexuality." Poets, he argued, could not be dictated to by the "Instruments of Instruction for the British Government" or "army Regulations." Firaq reminded "the Critic" that they were living in the twentieth century and not during the Inquisition. Threats do not work, Firaq said. Ghazal writers did not have to apologize for homosexual emotion in the ghazal or justify it as "sheer poetry" or as poetic "convention." The poet need not concern himself with the ignorant penal codes of any country.

Firaq reminded "the Critic" that "from Havelock Ellis to the present, writers all over the world who had done serious academic work or research, had accepted that some people love people of their own sex. Scientists do not fear slander." Religious or moral epithets condemning homosexuality which "the Critic" liberally used, Firaq argued, had nothing to do with the debate on ethics and aesthetics.

"Listen," Firaq told "the respected Critic,"

> are you aware of Socrates' autobiography, and his relationship with Alkibiades? Are you aware of Caesar's love affairs? Do you know what Walter Pater has written about Winckelmann in his book *The Renaissance* or what Edward Carpenter has written in his books *Friendship's Garland, The Intermediate Sex,* and *Civilization: Its Cause and Cure?* What about the life of this esteemed author? Sir, are you aware of Shakespeare's Sonnets and their motives? Do you know of Walt Whitman and his poem "To a Boy"? Have you heard Sappho's name? Do you know the meaning of Lesbianism? Do you know of the refined and pure book called *The Well of Loneliness?* Do you know of D. H. Lawrence and his works? And of Middleton Murry's *Son of Woman?* Do you condemn all these to fourteen years in jail? What punishment would you give Tennyson for writing *In Memoriam* because recently some researchers have brought to light his homosexual feelings and statements?

Firaq goes on to remind "the Critic" that he, with his "slavish mentality and pedestrian prejudice," has no right to condemn venerated Asians like Sa'adi, Abu Niwaas, Hafiz, Zahoori, Urfi, Mahmud Ghaznavi, Babur, Sarmad, and numerous Urdu poets whose words reflected their homoerotic leanings. Homosexuality, Firaq wrote, was not incidental or external

---

4. *Urdu Ghazal Goi,* 3–4.

to "their greatness" but an intrinsic part of it. Homosexuality, he argued, was "the most sensitive vein of their life." He pointed out how just the curl in the hair of Ayaz, Mahmud's beloved, is the soul of one of Iqbal's ghazals.[5] What is good and what is bad in art cannot, according to Firaq, be decided by those with a commonplace outlook. Shakespeare's heroines Rosalind, Olivia, Viola, Imogen and Perdita, Firaq insisted, would have lacked their impishness, vitality and grace, had beautiful young men not played the parts of women on the Renaissance stage.

Firaq pointed out that the ghazal was dynamic and had evolved away from external elements to an articulation of internal and spiritual romance "to the extent that the twentieth-century ghazal does not contain a word or even a verb which points to it being homosexual." He opined that it was a modern nazm, Josh's *Nasaza Jawani*, and not a ghazal, that contained one of the most evocative descriptions of homosexual life.

5. Firaq is referring to the ghazal that begins "*Kabhi ae haqiqat-i-muntazar.*"

Sharada: "Farewell" (Hindi)

Introduced and translated by Ruth Vanita

This short story, written by a young graduate of the Kanya Mahavidyalaya, Jalandhar, the first women's college in Punjab, appeared in the May 1938 issue of the *Jalvid-Sakha*, the college magazine, which had a large readership among former students and supporters of the college throughout India. The Kanya Mahavidyalaya, still in existence today, was an unusual institution for its time. Founded under the aegis of the Arya Samaj social reform movement, it produced a number of remarkable women, many of whom became teachers and never married. The college, which had grown out of a girls' school, had a hostel, widows' home and a girls' orphanage attached to it, and was supported by donations from well-wishers. Its journal regularly featured stories about outstanding women, both Indian and foreign, and initiated a number of interesting practices, such as prefixing women's and men's names with "Shri" instead of the gendered "Shriman" (Mr) and "Shrimati" (Mrs) or "Kumari" (Miss).

This story is an interesting early example of a genre of fiction that celebrates romantic friendship and love between girls. Its unembarrassed hyperbole, use of terms and tropes such as *sahvas* (cohabitation) and *viyog* (separation) normally used in the context of heterosexual romance, and simultaneity of the idea of sisterhood with the aspiration to live together forever, are noteworthy, especially in the context of emerging women's educational institutions where it was possible for women to stay unmarried and spend their lives together as teachers. That most women students were not destined for such a life but were compelled to enter a marriage structure inherently unequal lends poignancy to Sharada's description of the woman-woman relationship as one of equality and likeness doomed to brevity.

The story is written in self-consciously ornamental and Sanskritized Hindi, with a couple of English sayings, such as "A friend in need is a friend indeed," interspersed in Roman script. This is in accordance with the Kanya Mahavidyalaya's language policy which was to give girls the same education that boys were receiving in this late colonial period and to equip girls both with the national language, Hindi, as well as with the international language, English, so that they could operate with confidence in the world.

It was an evening in spring. Nature was peaceful, the sky was calm above. The many-hued flowers in the garden smiled gently. The birds sat quiet on the branches. Only the black cuckoo on the mango tree sang softly. It was as if all living creatures had taken a vacation from their daily work and were strolling in some garden or other. Veena too walked toward the garden, immersed in her serious, deeply felt problems. Despairing, sorrowful, and distressed, she went and sat near a bower overgrown with creepers. Question after question relating to togetherness and to separation arose in her heart. And one two-syllable word made her feel as if she was dissolving into nothingness. She felt as if the blood had stopped flowing in her veins, as she sat there perplexed, paralyzed.

Farewell—how these two syllables pierce the heart! One who ponders the depths of these syllables is bound to start shedding tears to calm the heart. And yet calm flees from such a one. Tears are a life-giving cordial—they prevent such a one from dying. Today Veena too was weeping bitterly.

Veena loved Prabha. Each of them was ever willing to give her life for the other. They were bonded with the pure thread of sisterhood. No worldly power, no force, no glamor could separate these two spirits. They were alike in manner, way of life, interests and emotions. There was equality, oneness and fondness in everything they did. Their two hearts were two flowers laughing in the wide garden of the world. They had blossomed together in one flowerbed. Their relationship was one of heavenly tenderness and joy. Like successful actors, they were happily playing their parts in the great drama of life. But days of happiness, days of pleasure, days of love are short, they pass away quickly, disappear in the twinkling of an eye. And one can hardly bear the days of deep sadness that follow.

So too, ever since Veena had made Prabha the object of her tender love, Prabha had never been aware that she would one day be parted from her beloved Veena. Their life of love was so unusual that it seemed impossible to even dream of separation. She believed that their hearts would always be united, bound together. She fully believed that God would keep them both in one place, and that the pure stream of their love would always flow like the Ganga through hundreds of delightful places. But "Man proposes, God disposes." These hopeful buds were only half open when Veena suddenly realized that Prabha was going to be parted from her forever. Veena had spent the long years of hostel life in the sweet company of Prabha. In these years they had experienced all the fulfillment, all the joys of life. Veena looked up at the sky—small drops were falling, and the thirsty soil drank them up, releasing vapors like the sighs of a lover parted from the beloved.

Prabha will leave tomorrow—Veena could not bear the thought. Just then Prabha entered.

Prabha: *Didi,* why are you here alone?[1] It's raining. Why these tears?

---

1. *Didi* is the word for "older sister" and conveys respect for an older person. Words with the same meaning in other languages include Chechi, Apa, Baji. These words are often used in the context of romantic relationships—see pp. 292, 299, 314.

Veena: Prabha, my heart is full, I feel dizzy. Are you really going home tomorrow?

Prabha (her head drooping): Oh, Didi, how could I be fated to see this day? Truly, I never even dreamed this day would come so soon. But, my queen, happy days pass away quickly. Their heavenly beauty shows itself for a moment and then vanishes with the blowing of the wind. Now how will we live through the long days of sorrow? Yes, tomorrow my brother is coming to fetch me.

Veena: Little one! Where now will I find a lovely laughing sister like you? Your sweet voice will be nothing but a memory. All my dreams of happiness will disappear now like the bursting of a bubble. I'll cry and cry whenever I remember your tender love. Who will smile when I succeed and weep with me when I fail? You are the only one in this world with whom I am intimate. Now I will have to deal with all my problems alone and fulfill my desires alone, too. Where are you going, emptying my life of all pleasure?

Prabha: Didi, tell me, whom am I to call my intimate? I will remember your pure sisterly love. To whom will I tell the uncompleted stories of my joys and sorrows, who will help me resolve them? Wherever I live, the place will be unfamiliar to me. Living with you, I have forgotten the great happiness of my mother's home. That was because I found in your love a heart sympathetic to my own. That was why I could love you as I did.

Today mother nature too sheds tears at the parting of two hearts. They had experienced so much together, traveled together several times, and had divided their work schedules between themselves like day and night. They had revealed their innermost desires to one another, and had given their deepest wishes and blessings to one another at festive times. Their relationship was based on the ideal "A friend in need is a friend indeed." This last evening was heaven for them and when night fell, Prabha said in an eager tearful voice: "Veena, please play the *veena* [musical instrument] for me." Veena sang sad songs that made Prabha's heartstrings quiver. She fell into Veena's arms and they both were covered by the still and silent night sky. Veena's heated breath brought in the dawn. As the sun rose, Prabha was told that her brother had arrived. She came to Veena with tears in her eyes.

Veena bade her farewell with tears of love; with infinite fondness they wiped each other's tears.

Veena said, "Farewell, my queen" and the two hearts were separated forever.

Suryakant Tripathi "Nirala": Kulli Bhaat (Hindi)[1]

Introduced and translated by Ruth Vanita

Suryakant Tripathi (1869–1961), who wrote under the pen name "Nirala" (Unique), is among the greatest modern Hindi writers. Best known as one of the founders of the *chhayavad* school of poetry, he was also a novelist and essayist.

First published in 1939, *Kulli Bhaat*, subtitled a "humorous novel of character," is a reminiscent sketch that tells the story of Pandit Patwaridin Bhatt's lifelong friendship with Nirala. In his foreword Nirala says: "Kulli was, first and foremost, a man—a man who will always be honored from a human point of view."

[At the age of sixteen, Nirala is sent to visit his wife in her village in Uttar Pradesh, after his father and hers have had a disagreement. At the railway station, Nirala meets a man, about twenty-five years old, fashionably dressed in a Lucknow style, who gives him a ride in his horse-drawn cart, stares at him all the way, and refuses to accept payment. As soon as he reaches his in-laws' house, his mother-in-law anxiously asks: "Did you come in Kulli's cart?" Thinking that Kulli might be a so-called untouchable, Nirala replies, "That's an outdated way of thinking." His mother-in-law examines him with great suspicion and sighs deeply. As soon as his wife appears, she too asks: "You came in Kulli's cart?" Nirala is bewildered.]

The next morning, I awoke quite late. . . . As I sat down with a book, my mother-in-law said: "Kulli came today, at sunrise. I told him you were sleeping. He said he would come again. But it's not good for you to be friendly with him."

"If he comes to meet me, I'll have to meet him," I replied.

---

1. This translation from *Kulli Bhaat* (New Delhi: Rajkamal Prakashan, 1997).

"But he's not a good man," mother-in-law said solemnly.

"Still, he's a man so—"

"I don't mean he has horns. It's among men that one measures a man."

"If you know him so well, you should have told him not to come."

"One can't say that to someone who belongs to the village. You are a relative—anyone in the village can meet you affectionately. It won't be good for me to stop them."

"So you mean if someone comes to meet me affectionately, I should be the one to stop them?"

"No, I mean that if you are seen with him, you may get a bad name."

"But" I replied, "maybe he will get a good name from being seen with me."

Mother-in-law scrutinized me as if looking for signs of a good name.

At that moment Kulli arrived and called out in a subdued voice: "Woken up?"

Mother-in-law frowned. My wife rapidly walked through the room. I have always been inclined to take the path of revolt. I went out, curious to know why Kulli was such a dangerous man. Kulli bowed and folded his hands, with a sweetly sympathetic smile. I responded to his greeting, thinking him a very civilized person.

. . . . We began to talk about the history of the town. I noticed that Kulli looked at me, especially at my eyes, as if I was very dear to him. I had never experienced such a look before. I was curious, and also pleased. . . .

[Kulli offers to come in the evening and take Nirala on a tour of the historical sites around the village. Nirala's mother-in-law tells him that Kulli is a wolf in sheep's clothing, and that he should take his servant along when they go out. Nirala has always been inclined to rebellion—as a child, he disobeyed his father and drank water given by people considered untouchables. Kulli arrives an hour early, extremely well dressed.]

Kulli said to me: "Why do you want to take the servant along?"

This heightened my curiosity. I said: "It's his duty to come along, but I will send him off on some errand or other."

Kulli interpreted this in his own way. He thought I had understood his intentions and was in agreement with them—I was just the kind of man he had taken me to be.

[Nirala's mother-in-law equips the servant with a stick. After they see a temple, Kulli keeps winking at Nirala, indicating that he should send the servant away, which he does. After showing him the fort, Kulli takes him to his house.]

Kulli lit a lantern and said: "This is my humble abode. I'm the only one left in my family. I have some land. No kids or wife. I own two horse carts. I live as I please, that's what others don't like. Suppose I do have a vice, what is it to anyone? It's my own money I waste."

I thought he was right. I said: "The world can't run unless it points fingers at others."

Kulli was pleased and said: "Yes, but there are people in the world like you and me, who don't care about fingers being pointed at us."

Kulli very affectionately gave me betel and pressed my finger gently as he did so. I was happy, thinking that Kulli, belonging to my in-laws' village, was my brother-in-law and was joking with me. Kulli stretched his limbs strangely when he saw me happy. Enjoying his excitement, he said: "Come and eat sweets with me tomorrow. But don't tell anyone about it, because people here see crooked meanings in straightforward matters. Come by nine tomorrow." Then, very humbly, he added: "One should be compassionate to the poor."

Today, people don't understand my irony; in those days I didn't understand others' irony. I accepted Kulli's invitation and got up to go.

Gazing at my face, Kulli said: "How beautiful betel makes you. You have wonderful lips. What can I say—the delicate lines of betel color make them look like a sword." . . .

[Next morning] Kulli embraced me, saying: "Come in, come in." I felt as if the Ganga and Yamuna had met.

Kulli very respectfully took me indoors. A large mirror was decorated with triple-stringed garlands of flowers. Kulli took hold of me and both of us stood in front of it. Although we were not wearing garlands, in the mirror it looked as if we were. I was delighted with Kulli's art. Kulli looked at me in the mirror and laughed. I smiled back. Kulli was very pleased and said: "Well."

He hastily went to the other room and returned with a tray of sweetmeats, which he put on a tall table next to the bed. Placing a jug of water and glass next to it, he requested me to eat.

As I ate, Kulli watched me with yearning eyes. When I finished, he helped me wash and wipe my hands, and gave me betel.

I ate the betel and sat on the bed. A beautiful bed, with a beautiful bedspread. Kulli showed me a bottle of perfume and said: "I got this. Not that we are going to do massage."

I looked at Kulli like an ignorant youth. Kulli remained motionless. I saw that his face had become distorted. I didn't understand why. Kulli made an impatient movement but remained where he was. I thought maybe he was unwell. Kulli gave me a very loving look and said: "I'll shut the door, then."

But as he said this, he sat down with a thud. I felt afraid of Kulli, not because he might do something to me but because he seemed to need a doctor at once. I got worried and asked: "Shall I call a doctor?"

"Oh! You are very cruel," Kulli said.

I wondered what Kulli's tension had to do with my cruelty. I just couldn't figure it out.

Kulli made another violent movement, and said: "I don't want to force—"

I started laughing. Kulli remained where he was and said in sepulchral tones: "I love you."

"I love you too," I replied.

Kulli came alive and grew tense, saying: "Come then."

I couldn't understand why he was calling me.

"I have come," I said.

Kulli asked me: "So have you never—?"

The less I understood what was going on, the more annoyed I grew. "Why don't you say plainly what you mean?" I asked.

Kulli was completely deflated.

"Very well, good day," I said and left. All I knew was I didn't like his behavior.

That was my first meeting with Kulli. I went home. A heavy silence surrounded me, as if I was not there even while being there.

[Later Kulli, with Nirala's support, marries a Muslim woman and is ostracized. When he dies, no priest will perform his last rites, so Nirala performs them himself.]

Josh Malihabadi: "There Will Never Be Another Like You" (Urdu)

Introduced and translated by Saleem Kidwai

Shabbir Hasan Khan (1896–1982), sometimes described as the *Shair-i inqilab* (poet of the revolution), wrote under the pen name Josh Malihabadi (Passion of Malihabad). The British government banned some of his poems. In 1956 he migrated to Pakistan. His last published work is his autobiography, *Yaadon Ki Baraat* (A Procession of Memories).[1] In it he admits to being in love eighteen times, twice with men. Josh wrote his first love poems for S. H., an Eurasian boy, whose tutor, himself attracted to the boy, played go-between. Josh's second beloved was A. H., a classmate. Josh recalls a train trip they took when they had "a great time" alone in a train compartment. Once, when A. H. tried to test Josh's love for him, Josh flew into a rage and tried to stab himself.[2]

There is no suggestion in Josh's autobiography that the poet Saghar was a special friend. Josh mentions Saghar twice. He quotes the poet Firaq Gorakhpuri (see p. 264): "God be praised, this lad Sagharwa[3] claims to be a poet. I swear my butler writes better poetry" (589). The second time he mentions that another poet, Majaaz Lakhnawi, flirted with Saghar while belittling him as a poet (562).

Josh's letters to Saghar Nizami, published after their deaths, tell a different story. The correspondence and interviews given by Saghar illuminate a friendship of fifty years and fill in many gaps in Josh's recollections.[4] Saghar was deeply hurt by Josh's version.

---

1. Josh Malihabadi, *Yaadon ki Baaraat,* (new and enlarged version) (Delhi: Media International, 1997).
2. *Yaadon ki Baaraat,* 653–58.
3. The addition of *wa* to a person's name indicates intimacy.
4. Khaliq Anjum, ed., *Josh banam-i Saghar: Josh Malihabadi ke khutut Saghar Nizami ke naam* (New Delhi: Monumental Publishers, 1991). These letters were first published in

Saghar Nizami[5] was the pen name of Samad Yar Khan (1905–1983), a young poet, who first met Josh on a train, most probably in 1922. Josh was already famous, had published widely in journals and had published his first collection of poems in 1921. Saghar was eager to meet him. Sixty years later Saghar recalled: "He was fair and his cheeks were sunken unlike the plumpness they acquired later. His face was very different then."[6]

Saghar had started writing poetry in his early teens and had adopted the poet Seemab Akbarabadi (died 1951) as his *ustad* (teacher).[7] Seemab was then at the peak of his popularity, and Saghar added Seemabi to his pen name, thus becoming Saghar Seemabi. He moved to Agra where Seemab lived. In 1922 Seemab financed a journal and their names appeared as coeditors. For the journal, Seemab chose the title *Paimana* (cup) to match Saghar's pen name. Saghar was a popular poet, good looking, always well dressed, and with a melodious voice.

Josh and Saghar continued to meet at poetry readings and began a correspondence. In Josh's first letter, dated November 1923, he apologizes for not having answered Saghar's earlier letters. He ends with the remark: "You have written 'For some reason life seems to be getting pleasanter.' I do not understand. Will you kindly explain. You are not a 'victim of desire' but the 'focus of desire'" (47–48). In his next letter he sent his "humble respects to respectable Seemab" (48–49).

In 1924 Saghar moved to Lahore with Seemab. His first collection of quatrains, *Shababiyat*, was published in 1925. His relationship with Seemab soured. Seemab returned to Agra in 1926 and Saghar stayed on in Lahore. Their relationship was to deteriorate until it reached a point of hostility.[8] In 1934 Saghar started editing the journal *Asia*. He revived his correspondence with Josh. In 1935 Saghar became a disciple of the Sufi Nizami order and changed his pen name from Saghar Seemabi to Saghar Nizami.

On October 16, 1935, Josh praised the journal: "And why should it not be? After all is it not impossible that anything that Saghar does should be anything but beautiful and elegant" (50–51). Two months later Josh was worried about Saghar's lingering illness. "Dear young

---

Z. A. Khan, ed., *Saghar Nizami; Fan aur Shaksiyat* (New Delhi: Saghar Nizami Memorial Academy, 1985). All references are to Anjum's edition unless otherwise stated. I have used this edition because it includes photocopied facsimiles of the letters. The letters as published are not complete. Portions have been censored with the plea that they are "moth-eaten." The interview, given soon after Josh's death, was published in installments in *Biswin Sadi* (1982).

5. *Saghar* is usually used for "wine-cup."
6. Anjum, *Josh banam-i Saghar,* 13
7. "This Master-disciple relationship was a formality even though Seemab Sahab counted him among his foremost pupils." Khan, ed., *Saghar Nizami,* 14.
8. Ram, "Saghar Nizami," in Khan, ed., *Saghar Nizami,* 75. While being interviewed for a documentary film, Saghar warned that he would walk out if any question about either Seemab or Josh was asked. Anjum, *Josh banam-i Saghar,* 44.

man, get well soon now. Your illness is an affliction for my heart." (51). A few months later Josh is much more expressive: " . . . Where are you? How are you? What are you up to?" And then, "That great poet of yours[9] . . . [supposedly indecipherable] . . . is unhappy and furious and is threatening to destroy me. Let's see if I survive? I hope you will not forget me in your prayers" (52). A week later Josh was still worried about Saghar's bad health. Addressing him as "my life" he pleaded: "For God's sake let me know how you are or my soul will stay in pain" (52).[10] Ten days later he again wrote: "For the sake of God and his Prophet, look after yourself, and if you are careless with yourself, I will die" (53).

In 1937 rumors regarding their friendship seem to have begun. Josh was furious at an unnamed gossipmonger:

⋈ ⋈ ⋈

. . . this person has really turned out to be wicked as well as a fool. There are enough trouble makers and slanderers among the Muslims but he beats them all. I do not even speak to him. Yet he shamelessly continues to visit me. This is nothing. He . . . [moth eaten] . . . things will be said, to both of us because . . . [moth eaten] . . . already know that our relationship . . . [moth eaten] . . . and he can only condemn as indecent the deepening of a relationship. Two people only have to meet and he starts getting suspicious." (55)

⋈ ⋈ ⋈

In June 1939 Josh wrote one of his longest letters to Saghar.

⋈ ⋈ ⋈

. . . Intimacy does not only have to come from depravity but can also be based on common virtues, even if the foundation of such intimacy is weaker. Compared to virtues, vices are more attractive and more durable. Therefore dear friend, if I desire to see you and you wish to spend time with me, then be assured there is no love and affection in these longings. Instead we happen to have many common vices and some common virtues. It is this that is behind the miracle of this intimacy. . . . Therefore be warned that when I invite you to Malihabad it is not because of love. I want you to come so that while it rains, our few weakly virtues and our numerous robust vices can wrestle to their heart's content and . . . [censored by Urdu editor] . . . get a chance to fulfill their ap-

---

9. Anjum thinks this allusion is to Seemab Akbarabadi; fn 1, 91.
10. Saghar removed the phrase "my life" when he reprinted the letter in an article. See Anjum, fns. 1 and 2, 91.

petites. Our wickedness will swing from the branches till it is so fat and smooth that when the raindrops of life's mundane existence fall on us, they will slip off unnoticed like water off a duck's back—do you get the point?

Therefore, come, you have to come. Come when it is raining, when the rain swirls as if intoxicated. The cuckoo will lament . . . and among the laden branches of the mango trees we will invoke the ancestors of our wickedness, we will idolize our depravity, acknowledge the sovereignty of our mischief and celebrate the anniversary of our carnality . . . Our vices will be far more intoxicated than our virtues. Come, please come . . . Forgive my bad handwriting. My hand trembles with the idea of mischief (57–60).[11]

When Josh wrote next in June 1940, he sounded angry and hurt that Saghar had not bothered to inquire after his health when he had been so unwell that his "heart could have stopped at any moment." Now, having heard from Saghar, he felt better. He wanted to see him and requested him to write back that very day (60–61). In November, Josh again invited Saghar: "I am restlessly yearning for a sight of you. . . . The cup of my life is filling up with frightening speed. Come, and come before it spills over, or else. . . ." (61–62).

In February 1942 Josh invited Saghar again: "It would be difficult for you to imagine how I yearn for you . . . We both have to and must go to Allahabad for Holi. It's very important—you know what I mean. . . ." (63) A couple of weeks later he reminded him, "On Holi, the third of March, I will be in Allahabad. You had promised Ram Pratap and Firaq[12] that you would come. If you do, then it will really become Holi—the days would be *Id* and the nights like *shab-e baraat* [all names of festivals]" (64).

On July 28, he writes his longest letter to Saghar:

. . . I am in Chail [foothills of the Himalayas] at the moment. I am alone in the bungalow. . . . The rain seems to be enjoying itself. Brown clouds hide the mountains. The misty clouds touch the windowpanes as they dance outside. The cold touches my skin and permeates my bones. There is life and freshness in the air; the atmosphere is delightful and fantasies dance around me. Every pore of mine is screaming Saghar, Saghar, Saghar, how can I find him this minute; what can I do to make Saghar appear this moment . . . [moth eaten, according to the Urdu editor] . . . Are the days of miracles over?

---

11. The letter ends with a few verses, some words of which have been censored.
12. The poet Firaq Gorakhpuri.

Can another miracle, that Saghar drop from the clouds, not happen? Uff! How immediate is this need for Saghar.

Suddenly the thought of Seemab, Saghar's former friend, interrupts these romantic longings: "I met Allama[13] in Agra. A handsome though slightly jaded young man was in the room with him. The *maulana* [Seemab] was beaming." Soon the earlier mood took over again: "Uff, what a romantic mist whirls around me. Saghar if you were to appear at this moment, I would cut off the nose of my intellect and start believing in God. Allah *Miyan* [invocation of God] you do not often get a chance like this. This is a great opportunity for you. A mountainlike infidel is insistent on believing in you. Send me Saghar in the fraction of a second and get this harder-than-iron neck to bend before you." He ends the letter with another dig at Seemab:

Damn it, talking of intellect, suddenly the face of a fool from Akbarabad appeared before me.[14] Listen to this quatrain:

> Why should I love the mentally dead,
> Why should I go near a walking corpse,
> A criminal I would never dread,
> But why should I be burdened with a dunce. (64–66)

Josh and Saghar had always lived in different cities and met mostly at poets' gatherings. In 1943 they arranged to work together for the film industry. With their families, employees, and pets, they moved to Poona, where they shared a luxurious house. Saghar was to later recall: "Until we became close our interests had not clashed. Until we lived together I felt serene and those times were very happy ones. However when we began living next to each other in the Tahir palace, acrimony began."[15] Things worsened when Saghar, on Josh's advice, and contrary to his new wife Zakiya's advice, resigned his job and moved to Bombay to look for a new one.[16]

---

13. Lit. "most learned." Probably refers to Seemab Akbarabadi.
14. Appears to refer to Seemab.
15. Anjum, *Josh banam-i Saghar,* 20.
16. Saghar had married Zakiya Sultana on March 28, 1943. Ram, "Saghar Nizami," in Khan, ed., *Saghar Nizami,* 77.

Josh moved to Delhi in 1948 when Prime Minister Jawaharlal Nehru appointed him editor of the government journal *Aaj Kal* and advisor to All India Radio. Saghar was still in Bombay. From Delhi Josh wrote:

◈ ◈ ◈

I have been an old victim of these pig-headed suspicions of yours. . . . Anyway, why should I care. I love the blessed Sagharwa whether he acknowledges it or not. . . . [censored by Urdu editor] . . . Since the pitter-patter of the rain has started, I long—and long achingly—for you to brighten all my evenings, that I could nourish my soul on your beautiful face. . . . this Khan loves you, my life. . . . There is a *mushaira* being planned at the radio station. You must come for it. It would be an excuse to meet but also a chance for physical intimacy, dear one. . . . I take my leave, my bride. (70)

◈ ◈ ◈

On April 15, 1949, Josh wrote to Saghar about his decision to go to Pakistan. The government of Pakistan, which had declared Urdu the national language, was very keen to induce this famous Urdu poet to emigrate. Josh was conflicted. To Saghar he wrote: "If I can be assured that I would be able to see you there, my decision would be easy . . . my beloved, I'm smitten" (75–76).

On June 15, 1949, Josh wrote: "I have written a thousand times that I am dying to see you." Then: "Serious matters over, let's indulge in some vulgarity.

"2. Aslam Khan of Rampur has a young poet staying with him. He has sent me an article in his praise for publication. The poor dove takes pains so that the crow gets to eat the eggs!"

"3. Firaqwa[17] is having a great time these days, and me, I'm starving" (76–78). The editor of these letters omitted points 1 and 4, but in a subsequent collection of Josh's letters he reproduced the entire letter. Point 1 was a joke about whether a female prostitute who mounted a man should be called a *gandu* (bugger). Point 4 was: "I thought of you last night and an earthquake erupted in the crotch of my trousers."[18]

Included in the volume is the undated draft of a letter by Saghar, found among his papers:

◈ ◈ ◈

Wise friend, absent lover,

It is two o'clock at night. I am encircled by echoing silence. Random, colorful memories appear and disappear rapidly. The mind handles these boulders as if they were

---

17. The poet Firaq Gorakhpuri.
18. Khaliq Anjum, ed., *Josh Malihabadi ke Khutut* (New Delhi: Anjuman Taraqqi Urdu, Hind, 1998), 34.

flowers but my heart is sinking. The entire past has descended on my soul like a land-slide. I am buried under an indescribable weight. There are millions of feelings, both of joy and grief. Let alone putting these into words, I do not even have the capacity to dwell upon them. Your personality pervades the atmosphere. . . .

. . . You know that it was not our art that brought us so close to each other. We were bonded and bound by our natures, by the harmony between our temperaments and by that single desire which is connected to our unique personalities—our love of transgres-sion, by our backgrounds and our all-quenching humanitarianism . . .

You were old even then and I was as young as I am now. I well remember that at no point did I allow you to feel that you were saddled with an immature friend. Rather, you, who were older and jaded with experience, came forward to embrace me with my youthful precocity, sharpness, drive and delicate ways. After that it seemed that thought had mingled with thought, mind with mind, heart with heart, as if they would never be parted until the day of judgment. From 1923 to 1941, our untainted relationship de-veloped and reached new heights. . . . We were intimate in every aspect of our lives and art but never had any professional or self-serving dealings. . . .

Then came the unfortunate moment when such a conflict did arise. Our proximity and closeness climaxed in Poona and this had an alienating effect. The fall-out was ugly and unpleasant, and why should I repeat what happened thereafter . . . Those were dark, ugly days for our relationship. I do not know if this troubled you in any way. As for me, I was so deeply shocked that my life grew as empty and bitter as a bad hangover. In Poona it became clear to me that proximity is the death of a relationship. The veil of dis-tance is very important for any relationship to continue. . . . It was not so much your behavior that made me unhappy as the shattering of that large, imposing idol which my affection had carved from your art and personality, and which, housed in my little heart, had kissed the heavens. The premature breaking of this image filled my heart with poi-sonous bitterness. This bitterness continued to corrode the colors of my life until feel-ings of hatred and revenge stirred up a war of nerves between us.

Leaving Shalimar[19] was the beginning of the destruction of my future. During 1944–45, I was in a dreadful state but for three years, from 1944 to '46, you did not even throw a glance my way. . . . My leaving Poona was not merely moving house; it was the destruction of my home in exile. . . . After January 9, 1944, you stopped meeting me and for two years you closed all doors of communication. There was a gulf between us for two years. Eventually, one day in Poona you sat me down to clarify matters. . . . For a short time after that we were once again inseparable like sugar and syrup. . . . Ex-pectations and dependence began again, and again they burst like a bubble. . . .

Then you became a government official. We met in Kashmir but you were unrecog-nizable. The decent, polite Josh I had known now had haughtiness writ large on his

---

19. The film studio in which the two worked in Poona.

brow. The change in your manner continued. . . . When I met you in 1950 it felt like entering the frigidity of the north zone. In 1951, in Calcutta, there was nothing of the old Josh left. . . .

On that trip of mine to Delhi that you now mention, you convinced me that you did not even want to see me again. You [came] to the *mushaira* at the radio station. I was sitting right in front and I watched carefully. You avoided looking at me and made sure that our eyes never met. In the end it was I who greeted you. After this you recited your ghazal and left. In our history of twenty-nine years this was the first time you left without meeting me or leaving a word for me. Two days passed after this event. I was only a visitor to Delhi; you, praise Allah, were a resident of the city and could have easily traced me if you had wanted. You could simply have picked up the phone in your office and asked the radio station where I was staying. After this we met on the night of the discussion. Even then you were unrecognizable. While I was trying to leave the room to find you, I learned that you had already left.

. . . Take note how properly I behaved when, in spite of all this, I came to pay my respects to you. With a clean heart I spent the evening with you, drank with you, ate with you, heard your new poetry and recited some of mine. I left, having made no complaints. . . .

. . . I was sure that you not only did not want to see me but were also deliberately humiliating me. This definitely cooled my desire for contact with you. Yet I decided that while protecting myself I had to put up with this coldness of yours. I had to stand up to your arrogance since our relationship, no matter in what form or at what cost, had to continue. . . . All your life you have been under the Himalayan delusion that rules of social behavior and etiquette do not apply to you but that the rest of the world has to follow them when they deal with you. . . . After twenty-nine years I know you and your life like a mirror. Shall I put it another way. I know the difference between what you know about yourself and that which you do not. . . .. My desire to see you has not been dulled and is still as sharp as ever. Nostalgia creates a longing that cannot be denied. However, I do not wish to bring our relationship to the level it was before Poona. You are a great poet, a philosopher. You come from a great family. You are an influential man—the Prime Minister of the Republic of India is your close friend. Beyond these, I am convinced that you are a man of great integrity and until a few years ago your manners and dealings with friends were warm and courteous. You should try to continue to behave as you used to do. You and your friends are now in the closing stages of their lives. This phase of our lives should not be tainted by bad behavior. . . . It is true there are many things about you that I dislike and with which I am very unhappy. Yet I also have a personal affection for you and respect your talent a great deal. I also know that whatever you are, there will never be another like you. . . .

Look, the mists of dawn have appeared. The trams are on the road. For me this morning is the beginning of a new life, the beginning of a new relationship with you. You worship the dawn. I swear, with this beloved of yours as witness, that I have not written a single word to hurt you. I have only wanted to remove misunderstandings so that before we die we are no longer in the dark about each other, that we live as friends and die as friends. (34–43)

◈ ◈ ◈

Saghar moved to Delhi in 1954 to join All India Radio. He recalled: "Josh was very happy when I moved to Delhi. He welcomed me warmly. . . . Once again he found my home. Spring was back in our lives. . . . Within a short time Josh had detached himself from his local friends and had started spending time at my place. But he seemed detached. It was as if he had extracted the pleasures of life the way strong hands would squeeze a bunch of grapes."[20]

Josh left for Pakistan in 1956. Saghar discovered that he had migrated only when he dropped in to see him at his office. "Everyone knows of the storm of protest that arose both in India and Pakistan over Josh's decision to migrate. But during this turmoil, the only person who became a victim of his Pathan rage was me. Josh wrote a few articles against me in Diwan Singh's paper *Riyasat*, and made Diwan Singh write some more. He attacked me and also did not spare Zakiya. He called her a '*sabz pari*' [the green fairy]. If that was so, then I was Gulfam. What kindness!"[21]

They continued to meet on Josh's visits to Delhi. "He always met me when he came and always accepted my invitation. A lump still rises in my throat when I look at that sofa. After having had his drinks, eaten a meal, he would relax cross-legged on that sofa. And before he left he would always sing a *qawwali*."

They probably met for the last time in 1967. The day that Josh died All India Radio recorded an obituary by Saghar. He broke down during the interview. In another interview soon after Josh's death, he said: "That magician who doused flames by showering flowers on them has left the world and another like him will never be born. I have no power over my own sorrow. I have cut out his last picture from the *Hindustan Times* and stuck it in my diary . . . the mango blossoms of Malihabad await their tender who has disappeared into the unknown."[22]

Saghar Nizami died on February 27, 1983.

20. Khan, ed., *Saghar Nizami*, 409–10.
21. Khan, 411. Gulfam is the name of the prince besotted by Sabz Pari in Amanat's nineteenth-century dance drama *Indra Sabha*.
22. Khan, 415.

Ismat Chughtai:
Tehri Lakeer *(Urdu)*

Introduced and translated by Saleem Kidwai

Major Urdu fiction writer Ismat Chughtai (1915–1991) came to public attention in 1944 when she was charged with obscenity for her short story "Lihaf" (The Quilt) published in the journal *Adab i-Latif* in 1942. The story depicts sex between a neglected wife and her maidservant, witnessed by a horrified girl child. The married woman's husband is interested only in boys. Although the story takes a very negative view of homosexual relations, people were shocked by its explicitness. Chughtai's family, including her husband, tried to persuade her to apologize, but she refused. She got support from the famous writer Saadat Hasan Manto, himself often charged for obscenity. Finally she was exonerated by a Lahore court.

In her writings, Chughtai boldly dealt with the situation of Indian women, particularly Muslim women. *Tehri Lakeer* (The Crooked Line), 1945, is the first important Urdu novel on Muslim women; it shows sex as an instrument both of women's oppression and of their rebellion. Its publication raised a storm of protest. The novel sketches the lives of a middle-class Muslim family in everyday language. Such language was not used in Urdu prose before Chughtai. In the following extract, many characters from her school days seem to make an appearance.[1]

[A new young teacher] Miss Charan continued to teach Shamman privately and Shamman was ever ready to perform the most arduous tasks for Miss Charan. She would even

---

1. Rasul Fatima is one example. In her autobiographical essays, Ismat describes her own similar interaction with such a girl, and mentions that her best friend in school was called Saadat. "Lohe ke chane," *Kaghazi hai Pairahan* (1985; New Delhi: Publications Division, 1994), 138–40.

have committed murder for her. All she could think about was Miss Charan. The girls began teasing her but the only result was to make her thoughts of Miss Charan turn romantic. Every time she saw Miss Charan she was magnetized by her.

No matter where Miss Charan was, Shamman constantly felt her presence as if she were her own heartbeat. If Miss Charan were to pass by, Shamman was sure to make a mess of whatever she was doing. When they came face to face, she did not know what to say. If Miss Charan was out in the field coaching a sports class, it would become impossible for Shamman to concentrate, or to ignore that laughter which sent shivers through her. Everyone thought Miss Charan dark and ugly. To Shamman she was a beauty and there could be no one more beautiful than her. Shamman was attached to her family in a way and feared God but she had never been preoccupied with either of them. Miss Charan became more important to her than her family and her faith. She now created an imaginary idol of Miss Charan and passionately worshiped it. . . .

She began to imagine that even her body was constantly close to Miss Charan's. She would be standing and suddenly the vision of Miss Charan would appear—Shamman was tucked in bed and Miss Charan was putting her to sleep; she was thirsty, her throat parched, and Miss Charan was pouring cold fragrant nectar into her mouth, her hands on her forehead; Miss Charan was made of ice and the thought of this made Shamman heavy with sleep. She saw herself wandering around in the dark at night, weeping, and lying shivering on cold wet grass; she saw Miss Charan putting her to sleep on her down-filled pillow while she continued to fake sleep for fear that if she woke up, the dream would shatter. . . .

One night when she awoke she was aghast. The principal, torch in hand and wearing a long gown, was also in Miss Charan's room. A worried Miss Charan was trying to hold Shamman upright. She did not realize that she was sobbing loudly. Suddenly she fell silent and began staring at Miss Charan. She was actually sitting on Miss Charan's bed. Not the one she had imagined but the real one, the one with the green embroidered pillow covers and the brown blanket with a gold trimming.

She was dragged to her own room.

The next day the principal questioned her relentlessly. But she said nothing, answered no questions. How could she tell her about all the things she felt, wanted and imagined.

Three days later Miss Charan left the school. She did not meet anyone before she left. The watchman suddenly appeared, carrying her luggage, and she followed, bag in hand, and walked out of the school gates.

[Shamman felt guilty about Miss Charan's departure. She could not stop thinking of her, lost interest in studying, and failed the exam. She was transferred to a Christian mission school. There, her interest in virgin birth alarmed her family. So she was sent back to the old school, where she had to share her room with a girl called Rasul Fatima whom she hated. Rasul Fatima was pious but unattractive, untidy, and infatuated with Shamman. Shamman continuously humiliated her, and Rasul Fatima happily accepted her scorn. Shamman's loathing increased when Rasul Fatima's fingers started roaming over her while she slept. Shamman wanted to complain to the matron but remembered that some younger girls had recently been punished for pretending to deliver each others' babies under their quilts. She tried to stay away from her room and began spending time in the room of Saadat, whom she liked a lot.]

She was sitting with Saadat doing her homework when a young girl called out to her from the door.

"Shamman Baji, will you come out for a moment." The young girls in the hostels were like slaves to the older girls. They willingly did small chores, carried messages, stole flowers from the garden and carried books for the older girls. In return they were rewarded with the privilege of being allowed to massage the heads or feet of the older girls. The more popular a girl was, the larger the number of those who were willing to serve her. Shamman was not very popular with these girls because she was considered brusque.

Walking to the door she curtly asked "What is it?"

"Rasul Fatima Apa has sent this. . . ." Bashfully, the girl handed her a piece of paper and ran away. Rasul Fatima must have had to bribe this girl heavily to act as her messenger because the younger girls despised her.

The paper trembled in Shamman's hands. Before Saadat could see it she hid it in the collar of her sweater and returned to her books. But she was too disturbed to study. She felt as though she had received a threatening letter and was in grave danger. She had to read the letter, so she pretended that she needed to go to the bathroom. The letter read:

> Goddess of my heart,
>   Oh, why are you displeased with the one who loves you? How long is this going to last? If you actually hate me, then will you please choke the life out of me with those beautiful hands of yours? You have bewitched me. At least let me put my head at your feet and ask for forgiveness.
>   The ardent lover of your beauty, Rasul Fatima.

Shamman was panic stricken at the idea of returning to her room. What a horrible letter! If only she could find an excuse for staying on in Saadat's room.

[Shamman devised all kinds of excuses to avoid spending the night in her room. Finally she succeeded in making the matron transfer her to Saadat's room. There she became obsessed with Saadat's intimate friend Najma.]

One day Saadat came to class wearing Najma's satin vest. When Shamman touched her back, she felt as if her hand had been singed. Quickly she withdrew her hand. But within a moment she was looking for an excuse to touch Saadat's back again. When she did she felt as if serpents were wriggling across her palm. In the afternoon, feeling warm, Saadat took off the vest, hung it on the back of a chair and went for lunch. When Shamman returned to the room after lunch she saw the vest and her heart started pounding. [Pretending to go to the bathroom, Shamman remained in her room.] Hesitantly she moved toward the vest, her heart beating too fast for its own good. A whiff of fragrance hit her and she felt faint. Someone knocked down a trash can outside. Alarmed, she flung the vest on the bed and moved to the door. Then she turned back. The vest was now on the bed instead of over the chair. What if Saadat saw this? It would be disastrous if she guessed. . . .

[The annual dinner and fancy dress party were to be held in the school. The girls decided to dress as men, and the day scholars helped provide the boarders with clothes. Shamman too got a man's suit.]

Dressed as males, the girls felt self-conscious and shy, particularly those who were wearing whiskers and beards. Some sat in their rooms, wrapped up in sheets. Others tried to drag them out. The girls went into peals of laughter as the fat Akhtar, wearing a cap and beard, strutted around looking like Maulana Shaukat Ali [a Muslim political leader]. One girl was dressed as an Arab youth yet she looked effeminate. Nearby, Noori was fluttering around in a silk sari. She had not yet begun wearing saris so this was a thrill for her. But the effeminate Arab youth was chasing Khursheed, who, in an Egyptian dress, looked like a Punjabi woman. Shamman, in her dark suit, was reluctant to leave her room. A few girls had even tried to drag her out but had then let her be. There were many other girls wearing suits but Shamman felt as if she was naked.

The guests were all in the hall. The girls in their costumes began to assemble. Shamman spotted Saadat dressed as a washerman—long whiskers, a white turban and a bundle of laundry over her shoulder. With her was Najma dressed as the washerman's wife. At least, she was supposed to be a washerwoman but her clothing was more suitable to a heroine like Padmini.[2] Her flashy clothes glittered with tinsel. She was wearing the same satin vest, and yes, there was the same fragrance of cloves. She was wearing lipstick and rouge. And her feet took Shamman's breath away. Her heels looked like the brown eggs of a peacock, flecked with red. Silver anklets shone on her bare feet. Shining on her forehead like a diamond was a *tika.* Shamman gaped unabashedly.

"Just look at Shamshad," Najma said with a loud laugh. The other girls joined her. Najma's face had soon gone red: "*Hai Allah,* she looks exactly like a boy."

"Why aren't you coming along?" Saadat asked unenthusiastically.

"You are a bumpkin, you washerman. Here is a Sahab Bahadur. I'd rather go with him." Najma caught Shamman's hand and drew her along. Shamman felt as if she was dreaming.

No one paid any attention to Shamman's attire but she did not care. Instead, she stared at Najma. And whenever Najma looked at her, she blushed and burst into giggles. Najma sat close to her—in fact so close that her gauze *dupatta* [veil] was constantly touching Shamman's hands.

Saadat sat, looking dejected. She was not at all pleased with the way Najma was laughing and freely talking to Shamman. Shamman, in her excitement, had lost her appetite. And then Najma's anklets would come undone and Shamman had to constantly fix them. Najma's ears too had started hurting under the strain of her heavy earrings and

---

2. A medieval Rajput queen famed for beauty. Alauddin Khalji supposedly subdued Chittor only to obtain her.

Shamman had to attend to them. Shamman did not say much in response to Najma's chatter, but Najma noticed the villainous mustache on her innocent face, the hair escaping from under her hat, her constant blushing and her embarrassed smiles. Najma relaxed and began calling her Shamman instead of Shamshad.

Shamman said something and Najma broke into a loud laugh. Saadat, pretending indifference, was talking to a teacher about the forthcoming exams. She had peeled off her mustache and her turban was unwound and lay across her shoulder as a dupatta. Instead of a washerman, she now looked like an elderly lady.

When the time came for the competition, Najma began looking for Saadat who had returned to her room. Najma ran to her room and Shamman's heart sank. She could not sit still so she followed her. There she found Saadat sprawled on the bed weeping loudly and Najma trying to console her. On seeing Shamman they fell silent. Just then a few other girls came running and said, "Najma Baji, Miss Jarmi is looking for you." Najma had to leave. Shamman gingerly followed her back to the hall. All the girls were now parading in pairs in front of the audience. When a pair caught their fancy, they applauded loudly.

Miss Jarmi was looking for Najma. "Where is the washerwoman?" Then, "Where is your washerman?"

"Saadat is not feeling well," Najma answered softly.

"That's too bad. Well, you had better find a new partner. Come on, hurry up."

All of a sudden, Najma caught hold of Shamman's hand and joined the parade. Shamman was walking on air. All she knew was that Najma was holding her hand and that she was floating. . . .

After accepting her prize, Najma quietly returned to Saadat's room. The last song of the evening was sung, but suddenly Shamman choked on her own voice. She saw Saadat and Najma singing, their heads together and Najma's hand around Saadat's waist. They were lost in each other, oblivious to the world.

That night Shamman wept herself to sleep. She lay for a long time on her bed, trying to stifle her sobs by biting into her palms. Saadat was not in the room. Since it was a holiday, the girls were allowed to spend the night in other rooms. Saadat was with Najma! . . .

[The examinations were approaching. Girls began wishing each other good luck and exchanging gifts days before the exams started. The more popular girls were inundated with presents. On the day of the exams they were presented with flower garlands.]

The night before the exam, Shamman had sent for a garland, costing a rupee and a quarter, for Najma.[3] As long as she was awake that night she had sprinkled it with water to keep it fresh. She kept touching those lucky petals that would embrace Najma the next day. She wished she could hide among them.

---

3. A rupee and a quarter is an auspicious amount, given at ceremonial occasions.

The next morning she was so tense that she did not even eat her breakfast. She kept fidgeting with the garland and thinking of the moment she would put it around Najma's neck. Perhaps even Sitaji had not been so nervous when she was about to garland Ramchandraji. But then she would not have had to worry about the jeering stares of the girls or the eagle eyes of the matron. And these coarse and unromantic girls were always ready to mock. They had never lost their hearts to anyone and therefore thought nothing of laughing at the nervousness and the garlands of those who were devoted to others. They would wound them with their words and even create unpleasantness. If the devoted ones retaliated, the mockers called them names, questioned their morals and said other hateful things. They would also broadcast their weaknesses to all.

But the devotees were not to be deterred by taunts or censure. Instead they became more determined and unabashed in their devotions.

In fact, the families of some of these girls were infuriated with their obsessions but if they tried to stop them, the girls became hysterical. They would then have to be allowed to indulge themselves in their devotions.

Najma emerged from her room, laden with garlands. With trembling hands Shamman garlanded her. Najma responded with a little smile. Then she headed to the sick room where Saadat was. Shamman followed her.

She left the room immediately, stung by what she saw. She felt as if someone had dumped tons of muck over her heart. Saadat was sitting in bed, healthy and beaming, Shamman's garland wrapped around the knot of her hair.

Saadat and Najma were back together as if nothing had happened. Najma's exams finished and Shamman and Saadat's exams began. Shamman had spent only a rupee and a quarter on the garland for Najma who now bought hundreds of garlands for Saadat but seemed to have forgotten all about Shamman. In fact no one had a garland for her. As she stood in the queue of flower-bedecked girls on their way to the exam, she wished she had bought a garland for herself.

"Listen, Shamman, I don't like garlands so I picked these flowers from my garden. Aren't they beautiful?" Bilqees, an eighth-class day scholar, said to her, handing her some flowers. Shamman suddenly felt as if someone had covered her naked shame with sheets of flowers.

Rajendra Yadav: "Waiting" (Hindi)[1]

Translated by Ruth Vanita

Leading novelist Rajendra Yadav (born 1929) edits *Hans*, the premier Hindi literary journal. His most famous novel, *Sara Akash*, has never been out of print since first published in 1951, has been made into a movie and has sold over 500,000 copies.[2] His novels and short stories have been translated into many Indian and foreign languages.

"Prateeksha" (Waiting) is a long story published in 1962.

When people have lived through a situation repeatedly they get accustomed to it. But this is not true of Geeta. Even today, waiting is the most torturous part of her life. It is as if she is split in two while she waits—one part of her waits quietly, untroubled, while the other, torn by nerve-wracking tension, starts at every sound. . . .

Ever since Harsh has come, Nanda seems to have gone crazy. She is not on this earth, she is floating in the air, above time. She scarcely remembers that Geeta exists. . . . How quickly this girl changes color! Doesn't take her a minute! When will this Harsh leave? God knows how much time he has taken off work? . . . By bringing him here from the hotel, Geeta has increased her own pain. When they are with her, she pretends to be happy, laughs at their antics and jokes, and sometimes teases them, but the anguish within her grows deeper. . . .

How does she put up with the brazen behavior of these two and swallow this humiliation? . . . Later she feels angry but when they are with her, she feels as if they are two children whom she must look after, feed and provide for. . . .

1. This translation from Rajendra Yadav, *Pratinidhi Kahaniyan* (Delhi: Rajkamal Prakashan, 1985).
2. English translation by Ruth Vanita, *Strangers on the Roof* (New Delhi: Penguin, 1994).

Nanda looked very helpless and simple when Geeta first met her. She had a pretty face and a clear complexion. But there was an oddness about her that wasn't temperamental. It derived from living in a small town and being isolated. She wore her hair tightly pulled back and never let the end of her sari go below her waist. She thought this was the way to look smart. With what difficulty Geeta had changed her tastes! Geeta herself wore simple white clothes but when she went out with Nanda she wanted people to look twice at the girl. That was when the first contradiction surfaced in Geeta. Without consciously willing it, she gave up her preference for simplicity in regard to Nanda, and today that same Nanda—a sleeveless black blouse, a sari with a peacock feather design, its end floating down to her heels, a long string of huge pearls, and hair loosely coiled in a figure of eight—what a figure and what grace! And these days, she is lost in dreams, floating on air, as she walks along, close to Harsh as she can get. . . .

The morning after Geeta had brought the two of them home from the hotel, she made tea but neither of them got out of bed. She kept doing one chore after another, hoping that the maidservant would not arrive and find them still in bed. She hadn't slept all night. She couldn't get to sleep without Nanda. The door to Nanda's room was open, the curtain half drawn across it. Finally, she knocked at the door a couple of times and said: "Get up Nanda, it's eight o'clock, tea is ready." All she heard was a faint whimper and a sound of tossing and turning. The third time, Nanda said: "Didi, please bring it in here." The same way she always says it, as she lies in bed. She must be lying just the same way, Geeta guessed. Geeta replied, as she did every day: "All right, I'll bring it, I was born to serve you, it seems." A cup in each hand, she pushed the door with her foot and entered, the curtain wrapping itself around her. Harsh sprang up with a start and covered himself with the sheet. He was busy searching for his slippers when Nanda turned in bed, stretching and yawning, put her arms round his waist and pulled him down again. Pushing her arms away, Harsh muttered, "Stop it, Nanda, Geetadi is here." Her eyes still closed, Nanda tightened her hold and replied in sleepy tones, "So what? As if she doesn't know—my Didi is very largehearted, she doesn't bother about such things." Highly embarrassed, Harsh remained sitting. Pretending to be absorbed in balancing the cups, Geeta stepped forward. Trying her best to act natural, she said, "Here, take your tea." Without raising her eyes she saw that Harsh was wearing a shirt with Nanda's sari wrapped around his waist and Nanda had on only a petticoat and blouse. She had now slid down and put her head on Harsh's thigh, and her long thick silken hair flowed from the edge of the bed to the pillow. It was hard for Geeta to contain herself—this was Nanda's daily habit. When the two women slept together, the milkman would knock at the door downstairs and Nanda would wrap her arms around Geeta's waist to prevent her from getting up and would put her head in her lap like a demanding child. Her soft thick hair would flow over the bed just as it was flowing now. Geeta would stroke it lovingly and say: "Let me get up now, Nandan, the milkman will get annoyed. If he goes away, how will I make tea for you?" But she felt a deep satisfaction in stroking the somnolent Nanda's hair and she knew that Nanda too enjoyed it very much. The sight of Nanda's hair awakened the habitual stirring in her hands—perhaps Harsh doesn't know how Nanda enjoys having her hair stroked in the morning!. . . .

[Geeta recalls how she felt when Nanda became intimate with Miss Raymond.]

She kept feeling that she had always loved people unilaterally but no one had ever fully reciprocated her love. Somewhere she had heard that love is by definition one-way. In an intimate long-term friendship or love, the two parties never love one another equally. It is always one who loves and the other who is loved. . . .

[When Nanda left Geeta for Miss Raymond, Geeta pursued her and brought her back.]

. . . Geeta bolted the door and went straight into Nanda's room. As Nanda raised her head from her hands, Geeta pounced on her, slipper in hand, and began showering blows and abuses on her. . . . Nanda tried to fight back but was defeated by that tempestuous rage. She kept suffering the blows and crying out: "Didi, Didi, I'll die! I beg of you, forgive me, I'll never do it again." She kept protecting herself with her elbows and crying, like a small child. Finally, Geeta flung the slipper aside and fell to the ground like a felled tree, sobbing and gasping for breath. Nanda lay limp in her arms and she covered her throat, temples, lips, and arms with kisses, crying: "Nandan! Nandan! [affectionate pet name] Nandan, my Nandan! Forgive me, my queen. I can't live without you, Nandan! I'll do whatever you say. You can do as you like, go where you like but don't leave me and go away! Who else do I have but you, Nandan? I'll take poison if you leave me." All night, Geeta lay clinging to her, crying and asking forgiveness.

Remembering her own passion that night, Geeta's eyes filled with tears once more. . . .

She had feared that Nanda and she might be alienated from one another after that episode. But she found with pleased surprise that they became even more intimate and inseparable thereafter. They took a fortnight's leave and went to Puri for a week.

. . . Hand in hand, they would walk along the seashore, enjoying the waves tickling their feet. Nanda would laugh and call out: "Hold me, Didi," and then they would lie for a long time on the sand. . . .

One moonlit night they were lying on the sand in front of their hotel, letting the sand run through their hands. . . . Geeta's glasses were sticky with moisture. The roar of the sea awakened a strange excitement in mind and body. After a long silence, Geeta asked tenderly: "Your aunt beat you a lot, didn't she, Nandan?"

"Yes. How do you know?" Nanda replied with a sigh.

"Because that day you cried out several times, 'Aunt, I won't do it again.'"

Tears rolled down Nanda's cheeks. She hesitated, then said: "I have suffered a lot, Geeta Didi. My father sent me to my uncle's house to save me from my stepmother's ill treatment. But there—" She sighed again.

Geeta drew the weeping Nanda to her, put her head on her breast and stroked her temples for a long time. Tears fell from her own eyes too.

"The scar on my chest, which I said was caused by a boil, was actually given to me by my aunt. One day I told my cousin that I was thinking of going away with Harsh or by myself. She told her mother and after that—Didi, I lay moaning in pain for a week. She burnt me with a hot spoon, saying 'Here, I'll cool your lust.'"

. . . Nanda went on: "Harsh was two years' senior to me in college. We acted in a play together and grew close to each other. He had told me from the start that he was already married. But I was so crazy, I said my love for him was more than just the desire to get married. Now they have a child too, but, Didi, I never feel that Harsh is not mine."

Geeta was carried away too: "You saved me, otherwise I don't know what might have become of me. Everyone in my family or among my acquaintances who had a child used to think that I would adopt it and will my provident fund and insurance money to it. I was so tired of them all, Nandan, of their selfish calculations. . . . I was the daughter of a big officer, so when I got involved with my tutor, my father had him beaten up by the servants while I was locked in my room and could only beat at the door. I still sometimes hear his voice promising to return and fetch me. In revenge, I never obeyed my father. I kept studying and kept waiting, and now I feel as if waiting has become a way of life. . . . When I turned thirty-five I felt as if I was waiting again but didn't know for whom I was waiting. Sometimes now I think, you were the one I was waiting for." She took off her glasses, covered her eyes with her arm and burst out crying. "I am old now, Nandan. You are my daughter, beloved, companion, husband, everything. When I die take everything and settle down with your Harsh." Tears of self-pity continued to flow from her eyes. "All I have is yours."

"Didi, don't talk like this, Didi!" Nanda slid nearer and kept kissing Geeta's lips, eyes and earlobes. Looking at the tears on Geeta's cheeks and at her closed eyes shining in the moonlight, the thought came to her that Geeta might look like this when she died. Pushing the thought away, she kept repeating, "I won't go anywhere, Didi."

The tide was high and the waves were close to them now. When a huge wave rolled up and wet the sand just below them, they stood up, brushing down their clothes.

That night, binding Nanda's naked, abandoned body with her eager arms and excited breath, repeatedly kissing the scar on her right breast, Geeta kept saying like a madwoman, "Nandan, don't leave me! I'll die without you, Nandan!"

Later feelings of guilt and self-hatred might nibble at the conscience like so many mice, but at such moments neither Geeta nor Nanda could restrain herself. Nanda would get so wildly excited that she would take to scratching and biting.

Whenever Nanda awoke that night, she found Geeta stroking her hair, her shoulders or her back. Perhaps the sensation awakened her. She lay awake, gazing at the ceiling, listening to the roar of the sea and then slowly fell asleep. Her eyes opened again before dawn. Sleepily she embraced Geeta and asked, "You didn't sleep all night, did you, Didi?"

"I don't know what happened to me. I want you to keep lying like this while I gaze at you and stroke your hair, your cheeks. I feel as if someone will snatch you away from me."

Nanda didn't say anything. She felt slightly bored. . . . She wondered whether her own future would be like Geeta's present. She kept saying, "Didi, I'll never leave you,

I'll never go away." Holding Geeta's gray-sprinkled head in her arms she kept patting it as one caresses a small child who has fallen and hurt itself. But deep beneath that pure emotion was someone calculating—she has insurance for ten thousand rupees, at least ten to twelve thousand in the provident fund and probably fifteen to twenty in the bank. . . .

When she got up, Geeta felt as if all that had happened was a dream. They went and stood on the balcony, their saris wrapped around their shoulders, under which they were wearing only their bras. . . . Her elbows resting on the railing, Geeta slid her sari a little way along her shoulder, laughed and said, "Look how hard you bit me! There's a mark here. Do you lose your senses at such moments?"

Nanda felt embarrassed. But she laughed, mischievously stuck out her tongue, and turned away. . . .

[When she meets Harsh and Nanda goes to stay with him at a hotel, Geeta concludes that "if she insisted on having it all she might lose it all one day. So wisdom lay in swallowing her sorrow and giving Nanda some freedom. Harsh wouldn't stay here all his life—he had to return to his family and his job." So she goes to the hotel and brings them both home with her.]

And Geeta would watch Nanda wholly absorbed in washing Harsh's clothes, ironing his shirts or emptying his ashtrays with an expression of housewifely care on her face as if she had been married to him for years. Nanda had never of her own accord ironed Geeta's clothes. If she was asked to oil Geeta's hair she would behave as if she was being forced to work like a bonded laborer. In fact, it was Geeta who would wash Nanda's smaller garments when she went to bathe, or fold up her clothes with her own or keep track of her laundry accounts.

Bow wow! When Bose Babu's dog barked, Geeta jerked into wakefulness. . . . Half reclining, her head turned toward the door, she saw herself in the mirror. For a moment a sort of doubt arose in her mind—was this reclining, keenly observant Geeta in the mirror the real one, or was this one on the bed real? This doubt ran through her like a lightning bolt so that for a moment she felt afraid, alone in this empty, brightly lit flat. Perhaps, perhaps that Geeta in the mirror, half rising at the sound of the door, is the real one, and the reflection is this one lying outside.

Bhupen Khakhar:
A Story (Gujarati)

Introduced by Saleem Kidwai

Internationally renowned painter Bhupen Khakhar was born in 1934. He is also a gifted writer of Gujarati fiction and drama. One of the few Indian celebrities to have spoken openly to the press about his homosexuality and the homoerotic themes in his work, he explains how when he was younger he kept his homosexuality a secret from friends and family: "I was very much ashamed of my sexuality. . . . Up to 1975 I felt that if my friends knew I am gay, I was prepared to commit suicide. . . . After my visit to England in 1979, I saw that homosexuality was accepted."[1] His increasingly stable attachment to his friend Vallavbhai also encouraged him to speak openly, and the death of his mother in 1980, itself a severe blow, allowed him a new freedom of public action. The untitled story translated here was first published in *Kriti* magazine in April 1968 and is typical in its understated depiction of a lower-middle-class man's ease with his bisexuality, double life, and liaison with a peon. It is remarkable too for its exposure of how alternative familial arrangements are often masked as conventional ones.

Translated by Svati Joshi

Ratilal liked to have his picture taken. He also liked to wear white clothes. So when Manjari asked him to go with her to get their picture taken, he got ready. Ratilal and Manjari stood close to each other. Ratilal's hair had thinned slightly in front and the hair near his ear was gray. They had fallen in love when they were very young, but both were

---

1. Timothy Hyman, *Bhupen Khakhar* (Bombay: Chemould, 1998), 68.

still mad about each other. He bought a jasmine garland for Manjari's hair and then they both went to the studio. They stood straight, clutching each other. There was no space even for a lotus leaf between them.

Mohanlal was Manjari's husband.[2]

Mohanlal was very regular in his habits.

Every morning he would reach the office on time.

His work routine there too was fixed.

He would wear black clothes to go to office and would reach the machine at ten past eight.

He would greet Shyamlal who sat next to him and would begin his work.

Tea at nine thirty.

Mohanlal was expert at working overtime.

When he arranged to work overtime, Manjari never failed to make millet *rotis* for him.

Mohanlal and Manjari's married life was happy. They had two children.

Now Mohanlal had had a vasectomy. So there was nothing to worry about. Ratilal often used to stay at their home. Manjari and Ratilal were old friends. Mohanlal was reserved—he would talk to Manjari only when necessary.

Manjari's fondness for watching Hindi films was taken care of by Ratilal. Mohanlal only saw religious films. He was uninterested in other new films. But Manjari knew all the film songs by heart. Very often, during Mohanlal's absence, in the afternoon, she would sing them to Ratilal. When both were lying in bed she would take Ratilal's head on her lap or sometimes cover Ratilal's face with her loose hair and sing love songs. When Mohanlal once saw them like this he was very amused, but he was certain that their relationship was like that of brother and sister and since both were happy, the incident slipped his mind.

He even saw the picture of her and Ratilal in her purse. In the picture, Ratilal's jaw jutted out. Ratilal was fair and taller than Mohanlal. Mohanlal's hair had grayed. His lower lip hung down and his face was wrinkled.

Mohanlal had to go out of town on office work. The atmosphere was pleasant at Nani Jithardi when he reached there at seven in the morning. Because it had rained the previous day, some areas were waterlogged. But Mohanlal was very familiar with the roads of Nani Jithardi. He knew the peon who worked at Desai Steel Industries. It was with him that he had tasted liquor for the first time in his life. It tasted like poison. He never touched it again.

Mohanlal was very particular about his work.

The machine had conked out. He had repaired many such machines. He started work at seven thirty sharp. He had tea at nine thirty. Again he went back to work. He started thinking as he worked.

---

2. Rati is the name of the god of love's wife, and connotes eros. Mohan, lit. the charming one, is one of the names of Shri Krishna.

"Damn it, I have slogged all my life but the boss has no feelings for me. Last month his sister got married but he did not invite me. If he had invited me I could have impressed Manjari.

"What do people say about Ratilal and Manjari? When I see them cling to each other, I laugh with amusement.

"The boss is pleased with Ratilal. This time he gave him two increments. His pay now totals Rs 227.50 including dearness allowance. I still haven't seen the figure 200.

"After the vasectomy, I decided to sleep only twice a week with Manjari. On Mondays and Thursdays.

"The elder son is now twelve. He really understands everything. That's why Manjari uses that sentence: 'Shall we do that?'

"This time I am going to tell the Sahab: 'I slog so much and only one increment?'"

In the afternoon when Mohanlal went to the canteen with the peon, Ratilal and Manjari were entering the cinema hall to see a film. When the film started, Ratilal's hands started moving on Manjari's thighs. Manjari was absorbed in watching the film. When love dialogs occurred, her hair would fall on Ratilal's shoulder. During the songs she clasped Ratilal's hand firmly and pressed his fingers into her palm. When the film was over at six, Mohanlal was putting his things into his bag and going to sit in the temple at the edge of Nani Jithardi. He participated in the worship with great faith and then entered the peon's room.

Mohanlal returned after three days.

He specially remembered to buy a jasmine garland for Manjari.

Today was a Thursday.

Manjari did not say what she used to say every Thursday night.

Mohanlal was a little surprised.

In any case, Mohanlal never talked very much.

On Friday night when Mohanlal returned from office, Ratilal and Manjari, who were talking to each other, stopped. Both suddenly were silent.

A little later, Manjari, with tears in her eyes, threw herself at Mohanlal's feet and started crying aloud. Then Mohanlal thought that this was something serious.

He bent and raised Manjari's face.

A face red with tears.

Ratilal, with bent head, was flipping through the pages of *Modern Love,* as if trying to read.

Mohanlal remained lost in thought.

Suddenly Manjari spoke. "We both are not brother and sister. We have kept you in the dark. We are lovers. We have loved each other since childhood. I am bound to you by *dharma.* I have given you my body but my love I have given only to Ratilal. So I won't be able to leave him now. If you allow me, I can lead a married life with Ratilal."

At first, Mohanlal wanted to laugh aloud. But this was a very serious matter and a question of his life, so with a serious face he began to think. If Manjari leaves what will happen to these two children? Who will make millet *roti* and tamarind water for him when he works overtime? What will happen to the sentence Manjari speaks on Thursdays? Manjari went on speaking without pause.

"You have often seen us together—we have many pictures of us wearing white clothes, taken at Rekha Studio. We were born for each other." Having said this, Manjari rushed to Ratilal and stroked his hair with her fingers. Ratilal lifted his head from the love letters and his eyes met Manjari's.

Mohanlal did not know what to make of this. Slowly he went up to Manjari. Drawing her toward him, he said: "But if you and Ratilal love each other, why should you therefore live separately from me? Can't we all live together? I love you as much as Ratilal loves you. And if you leave me what will happen to our children?" Manjari had been thinking only of Ratilal. She hadn't given a thought to the children. Suddenly, at the thought of them, her motherly love gushed forth. She ran to the next room and picked up both her children. Ratilal and Mohanlal, their arms on each others' shoulders, witnessed this display of motherly love with delighted hearts.

Mohanlal thought, "I am nearly fifty-five. Ratilal is about fifty. So how many years are left to live?" Manjari too did not have any objection to living with Mohanlal and Ratilal. Even when she lived with Mohanlal alone she spent most of the day with Ratilal. Ratilal had no objection at all. Thus the three of them and the children entered a happy family life.

When they had a picture taken at Rekha Studio on Thursday, Manjari, dressed in white, stood in the middle. On one side was Mohanlal with a new black cap and a white moustache, and on the other side was Ratilal. There was no space even for a lotus leaf between the three of them. In the picture, two innocent children sat in front.

Kishori Charan Das:
"Sarama's Romance" (Oriya)

Introduced and translated by Sumanyu Satpathy

Well known writer Kishori Charan Das was born in 1942. "Sarama's Romance" was first published in *Jhakara*, the most prestigious Oriya magazine and then anthologized in *Bhanga Khelana*,[1] Das's first collection of short stories. It did not create any controversy.

[Sarama, the vivacious fifteen-year-old daughter of wealthy parents, is drawn to an older girl called Meera who is quiet and withdrawn.]

Why was it, then, that she got so much pleasure from being friendly with a girl like Sarama, who was so unlike herself? Why did Meera *Apa's*[2] languorous eyes soften whenever she saw Sarama? Why was it that her eyes expressed the bittersweetness of recovering something long lost? . . .

But even though she couldn't find an answer to the questions, Sarama was pleased because she thought she had found something new. In her adolescent mind she looked from different angles at the picture of this new person. Her curiosity surpassed her feelings of love—she was like a child gifted with a new toy.

[At a party at Meera's house, Sarama sings a song, to much acclaim. Meera is not asked to sing because]

. . . there was an intimate pathos in her singing, reminiscent of the deepening darkness of evening or of a calf gone astray, or of the irrevocability of inevitable cruelty. Such singing would be out of place at a noisy party.

---

1. Jeypore, Koraput: Bikash Pratisthan, 1961.
2. *Apa* means "older sister" and is here used as an honorific by younger girls addressing older girls.

Meera looked at Sarama and said very softly: "Do you really enjoy my singing?" Sarama didn't quite know what to say. She could not grasp the unusual intensity behind this simple question. To escape the silence, she smiled.

Suddenly she saw Meera Apa's face turn pale, as if she hadn't gotten what she expected to get. There was a shade of frustration in her normally languid eyes. Meera tried to go away but Sarama caught her by the hand and pulled her back. She looked at her and said: "Meera Apa!"

That one simple phrase, and everything was solved. All that Sarama wanted was to ease a complex situation. But her little gesture was perhaps enough to relieve Meera Apa. It was as if her eyes were saying: "You haven't quite been able to fathom my anguish, but you don't want to hurt me and that is enough."

Meera held Sarama's hands in her own for some time. Then she said abruptly: "I must go now."

Sarama kept gazing after her, curious and wondering. Her heart had softened toward Meera Apa.

That night she stayed awake for a long time, thinking of Meera Apa. What did she expect of her? Affection, sympathy, or something different? She felt as if she had attained adulthood. She was no longer a frivolous teenager capable of sharing only fun and laughter. She could give shelter too, like a grown-up person. She too could give solace to bleeding hearts. She swelled with the pride of a woman. She felt that she was no mere flower, delicate and pleasure-giving, but was now a giant banyan tree casting a huge shadow.

But wherein lay Meera Apa's anguish? Why was she so very different from her sisters, Neera and Dheera? They were married, whereas Meera, although she was the oldest, continued to be unwed. Why? Had no one found her a suitable match? Or was it that she didn't find anyone to her liking? Sarama couldn't believe that being outside a commonplace social institution like marriage could cause such anguish. No, there was some other reason.

Sarama kept asking herself that one question, and it made her feel happy. Meera Apa expected something of her—the favor of a woman, the shelter of love. It again occurred to her that she was now past adolescence. She had become a woman.

[At the prize-giving ceremony, Sarama receives many prizes and congratulations but Meera is not around. She leaves the crowd, goes in search of Meera and finds her reading alone in the garden.]

Meera looked at her and said: "I knew you would come to me."

"Why?" fickle Sarama asked with the innocuous curiosity of a child. Meera did not respond. Dusk was about to fall—the dusk of winter. There was no unruliness in the air; instead, there was eager anticipation. The naturally scarlet sun rays looked as though someone had smeared them with a liberal dose of vermilion. Here there was no party, no riotous celebration. Instead there was the hint of a secret preparation. As if someone was about to arrive, alone. Hence this silent preparation.

Sarama's playful eyes and Meera's melancholy liquid eyes met and continued to probe each other, as if to say something.

Then Meera took Sarama's hands and very gently drew her close. Sarama's books fell from her lap. Suddenly the inexperienced virgin felt the warm touch of two lips. Unexpectedly. Startled, she drew back. The blush on her face turned out to be the most beautiful thing the evening possessed.

The books lay there. Sarama got up and hurried back into the school where the cacophony continued—the ordinary hilarity of uncomplicated, normal people.

That one moment. Today it has come back to Sarama after a long time. Before falling asleep, her husband, Ajit Babu, asked: "Wasn't there a girl in your class called Meera Mahapatra? Who used to sing well?"

"Yes. Why?"

"You don't know? I heard she is going to marry that middle-aged history lecturer. He must be at least twenty-five years older than her. Well, stranger things have happened." So saying, Ajit Babu changed the subject.

But Sarama couldn't forget the subject so easily. So, she thought to herself, Meera Apa is to get married. Is it a love marriage? Who knows? Anyway, she is saved. Perhaps she will change now. An upper-class socialite woman kindles no fire of passion, does not plunge into experience. She is just an institution, her symbol the vermilion mark, her purpose procreation. Sarama smiled. Sentimental Meera Apa, the embodiment of melancholy—what would she do now?

Unnatural. Is this marriage of Meera Apa unnatural? Sarama recalled the day and the moment. What could be more unnatural than that?

Sarama kept thinking, brooding. Today she has truly grown up. She is a real woman now. Her husband lying next to her, two children on the other side. Today, there is no doubt that behind Meera Apa's love lay the self-expression of failed youth. In Sarama she had found compensation for unfulfilled desire. The unnatural face of a normal hunger.

Yet, Sarama asked, wasn't that chapter wonderful, and especially that unique moment? There was in that loving the first blush and tingle of the flesh. The world of the husband is a boat of duty, lust and money. There is in it peace, satisfaction—everything. But romance? She doesn't know what romance is. But perhaps in the perverted love of Meera Apa there was a touch of romance. Sarama wanted to look more intently at that past. No, never—one ought not to think of such things. She turned on her side and tried to sleep.

But she heard a vague song in the distance. Perhaps it was Meera Apa's pathetic, piteous cry. No, Meera Apa has not gotten married. She cannot marry. She was born only to crave, and cry. She craves for her Sarama even now. Sighing, Sarama was about to forget present reality. Why this perverted, improper thought? She felt with her hands the present, concrete reality. Her husband's flesh. The touch of hardness, the hot breath.

Crime of Passion

Summarized by Saleem Kidwai and Ruth Vanita

In these extracts from a 1980s judgment by an additional sessions judge, we conceal the identity of all parties. The judgment is interesting not only for its extreme homophobia but for the judge's refusal to consider the possibility that the victim, a Hindu, may have had a relationship, possibly sexual, with the accused, a Muslim. Both youths were students in an industrial training institute and lived in its dorms. On appeal, the death sentence was commuted to life imprisonment. All grammatical and spelling mistakes are in the original.

The Rector testified that on the night . . . he . . . noticed both S and D were in their rooms alone . . . at about 11:05 P.M. he and some others saw S appear running, his appearance "ghastly" and his hands and clothes smeared with blood. The accused confessed to the Rector that he had stabbed D.

They found the severely injured D. . . . The Company Doctor declared D dead when he arrived at the spot. . . . S confessed in a written statement. He was arrested and a diary seized from his person. From the room of the deceased, the police took, among other things, his diary, letters written by S and S's towel. From the room of the accused they took . . . an issue of *Time* magazine.

. . . According to [S's written statement], earlier he and the deceased D were friends. However, since some months before the incident there had been quarrels between them because of certain incidents of teasing, etc. According to him he attempted many times to gain revival of friendship with the deceased D. He had done his best to apologise D [sic] and requested him to pardon him. Despite all that, D had treated him with all insult and high-handedness . . . he had gone to the room of D, just to make one more attempt to revive the friendship and at that time D scolded him. . . . S went on to say that D had threatened him with a knife and in order to protect himself from D he had attacked D. . . .

I clearly find, in view of the letters written by the accused, which are four in number that it is the accused in whom was embedded a very ugly and noxious desire and intention which cannot have parallel in the human history. . . . It appears probable that earlier D and the accused might have friendship . . . at times they might have cut jokes which was natural with the age in question but it can never be taken to mean that the deceased D was giving any response to the accused. . . . It clearly appears from these letters that the accused was overpowered by irresistible desire and probably loitering in wrong impression that without D's friendship he would not be able to pull on. This shows as to what extreme a man completely over-powered by carnal desire can go.

. . . we also have got on record magazine by name "Time" . . . This magazine contains an article to the effect homosexuality in America. It is not disputed that this magazine was brought by the accused from the reading room and it was in his cupboard when the room was searched. Thus this finding of the magazine having direct bearing to the question of homosexuality would be another very strong circumstance to show the ill-desire of the accused with reference to the carnal aspect.

Then . . . [G's] evidence that the accused had also stated that he wanted to convert the sex of D and wanted to marry him and live as husband and wife, clearly indicated that in any case, he would have communicated that aspect to D. . . .

. . . Evidence of B clearly shows that on certain occasions, i.e., while working in the factory on the common machine, the accused used to come and tease D to the effect, "Homo, Homo." Then on the next day in the night in room No. 16 when D and B were busy in common study, the accused had gone there and again tried to tease D. On this occasion, as the evidence of B stands, there was end of patience of D and D had given *chappal* [slipper] beating to the accused. . . .

. . . His diary entries show that D used to take regular exercise, used to go for swimming. The boy definitely had so many good habits which indicated that he had a healthy mind and healthy career. . . . The accused is before me and is appearing a very thin fellow as compared to the deceased who was healthy and stout as can be seen from his photographs also.

[The Judge refused to consider the Nanavati case as relevant . . .][1]

. . . the accused who is young has committed this ghastly act of murder of the innocent boy D . . . only because of his carnal lust and homosexuality both irresistible. . . . This case is also an illustration as to how the things are going in the young world in various hostels and educational institutions. . . . The young generation of this country, particularly the students for the last some years are flouting high and reach traditions of our Indian Universities. The basic idea of scholarship as it exists in the Indian thought is that the student spends certain minimum years of his life in pursuit of knowledge, cultivation of good habits and discipline and necessarily observe strict bachelorhood and abstinence from the physical lust . . .

---

1. Nanavati had shot his wife and her male lover. He aroused tremendous public sympathy and was not given the death sentence because the murder was seen as an impulsive crime of passion.

. . . in this country there might be thousands of parents who worry about their wards in colleges, schools and hostels. . . . Thus the deterrent theory if applied, this case would definitely warrant that ultimate penalty will have to be inflicted as provided by law. This is absolutely necessary to serve as an eye opener for the young generation.

. . . it is impossible to convince oneself in the matter of lesser punishment as persons like the accused S would take that for such unsanctifiable acts one can escape from the clutches of the Law only with life imprisonment. . . . The persons diseased with such unnatural tendencies towards carnal desires and homosexuality are nothing but a cancer that would prove disastrous to the society and consequently to the Nation. . . .

. . . the question of reformative aspect was tried to be urged by [the lawyer] for the accused. . . . Reformation of carnal tendencies is possible when a person is still on the threshold of boyhood from when such tendencies develop. The very age of the accused which is of 22 years shows that many years back he crossed the bar for reformation. He is in fact on the threshold of becoming a full-fledged man. . . . Such infection has to be thrown out from the society, as, such a man who can be over powered by irresistible carnal lust, is no better than a beast. . . .

. . . I think there can be no other fittest case for inflicting death sentence, keeping in view the interest of society and the Nation at Large. In this case everything was extreme and therefore, penalty has to be extremely deterrent.

. . . The accused shall be hanged by the neck till he is dead subject to the confirmation of the sentence by the Hon'ble High Court.

Shobhana Siddique: *"Full to the Brim" (Hindi)*[1]

Translated by Ruth Vanita

The author of this story, born Shobhana Bhutani, studied at the National School of Drama, Delhi. She wrote short stories and plays *Shayad Haan, To Phir,* and *Aur Kal* before her tragic death by drowning in 1974.

Madan has got up. A cigarette between his lips, he has put on his shirt. He has opened the window. I am lying unclothed on this wide bed. Below me is spread a dark brown satin sheet with large pink roses all over it. A pillow embroidered with "Sweet Dreams" has fallen on the floor. A soft pillow lies under my hips. It is perfectly still outside. A breeze enters the room, bearing the perfume of your armpits, a perfume that drives me crazy even today. Madan's way of smoking is very careless—he barely touches the cigarette with his forefinger and middle finger, so that it seems as if it is about to fall. You hold a cigarette tightly in a clenched fist. I draw deeply on a Simla cigarette. When you take a drag your small slanting eyes grow even smaller. You look exactly like a Chinese merchant. Taking a last pull you suddenly throw away the cigarette with a jerk—and the blood begins to race through my veins, continues tingling for a long time. Energy seems ready to explode from every small, big, and even unnecessary action of yours. As if lava bursts from within you, emerges boiling from your fingernails, and spreads all around you. It overshadows everything that is in your proximity. It crushes every bone in my body. This alone is your strength. For you are very ordinary looking. A flat dark face, small eyes, a broad nose, full lips that seem ready to burst into laughter, and a long tight plait that seems to defy people. But there is an aura around you—perhaps your

1. Published in the discontinued *Sreshtha Kahaniyan* series, Delhi: Stara Paket Buksa, no date.

eccentricity. I feel afraid of your beauty because it depends so completely on your energy. As soon as your energy ebbs, your beauty will begin to rot like a stale fish. Then you will look coarse and ugly. That is why I want to squeeze every drop from these moments. I want to suck the nectar out of you, swallow you whole as as a lizard does an insect. So that when I leave you or when you tire of me, your attraction will have vanished and no one will think you worth tasting. You sit down next to me like a fanfare of drums. Why are you looking at me as if you have never seen me before? I consider my body through your eyes. Small fair feet, long slim legs lightly sprinkled with golden hair, dirty knees, full fair thighs, wide but slender hips, a slightly darker waist with a blue mark on it from tying my *salwar* tightly. Without a salwar, my waist looks less slim. Long full pink breasts with two dark brown dots, oh how delicate. A big gap between the two breasts, more than is usual. Whichever part you glance at comes alive. Every part begins panting like a small puppy, begins desiring you, begins demanding you. You hide your face between my breasts and remain perfectly still. A cry leaps out from every pore in my body and rises upward through me. I want to disappear, but the cry keeps echoing like the sobbing of a hungry cat. You take my face between your hands and look at me with overflowing eyes. How sensitive your face becomes. The warmth of your hands makes my skin tender, very tender. I see in your eyes that I am beautiful. My head droops slightly to the right. With what pride you smile. A shameless smile that begins on your lips and spreads to your temples, keeps spreading. Your yellow teeth shine. You find it amusing to see me in this state. Drawing a line on my left cheek with the hand that is holding it, you ask, "Well, what's happening, little sexpot?" I feel terribly shy. That word vibrates through me like someone blowing on a spiderweb. The web keeps trembling. Fighting my sensations, I say, "Nothing" in a quivering voice. "Really? Nothing?" you say, running your lips over my ear, "And now?" A wave rises beneath my controlled voice: "No, nothing," and then I say loudly "What can happen?" You brazenly get up and bring over the mirror that is hanging on the wall. "Look here." When I see my face in the mirror, I feel surprise, anger, embarrassment. I hide my face in my hands and say, "No, no, it's nothing, I have a headache, I have fever, a high fever." You throw down my hand and hiss, "I have happened to you." You throw the mirror on the bed and burst out laughing. The walls and the roof vibrate. How distorted your sense of humor is. You don't understand that this is not a joke. You can make a joke of anything.

You are the most brazen girl in our college. The salt and spice of your attractiveness is your good health. When I walk with you I feel that I'm the most important girl in the world. You stride along, scattering energy all around you. You walk down the corridor as if the whole building belongs to you and all the girls are your subjects. And I the special slave whom you find charming. Your beloved slavegirl.

We sit on the lawn behind the college, under the mulberry tree. You are talking very freely to Umesh, Sinha, Kapoor. In your presence all these boys seem like cooing pigeons. One feels like pinching their cheeks as one does a child's. Srivastava brings two dozen bananas. You lean forward and break off one. This little movement of yours seems charged with significance—more significance than life itself. Every gesture, every posture, every expression of yours seems so vast, as if you have the capacity to capture, to embrace the whole world. You devour the banana and throw the skin into the air, it gets stuck on a branch above. Ramanujam offers peanuts, first to you and then to me. You give him a come-hither look and smile. Oh, how I hate you for that. . . . You constantly seek the company of boys so that people may be misled into thinking that you are interested only in boys. You send off all these wretched dogs on a wrong scent. I silently applaud your cunning. Umesh asks, "Nanu, what is your hobby?" You reply, "Politics and sex." Umesh doesn't know where to look. To hide his nervousness, he says, "Yesterday Mr. Chatterjee was really gazing at you." You say, "Oh, you naughty boy," and pretend shyness, to offset your earlier mention of sex. What cheap behavior. I wish I could tear you and Umesh to pieces, no, throw you to the jackals. One day I'll push you down from some high cliff. I feel ashamed of your behavior. At such times, I don't exist for you because you flirt with them in my presence. You become the focus of their appreciation. Even though I am prettier than you, it is you the boys always admire, and somehow this seems natural. "Who's for coffee?" says Umesh, and you immediately second him. You might refuse at least once in a way! In your place, I would have refused at once, and then we two could have gone off alone and talked to our hearts' content.

Ramanujam, Sinha and I quickly cross the road. You say in a girlish way, "Oh, there's a car coming," and then Umesh puts his arm around your waist and takes you across the road. Even after crossing the road, his hand stays there for quite a while, and you do not move away. Shameless creature. How you act the helpless little thing to allure the boys. You always want to appear feminine when they are around. Is it possible that you really like boys? I look at your blooming face and feel sick. The restaurant is so suffocating. I want to get up and run away.

I stop talking to you. I am filled with suspicion and doubt. I hate you—or is it that I want to hate you? So that when I come back to you after some days your strength will seem doubled to me and I will be helpless before you, helpless with desire to have you. You will assert your claim to me, conquer me at night and suck the pith from me, empty me out.

Whenever I stop talking to you, you spend a lot of time with Ramanujam, Umesh and Sinha. You also talk and laugh with Uma, Mehrunisa, Kiran and Prabha, but all the time you are very aware of me. You try to demonstrate in small ways how much you need me. Oh, how I hate the sight of you. As soon as I see you, I stand more erect and turn away my face. Your eyes are filled with pain. When I get back to my room, I feel like crying. No one tells me I am pretty these days. I wear pink yet the boys do not look at me. I cover my face with cream and powder. "Why are you whitewashing yourself?" the girls ask. I have to give up powder and acknowledge that I look sick. Perhaps my feelings are very obvious or else it seems to me that everyone knows what is the matter with me.

At bedtime, you come to our room to return one of Uma's books. You don't look at me. When it is your turn to serve the food in the dining hall, you bring crisp chapatis for me, you throw a piece of lemon into my plate, you serve me curd and sugar twice over. I feel very irritated by these strategies of yours. But I am very hungry so I eagerly eat the crisp chapatis. I behave as if I haven't noticed anything unusual. But when my stomach is full, I feel exasperated with myself. You never dare come and ask me directly why I am angry with you. But you lightly brush your body against me, as we are walking along. When I don't react, your ego is hurt. I am amused by your childishness, and feel quite detached from you.

But suddenly the energy vanishes from your stride. You begin to turn pale. The teachers and your male and female followers begin to pay more attention to me. Gradually, all the reasons why I couldn't bear you begin to fade. And then one day they disappear altogether. I have to look for reasons to continue being angry with you but I can't find any. I feel sorry for you when you carry on your act. After all, you are doing all this to placate me. Poor thing, what techniques she uses. What right have I to be so cruel to anyone? What wrong have you done me? How pale you look! I should be ashamed of myself. I can never forgive myself. Suddenly I leave the class and run, panting, to your room. You throw aside your book (how fond you are of throwing things) and ask, "Want some water?" These moments are unbearable for both of us. You look at me as if you have found a lost treasure, as if you had given up hope of my returning. But you should know that I always return to you in the end. You lie down on the bed. We lie for a long time with our backs to each other. It seems unnatural to start once more. But it also seems unnatural to do nothing. Sometimes your foot or your plait brushes against me. I quiver and remain still. This unintended contact excites me terribly. But you don't take me. I put up with this, although I want to pounce on you, crush you, chew your bones. The day passes. You keep reading. I hear the sound of the pages turning. Whenever the sound stops I stop breathing. Have you gone to sleep? I can never bear to look at you asleep. . . .

You have really gone to sleep. You do not move at all. All my nerves are on edge, waiting. It is not yet midnight. . . . I go out into the corridor and try to read in the dim light. The words turn into ciphers and a cold anguish settles in my stomach. Am I afraid? Or is this excitement? What will you say? How will you begin? What will I reply? Will I be able to speak or will I choke? And you? Will you stand far off, silent, making my predicament more difficult or will you lovingly embrace me? I will wait, head bent, like an offender. I will accept whatever punishment you mete out. I want to run away but I cannot. Even if I run away I will return at midnight to receive my punishment.

It is midnight. You take a candle and examine my face. I pretend to be asleep. Your eyes shine with victory. So you knew all along? I do not like this cool look on your face. You touch my left cheek with your hand, scratch my temples, blow softly into my left ear. Then you tap with your fingers on my eyelids. Your touch is very soft and light. My body yearns to grab hold of your touch. Helpless sounds burst from my throat. For a long time, you continue to tease me like this. When I can no longer bear your touch and begin to moan, you pounce on me like a tiger. You draw my tongue into your mouth, crush my lips and suck my teeth. Your big hands play with me for a while, and then gradually you enter me. I feel very proud. Because your lava, your energy, your blossoming health enter me. I slowly keep rising, keep rising, and then, when I climax, you are very loving. For some reason you seem very grateful when I come. Then you put your cool lips there. I am sinking into love. I feel as if my blood is slowly ebbing from a high place. I feel a slow sweet dizziness. At that moment I realize how deprived I was all these days. You like early mornings. I wake you up, you whimper and fight me, fight yourself, for a long time, then you are defeated by my tenderness and dependence. I bite your chin gently. Overwhelmed, you hide your face in my cleavage. Yes, your mother is a whore, your father is a drunkard, lying drunk in some alley, you are my lost son, are you not, my life. Before you come, you say, "Who are you, tell me who you are, where do you live, what do you do, why have you come here, what are you to me, why do you give me such happiness, why do you leave me, why do you come back again, what are you to me, why do you leave me, why do you come back again, tell me, answer me, who are you, where have you come from, where—" You talk like a mad person, first slowly, then faster and faster, merely touching some words and breathing life into others. Then your words become indistinct, broken. You leave words incomplete and seem to sink into a swoon, then just before you come you suddenly fall silent—only your pulse throbs. I lay my head on your feet and fall asleep. The next day you have a slight headache or a hangover from smoking too much dope. How irritable you become. Your enthusiasm for life, which is so attractive, suddenly vanishes. You complain like a sick child. Was your enthusiasm based merely on a healthy body? A little weakness and your confidence flies away like a pigeon. All the girls sit around, but you don't listen to anyone. Uma brought you two Anacins but you refused them. But you accepted a codopyrine from me. You close your eyes and lie still when I tell you to do so. You never stay with the same girl for more than two months, or three months at the very most. But we have been together seven months. It is becoming a challenge for me to keep you with me. The other girls are beginning to notice this.

A week later. You have started keeping three seats together in the class. I think you have kept a seat for Uma because she is my roommate. How blind human beings can be! One day I arrived first and forgot to keep a chair for Uma, yes I forgot, all right, I deliberately didn't keep a chair for her, what will you do to me? You looked at me, then joined two chairs and sat down between both of us.

Now Uma is always with the two of us. I am not hostile to Uma but I don't believe in friendship between three people. I don't think three people can be good friends at the same time without one of them feeling like an unwanted third. And that is what gradually happens. You two enjoy talking for hours about politics or about yourselves. You forget my presence. Uma doesn't forget. She deliberately keeps you entangled by her wiles. So I don't resent her behavior. But you actually forget that I am sitting there. When I catch you at it, you try to hide it, but your efforts only make it more evident. New buds have appeared on the mulberry tree. How fresh they are. What pure beauty! I don't consider Uma more beautiful than I am. She is not at all beautiful. Not in the least. No, she isn't. At least, you never have liked her kind of looks. When she sits in the sun scrubbing her small feet, with what innocent wonder you watch her. Alas, what attraction there is in novelty, in new desire!

I close my eyes like the proverbial ostrich. I try desperately to explain away your behavior. After all, why should you confine yourself to me? I am not your friend. You are interested in politics, so is Uma, but I am not. (My older sister says silliness is attractive in girls). Sometimes when you are sitting near me, before I have finished talking, you get up and go off: "Oh, I have to study with Uma." You study together till two in the morning. Sometimes you ask me something which tells me that you haven't heard what I told you a fortnight ago. You forget many important things I have told you. But I have begun to put up with these insults because I cannot live without you, even for a moment. You have become a very personal need of mine, like the need to urinate. You always were. But in the beginning, I used to fight this need in myself. Now I cannot even fight with you. I am beginning to feel fulfilled now that I have you. I have become very delicate, a bundle of tenderness. You are exasperated by my passivity in bed. You say irritably, "Love me, love me." But I enjoy lying silent. That initial mad eagerness for every free moment between classes, every night, is disappearing. Sometimes, a fortnight passes without my missing it. But you have begun to wander like a thirsty ghost. You can't sleep. Many girls have noticed your discontent and have started trying to seduce you. They never dared before. It is you who must have incited them now!

One dark evening, you were stroking my soft palms. At that moment I felt all that I had imagined was false, my delusion. Your hands were solid and cold. The perfume of your armpits disturbed me. At that moment you had really come back to me. A short figure approached us. Suddenly you dropped my hand, drew away and said: "Yes, yes, I understand your point but I don't think you are right, in fact I would say that—" Uma was standing next to us. "Umey"—your lips were trembling. You stood up without another word. In the darkness Uma's eyes shone with a cruel satisfaction.

As I entered the room my image leapt at me from the mirror. How pale I have become, how old I look, how wrinkled. How hard it is to take each step. Perhaps I have no beauty at all, it is you who give it to me. How quickly I tire these days. I don't feel like doing anything at all.

You are with Uma in my room. I am lying on your bed in your room. Whenever you kiss her, these walls echo. You return very late in the night. You look prepared for a fight. But I don't say anything. You are disappointed. You feel I am becoming indifferent to you. I know you so well. How transparent you are. Once I have sought out a reason for every action of yours, I no longer feel angry, just sad. Sometimes I feel that although you are going out of my orbit, you can never become part of Uma's being—perhaps one day you will realize this and return. You have started spending more and more time with Uma. I have withdrawn into the background. For the first time, I look closely at Uma. A very fair complexion, wide jaws that are no longer rigid these days, a small upturned nose, small slanting brown eyes, bright red full—no, thick lips, brown hair. How beautiful Uma is! At night, I wait for her to return to our room. She returns, mussed up, relaxed, happy, and lies down on her bed. I keep looking at her—enchanted. There is nothing I can do. I would like to be attracted to boys. But I feel disgusted by them, afraid of them, I remember that childhood incident. Is there not a cruelty lurking in their eyes? And then, such a complete union with them is not possible as it is between you and me. Should I get married? What will it be like? How will I feel? These days such futile questions fill my head. But as long as you are around I can never be attracted to Umesh, Ramanujam, any of them. Because you overshadow them, all of us, these trees, this building. One laugh of yours scatters them all.

I didn't return after the final exam. What is the use of doing an MA? What great things have I achieved with a BA? I don't want to take up a job. I don't have the courage to compete in a men's world. Mother keeps insisting that I get married. If I ask for a second roti, she looks reproachfully at me, she is constantly worried about me. Every now and then she says, "The prices are rising, how long will your father—?" Father does not say anything but he does not oppose Mother either. He did oppose my older sister's marriage. Mother stopped sleeping with him in protest. Father was forced to give in to her. Next year Father will retire and Mother will have to give tuitions to make money. Madan has a beautiful body, so beautiful that it is not attractive. If his glance ever falls on my naked body, he says, "Oh sorry," and turns away. I find this amusing. He never forgets to pat me before leaving for office. He takes great care of me. Gradually I will get used to this situation. Let's see. Everything will be fine once I have children. Perhaps after we live together for many years I will start loving Madan. That is what everyone does. I enlarge the bindi on my forehead. Today Madan's aunt is coming on a visit. How beautiful she is. Is my lipstick looking good? She will stay for two or three days. Sleeping with Madan is such a nuisance.

V. T. Nandakumar:
Two Girls (Malayalam)[1]

Translated by T. Muraleedharan

Well-known novelist Nandakumar was born in 1925 in a royal family in Kodungallur. His novel *Randu Penkuttikal* (Two Girls), published in 1974, went into three editions in the first year of publication and was filmed in 1978. It then went out of print but, following our inclusion of these extracts in this book, another Malayalam edition was issued in 1999, with an English foreword by T. Muraleedharan, recounting his experience of discovering and translating these extracts for us.

⬦ ⬦ ⬦

Author's Foreword to the Second Edition

. . . While working for *Yatra Weekly,* I used to handle a regular column under the title "Problem-Solution." Its purpose was to suggest solutions to the personal problems of the readers. That is how I came across the details of an unusual love story of two young girls studying at a tutorial college.

The problem was raised by a girl who had been in love with a friend whom she considered her "sweetheart" and whom she tried to dominate. She was shocked when she accidentally saw this friend engaged in love games with one of the male teachers in the college. Her letter sought advice on how to discourage her friend from such a relationship with a man. Through our subsequent correspondence unfurled the queer details of the love affair as well as the physical relationship these girls had shared. When I remembered the finer points of that affair, narrated to me without anything being withheld, the profiles of Girija and the pretty Kokila took shape in my mind. That became *Randu Penkuttikal* (Two Girls).

While *Two Girls* was being serialized in *Chitrakarthika Weekly,* those who read it eagerly were mainly women and girl students. I also remember a warden of a ladies' hostel

---

1. This translation from the third edition (Kodungallur: Devi Book Stall, 1985).

confessing to me that she had come across many cases similar to the lesbian relationship shared by Girija and Kokila.

Nowadays such instances are not treated with as much secrecy nor are they uncommon any more. . . .

Lesbianism—which means a love affair between women—is now ubiquitous. In my opinion this passion is likely to be widespread among the young women of Kerala who, by nature, are extraordinarily sensitive. Such relationships have some healthy and positive potential hence they are important.

I came to know that the film adaptation of my novel, which appeared recently, was rejected even by girls. Perhaps this was because lesbianism, which is the soul of my story, was absent in the film. On the other hand, this second edition of the novel—which consists of 3,000 copies—is a clear indication of the fact that *Two Girls* is being widely read.

Let me conclude by praying for the growth and prosperity of lesbianism.

[Girija, only daughter of a wealthy businessman, plays with the neighbor's son Gopi but is repulsed when he tries to kiss her. She wants to be strong like him and to kiss a beautiful girl. When Kokila joins her school, Girija realizes that this girl not only meets but surpasses her fantasy of a beautiful female. She becomes friendly with Kokila, her two siblings Usha and Raghu, and their mother, a widowed factory worker. One day Kokila visits Girija's house and is overwhelmed by the expensive decor. Both Girija and her mother admire Kokila's beauty and insist that she wear some of Girija's clothes that she has outgrown. Girija makes up Kokila's face and arranges her hair. She is violently attracted to Kokila and longs to tell her she loves her. They become intimate friends and are teased by the other girls who ask if they are going to marry each other.

Girija sees Kokila talking to Sarah, a senior student and basketball champion. She forbids Kokila to talk to Sarah and Kokila promises to obey but continues to meet Sarah secretly. When Girija catches them coming out of the toilet together, she flies into a rage, slaps Kokila, and leaves her crying. The next evening Kokila comes to Girija's house.]

Girija didn't speak as she ascended the stairs. Kokila followed her quietly. They entered the bedroom in silence. Girija quickly closed the door behind them. While Kokila looked on uncomprehendingly, Girija securely bolted the door and sat down on the bed.

"Come and sit here," Girija said, patting the bed. Kokila hesitated. Girija repeated in an authoritative voice: "Sit down." Kokila timidly approached the bed and sat down, some distance away from Girija. She smiled bashfully but seductively.

"Sit closer to me." Girija caught hold of her hands and pulled her closer. "What are you up to?" Kokila inquired, with an alluring lisp. Gently stroking her long hair, Girija said: "I want to talk to you."

Kokila waited patiently, stealthily watching Girija from the corners of her eyes. Girija gazed at her intently and suddenly asked: "Kokila, do you love me?"

"Yes," Kokila nodded.

"I want to know if you really *love* me."

Kokila nodded again.

"Do you love me, and only me?"

"Yes."

"Don't you love anyone else?" Girija asked uncertainly.

Kokila shook her head and quickly waved back the curls that bounced on to her forehead.

"Then why did you talk to that slut?"

"She always tries to pick up a conversation with me."

"Even after I told you never to talk to her, why did you do so?" Kokila did not reply. A shadow of fear ran across her face. Lowering her eyes, she started chewing her nails.

"Why did you go to the toilet with her?" Girija's voice became rough—the memory of the incident brought the embers back into her eyes. Kokila did not reply. With downcast eyes, she continued chewing her nails.

"Tell me." Girija forcibly lifted her face. Staring into her eyes, she insisted: "Tell me—I want to know everything."

. . . Kokila looked up helplessly, pulled down the lower hem of her blouse and said as if in soliloquy: "She touched my face."

"Then, then?" Girija's grip on her shoulder became tighter, almost crushing.

"She said something and touched me here." Kokila indicated her bosom. Girija glared at the spot with overwhelming jealousy. Kokila quickly pulled her half-sari over the cute projections there.

Girija was furious. "Why didn't you scream for help?"

Kokila turned her face to look at Girija and asked in a surprised voice: "Why should I scream? Isn't she also a girl?"

Girija remained silent for a few moments. Suddenly she asked: "Then why do you move away when I try to touch you? Am I not a girl too?"

"Yes, but—." Kokila paused and covered her face bashfully.

"But what? What is wrong with me?"

"When you touch me, I feel ticklish. That is the reason. Besides, the way you look at me, I feel as if—I feel—" As she continued, with her face covered, Girija's arms encircled her. Holding her close, she suddenly started showering kisses on her neck, her face, her lips, whispering: "Yes, yes, I love you, my dear. You are mine. I want you. I want all of you—your mind and body!"

Kokila started giggling uncontrollably and tried to wriggle out of the embrace. But Girija forced her on to her lap and Kokila, once again, covered her face with both hands. Forcibly removing the hands, Girija gazed into her eyes; stroking her breasts, she said: "Don't ever let anyone else touch these, they are mine and mine alone." Kokila kept struggling to push away Girija's hands and get up; she whispered breathlessly: "*Chechi* [older sister], please, please—let me go. What if someone—?"

Girija was lost in thought. When she turned her eyes back to Kokila a few moments later, a faint smile was on her lips, a smile declaring unconditional love.

Stroking Kokila's face and hair softly, she closed her eyes and murmured as if in deep meditation: "O God! Please, please let her be mine forever, forever—"

In the state of bliss that followed, the first ever explicit expression of her secret passions, Girija remained motionless for some time. Kokila had sprung up and started smoothing her hair and adjusting her clothes. Stealthily she glanced at Girija and saw that she was watching her intently. The expression on Girija's face did not make her nervous any more; instead, she quite liked it. It was calm and serene. She smiled with a sense of satisfaction. Taking Kokila's hands and pressing them against her own bosom, Girija asked: "Kokila, will you ever leave me?"

Kokila shook her head. "No."

"Will you ever get married?"

She did not respond immediately. After a few moments' reflection, she said: "What if mother decides—"

Pressing her hands closer to her bosom, Girija declared: "No, you and I will never marry. We will live together."

Kokila shifted her eyes to the wall and asked in a tone of surprise: "But shouldn't we have children?"

"No. We don't want any children. Just you and me."

[Vijayan, a male teacher at school, falls in love with Kokila and proposes marriage. Kokila is flattered but afraid to respond. To turn Kokila against Vijayan, Girija tells her that he had proposed to Girija as well. The two girls go to a studio to get themselves photographed together. The photographer, a handsome youth named Suresh, also starts pursuing Kokila, who slips out of the house to meet him, telling her mother she is going to meet Girija. Girija becomes suspicious but Kokila placates her by writing a love letter.]

My dearest Chechi. . . . I shall never forget you. My love for you grows with every passing day. The day you leave me I shall die of a broken heart. I cannot write down all that is in my mind. I shall visit you on Saturday and tell you all. We will spend the night together. . . . Then you can do all that you used to talk about. All your desires will be fulfilled. I am ready for everything. But, Chechi, you should never suspect or misunderstand me. I desire nothing but your love.

Every night before sleeping, I lie looking at your photograph for a long time. My kisses have made the photo wet many a time. Sometimes I even cry a bit, thinking of you.

[When Kokila visits Girija's house, Girija gives her some of her expensive gold jewelry—a necklace and some bangles—as a gift.]

Winking suggestively, Girija proceeded up the staircase. Kokila lingered for a while, not sure what to do; then she accompanied Girija. The two girls reached the bedroom door. Entering the room, Girija switched on the light and fan. She noticed that Kokila was standing outside, plotting unintelligible designs on the mosaic floor with her toe. Is she traumatized by mysterious fears or doubts? Girija wondered. Or are these merely signs of the natural bashfulness of an inexperienced maiden?

"Why don't you come in, Kokila?" invited Girija.

Kokila raised her head, blushed profusely, and delicately stepped into the room. Girija chuckled. She carefully closed and bolted the door. Kokila took care to remain beyond reach. Girija parked herself on the bed. Casting her eyes down in nervous bashfulness, Kokila kept moving away and was soon in front of the mirror.

"Kokila, come and sit here," Girija invited again.

"No, I would rather stand here."

"Come on, Kokila!" Girija pleaded in a sweet voice. Kokila reluctantly came and seated herself on a corner of the bed—away from Girija. When the breeze dislodged her half-sari, she readjusted it with a tense urgency. When it tried to betray her again, she tucked its end into her waistband.

"Are you frightened of me?" Girija asked. Kokila shook her head in the negative. Girija smiled. Tugging at her hands lightly, she repeated the entreaty: "Come on, sit closer to me." Kokila obeyed like a child, her face still lowered and one finger pressed hard against her own lips. The curls on her forehead were rioting in the fan's breeze. Girija tried to wave them back but failed and proceeded, instead, to stroke her hair.

"How much do you love me, Kokila?" asked Girija.

"Quite a lot!" Kokila murmured.

"Will you ever betray me?" Girija placed a hand on her shoulder. Kokila remained silent. She sat looking at the lamp hanging from the ceiling. Girija hugged her.

"Won't you be mine forever?" she whispered in Kokila's ear, resting her head on her shoulder.

Kokila nodded shyly, then returned her eyes to the lamp. Girija smiled as she realized the implication. She got up and switched off the light and the room plunged into darkness. She returned to the bed. The scent and warmth of Kokila's body, and her presence so close to herself, spread flames across Girija's mind and body. Her instincts went berserk. Wild desire broke tethers. To restrain it was no longer possible. Entwining her arms around Kokila, Girija pressed her hard against her bosom. Kokila whimpered mildly—a sweet, almost inaudible sound. It sounded like a luscious birdsong to Girija. Showering passionate kisses on her lips and face, Girija murmured: "My pet, you are mine. Mine and mine alone."

Kokila pressed her hands against Girija's bosom and said in a muffled voice: "My Chechi." Pushing her down on the bed and stroking her all over her body, Girija replied: "My Kokila." There came only a hiss in response from Kokila. Hugging each other, they rolled all over the bed. Girija continued to shower kisses all over Kokila's body. Kokila winced in mild protest as Girija's fingers crept over her back toward the hooks on her blouse. She quickly pulled the blanket over both of them.

"What is this for?" Girija asked in a low, panting voice.

"Think of the shame if anyone comes to know," Kokila whispered in her ear.

"My pet, my sweet darling." Girija crushed her warm nude body against her own. Kokila's fingers trailed all over Girija's bare back. Suddenly everything turned topsy turvy. The sun rose in the west and set in the east. Then he rose again in the east and set in the west. North and south became south and north. Both the girls sank in a shimmering whirlpool of passion. When they emerged, they were panting uncontrollably, drenched in sweat as well as the overflow of a rapturous ecstasy, still locked in a deep embrace.

"My dearest Kokila," Girija said in an exhausted yet overwhelming voice.

"Yes," Kokila responded enervatedly.

"Shall I call you 'Koki' from now on?"

Kokila smiled. With a kind of satisfaction never experienced before, she caught Girija's legs within her own bare ones. Stroked her bare back with her petal-soft fingers. Pressed her sweaty bosom against Girija's fleshy one. Her eyes were closed, but her fingers kept roaming all over Girija's body.

Dawn. Girija was the first to awaken. Not sure whether or not it was all a dream, she placed her hand on her own waist and realized that it was bare. With inexpressible satisfaction, she got up and gathered her clothes. Kokila was still under the blanket, lost in a cozy, dreamful slumber. The innocence of an infant gleamed on her face. Girija slowly lifted the blanket and for a moment, stood gazing at the nudity beneath it. Then she lowered the blanket, bent forward to press her lips softly on Kokila's forehead and murmured: "My Koki, my dearest Koki."

She picked up her clothes and walked toward the bathroom.

[Kokila feels torn between Girija and Suresh and commences a sexual relationship with Suresh as well. He promises to marry her and she reluctantly gives him Girija's necklace to help meet the nuptial expenses. He promises to return it soon. Meanwhile Girija's parents are trying to arrange her marriage to Babu, a doctor who has moved in next door. Suresh absconds with the necklace and also with money stolen from his employer. Shattered, Kokila confesses to Girija, who is furious and assaults her but later forgives her and they sleep together once more.

Girija refuses Babu's marriage proposal and tells Kokila that if there is no other way out, they should commit suicide together, an idea that terrifies Kokila. When Vijayan resumes his pursuit of Kokila, Girija tells him about Kokila's affair with Suresh, hoping this will lead him to lose interest in her. Meanwhile, Babu, who has been reading an English book titled *Lesbian,* tells Girija that Kokila is a woman who will inevitably seek out a man and that Girija herself is going through a temporary phase that will pass. Girija once again refuses his proposal of marriage and runs away, crying. Kokila accepts Vijayan's proposal and writes Girija a letter, begging forgiveness.

Girija almost faints when she receives the letter but sets off in a daze to Kokila's house, carrying all her gold jewelry and whatever cash she has. Kokila pretends that the marriage has been arranged against her wishes. Girija does not respond, but merely asks if Kokila is happy. In confusion, Kokila answers that she is. Girija then gives her the packet containing the jewelry, saying it is a wedding present, and walks out of the house. Kokila opens the packet and cannot believe her eyes. She calls to Girija but she does not stop. Kokila breaks down and weeps uncontrollably.

Girija tries to buy sleeping pills to commit suicide but no chemist is willing to sell them to her. In desperation she walks into a hospital where she meets Babu and pleads

with him to give her sleeping pills. Babu persuades her to lie down and have some coffee, and then talks to her about man-woman relationships. He persuades her that all that
has happened was destined to happen because all women need men. He reiterates his
willingness to marry her if she so desires. Girija feels a surge of relief and they embrace
each other.]

Vijay Dan Detha:
"A Double Life" (Rajasthani)

Introduced and translated by Ruth Vanita

Vijay Dan Detha is one of India's leading short story writers and among the most eminent writing in Rajasthani today. Winner of a Sahitya Akademi award, he is a founder of the Rupayan Sansthan, Jodhpur, an institution that documents Rajasthani folklore, art and music. He is the author of *Baatan Ni Phulwadi* (A Garden of Tales), a collection of short stories that draw on folklore. Some of Dan Detha's longer short stories, of which "Dohri Joon" (A Double Life) is one, have been published in Hindi in two volumes entitled *Duvidha* and *Uljhan*.

The story excerpted here has been translated from Hindi, which is very closely related to Rajasthani and is written in the same script, Devanagari.[1] A play based on this story and entitled "Beeja-Teeja" was performed in New Delhi in the early 1980s.

May Eros, the formless one, be gracious and give to each one of us a double life.

Once upon a time there were two villages at a distance of twenty-four and twenty-four, that is, forty-eight miles apart from each other. The moneylenders in these two villages were famous for their stinginess. . . . Though they lived far from each other, they were close friends. And as luck would have it, the two got married on the same night. Their hands were joined to two extremely beautiful brides and pearls were generated simultaneously in the two oysters. In their joy, the two moneylenders promised each other

---

1. This translation from *Duvidha aur anya Kahaniyan* (New Delhi: Rajkamal Prakashan, 1979), 147–77. For an English translation of the complete story, see Vijay Dan Detha, *The Dilemma and Other Stories*, trans. Ruth Vanita (New Delhi: Manushi Prakashan, 1997).

that regardless of which had a daughter and which a son, the offspring would be united in marriage. Thus, while still in the womb, the two children were linked together.

. . . In the ninth month, under the influence of the same planet, two girls were born. Intoxicated partly by his pledge and partly by greed, one Seth played false. He announced his daughter's birth by beating a copper plate instead of a winnowing basket and sent the barber to his friend's village with the news of a son's birth. Both Seths celebrated the occasion by distributing molasses.

[The girl is raised as a boy. Despite his wife's remonstrations, the Seth insists on going ahead with her marriage to the other girl, because he is unwilling to break his pledge and because he wants the dowry. The girl is told by a married friend, who has caught a glimpse of her naked, that she is not a man. She refuses to believe this and adds: "Even if I had been a woman instead of a man, I would not have refused this marriage. After all, marriage is a union of two hearts. If the hearts of two women unite, why should they not get married?" After marriage, the two girls spend two nights gazing into one another's eyes. On the third night, the groom removes her shirt and the bride realizes the truth. The groom feels guilty but the bride reassures her, saying: "We will have to find our own path to freedom. What is so wonderful about marriage between a man and a woman? Everyone knows that the sun rises in the east. Were it to rise in the west, that would be something really special!" Dressing the groom in women's clothes, she says, "From today your name is Beeja and mine is Teeja. How blessed we are that fortune has brought us together. Don't you ever say another word of regret in my presence!"

Beeja's father is furious when she appears in women's clothes. He insists that they remove all their jewels and leave the house. The village elders too take umbrage, saying: "If a woman marries another woman, what is a man to do—go and find a mouse hole for himself?" Beeja plants a scarecrow in the village square and tells the men they are no better than it. While the villagers are busy destroying the scarecrow, the two women walk away.]

Beeja and Teeja, arms around each other, went out of the village. The earth was green as far as the eye could see. In the fields millet stood head high, waving in the breeze. Flowering creepers lay across the borders between the fields. Small bushes and trees stood buried in webs of greenery. Clouds wobbled drunkenly in the sky. The beauty of this earth lay before them, limitless, stretching out in every direction. For the first time, these beloved daughters of nature met with nature. Leaping like does, they climbed a hill. Mad with joy, they chased each other to the highest peak and began to whirl round and round, holding hands. The houses in the village looked like pock marks on the face of the earth.

A group of clouds touched the mountain. Rain fell in torrents. The air vibrated as though with drumbeats of joy. Flashing around them, the lightning throbbed with eagerness to see the beauty of the two friends. Wiping Beeja's face, Teeja said: "The lightning is thirsting to meet us. Perhaps its thirst cannot be quenched through these veiling clothes."

Beeja answered: "What use have we for veils? Why keep the poor lightning thirsty?"

As the blouses fell open, the lightning flashed. As if it too, hidden in clouds, had been thirsting for centuries. The glimpse of these lotus pairs quenched its thirst. Once more the joyful drumbeats burst forth.

After a while, the lightning flashed again. This was a more prolonged wave of lightning. Like ladybirds, the two stood, embracing, lost to the world, longing to mingle with one another, drinking nectar from each other's lips.

Like the clouds, they discharged their passion and slackened their embrace. The inanimate life of the mountain was infused with new meaning, and a new glow dissolved into the lightning. When consciousness returned, they put on their clothes. The lightning growled and flashed once more, as if it bore a peculiar grudge against clothing. As the growls echoed, they again fell into each other's arms.

As they came down the hillside, gamboling in the rain, they felt light and fresh like the flowers that grew around. Streams of joy flowed around them. With relaxed limbs the soaked earth was blessed by the pure love of the clouds.

It was only when they reached the foot of the mountain that they fully realized the height of their love. If there was anything in the world clearer and purer than the untouched water shed by the clouds, surely it was the deep love between them!

But in this human world one cannot live by love alone, and then, they were two girls. They wanted to set up house together in a new way of their own, making enemies of the village men. One might as well hope to overturn the mountain. If they had a choice, they would have preferred not to look at any human habitation.

Unwittingly, busy talking to each other, they went straight to the haunted tank. Darkness was gathering on the face of the earth. When the rain ceased, they wrung the water out of their clothes.

The forest sighed in the wind. The deserted tank. A hundred and twenty-eight ghosts had their dwelling here. Not even a bird could flap a wing here after dark. Whoever ventured here never returned home alive. In broad daylight men trembled when they had to pass within a couple of miles of the place.

They sat down on the brink of the tank, chatting fearlessly. Above them the moon played hide-and-seek with the clouds. Suddenly Beeja said: "The moon just whispered a spell in my ear. If you give me a kiss I'll tell it to you." Teeja answered: "If you give me a kiss, I won't ask for the spell."

"Oh, the spell is worth asking for," replied Beeja.

"Tell me then, without my asking," said Teeja.

"The moon keeps asking me why I look at its plain face instead of looking at the moon who is sitting next to me."

"Nonsense, the moon whispered that to me, not to you." The two moons had just begun to drink each other's nectar, when suddenly a voice echoed around them.

"I knew you would come here." Startled, they looked around. A dazzling white man was standing nearby, smiling at them. He looked as if molded in moonlight. Smiling, he said: "Today, our deserted lake has been purified. But I'm astonished that you didn't feel afraid to come to this tank of ghosts."

Taken aback, they both stood up. Beeja replied softly: "There is reason to feel afraid of human beings. What is there to fear from ghosts?"

"You are absolutely right," said the ghost chieftain, smiling. "We are consigned to this existence because of the black deeds of dishonest humans. We avenge ourselves on the fearful ones by frightening them as much as we can. . . . We heard the humans whispering about your marriage. We love to have fun, so our whole tribe went down to watch the morning scene. We liked the two of you very much. It was we who arranged the scarecrow episode, otherwise do you think those savages would have let you escape? In fact, I stayed with you right up to the mountaintop, to protect you."

At this both of them were suffused with shyness. The ghost chieftain began to laugh and said: "You were not shy in the lightning's presence so why feel shy at my words? The sight of your love made me feel that life is worth living. I 'm the chieftain of the tribe of ghosts. You can live here without fear. Near this lake I will set up a palace that a king might envy. The state treasury may run dry but you will never be in want. All your wishes, small and big, will be fulfilled. Women can come here, but the shadow of a man will not be able to cast a sharp glance at you. You can now disport yourselves to your hearts'content in this palace."

Looking in the direction indicated by the chieftain, they saw a snow-white palace gleaming in the dark. What unique carving and what wonderful windows! Inside, the palace glowed with light. Outside, the moonlight wove its web.

They had not realized that their love was such a blessing! When they entered the palace they were struck speechless with wonder. Saffron courtyards. Crimson walls. Vermilion ceilings. A lotus bedstead. A bed of roses. They swung in the swings of joy. Brighter than saffron, those two birds so lost themselves in the joys of togetherness that they became altogether oblivious to this world and its affairs. After all, what can compare in bliss with that primeval trance of Eros? . . .

At dawn when they came out of the palace and saw the sun rise, they felt as if the sun were rising from the pure petals between their thighs. Ever since that night, the sun has forsaken its former dwelling and has begun to rise from this new abode, whence it rises even today. All the joys of the world throbbed with eagerness to dwell in the bed of that palace. The thirst of the whole universe was encompassed in that one thirst of theirs.

[They visit the village a fortnight later.]

Then, flying and fluttering in circles like a couple of butterflies, they reached the village of the humans. The same encirclement of walls and barriers. The same huts and roofs. Each with its own limits and boundaries. Each with its own kitchen and stove. Each with its own fire and smoke. The squabbles of thine and mine. Heaps of rubbish lying here and there.

Amid all the scrambling to secure peace and happiness, bankruptcy showed its face. Worries and anxieties over children. Stinking baby clothes. Filth everywhere. Conflicts and quarrels in every house.

How had they lived in this hell for so many years? How did they grow up here? Today, remembering that past life, they were filled with disgust. How dreadful! But the villagers remain immersed in their life. They decorate the courtyards with red and yellow patterns. They draw pictures on the walls. They sing songs on special occasions. They cook special dishes at festival time. They swing. They dance and sing. No one sees filth anywhere!

[The villagers and Beeja's father do not remonstrate with the girls because they are too scared of the ghosts. The girls invite Beeja's mother to their palace. The next morning she arrives with Beeja's married cousin. They try to persuade Beeja and Teeja to return home and get married to men, saying that all the men, including the king, feel threatened by their behavior and are willing to marry them. Beeja's cousin narrates her woes—her husband is impotent and violent, and her father-in-law and brother-in-law rape her. Her parents, for fear of dishonor, do not come to her aid. Beeja and Teeja invite her to stay with them but she refuses, saying she wants to produce a child to inherit her in-laws' wealth. The ghost chieftain then uses his powers to make her husband potent. This gives Beeja the idea that the ghost could turn one of them into a man. Teeja is opposed to it but gives in. The ghost agrees to turn Beeja into a man but says if she ever wishes to become a woman once more, she will be able to do so.]

. . . Closing the door, the two of them walked, anklets tinkling, to their bedroom. Teeja was in a great hurry today. She flung off all her clothes in the time Beeja took just to undo her blouse. Tugging at Beeja's hand, she cried: "Why are you so slow today? Usually you are always so impatient."

After that, the two pink flamingoes fluttered, entwined, and took not a moment's rest all night. Teeja wished that night would never end, but Beeja was longing for dawn to come before its time. . . .

As the sun rose, Beeja felt a tremor run through her body. All at once, her breasts flattened out and hair sprouted on her cheeks and upper lip. She felt her limbs and ran her hands down her thighs. Yes indeed, she was now a fully developed young man. Her body was covered with curly black hair. Bubbling over with joy, he looked at his face in the mirror. For a moment, he felt scared of those huge curling mustaches. But how could he allow himself to feel scared? The glory of curling mustaches lies in their ability to scare others!

Seeing a turban, shirt, and waistcloth hanging on a peg, he leapt forward. For years he had dressed himself in these manly garments. Hastily he donned the waistcloth and shirt, and tied on the turban. The knee-long fringe of the turban waved proudly. . . .

Catching hold of Teeja's arm, he said: "Today I will settle all the old accounts with you."

Teeja stood silent, with bent head. She wondered what made her husband use such language. To tease his wife further, he added: "Today no candle will be needed in the bedroom. I'll engender such light and heat as you will never be able to forget."

"That's enough," Teeja replied, rebuking her husband. "You've barely become a man and you've already learned all their ways!" . . .

Smiling, her husband said: "It looks as if I'll have to teach you the ways of the world, after all." And with that, he picked Teeja up in his arms. All her struggles were of no avail. Laying her down on the bed of roses, he fell on her. As darkness swam before their eyes, a new light spread. The petals of the lotus seemed about to break asunder but did not. Teeja felt as if the whole universe had entered her body. When they separated, it took awhile for them to return to consciousness.

Then the husband, his eyes still closed, remarked: "How many days we wasted, just fooling around."

Turning away, Teeja replied: "Wasted? What do you mean, wasted? Those joys can never be forgotten, not even after death."

The same scenes again at night! While enacting those scenes, a new knowledge gradually began to dawn in the husband's mind—that a man is stronger than a woman. In fact, a frail woman is of no account at all in the face of a man's unlimited strength. A man is indeed tremendously powerful.

That night Teeja received her husband's seed into her womb. In the last hour before dawn, both of them, exhausted, fell into a deep sleep. When the husband's eyes opened, the sun had already climbed into the sky. Its rays shone into the room. Seeing the rays, pride awoke in his heart, telling him that it is man's heat and power that rises in the heavens in the form of the sun. Woman is merely his shadow. Earlier, the two of them owned the palace equally. Both of them had the same rights and the same importance. Perhaps Teeja still thought in those terms! That would never do. . . .

"Right now, I want an answer to one question. Who is the owner of this palace? You or I?"

Teeja could not quite grasp the import of this. She did not answer at once, but sat in silence. Her husband impatiently repeated his question. Looking at his curled mustaches, Teeja answered: "Why are you worried about who owns it and who doesn't? The two of us live together in this palace. Isn't that good enough?"

"I'm not asking who lives or doesn't live together. Answer my question clearly. Who is the real owner of this property?"

"The ghost chieftain," said Teeja in a low voice.

This answer disconcerted him at first, but he soon recovered and said crossly: "Why are you beating about the bush? Now that it has been given into our possession, who is the owner? Answer me. To whom does this invaluable wealth belong? To you or to me?"

Teeja's brain felt benumbed. Such a change of color in one night! Beeja had never asked such questions or sought such answers. As soon as a man took over, everything went topsy-turvy. It would be fatal to prevaricate now. She said: "We have equal rights over this property, but if you are still in doubt over the matter, you can ask the ghost chieftain to clarify it."

The husband felt every nerve in his body grow tense. "Don't you try to frighten me with your talk of the ghost chieftain," he said tauntingly. "Why should he ever take my side against you? What will he gain by favoring me, pray? But I never realized you could harbor such infidelity in your heart."

"You've realized it now!"

This infuriated the man with the curled mustaches and he grew mad with anger. "Don't think I will be cowed down by this lover of yours," he shouted. "I'll establish my own kingdom. I'll collect unlimited hoards of treasure and prepare a huge army. I'll build a mighty fortress and hundreds of queens like you will wait on me in the women's quarters."

[Teeja decides to visit Beeja's married cousin, to give Beeja a chance to cool down, but this further infuriates Beeja.]

"Don't you give me any of your sauce! As if I don't know that you want to gang up with the troop of ghosts and make an end of me! I know the tricks of such whores as you! Get inside this minute or else—"

"Or else what will you do?" said Teeja, smiling.

The smile on her lips made him lose the little self-restraint he had. Dropping her veil, he grabbed her hair. One yank and Teeja fell to the ground. Dragging her by the hair, he proclaimed: "I am not one of those fools who become enslaved to their wives and put up with women's nonsense!" He dragged her in and threw her on the bed. She clenched her teeth and shut her eyes. Not a sound escaped her lips. She felt it would be degrading even to cry out in front of so base a husband. She felt as if she was suffocating. In a little while, she sank into a deep well of unconsciousness.

Leaving her unconscious, he went out of the palace. He bolted the door from outside and began to wander about in the forest like a madman. In the course of his wanderings he came to the same mountain and began to climb it. Unshapely like a heap of dry stones, the mountain seemed colorless and ugly to him. Nature, steeped in sorrow, seemed to be mourning a death.

As soon as he reached the peak, the memory of that earlier day came before his eyes. He could not get rid of that picture even by closing his eyes, so he opened them with a start. Oh for those showers pouring down from heaven! Those lips! Those unrestrained embraces! That unbroken trance of love! Every pore of his body throbbed with the yearning to become Beeja once more. And with that yearning his form changed. The same smooth cheeks. The two lotuses blooming in the blouse—eager for the touch of Teeja's hands!

Beeja ran down the mountain, unbolted the door of the palace and rushed in. Shaking the unconscious Teeja, she cried out: "Teeja, Teeja! I've given up being a man. Open your eyes and recognize your own Beeja." After much shaking, Teeja returned to consciousness. Her eyes opened to see Beeja leaning like a creeper over her. The same tender affection spilling over from the eyes! The same soft-as-saffron body! The two fell into each other's arms and that is where they still are today.

Thanks to the ghost chieftain's magic, not only the filthy seed of man but Teeja's womb too burned up for ever. The creature named man dare not venture within a distance of twenty-four and twenty-four, a total of forty-eight miles around that place. However, just once, I did manage to visit them, on Teeja's express invitation. I saw that wonderful palace with my own eyes and I wrote this story at Teeja's dictation, in her words. Would the ghost chieftain have spared my life if I had dared add a word to her account?

Vikram Seth:
Poems (English)

Introduced by Ruth Vanita

One of the writers who has put Indian writing in English on the international map, Vikram Seth (born 1952) won the Sahitya Akademi award for his verse novel *The Golden Gate* (1986). He has published a novel, *A Suitable Boy*, four books of poems, a travelogue, and a libretto. He divides his time between New Delhi and London.

These poems are from his first collection, *Mappings*, published by Writers' Workshop, Calcutta (1981) and reissued by Penguin India (1994).

Guest

I woke. He mumbled things in the next bed.
I lay there for an hour or so. At four
The alarm rang. He got out of bed. He wore
Nothing. I felt his sleepy classic head
And long-limbed body stir my quiescent heart.
I'd thought that I was free. Wrong from the start.
I found I loved him utterly instead.

There was no real hope. 'Guy loving guy?
Man—that's a weird trip—and not for me.'
I accepted that. But next day, warily,
We coiled to snap or spring. Rash truth. To lie
Still could have spared the trust; the warmth as well.
I left his room that day. I try to tell
Myself this sorrow like this ink will dry.

Dubious

Some men like Jack
and some like Jill;
I'm glad I like
them both; but still

I wonder if
this freewheeling
really is an
enlightened thing—

or is its greater
scope a sign
of deviance from
some party line?

In the strict ranks
of Gay and Straight
what is my status?
Stray? or Great?

Nirmala Deshpande: "Mary Had a Little Lamb" (Marathi)

Introduced and translated by Ruth Vanita

Award-winning novelist Nirmala Deshpande was born in 1917. This story appeared in the magazine *Shabdashree* in 1982. A Hindi translation appeared in a special issue on women writers of the now-defunct literary journal *Sarika*, (October 16–31, 1984, 27–34). The story is interesting for its depiction of an interracial relationship in terms that appear nonjudgmental until almost the conclusion. Once the relationship moves from being romantic to being explicitly sexual, a sudden reversal takes place, with the Caucasian girl being stereotyped as the sexually predatory lesbian and the Indian girl as a misled heterosexual.

[Shobhana, a high school student, is a lawyer's daughter in Lalitpur, a small princely state in colonial India. The widow of a British colonel works as a governess to the princess and often consults Shobhana's father on legal problems pertaining to her husband's property. She is referred to as the Memsahib. Her only daughter, Rosemary, is a second year student in a Catholic college in Dehradun, and is visiting her mother during the vacation.]

Rosemary returns from her riding lesson every day around this time. Her teacher, Bankey Bihari, rides on another horse behind her. Drops of sweat fall from her silky golden hair. . . . Shobhana waits for the sound of Rosemary's horse approaching. Perhaps Rosemary has never noticed Shobhana. . . .

Rosemary's face seemed to have been absorbed into Shobhana's bloodstream. The sight of her agitated Shobhana greatly. As Rosemary's horse disappeared into the cluster of trees, Shobhana's heart would reach a crisis of tumult. She felt as if she was being strangled, as if her blood was boiling. . . .

[Shobhana and her sister go to the governess's garden, at her invitation, to pick flowers for a family function. Rosemary returns from her ride while they are there.]

A khaki shirt designed like a police uniform, a leather belt, men's shoes—male get-up in general, but a fresh attractive beauty blooming like a rose—like her name! Shobhana was dazzled, seeing Rosemary so close up. There were flowers on the bush but her hand, raised to pick them, stayed paralyzed in motion! . . .

That day it was as if Shobhana had found a new world. She had been introduced to Rosemary, now all she had to do was transform the acquaintance into an intimacy. Shobhana wanted to find her own lost individuality in the depths of Rosemary's blue eyes. She wanted to come in contact with modern ideas, to absorb the self-confidence evident in Rosemary's way of speaking and behaving. . . .

A couple of days later the Memsahib invited Shobhana and her mother to a ladies' party for new year. . . .

Shobhana was just going up the steps when Rosemary came running out and embraced her. A white lace mini frock and a string of pearls round her neck. Fair legs beneath the frock and her navel visible through the transparent fabric. Shobhana was taken aback and confused. She felt relieved when the embrace ended. That embrace in the presence of so many women made her feel self-conscious. . . .

[Rosemary resists her mother's attempts to send her back to England or to Dehradun. She says she wants to set up a social organization to work for the poor. The friendship between the two girls develops rapidly. Shobhana finds pretexts to spend time at Rosemary's house.]

As soon as they meet, the two friends join hands and walk round the garden. They swing on the swing and play in the water. Rosemary's name gets shortened to Mary and Shobhana's to Shona. When they go in to drink tea, Rosemary remarks: "We must have been attached to one another in a former life, that is why we are friends in this life!"

Shobhana says: "Whenever I heard your horse galloping, my heart would beat fast. I longed to be friends with such a bold girl. I used to watch you every day, from the bathroom window or hiding behind the trees, but you never noticed me."

"Wrong, absolutely wrong! I used to watch you too but pretended not to see you. There's a saying in English: Kiss a girl and she will kick you, kick a girl and she will kiss you. That's what it was!"

"I don't understand."

"Oh my dear kid, or rather, lamb—"

"What do you mean? Stop teasing."

"A kid can be somewhat cunning, but a lamb is a lamb. You are my lamb. I've seen many beautiful girls but you are different from all of them," Rosemary said, embracing Shobhana.

Rose's body emitted a manly scent. Riding on waves of scented thought, Shobhana set off for home.

One day Shobhana discovered in the course of conversation that Rosemary had another friend here. Shobhana was taken aback—so, she had been deluded all along! Walking arm in arm in the garden, eating each other's leftovers, drinking from the same glass, lying together on one bed, making those vows of lifelong friendship! She had been under the illusion that she was Rosemary's only intimate friend here, but now when she discovered the reality, she fell from heaven to earth.

Hiding the moisture in her eyes, she said in a somewhat tearful voice: "To have friends in Dehradun is one thing—but here—"

"I've told you, she was a friend. We met for the last time at a Christmas party. After that, I never had time to visit her. I don't feel like going. I spend the days waiting for you!"

"What's her name?"

"She's Chameli, who lives near the pond. I used to give her hairpins, ribbons, brooches, and she would be very pleased with them. Whenever Mummy and I fought about my going to England or Dehradun, I'd go and see Chameli and she would calm me down."

"You shouldn't fight with your mother. I never argue with my elders. I quietly obey them."

"It's not as if I want to fight but why does she keep on and on about dating? Do I have any identity as a human being or not?"

"That custom should be cultivated in India too."

"Dating? I don't want to get married at all. That masculine grasp, hairy chest, beard and mustache, and the smell of sweat from all kinds of hairs everywhere on the body— I feel sick even thinking about it! I much prefer friends like you."

"Not like me—like Chameli!"

"I like you better than Chameli, Shona my lamb."

"Why?"

"Chameli was a rustic. You are educated, intelligent—and then one can't really say why one likes one person more than another."

A thrill ran through Shobhana when she heard this. . . . Often Mary would start up a dance tune on the gramophone and teach Shobhana how to dance.

"But doesn't one need a man to dance with?"

"It doesn't make any great difference if there is no man. Each dancer should decide in their own mind on being the man or the woman. Then it's easy."

A couple of days later, Rosemary proposed that they take a photo of the two of them together—Rose in a pant and shirt, tie and shoes, and Shobhana in a nine-yard sari. But Shobhana refused, saying: "Oh no, my father will eat me alive when he sees such a picture. Nothing in the world can remain hidden from him."

"Don't worry. No one will get to know. After Mummy goes to play bridge on Saturday afternoon, you come over and I will call a photographer here. But don't forget to wear that gold-edged sari and the earrings with pearl dangles."

"How can I leave the house dressed up like that? What will my parents say?." . . .

"All right, bring the clothes in your book bag and you can dress here."

[But when Shobhana sets out on Saturday, her mother stops her and insists that she prepare for the visit of a prospective bridegroom, Shridhar. Shobhana meets Shridhar and feels attracted to him, but when they are briefly left alone, tells him she does not want to marry.]

"I don't want to marry"—how had she dared to speak thus? Or was it Mary who had spoken through Shobhana? . . . Next day, she slipped away to Mary's house. . . .

"The son of the Dewan of Dhar had come to see me. If we had liked one another, we would have got married."

"So you didn't like one another?" Mary asked, coming closer.

"He liked me but—"

"You didn't like him? Isn't that so?"

"I don't know—Father should not have called him over without consulting me."

"You are right! What was the boy like as a person?"

"Good-looking and lively. But, Rose, I couldn't make up my mind."

"Right!"

"Now I feel it was foolish to refuse him. He was handsome and impressive, he had curly hair—"

"What are you saying? Just say that again. You want to carry on with some good-for-nothing from Dhar?" Rose was screaming in anger.

Was Rose joking? What had happened to her? Shobhana shrank into herself.

"Don't act so crazy, Rose." Shobhana stood up to go but stood still, staring at Mary's furious face.

"I have waited long enough," Rose said and pushed Shobhana on to the bed.

Shobhana lay still, as if helpless. Rose began to tear off her clothes as if squabbling with her, and Shobhana began to sob and cry, still lying there. Her body did not have the strength left to put up any resistance at all. When she finally got up Mary was lost in herself.

Insulted, humiliated, and soiled, Shobhana left the Memsahib's house. The world seemed a frightening and futile wasteland. She felt angry with herself. She wanted to erase her body that was covered with the marks of the squabble. At home, she spent a long time bathing and scrubbing herself and then lay down, pretending to have a bad headache.

[At night Shobhana is unable to sleep. She feels frightened and goes to her aunt's room. Her aunt tells her that one feels frightened when getting married, but later one gets used to it.]

But how did all this happen? Shobhana had not realized that a rough man was hidden in Rose's beautiful body. Had not realized? No, this was not the whole truth. It was Rose's manliness that charmed Shobhana and to which she had been unconsciously attracted. Not unconsciously. Quite consciously. But she hadn't realized things would go so far. Now she felt torn between extreme hatred for Rose and sympathy for her, irritation and compassion. She throbbed like a fly in a spider's web.

How to find a way through this dense dark forest? Was there any medicine to heal these physical and mental wounds? To wipe out these blots? To escape from drowning in this moss-covered pond?

Shobhana missed Shridhar a lot. She longed to meet him, to sit and talk to him, to hear him speak words of consolation. She was looking for an opportunity to wash the blot from her heart with a reassuring touch. . . .

[Shridhar sends a note congratulating Shobhana on her courage in refusing marriage and wishes her a happy future. Shobhana feels very happy and blushes. She begins to imagine ways of going secretly to the club that lies beyond Memsahib's house, without her family's knowledge.]

As evening approached she would begin to murmur, "I have to return Rosemary's books, she needs them." This murmur would reach her family's ears. Thrusting into her bag any books she came across, she would wear her embroidered sari and set out. In the dusk. With the gardener as escort. Naturally! Because along the way lay scorpions, thorns, snakes.

Vijay Tendulkar:
Mitra's Story *(Marathi)*

Introduced and translated by Ruth Vanita

Vijay Tendulkar (born 1928) is one of India's best-known living dramatists. His plays have been translated and enacted in almost all Indian languages, including English, and in several foreign languages. Among the most controversial plays were *Sakharam Binder, Ghasiram Kotwal,* and *Shantata Court Chalu Aahe* (Silence, the Court Is in Session) about a woman who becomes pregnant out of wedlock. He has won many awards including the Sangeet Natak Akademi Award.

In 1982 he wrote *Mitrachi Goshta* (Mitra's Story), which is perhaps the first play in a modern Indian language with a lesbian protagonist.[1] Mitra, which means "female friend," is a diminutive of Sumitra. Her story is narrated in retrospect by a shy male undergraduate nicknamed Bapu. They are fellow students in a college in a Maharashtrian small town, where Sumitra is notorious for her "manly" demeanor. Men are both attracted and intimidated by her, but her only friendship is with Bapu, who promises to be her faithful friend although she warns him that he may regret this when he gets to know her. Bapu is shocked when Mitra attempts suicide. She tells him it was precipitated by her family's attempt to get her married and her own realization that she is not attracted to men. As an experiment, she slept with a male servant and decided that heterosexuality was not for her.

Mitra discovers another aspect of herself when she takes the role of hero in a college play and falls passionately in love with Nama Deshmukh, who plays the heroine. Mitra tells Bapu that as a schoolgirl she had felt mild attractions to other girls but had not understood their meaning. When enacting a love scene with Nama, however, she felt "when she touched me, when she embraced me, a desire for her body, a kind of terrifying hunger, very very frighten-

---

1. First published in Pune by Neelkanth Prakashan in 1982. The present translation from the Hindi edition (*Meeta ki Kahani,* 1985) has been checked by the author.

ing, and very delightful, absolutely real." She suddenly realized "like a flash of lightning—I don't need a man, I want a woman. I am different." A semi-comic interlude is provided by Bapu's roommate Pandey, a crude rustic, who falls violently in love with Mitra when she is dressed as a man onstage and joins the army in despair when he discovers she is a lesbian. Complications result when Mitra pursues and wins Nama, using Bapu's room for their trysts. Mitra uses every weapon, including anonymous letters and blackmail, to outmaneuver Nama's boyfriend, a local goon named Dalvi. For some time, Nama continues to sleep with both Dalvi and Mitra. Bapu helps Mitra, lending her his room and money, and acts as go-between as well as confidant for both women. Mitra defies Dalvi's threats and disregards Bapu's advice to find another girlfriend, because she says Nama is the only one she loves. After Dalvi leaves Nama, the lesbian relationship seems happy but Bapu knows that Nama is actually restless and is considering marriage.

A scandal breaks when a local newspaper publishes a story about the two women. Bapu, eager to know the details, meets Mitra.

(Enter Mitra with her bicycle, wearing dark glasses)

Bapu: What's the news?

Sumitra (on the alert): Of what?

Bapu: Just generally. I've been away.

Sumitra: What have you heard after you got back?

Bapu: I? (Clearly lying) Nothing at all. You are the first person I've met.

Sumitra: Really? (Seeing through him) . . . Why don't you ask once and for all?

Bapu: What?

Sumitra (sharply): When I am going to be expelled—go on, ask! (Without giving Bapu a chance to deny this) That's the news you are dying to hear, isn't it?

Bapu: No, no—but I heard something like that—

Sumitra: Thank you—for telling the truth. (Contemptuously) Liar! You guys don't have the courage to live truthfully. Do you know what happened? She denied everything. Covered her ears and cut herself off from me. When that didn't work she wept and cried and said I had made a fool of her. I spoiled her. I blackmailed her. None of it was her fault, she had no such desires. (Tries to laugh hysterically but fails) Yes, she begged for forgiveness and got off scot-free.

(Silence)

Bapu: What have you decided?

Sumitra: I? I can expose her, with proofs! She'd have nowhere to hide. But I won't do that. Why not? I don't know, maybe I still have a soft corner for her. I still love her, Bapu, I still crave for her. My blood cries out to her. She, only she! (With disgust) Even though she is such a coward. Begging forgiveness! I don't object to her accusing me. That's all right. I understand why she did it. She had to save her skin, that's fine. But she has even stopped meeting me. She has stopped going out of the house, for fear of me. I waited for her three hours this morning. . . .

Bapu: Where?

Sumitra: At the hotel opposite her house. Last night I felt like going straight to her house and knocking at the door. They wouldn't have let me in, of course. They'd have abused me. But at least I'd have seen her.

Bapu: Mitra—

Sumitra: I set out, but then I got angry. What right has she now to my love? It's one thing to deny the relationship to get out of a tricky situation, but it's quite another to stop meeting me. Why won't she meet me? Do you know, last evening I went to our usual rendezvous and sat there, waiting for her, thinking she would surely come. . . .

Bapu: Where?

Sumitra: At the house of the cycle repairman who sits outside college. He lives in the slum behind the cinema. (Bapu is speechless.) I sat there till ten at night. After that it became impossible to stay on. He was drunk. I left. (Anguish on her face and in her voice) I can't bear it. I'll kill her, I'll cut her to pieces.

Bapu: Mitra, stay calm.

Sumitra (with biting sarcasm): Mitra, stay calm! (Laughs loudly) Calm, you apostle of peace! You are calm—cold as an icicle! (Continues to laugh)

Bapu (finally): What about the expulsion? That is a lie, isn't it?

Sumitra (cuttingly): You can't contain yourself, can you? Curiosity is killing you! Why a lie? It's true. They will expel me. What did you think they'd do, give me a medal?

Bapu: No, but they could give a warning—

Sumitra: The whole city knows. A talented filthmonger has even written a story about me. . . .

Bapu: He hasn't taken your name—

Sumitra: So you've read it! So soon? As soon as you got back—

Bapu: Someone gave it to me to read—

Sumitra: Don't make excuses. You must have had fun reading it.

Bapu: No. . . .

Sumitra: Must have enjoyed every word—so tell me, tell me the juicy details. . . .

Bapu (sincerely): No, Mitra, I swear by God, I was very disturbed. I felt embarrassed, deeply ashamed—

Sumitra: Of me? Yes, of me—don't try to deny it, you liar.

Bapu: No, of myself, for reading it. Ashamed that anyone can write such things and they can be published.

(Sumitra is silent.)

Bapu: What have you decided?

Sumitra: About what?

Bapu: About the story.

Sumitra: Why don't you do something? Do whatever you want. Why do you ask me? I haven't read it. Why should I? Let them write what they please. Why should I read it? I am what I am. I know myself. What can they do to me? What ?

Mitra's father withdraws her from college. Dalvi tells Bapu that he will not let that "lesbian bitch" gain admission to any college. Nama succumbs to a marriage arranged by her family. Mitra pursues her to Calcutta and returns defeated. Mitra's family throws her out, and Dalvi gets her evicted from a women's hostel. Angered by her refusal to change her ways and by her using him to her own ends, Bapu breaks off relations with her. Some time later he meets the triumphant Dalvi and Pandey, who tell him that Mitra is an alcoholic and drinks every evening at the army club, in the company of officers who exploit her sexually. Bapu sees her there, cursing him for having abandoned her and cursing herself for having destroyed their relationship. Two officers carry her off in a drunken stupor. Bapu is disturbed yet does not renew contact with her and soon hears from Dalvi that she has committed suicide. The play ends with a distraught Bapu alone on stage.

Sunil Gangopadhyay
Those Days (Bengali)[1]

Introduced and translated by Shormishtha Panja

Major poet and novelist Sunil Gangopadhyay (born 1934) won the Sahitya Akademi award for *Sei Samay* (Those Days) in 1982. It is set in the nineteenth-century Bengal Renaissance during which a number of litterateurs and social reformers set the agenda for a new Bengal and a new India. One literary giant of the period was Michael Madhusudan Dutt (1824–1873), who is "Madhu" in *Sei Samay*. Dutt was fascinated by the West, and all his early writings were in English. His extant letters to Gourdas Basak, from his days at Hindu College in 1837 to the year before his death in 1873, which are one of Gangopadhyay's main sources for his depiction of the relationship in the novel, are all in English. His poems in English regularly appeared in leading Calcutta periodicals. Dutt converted to Christianity in 1843. Some time later he switched to writing in Bengali and produced seven plays, five long poems and innumerable short ones. His most famous poem is *Meghnadbodh Kavya* (1861), a retelling of the Ramayana story with Ravana's son Meghnad as the hero instead of Rama. Dutt's introduction of blank verse into Bengali poetry, his superb handling of metrics, use of numerous Sanskrit words, and skill in dramatic characterization considerably enriched Bengali literature.

Dutt's friendship with Gourdas Basak, highlighted in the following extract, was one of the strongest bonds he ever formed. His letters to Gour from 1841 to 1843 are ardent and exuberant, for instance: "Your thundering letter of Saturday last came over me like a thunderbolt: Oh! With what a beating heart I read it! In every line, in every word there were Rage—Fury—Hell—& Death!" He calls Gour his "ever beloved friend" and in one letter says he is writing at midnight, "the hour for writing love letters." Several of Dutt's early English lyrics are dedi-

---

1. Text used for this translation: *Sei Samay*, 2 vols., (Calcutta: Ananda, 1981, 1982), vol. 1, 32–40.

cated to Gour or written at his request, although in some he is disguised as a female. One song proclaims, tongue-in-cheek, that it is "dedicated as usual, to G. D. Bysack."

In 1843 Dutt wrote to Gour: "At the expiration of three months from hence I am to be married—dreadful thought! It harrows up my blood and makes my hair stand like quills on the fretful porcupine [sic]! My betrothed is the daughter of a rich *zemindar* [landlord]—poor girl! What a deal of misery is in store for her in the ever inexplorable womb of Futurity!" Dutt avoided this marriage by his conversion, and left for Madras in 1848, where he became a schoolteacher and married the daughter of a British indigo planter. In 1855 he deserted his wife and four children and eloped with a Frenchwoman, Emilia Henrietta, by whom he had two children. They remained together despite long separations and social ostracism. She died in 1873 and Dutt died three days later.

A number of Madhu's books lay scattered on a marble table by the wall. Beni went to look even though he knew Madhu didn't like others messing up his books. Choosing two, Beni asked: "Madhu, can I borrow these?"

Madhu said: "Take as many as you like. Only don't take the *Life of Byron*. I'm reading that."[2]

Peering down from the window, Madhu said: "My palanquin bearers will go for their bath soon. If you like, they can take you home now. If you leave later, you will have to hire a palanquin."

Beni said: "No, no, in that case I'll leave right away. But what about you, Gour? Won't you come too?"

Madhu answered instead of Gour. ""No, Gour won't leave right now. He's going to spend the day with me. Perhaps even the entire night—who knows?"

Beni raised his eyebrows and said: "The whole night?"

Gour said: "You must be mad. Who said I'd spend the night? You go ahead, Beni. I'll leave after he cools down a bit. If we all leave at the same time, he'll start drinking again."

2. Thomas Moore ed., *The Life, Letters and Journals of Lord Byron,* 2 vols (London: John Murray, 1830). For an account of Lord Byron's erotic relationships with men and the way he became a cult figure of sorts among homoerotically inclined men in nineteenth-century England, see Louis Crompton, *Byron and Greek Love* (Berkeley: University of California Press, 1985). Like Dutt, Byron too wrote love poems to men and changed the male to female pronouns before publication. In a letter to Gour dated November 25, 1842, Dutt writes: "I am reading Tom Moore's Life of my favorite Byron—a splendid book upon my word!" He then goes on to imagine a time when Gour will write his biography as the Irish poet Moore did Byron's. In fact, Dutt's first official biography, *Madhusmriti* (Memories of Madhu) by Nagendranath Shome (Calcutta: Gurudas Cattopadhyaya, 1954), was written with Gour's help and contained as an appendix Dutt's letters to Gour.

Beni grinned and said: "You are the only one who can control him. Take good care of him. Hey, Madhu, promise you won't get angry if I ask you something?"

"What?"

"In the acrostic you've written to Gour, why do you address him as 'she'? Of course, Gour is so lovely he could easily pass for a girl."[3]

In a serious tone, Madhu said: "Who said that poem is about Gour? It's true that I dedicate most of my poems to Gour, but that doesn't mean that all of them are about him."

"But acrostics are dedicated to the one whose name the letters spell out. . . . I still recall some of the lines:

> Go! Simple lay! And tell that fair,
> Oh! 'tis for her, her lover dies! . . ."[4]

"Learn to read properly, Beni. That's not the way to read poetry. Remember you are reading lines written by a poet as great as Byron or Pope."

"I can't write poetry, otherwise I'd like to write poems to Gour too."

"If the palanquin bearers leave for their bath, you won't get a ride."

"No, no, I'm going, I'm going."

Beni left in a rush. After seeing him to the head of the stairs, Madhu returned and shut the door behind him. Erasing the irritated expression from his face, he said: "Bloody miser, son of a miser! Left at the thought of hiring a palanquin! Good riddance!"

Gour was sitting with his head bent and his cheeks aflame. Madhu ran to him, seized him in his arms and rapidly gave him a number of smacking kisses, saying: "Now there's just you and me, me and you. Gour and Madhu, Madhu and Gour. Aaah! What bliss!"

Gour disentangled himself with difficulty and said: "What mad things you do, Madhu! You embarrass me in front of the others."

"What's there to be embarrassed about? I am passionately fond of your company as I am of you."[5]

"Beni said such horrid things!"

"Beni be damned!"

---

3. In a letter to Gour dated November 25, 1942, Dutt writes of being "prepared (poor as I am) to receive so beautiful a guest as yourself" and then goes on to lament, "I know you won't [visit Dutt] - you have everything but inclination to honor my 'humble shed' with your handsome presence!!" Gangopadhyay comments on Gour's eye-catching, effeminate good looks when he first introduces the character in *Sei Samay.*

4. The poem continues: "Undone by her, his heart sincere/Resolves itself thus into sighs!/Dear cruel maid! Tho ne'er doth she/Once think, for her thus breaks my heart . . ." The first letters of each of the twelve lines spells out "Gour Das Bysac."

5. This last line is an exact quotation, minus the underlining of the words "of you," from what is probably Dutt's most ardent letter to Gour, dated November 25, 1842. In the letter Dutt

"No, Madhu, you're breaking all limits. You don't listen to anyone nowadays."

"Only to you. I listen to you."

"If you're going to be so childish, I'll stop coming here."

"Don't say that, Gour. Anything but that. I can't live without seeing you. Is this why you've been avoiding me of late?"

"We have so many friends. Why don't you dedicate a few poems to them for a change? Why only to me?"

"Why not? I like only you. See what I've brought for you. Open that drawer."

"What now?"

Madhu opened the drawer with a jerk. In it lay two jars. Holding them up, he said: "See, pomatum from the most exclusive French fashion house. And this is lavender water."[6]

"You've procured all this for me?"

"Didn't you say the other day that you love lavender?"

"That was just for the heck of it."

"I got the lavender with quite a bit of difficulty. It's not always available, you know."

"You spend so much on me, Madhu. Just the other day you sent me Forget-Me-Not."

"Yet you forget me! Why worry about the expense, Gour? I would willingly give everything I have to you. I want a portrait of you—and if I have to sell all my clothes in order to commission it, so be it."[7]

Spreading his arms wide and closing his eyes, Madhu said ardently: " 'All kind, to these fond arms of mine/Come! and let me no longer sigh!' That dolt Beni was right. I *have* written this acrostic about you."

As soon as Madhu advanced to embrace him, Gour retreated to the other side of the table and tried to change the subject . . .

"You haven't come to Maths class in a while."

---

says: "There is not in this wide world a soul I prize so much as *thine:* You have in you all that is noble, generous, disinterested, tender, and what not? God bless you, my dear lad! Never did I dream of finding a heart so true, so susceptible of *true friendship* as yours, in this 'deceitful' world of ours. As long as I live—in whatever climate may my Fates lead me, thou shalt be remembered and that with the tenderest feelings of friendship!" (emphasis in original).

6. A letter to Gour written a day after the one cited in the previous note says: "There's a bottle (or whatever you please to call it) of Pomatum for you. I don't require your thanks, but you must praise my readiness in obeying you. I am sorry, I am not yet able to procure Lavender for you."

7. This is another detail from the November 25, 1842, letter. " I am resolved to possess a picture of thy *sweet* self," Dutt writes. He wanted a miniature to take with him to England, and added that if necessary, "I will sell my very clothes for it."

"I detest Maths. What's the point of learning it? Anybody can learn Maths. I'm a poet. Why should I bother my head over Maths? Shakespeare could have been Newton if he so chose, but Newton could never have been Shakespeare."

"And you've altogether given up coming for Bengali?"

"You think I want to waste my time learning the language of menials? Fie on it."[8]

"We still speak Bengali at home. Why call it the language of menials?"

"You don't have to learn a language in order to be able to speak it. Even coolies can speak." . . .

"Bharat Chandra wrote in Bengali, Ishwar Gupta writes in it."

"Call Bharat Chandra a poet? He's nothing compared to Byron and Wordsworth. And as for Ishwar Gupta, I can write poems like his any day of the week."

"You—write poems in Bengali? Write one and show me."

"I'll show you this very instant. Take a pen and paper."

"Me?"

" . . . I don't love Bengali, but I do love you, Gour! You write, I'll dictate. Which subject should I choose? Mountains? The sea? A beautiful woman? Bengalis have hardly any beauty to boast of, anyway. It's cloudy. I'll write about the monsoon."

[Madhu dictates a poem to Gour.]

"Now read the whole thing together. Join the first letters of each line together and see what you get."

Head bent, Gour read the poem and immediately blushed crimson. "You've done it again. You are too much, Madhu."

Madhu laughed and said : "G-O-U-R D-A-S B-O-S-H-A-K—isn't that right? See, I can write acrostics even in Bengali. Tell Beni that this too is an acrostic and it spells out your name. But it isn't about you, it's about the monsoon. When I set my mind to it, I can accomplish anything—anything at all. But I don't even feel like touching any book written in your dirty language. Sanskrit smells of Brahmans, Bengali stinks of servants."

"Where did you learn all this stuff?"

"Why, from nobody."

"I heard you're often around Keshto Banerjee's these days?"

"Yes, I've been there a couple of times. Why?"

"Has some pretty daughters, does he, whose faces you hope to glimpse?"

---

8. One of Dutt's friends said that he apparently dismissed Bengali as "patois" in his college days when he was composing poetry exclusively in English. However, Dutt changed his mind on this. In an 1865 letter to Gour from Versailles, Dutt writes: "If there be anyone among us anxious to leave a name behind him, and not pass away into oblivion like a brute, let him devote himself to his mother tongue. That is his legitimate sphere—his proper element. European scholarship is good in as much as it renders us masters of the intellectual resources of the most civilized quarters of the globe, but when we speak to the world, let us speak in our own language."

"Heh, heh, heh. Gour, you're jealous. Yes, I'm right. You're blushing. Why don't you tell me you dislike me visiting a woman?"

Madhu drew Gour into his arms. Covering his face with kisses, he murmured: "But I love you best, Gour. Please don't be angry. Please don't."

"Oh, Madhu, please—let me go."

There was a door to the right. Beyond it was Madhu's bedroom. Madhu dragged Gour in there, pushed him down on the bed and said: "Thou hast forgotten thy promise of honoring my poor cot with the sacred dust of your feet.[9] Fulfill that promise today, Gour. Bless my bed with the dust of your feet."

Flustered, Gour said: "I have to go now."

"No, Gour, no. You can't go. Not now." Madhu sat on the floor, placed his hands on Gour's thighs and said: "Let me put my head in your lap."

"Madhu, stop this madness."

"The other day I tried to write on your lap but you threw the paper away.

> 'I thought I shall be able
> (Making thy lap my table)
> To write that note with ease—
> But ha! your shaking
> Gave my pen a quaking—
> Rudeness never I saw like this . . . '[10]

Why, why, why, Gour? I love you so, why don't you love me back? Why do you spurn me? I write so many poems about you, but still I can't win your heart. Today, I've got you all to myself after such a long time."

"Madhu, stop this drunken nonsense. Let me go."

"No, no, no."

Unable to tolerate these excesses, Gour gave Madhu a violent shove. Losing his balance, Madhu fell spread-eagled on the floor. His head hit the floor with a bang. Gour was truly incensed. He didn't try to give Madhu a hand.

After a while, Madhu got up and said in a desolate voice: "Even you push me away, Gour. I shan't bother you any more. One of these days I'll suddenly disappear, and you'll search and search but never find me."

---

9. An exact quotation from Dutt's letter to Gour dated October 7, 1842.
10. This is a poem Dutt wrote when he was in college.

H. S. Shivaprakash:
Shakespeare Dreamship *(Kannada)*

Introduced by Ruth Vanita

H. S. Shivaprakash, born in 1954, taught English in Karnataka for many years and is currently editor of the Sahitya Akademi journal *Indian Literature*. He has published four books of poems and eight plays in Kannada and has translated several poems and plays, including *King Lear*, into Kannada. He has won many awards, including the Sangeet Natak Akademy award for Drama in 1997.

Shakespeare Swapna Nauki was produced in Bangalore in 1988 and published in 1989 by Parisara Prakashana, Shimoga. It presents a modern Indian interpretation, in Kannada, of the life and work of the greatest writer in English. Shakespeare's plays and poems are taught all over India, in schools and colleges. From the early nineteenth century onward, his plays have been staged both in English and in translation in all the Indian languages. Shivaprakash's text is one of the few to foreground the romance between two men which is the subject of Shakespeare's sonnets. In this it is ahead of the recent Hollywood film *Shakespeare in Love* which heterosexualized the romance.

Shakespeare (1564–1616) wrote 154 sonnets, of which 126 deal with his intense love for a beautiful youth, Mr. W. H.[1] Some of these sonnets are among the world's greatest love poems. Critics have speculated for centuries about the identity of "Mr. W. H." and many theories have been put forward, of which one of the most popular, accepted here by Shivaprakash, is that he was the young and beautiful Earl of Southampton, to whom Shakespeare dedicated his two early poems, *The Rape of Lucrece* and *Venus and Adonis*.

Until recently many critics insisted anxiously on the "platonic," that is, nonsexual nature of Shakespeare's passion for his male beloved, while some claimed that the poems were con-

---

1. The remaining twenty-eight sonnets spring from the poet's and the young man's triangular involvement with an unnamed "dark lady."

ventional literary exercises with no biographical significance. The latter view is hard to uphold since, of the numerous sonnet sequences produced by male poets of the time, only one other addresses a male beloved.[2] Shakespeare's addressing a male beloved transgresses literary convention. Some editors of his sonnets even today turn the male pronouns female to disguise the sex of the beloved. Of late, however, most commentators acknowledge the homoerotic nature of the emotions expressed in the sonnets, not only in such forms of address as "Sweet boy," "Dear love," "My rose," but also in the romantic and sexual tropes used throughout.[3] Shakespeare's depiction of homoerotic relationships in his plays, such as that of Rosalind and Celia in *As You Like It*, Viola and Olivia and Antonio and Sebastian in *Twelfth Night*, and Antonio and Bassanio in *The Merchant of Venice*, have also been explored by many critics.[4]

In *Shakespeare Swapna Nauki* an aging and drunk Shakespeare is visited at Stratford by two other famous playwrights, Ben Jonson (1572–1637) and Michael Drayton (1563–1631).

Translated by Laxmi Chandrashekar

Drayton: But how many times you have held during an argument that life and art, the ideal and the real, are embodied in the persons we love. Do you remember that sonnet of yours:

> Shall I compare thee to a summer's day?
> Thou art more lovely and more temperate.
> Rough winds do shake the darling buds of May
> And summer's lease hath all too short a date.

Shakespeare: And every fair from fair sometime declines,
By chance or nature's changing course untrimm'd.[5]
Yes, I had seen all this beauty in my lover.
Drayton: In your lover? Not in your lady-love, then? Ben, you know, don't you, how Greene and Lilly would deride Will for being a homosexual?

---

2. Richard Barnefield's *The Affectionate Shepherd*, 1594.
3. An early example of such interpretation is Oscar Wilde's "The Portrait of Mr. W. H." More recent examples include Joseph Pequigney, *Such is My Love* (Chicago: University of Chicago Press, 1985).
4. A recent production of *The Merchant of Venice* in Delhi foregrounded the eroticism of Antonio's and Bassanio's relationship. It opened with them kissing onstage before the lights go up.
5. Sonnet 18.

Shakespeare: The chap who spread the rumor, that devil's disciple, Marlowe, was himself a homosexual.[6] How could he know that I have seen as many women as he had hairs on his head, and that they haunt me now like ghosts? . . .

Jonson: I told you to forget the past.

Shakespeare: If I had been a woman, I would have turned my lover into a bird and hidden him in my nest. But what could I do? I am a man, and so is he.

Drayton: Which man inspired in you such deep queer love? Tell us at least today.

Shakespeare: The Earl of Southampton. By then he was brimming with the youth I had lost. He was ripe for marriage. His mother was eager to get him married. But he detested the very mention of marriage. He wanted to excel in courage and be immortal in wisdom. Those were his dreams. His uncle pestered me to write poems in his praise and make him consent to marriage. I needed the money, so I agreed. He had just received my first sonnets. Once, in the garden, he—

(When stage left lights up, Earl of Southampton is seen leaning against a tree, gazing at his reflection in the pond and daydreaming. Shakespeare enters the stage on that side. Coughs a couple of times to attract attention and then stands silent for a while. Suddenly Southampton laughs and applauds. He comes out of the reverie and sees Shakespeare.)

Southampton: Oh! The bard!

Shakespeare: Your servant, my lord.

Southampton: Therefore, follow my orders. Let me test the power of your imagination. Tell me, why did I laugh? Either solve this mystery or be gone.

Shakespeare: On seeing yourself, my lord.

Southampton: Good, but that is not all. Where did I see myself? In water, clouds or the sky?

Shakespeare: The sky and clouds were mirrored in water along with your face. You, unfortunately, saw yourself in the sky, my lord.

Southampton: Fortune had nothing to do with it. I don't believe in Fortune.

Shakespeare: You will when you live to be my age, my lord.

Southampton: Then I don't want to live to be your age. Only a minute ago, that golden cloud pierced my eyes like Her Majesty's throne. A butterfly flew from one flower here to another. When I turned to the sky again, that same cloud had vanished like your tattered livery. Then I decided, I am not a cloud, I am the sky. I want the expanse, the height and depth of the sky.

---

6. The word used in Kannada is the Sanskrit *samlingrati* (one who loves the same sex). Poet and playwright Christopher Marlowe (1564–1593), who was accused of being an atheist and a sodomite, was reported to have remarked that "all they who love not tobacco and boys be fools." He was stabbed to death in a tavern brawl.

Shakespeare: But the cloud takes on another form now—it resembles a deer. The larks seem to be its young ones. The cloud is rolling now. If you are the sky, how can you have the grace and magic of a beauty that changes minute by minute. So—[7]

Southampton: So I must get married! My mother's words. My uncle's advice.

Shakespeare: But, before your youth, ambition, power and beauty begin to wrinkle, if you have a child who inherits these qualities—

Southampton: I will be only a father then. Like you. How many children have you?

Shakespeare: Three.

Southampton: Don't you see? You had to come to London because you couldn't feed them. Besides, your wife must be quite disgusted with you. If you hadn't married, you wouldn't have had to tend our horses at the theater.

Shakespeare: But I don't tend horses for my livelihood. I write plays about kings and queens.

Southampton: And how much money does that fetch you? Look at this ring on my little finger. (Shakespeare looks). This ring is made of pure gold which came from a country across the seas. The emerald, shining like a star in its center, is from another country. Can all your plays and poems equal this in value?

Shakespeare: I do not know the value of my plays and poems, my lord. But your youth is more valuable than this ring. . . .

Southampton: You can have it. Sell it if you like. Marry as many as you wish to. Fill the world with your breed. But don't write another poem asking me to marry.

Shakespeare: Your heart has the largesse of the sky. Let this ring, like your youth, stay with you.

Southampton: Do you, a mere actor, have the audacity to refuse what I give? Who's there? Throw the fellow out.

Shakespeare: Please do not be impatient. I am your vassal. Your heart is bounteous as the sky, but your youth transient. Look there, my lord, how the thick cloud, in a moment, is scattered and formless.

Southampton (Suddenly embracing Shakespeare): You really are my friend.

Shakespeare: Your servant.

Southampton: I don't need a servant. I have enough of them in this mansion. You are my poet and friend. (Forcibly, he pushes the ring onto Shakespeare's finger. As stage-left darkens, Shakespeare, gazing at the ring, moves to stage-right which is lighting up.) . . .

Southampton: Will, where are you setting out to, so suddenly?

---

7. The trope of the ever-changing cloud shapes that are like the ever-changing self is found in *Hamlet* III. ii. and, most famously, in *Antony and Cleopatra* IV. xiv: "Sometime we see a cloud that's dragonish . . . /That which is now a horse, even with a thought/The rack dislimns, and makes it indistinct/As water is in water. . . . Here I am Antony/Yet cannot hold this visible shape. . . ."

Shakespeare: London is infested with plague. Theaters are closed down for the time being. We shall, at least, go to the country and make a living putting up plays there. . . .

Southampton: Are you going away then? What shall I do? If I don't listen to a new poem by you every day, I can't digest my food, I don't have any pleasant dreams—why, I can't even sleep.

Shakespeare: I will be back again soon, my lord.

Southampton: How soon?

Shakespeare: As soon as the plague is over, I shall be with you. Even when I am away, I have the token of your love with me. This ring will stay with me through day and night.

Southampton: You will write poems about me wherever you are, won't you?

Shakespeare: Certainly. But by the time I return, will you have a child who looks like you?

Southampton: Let the plague devour you! Get away! (Shakespeare begins to leave.)

Southampton: Will! Please stay! This anger is an expression of my love. Do compose a new sonnet about me before you leave.

Shakespeare (stands gazing at Southampton): I can't even speak. What poem can I compose now?[8]

The play ends with Shakespeare, near death, casting the ring given by Southampton into the sea, so that its elements, the emerald and the gold, may be washed back to the shores of Africa and India, from where they came.

---

8. Shakespeare often claims that his love strikes him dumb and he finds it impossible to put either his emotions or the beloved's virtues into words. Ironically, the claim is made with great eloquence, for example, in Sonnet 23, after comparing himself to a nervous actor who forgets his lines, he concludes: "O learn to read what silent love hath writ:/To hear with eyes belongs to love's fine wit."

Inez Vere Dullas: Poems (English)

Introduced by Ruth Vanita

Inez Dullas, (1914–1994), was a journalist and later editor of *The Onlooker* and of *Eve's Weekly* in Bombay. A prolific writer of short stories, plays and poems, she also wrote film scripts and worked with radio and television. These two poems are taken from her collection of poems, entitled *A Poem Happens* (Calcutta: Writers Workshop, 1986), 24–25. She lived for over forty years with her friend Erna Vatchaghandy.

Mitylene in Bombay

No Lesbos this, our sea-girt isle,
and Sappho does not sing
her songs of love with silvern tongue
yet nonetheless they still are sung
by voices new, in tropic clime.

Removed from ancient Grecian time
in dim cafes they meet—
svelte versions of the classic gay,
they come to watch the cabaret
perchance to cruise the clientele.

and some fall victim to the spell
the Tenth Muse used to Weave
that now is woven by the girls
in slacks, who smile through blue smoke whorls
their message, while the music plays.

Back Bay Tower

The topmost tower, it soars above
the diamond-prickled crescent sweep
caressing steel-smooth bay . . .

The gay, the lone, meet here to drink,
bemused with music, word-beguiled,
from seven-storied height

take flight to a world that denies
the square, the normal, and the straight,
for the most blatant queer

is here at home. The curious glance,
the prying question and knowing leer
are absent. Only friends

whose trends, like yours, are unconcealed,
make talk intriguing, laughter flow
in stimulating stream;

the dream of attic Greece come true
and Plato lives. Stubs glow; lights dim,
and mouth approaches mouth . . .

Hoshang Merchant:
Poems for Vivan (English)

Introduced by Ruth Vanita

Hoshang Merchant, born in 1947, teaches English at the University of Hyderabad. Writers' Workshop, Calcutta, has published ten books of poems by him. In the biographical note attached to *Hotel Golkonda* (1991), a cycle of poems written for a young waiter whom he befriended, he describes himself as "still searching for the ideal friend." In *Yusuf in Memphis* (1991), he evokes many traditions of homoerotic writing, including those of Greek love, modernist English poetry and the Persian-Urdu ghazal. *Flower to Flame*, from which the poems here are taken, was published by Rupa & Co. in 1992. Merchant is the editor of *Yaraana: Gay Writing from India* (Delhi: Penguin, 1999), a collection of contemporary writings on gay male experience.

I
Vivan!
A voice on the soundtrack
of the Sher-Gil family
A soft voice a woman's voice
A voice I have often heard
calling   Hoshi!
Vivan and I are brothers
under the skin
The lights go up
our eyes meet And the voices
are drowned

The boat has run aground
I must push it
The stern fathers look
from the colonnaded portico
across the lawn furniture
to the servants' quarters

Where the sons are at play
with the Pandus
or a quintal of hay
Or makers of beams
10 ft. across
There there be the hewers
of wood
And the milkers of cows
and of men
in cages in cities
at burning ghats
at Buchenwald

Eli Eli lama sabbakthani? Where
Liberty to lead a people?
Arms? Give me the feel of arms:
I shyly withdraw my palm from his palm . . .

IV
I forget dinner   I sleep
through the muezzin's dawn call to prayer
Morning: Vivan!
[Even the mafiosi are benign this morning!]

If I were to paint him
I'd touch upon his feet
with the manicured left toe-nail

Then I'd concentrate
on his grip
of the first time
[This last time
I gave him the slip]
The black bushy brows
The graying hair
Do I detect some colour there?

Then I'd look at his broad back
concealed in flowing robes
and how the pyjamas fall
in folds at the foot

His carpenter and milkmen
His mowers and haulers
have big feet and hands
The forest fire has a long tongue

The boys he beds (or doesn't)
have broad backs

and long legs
The arm of gossip has a far reach

But he only listens
to what the flood's vortex spoke
to Leonardo
Or listens to the whisperings under
the eaves of the Siennese

He's no Indian:
Kill him!
He dared to die
at Auschwitz . . .

Dear Vivan,
Why did you forget
my Palestinian?
They hung him upon a beam
Then they nailed him

Then he thanked them
for a good scaffold
Then they laughed a laughter
That still haunts our dreams

Mine and yours
come out as perfect visual puns
red paint in a bath = Blood Bath
big splash in a tub = The Big Splash

And in coquelle brush
or soft pastel
you FIX
all the blood congealed
below all the Macchu Picchus

be they at Delhi or Doon
The Andes or the Sorbonne
Or Amritsar: on garish lit streets
of advertisement hot rods
and elephant-gods

If I had to paint him
I'd paint a blob of drooling white
on his lap
And the mirrors can make

an endless quotation
in an empty colonnade.

Ambai:
"One Person and Another" (Tamil)

Translated by Kanchana Natarajan

This story was published in the Tamil journal *Sathangai*, no. 12 (July-September 1997). "Ambai" is the pen-name of C. S. Lakshmi. Born in 1944, she has published two collections of short stories in Tamil and a collection translated into English, *A Purple Sea* (1993). She currently runs an organization called Sound and Picture Archives for Research on Women.

When this story first appeared, a popular Tamil newspaper accused Ambai of vulgarity and added that a journal which claims to be literary should not publish stories about homosexuals.

The small bus climbed the narrow zigzag mountain path.

Sacks of vegetables from the plains—cabbage, coriander leaves, tomatoes, gourds, carrots, onions and ginger, together filled the bus with a particular odor. In a little while the sun would set. The dim red light of dusk lit up passengers as well as vegetables. A very fair child with brown hair was fast asleep behind a sack from which red tomatoes protruded. A figure in a white turban sat, clutching a sack of onions to his chest. Her face covered with a deep green veil, a woman sat, resting her yellow, green and red bangled wrist on a sack of gourds. The people in that bus looked like paintings executed by an artist with devoted care.

Looking at them, Arulan wondered how many of these figures had appeared in Matthew Nathan's paintings in the form of abstract colored lines, floating eyes, spreading veils, and even as unclothed figures. Next to him, holding his shriveled hand, sat the small boy, Veeru. As if guessing his thoughts, Veeru looked up at him, and Arulan's long gray hair touched Veeru's forehead. Veeru's eyes ran over the completely gray hair tied with a piece of jute string. Usually he did not tie his hair up. It would fly in the wind, almost touching his shoulders. But today was a special day, a day when the flowing hair was tied with a jute string. This was the day Matthew Nathan's body was buried under a tall fir tree which almost touched the sky. Arulan smiled at the boy who was looking up at him. Veeru moved closer to him.

Veeru was employed at a potato farm but he lived in the house with these two like their son, a very close relative. Today too, they had gone to the plains to buy paints, as they did every Friday. Although Nathan was not there, this Friday too they had completed the ritual. They had bought two small canvases and some paper for Veeru to practice painting. These were safely lodged on Veeru's lap.

About forty years ago, he and Nathan, seated in a bus just like this one, had come to settle down in a mountain village. Just a week before that, they had met at a party. Arulan's father, who was a soldier many years before, had come to live in the lap of this mountain. In the mornings, quite often, looking at the mountains, he would roar out, "In the north are the Himalayas, *pappa,* and in the south is the Kumari edge, *pappa.*"[1] Arulan's memory of this was blurred like a dream sensation. When the father uttered the words "Kumari Munai," his voice would choke with emotion. That was the only intimation Arulan had of his father's native place. After the demise of his parents, Arulan continued to live in the town in the foothills of the Himalayas and spent his time in music and writing. He had friends among those who visited the hills in the summer. It was at a party hosted by one such visitor that he first met Matthew Nathan. Nathan was surrounded by women and men who were chatting and laughing.

Recently, he had been described in the newspaper as a painter born of an Indian father and a foreign mother. When asked by a journalist if he had come in search of his roots, he replied, "Search for specific roots would restrict my quest. People like us have their roots spread all over the world. All those airports where we have waited as transit passengers to change planes, are our temporary dwellings. My father left this country in the early years of the twentieth century, after the First World War. At that time he carried with him a pouch containing two handfuls of earth from his garden in Pondicherry. When he stayed in Paris he mixed that soil in a pot and grew a plant in it. Wherever he went and lived, he carried that pot and in spite of the pot receiving soil from various countries, he still believed that it contained the soil from his country. The roots of the plant that had grown in that pot are firmly and deeply rooted in our garden in Paris. I have not come here in search of roots."

That was an era when people did not feel an emotional need to go in search of their roots. It would be many years before Alex Hailey would write about African roots. Individuals had not become completely fragmented at that time. It was the second decade after the Second World War, when the persecuted Jews, who bravely survived the horrors of the war and its aftermath, were trying to spread their roots all over the world. At that time too, many people, inspired by humanistic ideologies or by a desire for personal growth, quit their own lands. It was a time when many still believed that one could live

---

1. A well-known song by the famous Tamil poet Subramania Bharati (1882–1921). *Pappa* songs are addressed to *pappas* (little girls).

as a citizen of a world not limited by geographers' maps. The journalists were therefore not surprised to hear Nathan's views on roots, but what he said next set off waves of shock in the minds of the assembled intellectuals.

"Maybe you have come to India in search of a wife?" asked a journalist.

"No, not a wife. I am not interested in women," he announced casually.

Arulan had by now understood that Nathan had been invited to the party so that others could observe this unique specimen. The subject was not explicitly discussed because people who thought in this way at that time were like owls living in tree hollows.

Among many subjects discussed that evening was that of death. Sudden death, death from disease, death by accident and many other kinds of death were talked about.

"I don't want to die alone—someone should be with me when I die," said Matthew Nathan.

"Whether or not anyone is with you, you have to die by yourself," said Arulan.

Still sitting on the chair, Matthew Nathan looked up at Arulan standing next to him. There was a tender look in his blue eyes.

"How do you wish to die?" Nathan asked.

"Just like a bird—no one to look after me, no one to nurse me, without any plan, suddenly, without anyone to remember me."

"Do birds die like that?"

"I suppose so. I can't imagine any other way."

After the party, Arulan invited Matthew to his house. They continued to talk about painting and poetry. Arulan drowned in Matthew Nathan's blue eyes, long slender fingers, and soft face. Later, Matthew Nathan often remarked that he had been entangled by Arulan's dark skin, sharp eyes and long curly hair. Very soon they decided to live together. Crossing the rocky and steep mountains, traveling several miles by bus and by motor cycle and also trekking on foot, they selected this small mountain village. Some had commented rather caustically that this was their "hiding place" but Matthew Nathan was not bothered by such remarks. Arulan would tell his friends, "This is our nest."

Before he could take note of how much time had passed—painting, writing, protecting the environment in the hilly areas by preventing the felling of trees, teaching little girls and boys like Veeru—Matthew Nathan fell seriously ill.

The paintings done in those last few months were very different from his others. When hung on the wall, they looked as if they could fly like cotton. "They have no density, they are light, and indeed there is no need for weight," he once commented to Arulan. He sketched Veeru every evening. Veeru would come and pose as Matthew Nathan desired. In one painting, Veeru lay on his side. Naked. Laughing. A white smile. No tension in his body. His penis rested like a tender flower bud. He looked like a celestial being who, because of his weightlessness, could rise upward from earth to sky.

Matthew Nathan was bedridden for only a few days. Sponging his ailing body every day felt to Arulan like recalling a very familiar poem.

Matthew's white skin was more wrinkled because of his European blood. Green veins stood out on his fragile hands. Like a newly hatched bird, Matthew Nathan had no flesh on his neck. His jaw bone jutted out of his cheeks. His eyes were a shadowy blue, his moistureless lips like the dried leaves of a coconut palm. A receding forehead and his soft hair of mingled gold and gray coming down to his back. Hairless, narrow chest. Since he did not wear any tight clothes, he had no marks on his waist. His thighs and legs were like the descent of a dried-up waterfall. His organ was like a withered fruit—light, pink in color.

Once, when Arulan dipped a towel in hot water and sponged every part of his body, Matthew held Arulan's hand and said, "Arul, death is very strange, isn't it?" So saying, he lifted Arulan's palm to his dried lips and held it there. "Arul, forgive me, I have to do this alone," he said.

Eyes filled with tears, Arulan patted Matthew's back. When he awoke in the middle of the night, he saw Matthew sitting up and gazing at him.

"It feels as if the earth is slipping from under one's feet, Arul. It is like drawing a paintbrush up to the top corner of a canvas, and then letting the color drip down sideways, beyond the frame of the canvas." Matthew continued, "Will you bury me under a fir tree?"

"Yes, Matthew."

They remained silent for a long time.

The bus moved on.

Matthew Nathan died like a morning painting. When Arulan woke up in the morning, he saw Matthew's golden gray hair spread all over the pillow. His eyes were closed as though he was fast asleep. His head was tilted and his face reflected eternal peace.

Arulan stroked Matthew's forehead with a limp hand.

"Sahib, sahib," sobbed Veeru.

All the paintings had been sent to a museum a fortnight before his death. Only a big portrait of Veeru was kept in front of the bed. It was like their dream.

Under the huge fir tree reaching out as if touching the sky with its branches swishing in the winds, Veeru dug a hole in the ground. The body, covered with a white cloth, was laid to rest. In the background, women could be heard wailing. After they laid the body down, covered it with earth and flattened the soil, from somewhere a baby girl appeared and rolled about on the soil.

Outside the window the sun was setting. The Himalayan mountain tips glowed as if touched by fire. Smoke rising from chimneys in the valley looked like streaks of gray.

The bus stopped and some passengers alighted. Arulan rose suddenly and Veeru too got up with a jolt. But this was not their destination. Arulan got off the bus. Veeru too got down, carrying the bag containing the canvas and the paint tubes. Arulan stood at the edge of the mountain path and looked at the mountains. He had on a white dhoti and kurta. His gray hair shone like a white crown. He stroked Veeru's head and then let himself slide off the cliff. He spread his arms as though trying to grasp something. The dhoti and kurta moved like a wave in the air. In the light of dusk, his falling body looked like a monstrous white bird, wings outspread, flying slowly to its destination. He crashed down on a rock. Even as the stunned Veeru tried to cry out "Sahib!" red color began to spread on Arulan's white clothes as though a painter had mindlessly splashed paint with a rough brush.

Glossary

ASHRAM   The home of a guru, usually in the forest, where he or she practices austerities and also instructs his or her disciples who form a familylike community

ASVINS   Twin brother gods in the *Rig Veda Samhita*. In post-Vedic texts they are symbols of male youth and beauty in pairs. Krishna and Arjuna and Rama and Lakshmana are frequently compared to them. The Asvins are the fathers of the Pandava twins Nakula and Sahdeva, who are always together and are extolled for their exceptional beauty as well as their skills with horses and cows.

BODHISATTA   An infinitely compassionate being who is dedicated to the attainment of perfect awakening for the benefit of not just him- or herself but of all sentient beings. A necessary step toward becoming a Buddha.

BHAGVAD GITA
A.K.A. *GITA*   (literally, "Song of the Lord") In this part of the *Mahabharata*, (possibly interpolated later) when Arjuna hesitates to go to war against his kinsmen, Krishna instructs him on the nature of action, devotion, reality and the Self.

BRAHMA   First of the Hindu trinity: Creator god.

BUDDHISM   A religion that arose in India in the sixth century B.C. Although not named "Buddhism" any more than "Hinduism" was so named at that time, and similar to Hinduism in many of its doctrines, such as the doctrine of karma and of rebirth or transmigration, it developed into a separate religion with its own distinctive theory and practice, and spread to surrounding countries. It developed many different forms in India too but began to decline in the medieval period and practically disappeared from the Indian mainland by the end of the twelfth century A.D. when monasteries and libraries in Bihar and Bengal were destroyed by Turkish invaders. Despite some violent conflict, especially with Shaivites and followers of Shankara, Buddhism, and Hinduism had coexisted, as is evidenced by monasteries, schools of philosophy, and the acceptance of Buddha by Vaishnavites as one of the incarnations of Vishnu. Organized around institutions such as monasteries, Buddhism was more vulnerable to attack than relatively more individualized Hindu ascetic practice.

DHARMA   Often translated as "duty," "religion," or "righteousness," it can connote "the law of one's being." Thus the *dharma* of wood is to float on water. A person's being and *dharma* can be defined in various ways, according to social and familial position, caste and community, and in relation to the universe, divinity and other humans. Every creature is required to be true to its *dharma* which is also the way to fulfillment and liberation.

DUPATTA   Veil worn by north Indian women over the head and/or breasts.

FAQIR   Mendicant ascetic.

GHAZAL   Persian/Urdu love poem.

JAIN   Follower of Jainism. The Jains, who number about four million, are based mainly in Gujarat and Rajasthan, in western India. They are strict vegetarians.

JAINISM   A religion founded by Mahavira in the sixth century B.C. It has a continuous tradition in India. Its teachings, which emphasize nonviolence toward all living beings, influenced Mahatma Gandhi.

JATAKAS   Stories, in Pali, of the former lives of the Buddha, when he was incarnated as different human and nonhuman creatures, all male. Many of these stories were based on pre-Buddhist folktales. The *Jatakas* were well known by the third century B.C. although they were not compiled until the fifth century A.D.

KALI YUGA   The last and most degenerate age of the Hindu four ages. All recorded history occurs in the Kali Yuga. The cycle repeats itself when the Kali Yuga ends.

KAMIZ/KURTA   Different types of shirts, worn by both sexes in north India.

KARMA   Literally, action. Refers also to patterns of action carried over from previous births, which influence the present life. It has to be exhausted for liberation to be possible.

KATHA LITERATURE   *Katha* means "story." *Katha* literature consists of story cycles, compiled in many languages, from oral sources or from earlier, now-lost, texts. Examples of such compilations are the *Kathasaritsagara,* the *Vetalpanchavimsati,* the *Panchatantra.*

KHAYAL   Reflective song.

MAHABHARATA   Sanskrit epic attributed to Vyasa. Its dating is disputed; scholars place it anywhere from the eighth century B.C. to the fifth century A.D. The core story focuses on the war between two sets of cousins, the five Pandavas (Yudhishthira, Bhima, Arjuna, Nakula and Sahdeva) and the hundred Kauravas. Arjuna, the greatest Pandava warrior, is aided by Krishna, a chief of the Yadava clan, who is the incarnation of the preserver god Vishnu. The Pandavas are married to Draupadi, whose humiliation by the Kauravas is one of the chief reasons for the war, the other being the Kaurava usurpation of the Pandava kingdom.

MARSIYA	Lament for the martyr Husain, the Prophet's grandson.
MASNAVI	Long narrative poem.
MEHFIL	Gathering around a pir, more often devoted to mystical poetry and music than to religious discourse. In later Urdu, it meant any gathering of musicians, poets, or dancers.
MURID	Sufi disciple.
MUSHAIRA	Poets' gathering, where they recite their poetry aloud.
NAZM	Urdu verse.
PRASAD	Food distributed among devotees after being offered to the gods. In worship, this food, the leavings of the gods, is pure and is eaten with devotion.
PIR	Sufi master.
QAWWALI	Sufi devotional music.
QAWWAL	One who sings qawwalis.
RADHA	Cowherd woman, beloved of Krishna but married to another man. An incarnation of goddess Lakshmi.
RAGAS	Indian musical modes.
RAKSHASA	Demon.
RAMAYANA	Lit. the Rama Story. Sanskrit epic by Valmiki. Dating disputed; scholars place it anywhere from the fifth century B.C. to fifth century A.D. Tells the story of the just king Rama of Ayodhya, incarnation of the god Vishnu. Exiled for fourteen years by his stepmother's fiat, he is accompanied into exile by his wife Sita, daughter of the Earth goddess, and brother Lakshmana. Sita's abduction by the demon king Ravana leads to a war between Rama and Ravana. After Sita is rescued, she is subjected to a fire ordeal to test her purity. Although she survives this ordeal, Rama abandons her later, when his subjects doubt her chastity. When he finally asks her to return, she chooses to sink into the earth instead. There are many medieval *Ramayanas* in different Indian languages.
RAMCHARITMANAS	This sixteenth-century Hindi retelling of the Rama story by poet Tulsidas ends happily with Rama and Sita reigning in Ayodhya. It is the most popular north Indian version today and was the basis of a TV serial in the 1980s.
RASA	In ancient Indian poetics, nine types of aesthetic emotion expressed in different combinations in any art work and evoked in its recipient. Rasa theory is still used in Indian criticism today.

RASALEELA	Mystical dance of Krishna with the cowherd women, in which each woman thinks he is dancing with her alone. Signifies the way god, although one, appears in many forms to devotees.
RUBAI	Quatrain.
SAKHI/SAKHA	Female friend/male friend.
SALWAR	Loose trousers with drawstring, worn by both sexes in parts of north India.
SANSKARAS	Like *karma,* patterns of action carried over from previous births, which influence the present life. They can be related to individual, caste or community. They have to be lived through and exhausted for liberation to be possible. Also refers to rites of passage such as marriage.
SHAIVA	Worshipers of Shiva.
SHAKTA	Worshipers of the female principle Shakti, in her embodiments as various goddesses such as Durga, Kali, and Saraswati.
SHAKTI	Power, gendered female, of which all goddesses are embodiments. The consorts of male gods are called their Shaktis.
SHIVA	Third in the Hindu trinity, the destroyer god.
SUFISM	Islamic Mysticism that developed into a major social movement in the early centuries of Islam. Islam in India tends to be closer to Sufism than to Orthodox Islam.
TANTRA	A development within Mahayana Buddhism, which spread widely in India from the fifth century A.D. In the Hindu Shakta tradition, Tantrism, practiced by small groups of initiates, developed yogic, magical and sexual practices designed to lead to liberation. In both traditions, it emphasizes a structured heterosexual intercouse as a means of liberation.
TIKA	Mark on forehead; may be indicative of caste, community, religious or marital status.
UPANISHADS	Philosophical texts that function as commentary on and explication of the *Vedas.* Most of them were probably composed by 600 B.C., prior to the rise of Buddhism. There are eighteen major *Upanishads.*
VAISHNAVA	Worshipers of Vishnu, especially in his incarnations as Rama and Krishna.
VEDA	(from the root *vid,* knowledge) Sacred knowledge transmitted orally by a complex system of mnemonics and compiled later in four *Samhitas* or collections. Of these, the *Rig Veda Samhita* is the oldest and most important, the other three being the *Sama Veda Samhita,* the *Yajur Veda Samhita* and the *Atharva Veda Samhita.* The *Rig Veda Samhita* is a collection of 1,028 hymns, composed approximately between 1500 and 1000 B.C.

VEDIC LITERATURE   Written in early Sanskrit (different from the later epic and Puranic Sanskrit), this consists of the four *Veda Samhitas* and the commentaries, explications, and philosophical speculations contained in the *Brahmanas, Aranyakas* and *Upanishads*.

VISHNU   Second in the Hindu trinity, the preserver god.

Translators and Contributors

ADITYA BEHL is assistant professor of Hindi and Urdu, Department of South and Southeast Asian Studies, University of California at Berkeley.

LAXMI CHANDRASHEKAR is reader in English at N. M. K. R. V. College for Women, Bangalore.

SHOHINI GHOSH is reader in Video and TV Production at the Mass Communication and Research Centre, Jamia Millia Islamia University, Delhi.

SVATI JOSHI is reader in English at Miranda House College for Women, Delhi University.

SCOTT KUGLE is a research scholar at Duke University, Gradutate Program in Religion.

MURALEEDHARAN is lecturer in English Literature at St. Aloysius College, Elthuruth, Kerala.

KANCHANA NATARAJAN is reader in Indian Philosophy at Daulat Ram College for Women, Delhi University.

SHORMISHTHA PANJA is reader in the Department of English, Delhi University.

KUMKUM ROY is reader in Ancient Indian History in the Department of History, Delhi University.

SUMANYU SATPATHY is reader in the Department of English, Delhi University.

Name and Place Index

Page numbers in bold indicate a particular focus on or extended discussion of the particular author or text